Prentice-Hall Dictionary of Business, Finance and Law

by
Michael Downey Rice

Prentice-Hall, Inc.
Englewood Cliffs, New Jersey

Prentice-Hall International, Inc., *London*
Prentice-Hall of Australia, Pty. Ltd., *Sydney*
Prentice-Hall Canada, Inc., *Toronto*
Prentice-Hall of India Private Ltd., *New Delhi*
Prentice-Hall of Japan, Inc., *Tokyo*
Prentice-Hall of Southeast Asia Pte. Ltd., *Singapore*
Whitehall Books, Ltd., *Wellington, New Zealand*
Editora Prentice-Hall do Brasil Ltda., *Rio de Janeiro*

Library of Congress Cataloging in Publication Data

Rice, Michael Downey.
  Prentice-Hall dictionary of business, finance, and law.

  1. Commercial law—United States—Dictionaries. 2. Corporation
law—United States—Dictionaries.   3. Finance—Law and
legislation—United States—Dictionaries. I. Prentice-Hall, Inc. II.
Title. III. Title: Dictionary of business, finance, and law.
  KF887.R53 1983   346.73'07'0321   83–3022
                   347.30670321

ISBN 0-13-696583-0

Printed in the United States of America

Preface

The Language of Business, Finance, and Law

The law, perhaps more than any other discipline, depends on its vocabulary—words of art, terms defined in statutes, jargon, shorthand expressions for complicated concepts. Law has always depended on words and short phrases to identify important principles—**anticipatory breach, constructive notice, specific performance**—but legal jargon has virtually exploded in the last several decades of expanding federal regulation of business. The applicability of a federal statutes, with enormous legal ramifications, might turn on the definition of a single term such as **security**. Tax law is based on terms defined in the Internal Revenue Code and given interpretive gloss by courts over the years. Familiarity with terms such as **collapsible corporation, recapture,** and **half-year convention** are essential to communication among, and with, tax professionals. The proliferation of government programs has brought with it a proliferation of acronyms and initials to identify those programs. What is **FERC?** An **ESOP?** What does the **CFTC** do? What do you have to fear from the **EPA?**

The field of accounting has an equally arcane vocabulary, and accurate presentation of accounting efforts depends on accurate usage of that vocabulary. Much of that vocabulary is the same as that of the business lawyer, and that is why it is in this book. Terms such as **current assets** and **monetary liability** have complex meanings spelled out in accounting literature, and misuse of accounting terms can mislead business decision-makers.

The intensity of activity in the financial markets has led to the development of an entire vocabulary of short expressions packed with meaning. What do brokers mean when they sell a security **ex-dividend** or **flat?** What's a **put?** A **straddle?** A **debenture?**

Who Needs This Dictionary?

This book is for the business and financial community and all who inhabit and serve it, regardless of particular discipline or training. In particular, it is for business people who deal with the law, and for lawyers who deal with business. This must include virtually all business people, and certainly most lawyers.

For business people—accountants, bankers, brokers, corporate officers, financial officers, line managers—we have provided, in one place, a source of the meanings of terms that so often fly through the air in business meetings and speckle the pages of memoranda and publications. Here can be found definitions for such terms, packed with hidden meaning, as **wrap-around, leveraged buy-out,** and **negative pledge.** This book explains what lawyers mean when they warn against **resale price maintenance** and **accumulated earnings tax.** Meaning is given to commonly used, but often mysterious, acronyms and initials: **ASPR, DISC,** and **CEQ,** for example.

For lawyers we have gone beyond simple definitions. Lawyers must know the source of the special terms of business law, where they can look for more information. Thus this dictionary is a research tool: we have included extensive references to statutory materials and sources of terms, leading cases, and articles in the legal and business literature. This dictionary can be the starting place for many inquiries.

For students, not only of business and law, but also of related disciplines, engineering, accounting, economics, and public administration, we have designed this dictionary as a reference tool—sufficiently accurate and comprehensive to be a reliable and effective handbook, an essential part of any student's basic library.

What Does This Dictionary Cover?

This dictionary covers business law, but while that topic is perhaps narrower than the simple term "law," it encompasses an extraordinary range of subjects, some relatively new, and all rather complex. Corporate law, taxation, contracts, commercial paper, secured transactions, securities regulation, antitrust, bankruptcy, labor and other topics in a traditional law school curriculum with a business orientation are accompanied by more recent products of federal legislation: administrative law, environmental law, pension and profit sharing plans, banking regulation, and transportation regulation. We have not included some traditional legal topics that are not particularly relevant to business problems: trusts and estates, torts, and criminal procedure, for example—topics better left to the traditional legal dictionaries.

Using This Dictionary

The use of a dictionary needs little explanation—the term in question is simply found in the alphabetical order. Precision is not always important to start; we have included common variations of many terms, and have tried to provide sufficient cross-references to permit the reader to develop quickly the information on a point that this book has to offer.

In the case of proper names—statutes, government agencies, and cases—we have put the principal definitions under the correct name, but we have also inserted in correct order the acronym or other common name. Thus the **Government National Mortgage Association** is defined and explained under that name, but if that name is not known, it can be found by inspecting **GNMA** or even **Ginnie Mae**.

Order

The letter-by-letter style of alphabetization is used in this dictionary. That means that hyphens and spaces between words are ignored; thus **callable** appears before **call date**. Acronyms are included in the order as if they were words; periods in acronyms and abbreviations for names are disregarded. Terms including numbers, such as **form 8-K**, are in numerical order following the first usage of the initial word in the term; numbers precede letters, so that **form 8-A** appears before **form S-8**. Organizations are listed by the full name, except that "Office," "Department," "Bureau," and "United States" are disregarded.

Cross References

Because each definition involves words of art, themselves found in this dictionary, we have not identified each instance in which a term used in a definition has its own definition, out of fear of impairing the presentation. Nevertheless, the reader should examine other terms found in a definition where they seem to be terms of art. Thus the definition of **accelerated depreciation** will suggest inspecting the definition of **sum-of-the-years' digits** and **declining balance**. Acronyms usually are defined simply as the spelled-out term; the reader may then wish to inspect the definition of the spelled-out term. Thus **FERC** would lead the reader to examine the definition of **Federal Energy Regulatory Commission**.

Many definitions also have specific cross references, indicated by bold-face type. Introductory signals have these meanings:

See: Inspection of the cross-referenced term is important to an understanding of the term in question.

See also: Inspection of the cross-referenced term may be helpful.

Compare: A different but related definition of opposite or contrasting tenor should be examined for comparison with the defined term.

These signals are not the same as the signals used for citations, which appear in italics.

Citations

The citations found in most definitions are in the usual form for legal materials, following the "Blue Book" of the Harvard Law Review, *A Uniform System of Citation*. Cases are cited by volume and page of the appropriate reporter. Books are cited to author, title, and date, preceded by the volume number in the case of a multi-volume work. Articles in legal and business periodicals are cited to author, title, volume, title of the periodical, page, and year of publication, for those journals running consecutive page numbers for all issues in a given year or volume. For other periodicals that number pages in each issue, the date of the issue is identified.

For statutory materials, we have taken some liberties with the Blue Book rules, because the United States Code, the official compendium of federal laws, is revised only every six years and is always several years late coming out. We have thus cited the United States Code (U.S.C.) for federal laws, even though a particular law may be too new to appear therein, but we have also cited the volume and page in the session laws. The newest laws can be found in the unofficial reporters pending incorporation in the official publication.

Likewise, the Code of Federal Regulations, although revised annually, can be a bit tardy, and citations to regulations announced in the Federal Register at the time of publication that are not yet included in the appropriate code volume include the Federal Register citations.

Abbreviations

Some of the statutory and regulatory references may seem somewhat cryptic to those unfamiliar with legal bibliography. Here are some common abbreviations:

C.B.	Cumulative Bulletin (Internal Revenue Service)
C.F.R.	Code of Federal Regulations
Fed. Reg.	Federal Register
I.R.B.	Internal Revenue Bulletin
I.R.C.	Internal Revenue Code
Treas. Reg.	Treasury Regulations
U.S.C.	United States Code

Other abbreviations can be deciphered by looking them up in this dictionary. (For that matter, so can these.)

References to the Uniform Commercial Code and other uniform state statutes mean the version promulgated by the sponsoring body. Many states, in adopting uniform laws, have made changes from the "official" version, and we have not attempted to identify those variations.

AAA: American Arbitration Association.

AAP: Affirmative Action Plan.

AAR: Association of American Railroads.

AB: *Aktiebolag,* a joint stock company organized under the laws of Sweden.

ABA: 1. American Bankers Association. 2. American Bar Association.

Abandoned: A registered trademark is deemed to be "abandoned"

(a) When its use has been discontinued with intent not to resume. Intent not to resume may be inferred from circumstances. Nonuse for two consecutive years shall be prima facie abandonment.

(b) When any course of conduct of the registrant, including acts of omission as well as commission, causes the mark to lose its significance as an indication of origin.

15 U.S.C. § 1127.

Abandonment loss: Loss, deductible from federal income tax, due to the sudden loss of usefulness and abandonment of a business asset. The deduction allowed is the difference between the asset's undepreciated cost and the salvage value, if any. I.R.C. § 165; *see* Treas. Reg. § 1.165-2.

ABC transaction: Method of financing used in the oil and gas industry, involving three parties: "A," the owner of oil or gas leases, "B," the operator and developer, and "C," the financer. A sells the leases to B; B pays only a portion of the price, and A retains the right to an oil payment as security for the balance. A then sells that right to C. A is thus paid in full for the leases, and receives capital gain treatment on the sale of both the lease and the right to the oil payment. All the income from the property is taxed to B, who is entitled to depletion allowances. *See* I.R.C. §§ 614, 636.

Absolute priority: Rule governing distribution of a bankrupt debtor's property that requires that creditors of a given class be compensated in full before any participation by a junior class of creditors. The rule is applied by starting with the highest class of creditors and working down through the classes of creditors, then through the classes of stockholders, until the assets are exhausted. *See Consolidated Rock Products Co. v. DuBois,* 312 U.S. 510 (1941). The absolute priority rule prevailed in reorganizations under Chapter X of the old Bankruptcy Act, but has been modified by the current Bankruptcy Code to permit some flexibility for senior creditors to grant concessions to junior classes of creditors in order to expedite acceptance of a reorganization plan. 11 U.S.C. § 1129. *See* H.R. Rep. No. 95-595, 95th Cong., 1st Sess. 412 (1977).

Abstract: Summary of a record, usually the record of conveyances of land.

Abusive tax shelter: Investment plan or arrangement, in connection with which the organizer or seller makes a statement that such person knows to be false or fraudulent as to any material matter with respect to the availability of any tax benefit, or such person overvalues a material matter by more than 200%. I.R.C. § 6700, added by the Tax Equity and Fiscal Responsibility Act of 1982.

Accelerated cost recovery system: System of capital cost recovery deductions from federal income taxes, established by section 201 of the Economic Recovery Tax Act of 1981, to replace other methods of depreciation for property placed in service in 1981 and later. The accelerated cost recovery system permits "recovery" of capital costs for most types of tangible personal property using accelerated methods over statutorily established periods unrelated to, but generally shorter than, actual useful lives. Salvage value is disregarded. I.R.C. § 168. *See* S. Rep. No. 97-144, 97th Cong., 1st Sess. 39 (1981). The accelerated cost recovery system has been modified by section 206 of the Tax Equity and Fiscal Responsibility Act of 1982 for property placed in service after 1984.

Accelerated depreciation: In the federal income tax sense, a method of depreciation that permits income to be reduced by amounts attributable to the reduction in value of an asset, at a rate that exceeds the actual rate of such reduction. *See* I.R.C. § 167. In the accounting sense, accelerated depreciation may refer to a method of depreciation that permits the writing off of the cost of an asset at a rate faster than the straight-line method. Sum-of-the-years' digits and declining balance are the most common methods of accelerated depreciation, but straight-line depreciation may be an accelerated method if a depreciation period shorter than the actual useful life is used. See accelerated cost recovery system.

Accelerated paper: Commercial paper or other debt instrument that is overdue and has been accelerated.

Acceleration: 1. In the case of a debt instrument, "acceleration" means declaration by the creditor that the debt is immediately due and payable, before its stated maturity, usually occasioned by the default of the debtor. Except in the case of instruments due on demand, a party may accelerate "at will" or "when he deems himself insecure" only if he in good faith believes that the prospect of payment or performance is impaired. UCC Section 1-208. Most debt instruments specify the circumstances in which the debt may be accelerated. 2. In the case of the registration of securities with the Securities and Exchange Commission, "acceleration" means permitting the registration to become effective prior to the expiration of the 20-day waiting period usually required after the filing of amendments to the registration statement. Acceleration is normally requested in connection with filing of the price amendment, so that the pricing of the securities is done close to the effective date. *See* SEC Rules 460, 461; 17 C.F.R. §§ 230.460, 230.461.

Acceptance: 1. With respect to a contract, the manifestation of assent by the offeree to the terms offered which binds the parties; *see* acceptance of offer. 2. With respect to the sale of goods, the taking by the buyer of particular goods which have been appropriated to the contract as his own, by signifying to the seller that the goods are conforming to the contract of sale, failing to make an effective rejection, or doing any act inconsistent with the seller's ownership. UCC Section 2-606. *See* UCC Section 2-207; **battle of the forms.** As to a partial acceptance, *see* UCC Section 2-601; for revocation of acceptance, *see* UCC Section 2-608. 3. With respect to a draft, the drawee's signed engagement to honor the draft as presented. UCC Section 3-410. 4. Draft that has been accepted by the drawee by affixing the word "accepted," the date the draft is payable, and the drawee's signature on the instrument. See **acceptance of offer.**

Acceptance credit: Trade credit or letter of credit that has been endorsed or "accepted" by a bank, and is thus an obligation of the accepting bank.

Acceptance liability: Liability of the drawee of a draft.

Acceptance of offer: With respect to contracts, "Acceptance of an offer is a manifestation of assent to the terms thereof made by the offeree in a manner invited or required by the offer." Acceptance may be by performance or promise. *Restatement, Second, Contracts* § 50 (1981).

Acceptor: Drawee of a draft, after acceptance.

Access, right of: Right of an antitrust agency to access to the books and records of a corporation being investigated. *See FTC v. American Tobacco Co.,* 264 U.S. 298 (1924); *United States v. Morton Salt Co.,* 338 U.S. 632 (1950); see also **Antitrust Civil Process Act.**

Accession: Something added by growth or attachment to other property, as cargo handling equipment to a vessel; the process of such addition. *See* UCC Section 9-314.

Accommodation contract: Guaranty of a negotiable instrument, usually simply by signing the instrument.

Accommodation endorsement: 1. The guaranty of a negotiable instrument, by endorsement of the instrument. 2. The endorsement of an acceptance by a bank for another bank.

Accommodation paper: Negotiable instrument bearing the endorsement of an accommodation party as surety or guarantor.

Accommodation party: Party who signs an instrument in any capacity for the purpose of lending his name to another party to that instrument, as a surety or guarantor. *See* UCC Section 3-415. Traditionally, the term referred to a party supplying the endorsement or guaranty without consideration.

Accord and satisfaction: Assent to proposed compromise of a dispute by acceptance of or promise to accept tendered payment or stated substitute performance. *See Restatement, Second, Contracts,* § 281 (1981).

Account: Statement or record of transactions between parties, usually involving an unfulfilled obligation on the part of one to the other. For the purpose of Article 4 of the Uniform Commercial Code—Bank Deposits and Collections, an "account" is any account with a bank, including a checking, time, interest, or savings account. UCC Section 4-104. For the purpose of Article 9 of the Uniform Commercial Code—Secured Transactions, "account" means "any right to payment for goods sold or leased or for services rendered which is not evidenced by an instrument or chattel paper, whether or not it has been earned by performance." Vessel charters are regarded as accounts, not chattel paper, under Article 9. UCC Section 9-106.

Account debtor: For the purpose of Article 9 of the Uniform Commercial Code—Secured Transactions, an "account debtor" is a person who is obligated on an account, chattel paper, or general intangible. UCC Section 9-105(1)(a).

Accounting income: Aggregate income or loss for a period, including unusual items as reported in the income statement, before deducting related tax expense or adding related tax saving. International Accounting Standards Committee, Statement of International Accounting Standards 12, *Accounting for Taxes on Income,* paragraph 3 (1979).

Accounting Principles Board: Body formed by the American Institute of Certified Public Accountants to establish and publish accounting principles. The APB was superseded by the Financial Accounting Standards Board in 1973.

Account party: Party for whose account a letter of credit is issued. Other parties to a letter of credit transaction are the issuer, who issues the credit at the request and for the account of the account party, and the beneficiary, who is entitled to draw on the letter of credit.

Accounts payable: Record of amounts owed by an entity on a current, or short-term basis.

Accounts receivable: Record of amounts owed to an entity on a current, or short-term basis.

Account stated: "Manifestation of assent by debtor and creditor to a stated sum as an accurate computation of an amount due the creditor. A party's retention without objection for an unreasonably long time of a statement of account rendered by the other party is a manifestation of assent." *Restatement, Second, Contracts* § 282(1) (1981).

Accredited investor: The Small Business Issuers' Simplification Act of 1980, Pub. L. No. 96-477, 94 Stat. 2275,2294 (1980), amended the Securities Act of 1933 to provide an additional exemption from registration, in new section 4(6), for transactions involving offers or sales to "accredited investors," if the aggregate offering price does not exceed $5,000,000, there is not any advertising or solicitation, and a notice is filed with the Securities and Exchange Commission. 15 U.S.C. § 77d. "Accredited investor" is defined in new section 2(15) as:

(i) a bank as defined in section 3(a)(2) of the Act whether acting in its individual or fiduciary capacity; an insurance company as defined in section 2(13) of the Act; an investment company registered under the Investment Company Act of 1940 or a business development company as defined in section 2(a)(48) of that Act; a Small Business Investment Company licensed by the Small Business Administration; or an employee benefit plan, including an individual retirement account, which is subject to the provisions of the Employee Retirement Income Security Act of 1974, if the investment decision is made by a plan fiduciary, as defined in section 3(21) of such Act, which is either a bank, insurance company, or registered investment advisor; or

(ii) any person who, on the basis of such factors as financial sophistication, net worth, knowledge, and experience in financial matters, or amount of assets under management qualifies as an accredited investor under rules and regulations which the Commission shall prescribe.

15 U.S.C. § 77b(15). *See* SEC Regulation D, 17 C.F.R. §§ 230.501–506, 47 Fed. Reg. 11251 (1982).

Accretion of discount: Accumulation of capital gains on discount bonds in anticipation of receipt of payment of par value at maturity.

Accrual accounting: Determination of periodic income and financial position by measuring economic resources and changes in them as the changes occur rather than simply by recording receipts and payments of money. American Institute of Certified Public Accountants, Accounting Principles Board Statement No. 4, Ch. 5, *Basic Features and Basic Elements of Financial Accounting,* paragraph F-6 (1970). This method of accounting treats income as having occurred when the right to receive it comes into being, and expenses as having occurred when the liability arises, in each case regardless of the date on which the cash transaction occurs. The alternative is the cash basis, in which income and expenses are reported only when actually received or paid.

Accrual benefit: As used in ERISA, in the case of a defined benefit plan, the individual's accrued benefit determined under the plan and expressed in the form of an annual benefit commencing at normal retirement age, or if it cannot be so expressed, the actuarial equivalent thereof; in the case of an individual account plan, the balance of the individual's account. ERISA §§ 3(23), 204(c)(3); for "accrued benefit," *see* Treas. Reg. § 1.411(a)(7).

Accrued dividends: Dividends accrued on preferred stock since the last dividend payment was made, or anticipated regular dividends on common stock.

Accrued interest: Interest accrued on a bond or note since the last interest payment was made.

Accrued liability: For the purpose of ERISA, the excess of the present value, as of a particular valuation date of a pension plan, of the projected future benefit costs and administrative expenses for all plan participants and beneficiaries over the present value of future contributions for the normal cost of all applicable plan participants and beneficiaries. ERISA § 3(29).

Accumulated dividends: Dividends on cumulative preferred stock not yet paid.

Accumulated earnings tax: Special federal tax, intended as a penalty, on earnings retained by a corporation in excess of what is needed for the reasonable needs of the business for the purpose of avoiding income tax on distributions to shareholders. I.R.C. §§ 531–537. *See United States v. Donruss Co.,* 393 U.S. 297 (1969).

Accumulated interest: Interest past due and unpaid.

Acid-test ratio: Current ratio; the ratio of quick, or liquid assets to current liabilities. An acid-test ratio of less than one is cause for serious concern.

Acquiescence: Indication by the Commissioner of Internal Revenue that the Internal Revenue Service will follow a decision of a court on a tax matter.

Acquisition indebtedness: Indebtedness in connection with the acquisition of a business by a tax-exempt organization. *See* I.R.C. § 514.

Acquisition of assets: Form of merger in which the acquiring company purchases all or most of the assets of the company being acquired, instead of purchasing the stock. The corporate shell of the acquired company remains after the acquisition, having as assets the stock or other consideration paid by the acquiring company and any other assets not acquired. See **reorganization.**

Acquittance: Written instrument evidencing the discharge of an obligation, by full payment, or a release from an obligation, even though not fully paid.

ACRS: Accelerated cost recovery system. *See* I.R.C. § 168.

Action: Proceeding to enforce rights by judicial process. For purposes of the Uniform Commercial Code, a judicial proceeding including recoupment, counterclaim, set-off, suit in equity, and any other proceedings in which rights are determined. UCC Section 1-201(1).

Act of bankruptcy: Prior to the effective date of the Bankruptcy Code in 1979, the federal Bankruptcy Act required proof of one of six "acts of bankruptcy" for involuntary bankruptcy: fraudulent transfer, preference, judicial lien, assignment for the benefit of creditors, appointment of a general receiver, or written admission of inability to pay debts together with a willingness to be adjudged a bankrupt. The Bankruptcy Code has abolished the concept; 11 U.S.C. 303.

Act of God: Natural and unpreventable accident or disaster, such as deluge, that would excuse delay or failure to perform a contractual duty, or excuse liability for loss. *See* 10 S. Williston, *Contracts,* §§ 1083, 1102A (3d ed. 1967). An act of God must be attributable exclusively to natural causes, without human intervention. *See* Carriage of Goods by Sea Act, Pub. L. No. 521, ch. 229, 49 Stat. 1207 (1936), section 4(2)(d), 46 U.S.C. § 1304(2)(d). See also force majeure.

Actual total loss: In the case of marine insurance, circumstances in which the insured goods or the ship cannot arrive at their destination in the form they were in when insured:

The underwriter engages that the object of the assurance shall arrive in safety at its destined termination. If, in the progress of the voyage, it becomes totally destroyed or annihilated, or if it be placed, by reason of the perils against which he insures, in such a position, that it is wholly out of the power of the assured or of the underwriter to procure its arrival, he is bound by the very letter of his contract to pay the sum insured.

Roux v. Salvador, 3 Bing. N.C. 266, 285 (1836). *See* G. Gilmore & C. Black, Jr., *The Law of Admiralty* 83 (2d ed. 1975).

Actuarial cost method: See advance funding actuarial cost method.

ACU: Asian currency unit.

ADB: Asian Development Bank.

Additional depreciation: Excess of depreciation claimed for federal income tax purposes over straight-line depreciation.

Add-on interest: Method of calculating interest on a loan whereby interest is calculated for the duration of the loan and then added to the principal; periodic payments are calculated by dividing that total by the number of payments. This method of calculating interest, sometimes called "flat," disregards the reduction in the outstanding principal balance.

Add-on minimum tax: 15% minimum tax on a corporation's tax preferences. I.R.C § 56(a); tax preferences are income that is sheltered from tax by certain deductions and other special tax benefits. *See* Treas. Reg. §§ 1.56-1, 1.57-1.

Adequate assurance of performance: Assurance furnished by a party to a contract that performance will be rendered, furnished when the other party has grounds to believe that the ability of the party to render such performance has been impaired. The adequacy of such assurance is to be determined by commercial standards. UCC Section 2-609. *See James B. Berry's Sons Co. of Ill. v. Monark Gasoline & Oil Co.,* 32 F. 2d 74 (8th Cir. 1929).

Adequate consideration: For the purpose of ERISA:

(A) in the case of a security for which there is a generally recognized market, either (i) the price of the security prevailing on a national securities exchange which is registered under section 6 of the Securities Exchange Act of 1934, or (ii) if the security is not traded on such a national securities exchange, a price not less favorable to the plan than the offering price of the security as established by the current bid and ask prices quoted by persons independent of the issuer and of any party in interest; and (B) in the case of any asset other than a security for which there is a generally recognized market, the fair market value of the asset as determined in good faith by the trustee named fiduciary pursuant to the terms of the plan and in accordance with regulations promulgated by the Secretary.

ERISA § 3(18). In other contractual contexts, the phrase "adequate consideration" has little meaning, because there is no requirement that consideration be "adequate" to support a contract (although courts may refuse to grant equitable relief if consideration is grossly inadequate, or inadequacy of consideration may be relevant to certain defenses, such as mistake, misrepresentation, duress, or undue influence). *Restatement, Second, Contracts* § 79 (1981).

Adequate protection: Creditor protective provision in the Bankruptcy Code, providing for payments or other measures intended to protect the interest of secured parties in equipment remaining in the possession of the bankrupt and whose repossession is restrained by law. "Adequate protection" may be provided by cash payments to the extent of the decrease in value of the property while in the hands of the bankrupt entity, additional or replacement liens, or other relief. 11 U.S.C. § 361; *see* H.R. Rep. No. 95-595, 95th Cong., 1st Sess. 338 (1977).

Adjudication: For the purpose of the Administrative Procedure Act, "agency process for the formulation of an order." 5 U.S.C. § 551(7). *See* 5 U.S.C. § 554.

Adjudicative facts: Facts about particular parties to an administrative agency proceeding, and the particular facts in controversy. See Davis, *An Approach to Problems of Evidence in the Administrative Process*, 55 Harv. L. Rev. 364, 402 (1942) Compare **legislative facts.**

Adjusted basis: Basis of property for the purpose of determining the gain or loss from a sale or disposition. The adjusted basis is the cost (I.R.C. § 1012) adjusted for depreciation and other costs (I.R.C. § 1016). *See also* I.R.C. §§ 1031, 1033.

Adjustment assistance: Federal program of direct compensation to groups of workers or firms that are directly injured by increased imports, under the Trade Expansion Act of 1962, Pub. L. No. 87-794, 76 Stat. 872 (1962). *See* Metzger, *Escape Clause and Adjustment Assistance,* 2 Law & Policy in Int'l Bus. 352 (1970).

Admeasure: To assign to a vessel a given capacity or measure. A vessel must be admeasured by the United States Coast Guard in connection with the preparation of documentation upon completion of construction or modification. *See* 46 U.S.C. § 71.

Administrative law: Branch of the law concerned with the actions of government agencies and judicial review of those actions. *See generally* K. Davis, *Administrative Law Text* (3d ed. 1972). K. Davis, *Administrative Law Treatise* (2d ed. 1978).

Administrative law judge: Officer of an administrative agency empowered to hear and decide disputes; formerly called a hearing examiner.

Administrative Procedure Act: Federal statute governing the procedures for actions by and before federal administrative agencies, and judicial review of agency decisions, including rule-making, adjudication, licensing, and imposition of sanctions. Pub. L. No. 404, ch. 324, 60 Stat. 237 (1946), 5 U.S.C. §§ 551–59, 701–06, 1305, 3105, 3344, 6362, 7562. States also have legislation concerning procedure of state administrative agencies, often based on the Model State Administrative Procedure Act promulgated by the National Conference of Commissioners on Uniform State Laws. *See generally* K. Davis, *Administrative Law Treatise* (2d ed. 1978), *Administrative Law Text* (3d ed. 1972).

Administrator: For the purpose of ERISA, the person specifically designated under the terms of the instrument under which the plan is operated, the plan sponsor, or such other person as the Secretary of Labor may by regulation prescribe. ERISA § 3(16)(A); *see* Treas. Reg. § 1.414(g)-1.

Admiralty law: System of jurisprudence covering maritime matters, acts done upon or relating to the sea and the carriage of goods and passengers by water. Admiralty has roots different from the law relating to other matters, has many principles different from and sometimes inconsistent with such other law, and until recently admiralty disputes were heard in different courts. *See generally,* G. Gilmore & C. Black,

Jr., *The Law of Admiralty* (2d ed. 1975); Knauth's *Benedict on Admiralty* (7th ed., rev. 1981). Admiralty matters are handled in the United States by the federal courts. U.S. Const., art III, sec. 2, cl. 1; *The Lottawanna,* 88 U.S. (21 Wall.) 558 (1875). The admiralty jurisdiction of the United States federal courts extends to all waters, including inland waters, that are navigable in interstate commerce, but for some purposes, admiralty jurisdiction is limited to vessels. *See, e.g., Foremost Insurance Co. v. Richardson,* 457 U.S. ____, 102 S. Ct. 2654 (1982); *Keller v. Dravo Corp.,* 441 F. 2d. 1239 (5th Cir. 1971), *cert. denied* 404 U.S. 1017 (1972).

Admitted assets: Those assets of an insurance company subject to the laws of the state of New York that can be counted in determining the financial condition of that insurer. New York Ins. Law § 70.

ADR: 1. Asset depreciation range. 2. American Depositary Receipt.

Ad valorem: According to value; system of taxation based on the value of the thing taxed.

Advance funding actuarial cost method: For the purpose of ERISA, an actuarial technique for establishing the amount and incidence of the annual actuarial cost of pension plan benefits and expenses. Acceptable methods include the accrued benefit cost method (unit cost method), the entry age normal cost method, the individual level premiums cost method, the aggregate cost method, the attained age normal cost method, and the frozen initial liability cost method. The terminal funding cost method and the current funding (pay-as-you-go) cost method are not acceptable. ERISA § 3(31). *See* American Institute of Certified Public Accountants, Accounting Principles Board Opinion No. 8, *Accounting for the Cost of Pension Plans,* Appendix A, paragraph 9 (1966).

Advance refunding: 1. In the case of corporate or municipal debt securities, the sale of an issue of new securities intended to refund the existing securities before the call or maturity date, with the proceeds held in trust pending redemption or payment at maturity of the existing securities. 2. In the case of government securities, an arrangement whereby the government will offer holders of outstanding securities an opportunity to exchange the securities prior to maturity for other, longer-term securities.

Adverse claim: With respect to the transfer of investment securities under Article 8 of the Uniform Commercial Code—Investment Securities, an "adverse claim" includes a "claim that transfer was or would be wrongful or that a particular adverse person is the owner of or has an interest in the security." UCC Section 8-301.

Advice: When given by a bank, a written acknowledgment of a particular transaction.

Advising bank: With respect to letters of credit, the bank that gives notification to the beneficiary of the issuance of a credit by another bank. UCC Section 5-103(1)(e).

Advisory Circular: Publication of the Federal Aviation Administration providing technical information, statements of policy, information for testing and certification of pilots and mechanics, and other information related to the activities of the FAA.

Advisory funds: Funds deposited with a bank for investment for the account and in the name of the depositor, but only after consultation with that depositor.

Advisory opinion: Advice furnished by an administrative agency, with various degrees of formality and binding effect, depending on the agency. The Federal Trade Commission has a relatively formal procedure for the issuance of an "Advisory Opinion" concerning the legality of or likelihood of remedial action against a course of action that a business proposes to pursue. 16 C.F.R. §§ 1.1–1.4; *See* Section of Antitrust Law of the American Bar Association, *Antitrust Law Developments* 210 (1975).

Affected with a public interest: In the case of a private business enterprise, having monopoly characteristics and being of a nature essential to the public, such that a duty arises to furnish certain levels of service at reasonable rates, and perhaps justifying government regulation. Utility companies have traditionally been regarded as being "affected with a public interest." The phrase was coined by Lord Chief Justice Hale in about 1670:

3. If the king or a subject have a publick wharf, unto which all persons that come to that port must come and unlade or

lade their goods . . . in that case there cannot be taken arbitrary and excessive duties for cranage, wharfage, pesage & c. neither can they be enhanced to an immoderate rate, but the duties must be reasonable and moderate, though settled by the king's license or charter. For now the wharf and crane and other conveniences are affected with a publick interest, and they cease to be juris privati only; as if a man set out street in new building on his own land, it is now no longer bare private interest, but it is affected with a publick interest.

De Portibus Maribus, 1 Hargrave, Tracts, 77–78.

Affecting commerce: The term "affecting commerce," as used in federal legislation, is intended to provide jurisdiction over matters to the extent permitted by the commerce clause of the Constitution, and is regarded as broader in scope than "in commerce." *E.g.,* section 5 of the Federal Trade Commission Act, as amended by the Magnuson-Moss Warranty–Federal Trade Commission Improvement Act (15 U.S.C. § 45(a)), prohibits unfair methods of competition "affecting commerce." For the purpose of federal labor legislation, "affecting commerce" means "in commerce, or burdening or obstructing commerce or the free flow of commerce, or having led or tending to lead to a labor dispute burdening or obstructing commerce or the free flow of commerce." National Labor Relations Act, section 2(7), 29 U.S.C. 152(7). See **commerce, commerce clause.**

Affiant: Person who makes a statement by affidavit.

Affidavit: Statement of facts confirmed by oath or affirmation.

Affiliate: For the purpose of the Securities Act of 1933, a person directly or indirectly controlling, controlled by, or under common control with an issuer of securities. *See* SEC Rule 405, 17 C.F.R. § 230.405, 47 Fed. Reg. 11390, 11435 (1982); *see also* SEC Rule 144, 17 C.F.R. § 230.144; SEC Regulation S-X, 17 C.F.R. 210.1-02(b); Cal. Corp. Code § 150. For the purpose of the Bankruptcy Code, an affiliate is an entity that controls 20 per cent or more of the voting stock of the debtor, or 20 per cent or more of whose voting stock is controlled by the debtor, or controls or is controlled by the debtor through a lease or operating agreement; the term also includes a business operated by the debtor under lease or operating agreement, or the operator of the debtor under such an agreement. 11 U.S.C. § 101(2); *see* H.R. Rep. No. 95-595, 95th Cong., 1st Sess. 308 (1977). See also **affiliated group.**

Affiliated group: Group of corporations entitled to file a consolidated federal income tax return. I.R.C. §§ 1501–1505. An affiliated group is a chain of corporations connected through stock ownership with a common parent, where the parent owns 80% of the stock of the controlled corporation. I.R.C. § 1504(a). Affiliated corporations that do not file consolidated returns have available deductions for dividends paid and received. I.R.C. §§ 562, 243.

Affiliated person: For the purpose of the Investment Company Act of 1940, an "affiliated person" is a person directly or indirectly owning or controlling five per cent or more of the voting stock of the subject company, a corporation of which the subject company directly or indirectly owns or controls five per cent or more of the voting stock, "any person directly or indirectly controlling, controlled by, or under common control with" the subject company, and officers, directors, partners, and employees. Section 2(a)(3); 15 U.S.C. § 80a-2(a)(3); *see also* section 3(a)(19) of the Securities Exchange Act of 1934, 15 U.S.C. § 78c(19).

Affirmative disclosure: Remedy of the Federal Trade Commission in deceptive advertising cases, requiring advertisers to disclose possible adverse characteristics of products or services advertised. *See generally* Section of Antitrust Law of the American Bar Association, *Antitrust Law Developments* 204 (1975).

Affreightment, contract of: Contract for the carriage of specific goods, usually by water, and usually by designation of a specific vessel or vessels to the contract. A contract of affreightment is similar to a charter party, and may include a charter party.

After-acquired property clause: Clause in a mortgage or security agreement purporting to attach the lien of the mortgage or the security interest to property not in the possession of the debtor at the time of creation of the instrument, when and as such property is acquired. After-acquired property clauses are often found in mortgages covering an entire railroad or utility system to reach equipment brought in later to supplement or replace existing equipment. *See* UCC Sections 9-108, 9-204. *See also* Cohen & Gerber, *The After-Acquired Property Clause,* 87 U. of Pa. L. Rev. 635 (1939).

After-market: Market for securities after the original issuance. In the international setting, the term refers to the period after issue but before the selling syndicate has been disbanded.

Afternoon: For the purpose of Article 4 of the Uniform Commercial Code–Bank Deposits and Collections, "afternoon" means "the period of a day between noon and midnight." UCC Section 4-104(1)(b).

After notice and a hearing: As used in the Bankruptcy Code, this phrase does not mean that a hearing must be held, but only that an opportunity for a hearing is afforded. As set forth in the Code, the phrase "after notice and hearing":

(A) means after such notice as is appropriate in the particular circumstances, and such opportunity for a hearing as is appropriate in the particular circumstances; but

(B) authorizes an act without an actual hearing if such notice is given properly and if–

 (i) such a hearing is not requested timely by a party in interest; or

 (ii) there is insufficient time for a hearing to be commenced before such act must be done, and the court authorizes such act;

11 U.S.C. § 102(1); *see* H.R. Rep. No. 95-595, 95th Cong., 1st Sess. 107, 315 (1977).

After sight: After acceptance, usually referring to the date of payment of commercial paper, as a certain number of days "after sight."

AG: 1. *Aktiengesellschaft,* joint stock company organized under the laws of Germany. 2. Attorney General.

Agency: With respect to government agencies, under the Administrative Procedure Act agency means "each authority of the Government of the United States, whether or not it is within or subject to review by another agency, but does not include ..." Congress, the courts, the governments of territories or the District of Columbia, or for most purposes, military commissions, courts martial, or military authority on foreign soil in time of war. 5 U.S.C. § 551(1). The Freedom of Information Act expands on this definition to include "any executive department, military department, Government corporation, Government controlled corporation, or other establishment in the executive branch of the Government (including the Executive Office of the President), or any independent regulatory agency." 5 U.S.C. § 552(e). *See Forsham v. Harris,* 445 U.S. 169 (1980). *See also* 5 U.S.C. § 552b(a), 18 U.S.C. § 6001.

Agency action: For the purpose of the Administrative Procedure Act, "the whole or part of an agency rule, order, license, sanction, relief, or the equivalent or denial thereof, or failure to act...." 5 U.S.C. § 551(13). "Agency action" is broader in scope than "agency proceeding."

Agency for International Development: Division of the International Development Cooperation Agency, a part of the executive branch of the United States government, which carries out programs of assistance for less-developed countries under the Foreign Assistance Act of 1961 and the Agricultural Trade Development and Assistance Act of 1954. *See* 45 Fed. Reg. 54149 (1980); Grant, *The Foreign Economic Assistance Program,* in II W. Surrey & D. Wallace, Jr., ed., *A Lawyer's Guide to International Business Transactions* 195 (2d ed. 1979).

Agency proceeding: For the purpose of the Administrative Procedure Act, agency proceeding means rule-making, adjudication, and licensing. 5 U.S.C. § 551(12). "Agency proceeding" is narrower in scope than "agency action."

Agency records: The Freedom of Information Act provides for public access to certain "agency records." 5 U.S.C. § 552. The term has been narrowly construed to mean writings or transcriptions that perpetuate knowledge. *Nichols v. United States,* 325 F. Supp. 130, 135 (D. Kan. 1971), *aff'd on other grounds,* 460 F. 2d 671 (10th Cir. 1972), *cert. denied,* 409 U.S. 966 (1972). *See Kissinger v. Reporters Committee for Freedom of the Press,* 445 U.S. 136 (1980); comment, *The Definition of "Agency Records" Under the Freedom of Information Act,* 31 Stan. L. Rev. 1093 (1979).

Agency shop: Employment situation where the employees are represented by a union but with nonunion employees also employed and being represented by the union; the nonunion employees must pay union dues, but are not required to become members.

Agent: Person who acts for another (the principal), with the authority to bind the principal on matters within the scope of the agency relationship, expressed or implied. In determining whether a person is acting as "agent" so as to bind the principal under the National Labor Relations Act, "the question of whether the specific acts performed were actually authorized or subsequently ratified shall not be controlling." Section 2(13), 29 U.S.C. § 152(13).

Agent bank: In international debt transactions, a bank acting for the lenders and bondholders, providing services and functions similar to the indenture trustee in a debt financing in the United States. An agent bank is also used in conditional sale financing of railroad equipment in the United States, to hold the security interest in the equipment and to collect and disperse the funds on behalf of the investing participants.

Agent for service: Party named in a registration statement for securities as the party to whom the SEC should send communications regarding the registration statement. *See* SEC Rule 478, 17 C.F.R. § 230.478.

Aggregation rules: 1. Rules for the disposition of stock under SEC Rule 144 whereby sales by a donee are aggregated with sales by its donor in determining whether the maximum number of sales in a given period has been exceeded. 17 C.F.R. § 230.144.

Aggrieved party: Party entitled to resort to a remedy. UCC Section 1-201(2).

Agio: In international debt transactions, a premium paid by the borrower for prepayment of the obligation.

Agreement: "Manifestation of mutual assent on the part of two or more persons." *Restatement, Second, Contracts* § 3 (1981). The *Restatement of the Law, Second, Contracts,* gives a wider meaning to "agreement" than to "contract," an important difference being that the word "agreement" does not imply that legal consequences are produced. It is possible to have a contract without an agreement and an agreement without a contract. The Uniform Commercial Code defines "agreement" as "the bargain of the parties in fact as found in their language or by implication from other circumstances including course of dealing or usage of trade or course of performance ... ." UCC Section 1-201(3). See **contract; bargain.**

Agreement among underwriters: Agreement among the underwriters participating in an issue of securities, appointing a managing underwriter, setting forth the manager's duties and authority, and covering the allocation of shares among the underwriters, the price of the shares, the spread between the offering price and the price to the issuer, the terms of payment, stabilization, and other matters. On behalf of the underwriting group, the managing underwriter will enter into a separate agreement, an "underwriting agreement," with the issuer.

Agreement corporation: Corporation, organized under state law, authorized under section 25 of the Federal Reserve Act to engage in international banking and financial operations. *See* Pub. L. No. 106, ch. 18, 39 Stat. 755 (1919); 12 U.S.C. §§ 601–604a. *See* Regulation K, 12 C.F.R. § 211; see also **Edge Act Corporation.**

Agreement of rescission: See rescission.

Agricultural cooperative: Organization to collectively prepare for market, handle, and market agricultural products. *See* Cooperative Marketing Act of 1926, Pub. L. No. 450, ch. 725, 44 Stat. 802 (1926), 7 U.S.C. § 455; Robinson-Patman Act, 15 U.S.C. § 13b; see also **Capper-Volstead exemption.**

Agricultural Stabilization and Conservation Service: Division of the United States Department of Agriculture responsible for programs for voluntary production adjustment, resource protection, and price, market, and farm income stabilization.

Agriculture, United States Department of: Cabinet-level department of the executive branch of the United States government responsible for agricultural and rural development. Important divisions are the Farmers Home Administration, the Rural Electrification Administration, the Agricultural Marketing Service, the Animal and Plant Health Inspection Service, the Federal Grain Inspection Service, the Food Safety and Quality Service, the Agricultural Stabilization and Conservation Service, the Commodity Credit Corporation, the Federal Crop Insurance Corporation, the Forest Service, and the Soil Conservation Service.

AIBD: Association of International Bond Dealers.

AICPA: American Institute of Certified Public Accountants.

AID: Agency for International Development.

Airbill: Document evidencing the receipt of goods for shipment issued by an air carrier or air freight forwarder, similar in function to a bill of lading issued by a marine or rail carrier. The term includes air consignment notes and air waybills. UCC Section 1-201(6).

Air consignment note: See airbill.

Aircraft: Any contrivance used or designed for navigation or for flight in the air. Federal Aviation Act, section 101(5), 49 U.S.C. § 1301(5). Hovercraft are not considered aircraft under United States law, but are treated as vessels. For the purpose of the Convention on International Recognition of Rights in Aircraft, the term "aircraft" includes "the airframe, engines, propeller, radio apparatus, and all other articles intended for use in the aircraft whether installed therein or temporarily separated therefrom."

Airline Deregulation Act of 1978: Federal legislation reducing CAB control over airline rates and initiation and termination of service, and covering related matters. Pub. L. No. 95-504, 95th Cong., 2d Sess., 92 Stat. 1705

(1978). *See* H.R. Rep. No. 95-1211, 95th Cong., 2d Sess. (1978).

Air waybill: See airbill.

Alaska Power Administration: Division of the United States Department of Energy responsible for operating and marketing hydroelectric power in Alaska.

Alienate: Convey or transfer.

Alienation clause: Clause in a mortgage or secured debt instrument causing the debt to be accelerated, and be payable in full, upon the sale or transfer of the property that is subject to the mortgage or secured debt instrument.

ALJ: Administrative law judge.

All-inclusive: Method of accounting for unusual items in which nonrecurring items are included in net income, but separate disclosure may be made of individual amounts. International Accounting Standards Committee, Statement of International Accounting Standards 8, *Unusual and Prior Period Items and Changes in Accounting Policies,* paragraph 6 (1978). Compare current operating performance.

All-in rate: Interest rate on a loan including the cost of compensating balances, commitment fees, and other charges for the loan.

Allocation: 1. Under Section 2-615 of the Uniform Commercial Code, a seller of goods whose capacity to perform is partially impaired by the occurrence of certain contingencies has a duty to allocate production and deliveries among his customers, "in any manner which is fair and reasonable." 2. Portion of an issue of securities allocated to one of the members of the underwriting or selling syndicate. Also called allotment.

Allocation of customers: See vertical restraint.

Allocation of geographic markets: See territorial restriction.

Allonge: Attachment to a negotiable instrument used to make endorsements when there is no room on the instrument itself.

Allotment: See allocation.

Alpha: The excess return (the return in excess of a risk-free rate) of a given stock when the excess return of the stock market as a whole (or a selected segment of the market) is zero. See J. Van Horne, *Financial Management and Policy* 59 (4th ed. 1977).

ALTA: American Land Title Association.

Alteration: Change in the contract of a party to an instrument. An alteration that is material and fraudulent discharges the obligation of the party whose contract is thereby changed. UCC Section 3-407. The alteration of a warehouse receipt or bill of lading leaves it enforceable according to its original terms. UCC Sections 7-208, 7-306.

American Arbitration Association: Nonprofit organization that publishes rules for arbitration and provides for the administration of arbitration.

American clause: Clause in a marine insurance policy to the effect that subsequent insurance obtained by the insured shall not reduce the liability of the insurer, or give rise to a right of contribution against the subsequent insurers.

American Depositary Receipt: Certificate of deposit issued by an American bank against the deposit of foreign securities with a foreign branch of that bank or with a foreign depositary bank affiliated with the American bank. Transactions in the securities among United States investors are evidenced by transfer of the depositary receipts instead of the actual securities. *See generally* Tomlinson, *Federal Regulation of Secondary Trading in Foreign Securities,* 32 Bus. Law. 463 (1977).

AMEX: American Stock Exchange.

Amortization: Reduction of a debt balance by the payment of periodic installments of principal; the periodic charging to expense of some amount of cost. Amortization sometimes is used in the sense of depreciation, but usually only for intangible assets. The term amortization is used in the sense of depreciation in certain federal income tax provisions permitting "rapid amortization," depreciation of an asset in a period that is short relative to the economic life of the asset. *See, e.g.,* I.R.C. §§ 169, 184. As to amortization of bond premium, *see* I.R.C. § 171.

Amtrak: Pseudonym for the National Railroad Passenger Corporation.

Ancillary relief: Supplemental or ancillary prohibitions used to accomplish effective equitable relief in antitrust cases brought against mergers and acquisitions under section 7 of the Clayton Act. For example, if divestiture of an acquisition is ordered, the divesting company may be required to provide patent rights or business or technical assistance to the purchaser of the divested assets. *See* American Bar Association, Section of Antitrust Law, *Antitrust Law Developments* 100 (1975).

Ancillary restraint: Restraint of trade that is not considered a violation of section 1 of the Sherman Act because it is merely ancillary to and supportive of legitimate activity, and is necessary if the main purpose of the legitimate activity is to be achieved. *Addyston Pipe & Steel Co. v. United States,* 175 U.S. 211 (1899). *See Restatement, Second, Contracts* § 188 (1981).

ANCOM: Andean Common Market.

And interest: In connection with a quotation of a bond price, meaning the purchaser will also have to pay the accrued interest.

Annualize: To express, as an annual rate, the return on an investment or interest on a loan that is earned or accrued for a period of more or less than one year.

Annuity: Contract providing for the payment of a specified sum at specified intervals, either for a certain period or for the life of the holder.

Annuity bond: Perpetual bond; a bond that does not mature, and bears interest perpetually.

Anti-churning rules: Provisions of the Internal Revenue Code prohibiting use of the accelerated cost recovery system for property sold and leased back to the person who previously owned or leased the property. I.R.C. §§ 168(e)(4)(A), 168(e)(4)(B).

Anticipatory breach, anticipatory repudiation: Repudiation of a contract with respect to a performance that is not yet due, giving the other party the right to seek remedies or suspend its own performance. *See Restatement, Second, Contracts* §253 (1981); UCC Sections 2-610, 2-713, 2-723, 5-115; Jackson, *"Anticipatory Repudiation" and the Temporal Element of Contract Law: An Economic Inquiry into Contract Damages in Cases of Prospective Nonperformance*, 31 Stan. L. Rev. 69 (1978); Note, *U.C.C. § 2-713: Anticipatory Repudiation and the Measurement of an Aggrieved Buyer's Damages*, 19 Wm. & Mary L. Rev. 253 (1977).

Antidilution: Increase in the amount that would otherwise be reported as earnings per share or a decrease in the amount of net loss per share. American Institute of Certified Public Accountants, *Reporting the Results of Operations,* Accounting Interpretation of APB Opinion No. 9, paragraph 58 (1971).

Antidilution provision: Covenant of a corporation to a stockholder, or a provision in a warrant or option to purchase stock, designed to protect the holder of the stock, warrant, or option from dilution of his position by subsequent issuance of additional stock. Antidilution provisions customarily provide a right to participate in a future issue of stock, in proportion to the current holdings of stock, warrants, or options.

Antidilutive security: Security that would result in an increase in the amount reported as earnings per share or a decrease in the amount reported as net loss per share. American Institute of Certified Public Accountants, *Reporting the Results of Operations,* Accounting Interpretation of APB Opinion No. 9, paragraph 58 (1971).

Antidumping law: The Trade Agreements Act of 1979, Pub. L. No. 96-39, 93 Stat. 144 (1979); 19 U.S.C. § 2501–2581, which replaces the Antidumping Act of 1921. The antidumping law provides for the imposition of special duties on imported goods "sold in the United States at less than its fair value," if an industry in the United States is being or is likely to be injured. *See* Simons, *"Non-Sale" Transactions and the Antidumping Laws of the United States,* 35 Bus. Law. 1611 (1980).

Antidumping order: Order by the International Tariff Commission to maintain the price of imports by imposing a tariff on imports sold at less than fair value. *See* section 751 of the Tariff Act of 1930, as amended by section 101 of the Trade Agreements Act of 1979, 19 U.S.C. § 1675.

Antifraud provisions: Remedies for fraud in the issuance of securities provided by sections 12 and 17 of the Securities Act of 1933.

Antimanipulative rules: Rules of the Securities and Exchange Commission regarding the maintenance of an orderly market and the prevention of market manipulation in securities offerings. SEC Rule 10b-6, 17 C.F.R. 240.10b-6; *see* SEC Release 34-18528, 47 Fed. Reg. 11482 (1982).

Antitrust Civil Process Act: Federal statute giving the Antitrust Division of the Department of Justice the power to compel a prospective defendant to produce documents at the investigative stage, before a complaint has been filed. Pub. L. No. 87-664, 76 Stat. 548 (1962), 15 U.S.C. §§ 1311–1314, 18 U.S.C. § 1505. *See* American Bar Association, Section of Antitrust Law, *Antitrust Law Developments* 233 (1975).

Antitrust division: Division of the United States Department of Justice, headed by an Assistant Attorney General, responsible for enforcement of the Sherman Act, the Clayton Act, and certain other antitrust laws. The Bureau of Competition of the Federal Trade Commission has concurrent jurisdiction over many antitrust matters, but criminal matters are handled by the Antitrust Division exclusively. *See* American Bar Association, Section of Antitrust Law, *Antitrust Law Developments* 229 (1975).

Antitrust laws: For the purpose of private treble damage and injunctive relief under the Clayton Act, "antitrust laws" are defined in section 1 of the Clayton Act as the Sherman Act, the Clayton Act, and parts of the Wilson Tariff Act. 15 U.S.C. § 12; *see Nashville Milk Co. v. Carnation Co.*, 355 U.S. 373 (1958). For other purposes, the term may include related laws, such as the Robinson-Patman Act, the Federal Trade Commission Act, and other laws designed to prohibit monopolization or restraint of interstate or foreign trade or commerce and unfair trade practices, and otherwise to ensure the operation of competitive markets. *See* section 2 of the Antitrust Civil Process Act, 15 U.S.C. § 1311. Antitrust laws are administered by the Antitrust Division of the Department of Justice and the Bureau of Competition of the Federal Trade Commission. Private remedies are also available, and state agencies may bring actions under the federal antitrust laws. *See generally* American Bar Association, Section of Antitrust Law, *Antitrust Law Developments* (1975); Areeda & Turner, *Antitrust Law* (1980). States also have antitrust laws; *see, e.g.,* N.Y. Gen. Bus. Law §§ 340–347.

Antitrust Procedures and Penalties Act: Amendment to section 5 of the Clayton Act creating a mechanism for public challenge of settlements of civil antitrust suits brought by the Justice Department, known as the Tunney Act for its sponsor, Senator John Tunney. Pub. L. No. 93-528, 88 Stat. 1706 (1974); 15 U.S.C. § 16(b)–(h). *See* S. Rep. No. 93-298, 93d Cong., 1st Sess. (1974); H.R. Rep. No. 93-1463, 93d Cong., 1st Sess. (1974); Sierk, *The Increased Potential for Challenges to Settlements of Government Antitrust Cases,* 32 Bus. Law. 451 (1977).

AOD: Action on decision, a document of the Internal Revenue Service.

APA: Administrative Procedure Act.

APB: Accounting Principles Board of the American Institute of Certified Public Accountants.

API: American Petroleum Institute.

Appraisal right: Right of a dissenting corporate shareholder to have shares appraised and to receive fair value therefor, if such shareholder objects to a statutory merger that he cannot block. Model Business Corporation Act § 81; N.Y. Bus. Corp. Law § 623; Del. Code Ann. Tit. 8 § 262; Cal. Corp. Code §§ 1300–1312. See squeeze-out merger.

Arb: Risk arbitrageur.

ARB: Accounting Research Bulletin.

Arbitrage: Transaction based on the difference in price of a commodity or security between markets by simultaneous buying and selling of the same commodity or security in different markets. *See* M. Stigum, *Money Market Calculations: Yields, Break-Evens, and Arbitrage* 128 (1981). See also **risk arbitrage.**

Arbitrage bond: Obligation issued by a state or local government, the proceeds of which are invested in securities generating taxable interest, expected to have a higher yield than the rate on the bonds. Interest on arbitrage bonds is not exempt from federal income tax, as is interest on other types of municipal bonds. I.R.C. § 103(c).

Arbitrageur: One who engages in arbitrage.

Arbitration: Resolution of a dispute by a proceeding before an expert or panel of experts, rather than a proceeding in court. Arbitration is often specified in contracts as the means of settling disputes, and is quite common in the maritime setting. *See* Federal Arbitration Act, Pub. L. No. 401, ch. 213, 43 Stat. 883 (1925), 9 U.S.C. §§ 1–14, 201–208; *see generally* G. Goldberg, *A Lawyer's Guide to Commercial Arbitration* (1977); Higgins, Brown, & Roach, *Pitfalls in International Commercial Arbitration,* 35 Bus. Law. 1035 (1980).

Arbitration Act: Federal statute covering arbitration of maritime and commercial disputes; Pub. L. No. 401, ch. 213, 43 Stat. 883 (1925), 9 U.S.C. §§ 1–14, 201–208.

"A" reorganization: Statutory merger or consolidation. See **reorganization.**

Arrangement: Agreement among a debtor and its creditors to extend the time of payment or reduce the amount of debt. *See* Del. Code Ann. Tit. 8 § 302(b).

Arrears, in: 1. Overdue and unpaid. 2. In the case of rent, not due until the end of the period of occupancy for which the rent is calculated.

Arrest: Seizure of a vessel pursuant to an action in rem for a claim against the vessel in admiralty. *See* Federal Rules of Civil Procedure, Supplemental Rules for Certain Admiralty and Maritime Claims, Rule C.

Articles of incorporation: Document filed with the secretary of state to create a corporation in those states with a business corporation law based on the Model Business Corporation Act. The articles of incorporation must contain certain information required by the state business corporation laws, such as the name of the corporation, the authorized capital structure, the purpose for which the corporation is formed, and the location of the principal office in the state. Model Business Corporation Act § 54 (1979). The term usually includes all amendments; Model Business Corporation Act § 2(c) (1979); Cal. Corp. Code § 154. See **certificate of incorporation.**

Articulation: Relationship between balance sheet items—assets, liabilities, and equity—and income and its components—revenues, expenses, gains, and losses. Financial Accounting Standards Board, Statement of Financial Accounting Concepts No. 3, *Elements of Financial Statements of Business Enterprises,* paragraph 15 (1980).

A/S: 1. *Aktieselskab,* joint stock company organized under the laws of Denmark. 2. *Aksjeselskab,* joint stock company organized under the laws of Norway.

Ashbacker doctrine: Doctrine that two parties making mutually exclusive applications to an administrative agency are entitled to comparative hearings. *Ashbacker Radio Corp. v. FCC,* 326 U.S. 327 (1945). *See also Northwest Airlines v. CAB,* 194 F. 2d 339 (D.C. Cir. 1952).

Asiadollar: Asian currency unit.

Asian currency unit: United States dollar held in Singapore.

Asian Development Bank: International organization to finance development in member countries of Asia. Loans are made only to member countries or their central banks, or are guaranteed by the member country. The bank borrows money in various countries, and has offered bonds and notes in the United States. *See* Asian Development Bank Act, Pub. L. No. 89-369, 80 Stat. 71 (1966), 22 U.S.C. § 285; Rea & Ilyeas, *The Asian Development Bank,* in II W. Surrey & D. Wallace, Jr., ed., *A Lawyer's Guide to International Business Transactions* 155 (2d ed. 1979).

Asian dollar CD: Certificate of deposit issued by a Singapore branch of a United States or Japanese bank, denominated in dollars.

As is: Language in a contract of sale meaning that the buyer takes all risk as to the quality and condition of the property involved. In a transaction for the sale of goods, such language acts to exclude implied warranties. UCC Section 2-316. See **implied warranty.**

As per recital: Recital on an instrument citing the circumstances that gave rise to the instrument, which does not make the instrument unconditional (and hence does not impair the treatment of the instrument as a negotiable instrument). *See* UCC Section 3-105(1)(b).

ASPR: Armed Services Procurement Regulation.

ASR: Accounting Series Release.

Assessed value: Value of property for the purpose of levying a tax that is based on value; assessed value may be an arbitrary value, unrelated to current market value.

Assessment: Claim against stockholders for any unpaid balance of the purchase price of stock, in the event that the assets of the corporation are insufficient to satisfy the claims of its creditors. Del. Code Ann. Tit. 8 § 162; Cal. Corp. Code § 423. *See Cooney Co. v. Arlington Hotel Co.,* 11 Del. Ch. 286, 101 A. 879 (1917), *aff'd sub. nom. duPont et al. v. Ball et al.,* 11 Del. Ch. 430, 106 A. 39 (1918).

Assessment ratio: Ratio of assessed value to current market value.

Asset: The property of an entity that can be expressed in monetary terms; the property of an entity that is available to pay creditors. As defined by the Financial Accounting Standards Board, "Assets are probable future economic benefits obtained or controlled by a particular entity as a result of past transactions or events." Financial Accounting Standards Board, Statement of Financial Accounting Concepts No. 3, *Elements of Financial Statements of Business Enterprises,* paragraph 19 (1980). *See also* American Institute of Certified Public Accountants, Accounting Principles Board Statement No. 4, Ch. 5, *Basic Features and Basic Elements of Financial Accounting,* paragraph 19 (1970).

Asset-based loan: Loan based on the security of specific assets, rather than the general credit of the borrower.

Asset case: Bankruptcy case in which the assets are sufficient to pay administrative expenses and make some distribution to creditors.

Asset depreciation range and class life system: System of specified ranges of useful lives of various classes of property for use in taking depreciation deductions from income for federal tax purposes under section 167 of the Internal Revenue Code. *See* Rev. Proc. 72-10, 1972-1 C.B. 721; Rev. Proc. 77-10, 1977-1 C.B. 548. See also **accelerated cost recovery system.**

Asset guideline class: Class of assets with a certain guideline period of useful life for depreciation purposes under the asset depreciation range system.

Assets of the plan: For the purpose of ERISA, the assets of an employee pension benefit plan or employee welfare benefit plan that are subject to the fiduciary responsibility provisions of sections 401–414 thereof.

Assign: 1. To convey or transfer rights. 2. Assignee, usually prospective and as yet unidentified, as in "successors and assigns." See **assignment.**

Assignee: Party to whom an assignment is made.

Assignment: Transfer of a given piece of property or right, usually limited to transfers of contractual rights. In certain cases, an assignment may be distinguished from a transfer, in that transfer implies substitution of the beneficiary of the contractual rights, whereas assignment refers to an alienation by a party of contractual rights to which it will be entitled upon performance of obligations under the contract. Thus an assignment is usually limited to rights, and excludes duties. Under most circumstances, contractual rights can be assigned unless the parties to the contract agree otherwise. *See Restatement, Second, Contracts* §§ 316–343 (1981); UCC Sections 2-210, 5-116. Delegation of duties is altogether different from an assignment, although an assignment may involve a delegation of duties; an assignment of a contract of sale subject to Article 2 of the Uniform Commercial Code–Sales, in general terms delegates to the assignee the duties of the assignor under the contract, and the assignee's acceptance of the assignment constitutes a promise to perform those duties. UCC Section 2-210(4).

Assignment of wages: Assignment by a debtor to a creditor of the right to collect and receive a portion of the debtor's wages if a default occurs on the debt in question, without resort to judicial process.

Assignor: Party by whom an assignment is made.

Associate company: For the purpose of the Public Utility Holding Company Act of 1935, an "associate company" of a company means any company in the same holding-company system with such company. "Company" and "holding company system" are both specifically defined in the act. Section 2 of the Public Utility Holding Company Act of 1935, 15 U.S.C. § 79b(a); *see also* I.R.C. § 1083(b).

Associated company: For the purpose of International Accounting Standard 3, *Consolidated Financial Statements*:

An "associated company" is an investee company that is not a subsidiary and in respect of which

(a) the investor's interest in the voting power of the investee is substantial, and

(b) the investor has the power to exercise significant influence over the financial and operating policies of the investee, and

(c) the investor intends to retain its interest as a long-term investment.

There is a presumption against "significant influence" if the investor holds less than 20% of the voting power of the "investee." International Accounting Standards Committee, Statement of International Accounting Standards 3, paragraph 4 (1976).

Association: Organization whose characteristics require it to be taxed as a corporation rather than another type of organization such as a partnership or trust. These characteristics are (a) associates, (b) an objective to carry on business and divide the gains therefrom, (c) continuity of life, (d) centralization of management, (e) liability for debts limited to the organization's property, and (f) free transferability of interests. Treas. Reg. § 301.7701-2; *see Morrissey v. Commissioner,* 296 U.S. 344 (1935).

Association of American Railroads: Private organization of railroad companies in North America which provides a variety of functions for member railroads, including arrangements for interchange of equipment, setting of standards for equipment and facilities, preparation of statistics, and promotion of railroad interests in Washington.

Association of International Bond Dealers: Association, with headquarters in Zurich, formed to establish uniform practices in international bond markets.

Assurance of voluntary compliance: Affidavit given by the subject of an FTC investigation promising to discontinue the challenged practices, without an admission that the practices are illegal. *See* American Bar Association, Section of Antitrust Law, *Antitrust Law Developments* 212 (1975).

Assured: Person insured.

At par: At the face, or nominal amount.

At-risk rules: Provisions of the Internal Revenue Code that limit the amount a taxpayer can deduct for business losses to the amount of the taxpayer's actual liability and amount "at risk." I.R.C. § 465. With respect to investment credit, *see* I.R.C. § 46(c)(8).

Attach: Used in connection with a security interest under the Uniform Commercial Code to mean to become enforceable against the debtor with respect to the collateral. A security interest attaches to collateral when the debtor has signed a security agreement containing a description of the collateral, the secured party has given value, and the debtor has rights in the collateral. *See* UCC Section 9-203. A security interest that has attached may not be valid against third parties until it has also been "perfected."

Attachment: Lien on property established at the commencement of a legal action as security for the payment of any judgment recovered in the action.

At the close: In connection with an order to buy or sell securities, at or as close as possible to the price of the security at the close of the trading session on the exchange on which the security is traded.

At the market: At the currently prevailing market price. Usually, in connection with an order to by or sell securities, "at the market" means the price that prevails when the order is received.

At the opening: In connection with an order to buy or sell securities, at the opening of the next trading session on the exchange on which the security is traded, or not at all.

Attorney-in-fact: Party acting for another under a power of attorney.

Attornment: Acknowledgment by a tenant of a new landlord.

Attribute: In accounting terminology, a trait or aspect of an accounting element to be measured. *See* Financial Accounting Standards Board, Statement of Financial Accounting Concepts No. 1, *Objectives of Financial Reporting by Business Enterprises*, paragraph 2, n. 2 (1978). For example, historical cost and replacement cost are attributes of an asset.

Attribution rules: Provisions of the Internal Revenue Code for constructive ownership of stock whereby stock nominally owned by family members is attributed to an individual, and stock owned by partnerships, trusts, and corporations may be attributed to partners, beneficiaries, or majority stock-holders. I.R.C. § 318.

Auction: Sale in which the seller or his agent (the "auctioneer") invites offers from successive bidders in an effort to obtain the most favorable bid. *See Restatement, Second, Contracts* § 28 (1981); UCC Section 2-328.

Audit committee: Committee of the board of directors of a corporation, usually composed of directors who are not members of management, that performs certain auditing functions such as selection of independent auditors, review of the plan of audit, review of the results of audit, review of internal controls, review of interim financial information, review of press releases, special investigations, and internal audits. Securities and Exchange Commission, *Staff Report on Corporate Accountability* F60 (1980). *See* Connecticut Stock Corporation Act, 33 Conn. Stat. Ann. § 318(b); *see generally,* J. Bacon, *Corporate Directorship Practices: The Audit Committee* (1979); Baruch, *The Audit Committee: A Guide for Directors,* Harv. Bus. Rev. 184 (May–June, 1980); *The Overview Committees of the Board of Directors,* 35 Bus. Law. 1335 (1980); Greene & Falk, *The Audit Committee—A Measured Contribution to Corporate Governance: A Realistic Appraisal of Its Objectives and Functions,* 34 Bus. Law. 1229 (1979).

Auslandskassenverein: System of clearing foreign securities in Germany.

Authenticate: See signed.

Authority to pay: Authorization given by the issuer (or confirmer) of a letter of credit to a third party to pay drafts drawn under the credit.

Authority to purchase: Advice that the writer has been authorized by a third party to deal in a specified way with specified instruments, such as purchasing documentary drafts. *See* H. Harfield, *Letters of Credit* 17 (1979).

Authorized capital stock: Total number of shares of stock which a corporation is authorized to issue, whether or not the total number of shares that may be outstanding at any one time be limited to a lesser number. Del. Code Ann. Tit. 8 § 391(b).

Authorized shares: Shares of all classes of stock which a corporation is authorized to issue. Model Business Corporation Act § 2(g) (1979).

Automated clearinghouse: Computer-based bank clearing and settlement operation for the exchange of electronic, paperless transactions among participating banks. The transactions cleared through an automated clearinghouse are usually recurring payments for which paper checks are not considered necessary.

Automatic stay: 1. Stay of any action to enforce claims or recover property from a debtor, occurring automatically with the filing of a petition under the Bankruptcy Code. 11 U.S.C. § 362. *See* H.R. Rep. No. 95-595, 95th Cong., 1st Sess. 174, 340 (1977). 2. Stay of a bank merger upon commencement of an action by the Antitrust Division of the United States Department of Justice. The Bank Merger Act of 1966, 12

U.S.C. § 1828(c)(7)(A); *see United States v. First City National Bank of Houston,* 386 U.S. 361 (1967).

Automobile Dealers' Franchise Act; Automobile Dealers' Day in Court Act: Law permitting automobile dealers to bring suit in federal court against automobile manufacturers in matters related to dealer franchises. Pub. L. No. 1026, ch. 1038, 70 Stat. 1125 (1956), 15 U.S.C. §§ 1221–25. *See Schnabel v. Volkswagen of America Inc.,* 185 F. Supp. 122 (N.D. Iowa 1960).

Average life: Average maturity of a debt instrument with sinking fund or principal amortization provisions, determined by taking an average of the periods until principal is repaid, weighted by the amount of principal repaid at the end of each such period.

Averaging convention: Convention permitting the assumption, for the purpose of depreciation under section 167 of the Internal Revenue Code, that all acquisitions and retirements of depreciable assets in a given tax year occurred on the first day of the second half of that year (the half-year convention) or that the acquisitions and retirements in the first half of the tax year occurred on the first day of that year, and the acquisitions and retirements in the second half of the tax year occurred on the first day of the next tax year (the modified half-year convention). Treas. Reg. § 1-167(a)-11(c)(2). See also **accelerated cost recovery system.**

Avoiding power: Power of a trustee in bankruptcy to avoid a transfer of the debtor's property for the benefit of creditors made while the debtor was insolvent or within 90 days of the filing of the petition for bankruptcy. 11 U.S.C. § 547(b); *see* H.R. Rep. No. 95-595, 95th Cong., 1st Sess. 177 (1977).

B

Baby bond: Bond with a par value of $100 or less.

Bad debt: Debt that becomes worthless. *See* I.R.C. §§ 166, 111.

Bailee: Person holding goods under a bailment. In the case of transactions evidenced by documents of title covered by Article 7 of the Uniform Commercial Code, "bailee" means "the person who by a warehouse receipt, bill of lading or other document of title acknowledges possession of goods and contracts to deliver them." UCC Section 7-102(1)(a).

Bailment: Delivery of personal property in trust to another, for a specific purpose, pursuant to a contract (express or implied), in contemplation of eventual return of the property to the owner.

Bailment-lease: Legal device of the nineteenth century for financing of a sale whereby personal property, owned by one, is delivered to another who could retain the property so long as regular payments are made. At the end of a specified period, the possessor of the property would become the owner, perhaps upon payment of a nominal sum. A bailment-lease was the equivalent of a conditional sale, and was used in jurisdictions where the title-retention feature of the conditional sale device was not given legal effect. *See* Montgomery, *The Pennsylvania Bailment Lease,* 79 U. of Pa. L. Rev. 920 (1931).

Bailor: Party who surrenders property to a bailee.

Bailout: Removal by shareholders of corporate profits at capital gains rates by borrowing funds secured by the corporation's stock and exchanging that stock for the stock of a newly formed holding company and the assumption by the holding company of the liability for the borrowed funds. Sections 304 and 306 of the Internal Revenue Code (as amended by the Tax Equity and Fiscal Responsibility Act of 1982) have anti-bailout provisions.

Balance sheet: Statement of financial position; statement of the assets, liabilities, and capital of an entity at a specified time; sometimes called a statement of condition.

Balleisen contract: Contract of employment that appears to give recognition to rights to collective bargaining but effectively denies such rights.

Balloon maturities: Bonds maturing last in an issue of bonds with serial maturities, in which the last maturities are a substantially greater proportion of the issue than the earlier maturities.

Balloon note: Note whose regular principal amortization features are insufficient to retire the indebtedness fully before maturity. All or a major portion of the principal will then be payable at the maturity of the note in a single, "balloon" payment. See also **bullet loan.**

Balloon payment: Payment at the maturity of a balloon note. Such a payment is substantially larger than the other payments on the note.

BAN: Bond anticipation note.

Bank: Institution that accepts funds for deposit, lends money, and may perform financial operations such as handling checks, bills of exchange, and other instruments of credit. For the purpose of the Federal Reserve Act, "the word shall be held to include State bank, banking association, and trust company, ..." Pub. L. No. 43, ch. 6, 38 Stat. 251 (1913); 12 U.S.C. § 221. *See also* section 2(b) of the Bank Holding Company Act. The Securities Exchange Act of 1934, section 3(a)(6), defines a bank as:

(A) a banking institution organized under the laws of the United States, (B) a member bank of the Federal Reserve System, (C) any other banking institution, whether incorporated or not, doing business under the laws of any State or of the United States, a substantial portion of the business of which consists of receiving deposits or exercising fiduciary powers similar to those permitted to national banks under section 11(k) of the Federal Reserve Act, as amended, and which is supervised and examined by State or Federal authority having supervision over banks, and which is not operated for the purpose of evading the provisions of this title, and (D) a receiver, conservator, or other liquidating agent of any institution or firm included in clauses (A), (B), or (C) of this paragraph.

15 U.S.C. § 78c(a)(6). For the purposes of special tax rules for banks, the Internal Revenue Code defines a bank as

a bank or trust company incorporated and doing business under the laws of the United States (including laws relating to the District of Columbia) or of any State, a substantial part of the business of which consists of receiving deposits and making loans and discounts, or of exercising fiduciary powers similar to those permitted to national banks under authority of the Comptroller of the Currency, and which is subject by law to supervision and examination by State, or Federal authority having supervision over banking institutions. Such term also means a domestic building and loan association.

I.R.C. § 581. Under the Uniform Commercial Code, a bank is "any person engaged in the business of banking." UCC Section 1-201(4). The Delaware law provisions that deny "banking power" to corporations organized under the Delaware Corporation Law speak of the power of "issuing bills, notes, or other evidence of debt for circulation as money, or the power of carrying on the business of receiving deposits as money," but corporations organized to "buy, sell and otherwise deal in notes, open accounts and other similar evidences of debt, or to loan money and to take notes, open accounts and other similar evidences of debt as collateral security therefor..." are not regarded as engaged in the business of banking. Del. Code Ann. Tit. 8 § 126.

Bank check: Check drawn by a bank on itself or on its account at another bank.

Bank discount: Method used by banks to calculate the discounted price of an instrument at a given annual rate. Bank discount is based on the face amount of the instrument, and is figured on the actual number of days to maturity, but uses a 360-day year for the daily equivalent of the annual rate. Thus, the discount is the number of days to maturity, times the annual rate, divided by 360. The price is the face amount less the discount. For a given price, the bank discount rate is lower than the bond-equivalent yield. Treasury bills are quoted on a bank discount basis.

Bank draft: Draft written by a domestic bank on funds on deposit in its account at a foreign correspondent bank.

Banker's acceptance: Form of bill of exchange, a draft drawn on a bank, that has been accepted by the bank; that is, the bank has agreed by its en-dorsement on the face of the draft to pay the draft at maturity. Banker's acceptances are negotiable instruments, and when a banker's acceptance has been negotiated, the drawer who has endorsed the acceptance and the accepting bank are both obligors on the draft. Banker's acceptances usually arise from letters of credit in foreign trade transactions when a draft is drawn by a foreign seller of goods pursuant to the authority of a letter of credit issued on behalf of the buyer of the goods. *See* Joines, *Bankers' Acceptances,* in T. Cook, ed., *Instruments of the Money Market* 77 (4th ed., 1977). Bankers' acceptances meeting the requirements of section 13 of the Federal Reserve Act are acceptable for borrowing from the Federal Reserve by member banks. Regulation A of the Federal Reserve, 12 C.F.R. § 201.4.

Banker's credit: Letter of credit; in Article 2 of the Uniform Commercial Code—Sales, a banker's credit in a contract of sale means "an irrevocable credit issued by a financing agency of good repute and, where the shipment is overseas, of good international repute." UCC Section 2-325.

Bank for Cooperatives: Bank organized under the Farm Credit Act of 1933 to make and service loans to eligible cooperative associations, owned and controlled by farmers and persons engaged in farm-related activities. There is a Central Bank for Cooperatives which participates in the larger loans made by the district banks. Banks for Cooperatives are supervised by the Farm Credit Administration. *See* Title III of the Farm Credit Act of 1971,

Pub. L. No. 92-181, 85 Stat. 583 (1971).

Bank for International Settlements: Independent financial organization located in Basle, Switzerland, which performs a variety of banking, trustee, and agent functions, primarily with central banks. The BIS provides a forum for representatives of central banks to meet monthly, and is the only international financial institution in which Eastern European countries are represented.

Bank holding company: Company that owns or controls one or more banks. For the purpose of the Bank Holding Company Act, a company has control over a bank if it has the power to vote 25% or more of the voting stock, controls the election of the board of directors, or exercises a controlling influence over the management or policies of the bank. Section 2(a) of the Bank Holding Company Act, 12 U.S.C. § 1841(a). Bank holding companies are supervised by the Federal Reserve Board. *See also* Regulation S-X, 17 C.F.R. 210.1-02(e).

Bank Holding Company Act of 1956: Federal statute subjecting bank holding companies to supervision by the Federal Reserve Board. Pub. L. No. 511, ch. 240, 70 Stat. 133 (1956); 12 U.S.C. §§ 1841–1850. *See* American Bar Association, Section of Antitrust Law, *Antitrust Law Developments* 92 (1975).

Banking Act of 1933: Federal legislation prohibiting banks from engaging in the sale of securities and other activities reserved to investment banking firms; usually called the Glass-Steagall Act. Pub. L. No. 66, ch. 89, 48 Stat. 162 (1933).

Banking day: For the purpose of Article 3–Commercial Paper and Article 4–Bank Deposits and Collections of the Uniform Commercial Code, "banking day" means "that part of any day on which a bank is open to the public for carrying on substantially all of its banking functions." UCC Section 4-104(1)(c).

Bank Merger Act of 1966: Amendment to the Federal Deposit Insurance Act requiring bank regulatory agencies to take into account antitrust considerations in approving bank mergers. Pub. L. No. 89-356, 80 Stat. 7 (1966), 12 U.S.C. § 1828. *See United States v. First City National Bank of Houston,* 386 U.S. 361 (1967). *See generally* American Bar Association, Section of Antitrust Law, *Antitrust Law Developments* 89 (1975); Austin, *The Evolution of Commercial Bank Merger Antitrust Law,* 36 Bus. Law. 297 (1981).

Bank reserves: Balances set aside by banks to meet reserve requirements. Banks that are members of the Federal Reserve System keep reserves in the form of cash and deposits at the Federal Reserve Banks.

Bankrupt: One who comes under the protection of the bankruptcy laws, whether voluntarily or involuntarily.

Bankruptcy: Circumstances of financial distress such that the protection of the bankruptcy laws is employed for the orderly disposition of assets and settlement of creditors' claims. Bankruptcy was once distinguished from insolvency in that bankruptcy was involuntary, initiated by creditors, whereas insolvency was voluntary and initiated by the debtor. In current usage, the term "bankruptcy" and the bankruptcy laws cover both voluntary and involuntary situations.

Bankruptcy Act: Act of July 1, 1898, Pub. L. No. 171, 55th Cong., 30 Stat. 544, as amended from time to time, and finally, in 1979, superseded by the Bankruptcy Code.

Bankruptcy Code: An Act to establish a uniform Law on the Subject of Bankruptcies, Pub. L. No. 95-598, 92 Stat. 2549 (1978); effective October 1, 1979, and codified at 11 U.S.C. §§ 101–151326. *See* S. Rep. No. 95-989, 95th Cong., 2d Sess. (1978); H. R. Rep. No. 95-595, 95th Cong., 1st Sess. (1977); 124 Cong. Rec. S 17406 (1978); 124 Cong. Rec. H 11809 (1978). *See generally Structuring and Documenting Business Financing Transactions Under the Federal Bankruptcy Code of 1978,* 35 Bus. Law. 1645 (1980).

Bank wire: Electronic communication system owned and operated by participating banks, for the transmittal of information regarding funds transfer and other information. The bank wire is much like the Fed wire, but is private, and permits the transfer of information not handled by the Fed wire. See also **Fed wire.**

Banque d'affaires: French investment banking firm. A banque d'affairs has greater authority to conduct banking activities than American investment banking houses, and is similar to a British merchant bank.

BarChris: *Escott v. BarChris Construction Corp.,* 283 F. Supp. 643 (S.D.N.Y. 1968).

Bare-boat charter: Charter of a vessel in which the charterer supplies the crew, pays all expenses, and controls the course of the voyage. A bare-boat charter can be written with the same features as a finance lease, and can be used as the basis for a financing.

Bargain: "Agreement to exchange promises or to exchange a promise for a performance or to exchange performances." *Restatement, Second, Contracts* § 3 (1981). The Restatement uses the terms "bargain," "agreement," and "contract"; "bargain" is narrower than the other terms, its essential characteristic being the exchange. See **agreement; contract.**

Bargain purchase option: Provision in a lease allowing the lessee, at his option, to purchase the leased property for a price that is sufficiently lower than the expected fair value of the property (at the date the option can be exercised) that such exercise appears, at the inception of the lease, to be reasonably assured. Financial Accounting Standards Board, Statement of Financial Accounting Standards No. 13, *Accounting for Leases,* paragraph 5d (1976).

Bargain renewal option: Provision in a lease allowing the lessee, at his option, to renew the lease for a rental that is sufficiently lower than the expected fair rental of the property (at the date the option can be exercised) that such exercise appears, at the inception of the lease, to be reasonably assured. Financial Accounting Standards Board,

Statement of Financial Accounting Standards No. 13, *Accounting for Leases,* paragraph 5e (1976).

Base rate: In international debt transactions, the interest rate to which is added the lending margin to borrowers.

Basic facts or basic findings: Factual conclusions upon which the ultimate finding is based. *See, e.g., California Motor Transp. Co. v. Public Utilities Com.,* 59 Cal. 2d 270, 379 P. 2d 324 (1963). Compare **ultimate facts.**

Basis: Value placed on property for the purpose of determining gain or loss under the Internal Revenue Code. In general, the basis is the cost, less depreciation deductions taken. *See* I.R.C. §§ 1011–1016.

Basis point: Measure of the difference between interest rates; a basis point is one one-hundredth of one percent.

Basis price: Price of a security expressed in terms of yield to maturity or annual rate of return.

Basket clause: 1. Clause in a legal investment law governing the investments of insurance companies or savings banks, permitting investments that do not fit within any of the other specifically described and permitted categories. The use of the basket clause is usually limited to one or two percent of the assets of a bank or insurance company subject to the law. *See, e.g.,* New York Banking Law, section 235, subdivision 29; New York Insurance Law, section 81, subdivision 17. 2. Protective clause in a contract tying future

payment to the dollar price of a basket of goods or services or a basket of currencies. *See* Carter, *Maintenance of Value "Equal Protection" for Small Savers: Foreign Currency Accounts Versus Basket Clause Accounts,* 34 Bus. Law. 233, 249 (1978).

Basket lien: Lien on a described group of property, without specific identification of individual pieces, and permitting the movement into and out of the group at the control of the debtor. Basket liens are used for spare parts in connection with aircraft financing. *See* Federal Aviation Act, section 503(a)(3), 49 U.S.C. § 1403(a)(3); UCC Section 9-205.

Battle of the forms: Controversy that arises in sales transactions when a seller supplies a quotation or makes an offer to sell on its quotation form, and the buyer accepts by issuing a purchase order on its form, and the terms on the buyer's form are inconsistent with the terms on the seller's form. *See* UCC Section 2-207; *Doughboy Ind., Inc. v. Pantasote Co.,* 17 App. Div. 2d 216, 233 N.Y.S. 2d 488 (1962); Duesenberg, *Contract Creation: The Continuing Struggle with Additional and Different Terms Under Uniform Commercial Code Section 2-207,* 34 Bus. Law. 1477 (1979).

BCR: Benefit/cost ratio.

Bearer: When used to describe a security, means payable to the bearer or person in possession, as a "bearer" bond. The bearer, under the Uniform Commercial Code, means "the person in possession of an instrument, document of title, or security payable to bearer or indorsed in blank." UCC Section 1-201(5). Under Article 8 of the Uniform Commercial Code–Investment Securities, a security is in "bearer" form "when it runs to bearer according to its terms and not by reason of any indorsement." UCC Section 8-102(1)(d).

Bellotti: *First National Bank of Boston v. Bellotti*, 435 U.S. 765 (1978). Case striking down a Massachusetts statute that prohibited corporations from making expenditures for the purpose of influencing legislation.

Benedict v. Ratner: Case holding that floating liens (liens on property in the control of the debtor and subject to sale and replacement, such as inventory or spare parts supplies) were ineffective. 268 U.S. 353 (1925). The rule of *Benedict v. Ratner* was reversed by the Uniform Commercial Code. UCC Section 9-205.

Beneficial owner: 1. Section 16 of the Securities Exchange Act of 1934, 15 U.S.C. § 78p, requires reporting by "every person who is directly or indirectly the beneficial owner of more than 10 per centum of any class of any equity security... ." In this context, the term "beneficial owner" has been broadly construed to include parties with overlapping economic interests. *See Whiting v. Dow Chemical Co.*, 386 F. Supp. 1130 S.D.N.Y. 1974), *aff'd*, 523 F.2d 680 (2d Cir. 1975). The Williams Act amendments to the Securities Exchange Act of 1934 impose certain disclosure obligations on any person who is "directly or indirectly the beneficial owner of more than 5 per centum" of classes of securities registered under the Act (section 13(d)), and

in connection with tender offers (section 14(d). Elaborate definitions are provided in the regulations: SEC Rule 13d-3, 14d-1(b)(4), 17 C.F.R. §§ 240.13d-3, 240.14d-1(b)(4), but the definitions are not necessarily applicable to section 16. SEC Release No. 34-11616 (1975). *See* Shreve, *Beneficial Ownership of Securities Held by Family Members*, 22 Bus. Law. 431 (1967). 2. Beneficiary of a trust that owns and leases equipment in a leveraged lease transaction. If the trust is properly arranged, the tax incidents of ownership of the equipment will pass through to the beneficial owner or owners.

Beneficiary: 1. With respect to contracts, a person that will benefit from performance, other than the promisee. *Restatement, Second, Contracts*, § 2(4) (1981); *see* §§ 302–315. 2. With respect to a letter of credit, "a person who is entitled under its terms to draw or demand payment." UCC Section 5-103(1)(d).

Benefit/cost ratio: Ratio of benefits to costs of a project, usually a public works project. If the benefit/cost ratio is greater than one, the project is justified by this measure. See **cost-benefit analysis**.

Benefit of the bargain: See **expectation interest**.

Berne Union: International Union for the Protection of Literary and Artistic Works, with headquarters in Berne, Switzerland.

Best-efforts underwriting: Underwriting arrangement for an issue of securities whereby the underwriters agree to use their "best efforts" to sell the securities, but if all or a specified percentage cannot be sold, the underwriters have no obligation to purchase the securities. Compare firm commitment underwriting.

Beta: The slope of the "characteristic line" of a stock. The "characteristic line" is a plot of the relationship of the excess return of a stock (the amount by which the rate of return on the stock exceeds a risk-free rate of return) to the excess return of the stock market as a whole. A beta of greater than one indicates that the stock's excess return varies more than proportionately with the excess return of the market, and thus presents greater opportunity for gain and greater risk than the market as a whole. *See* J. Van Horne, *Financial Management and Policy* 59 (4th ed. 1977).

Between merchants: In Article 2 of the Uniform Commercial Code–Sales, a transaction "between merchants" is any transaction "with respect to which both parties are chargeable with the knowledge or skill of merchants." UCC Section 2-104(3).

Bill of exchange: Draft or order to pay a specified amount at a specified time drawn on, and payable by, an individual, a business, or a financial institution.

Bill of lading: Under the Uniform Commercial Code, the term "bill of lading" means "a document evidencing the receipt of goods for shipment issued by a person engaged in the business of transporting or forwarding goods, and includes an airbill." UCC Section 1-201(6). A bill of lading may be negotiable (order bill) or nonnegotiable (straight bill). For forms used by railroads, *see* 49 C.F.R. § 1035. *See generally* R. Riegert & R. Braucher, *Documents of Title* (3d. ed. 1978).

Bill of Lading Act: Federal statute covering bills of lading, similar to the Uniform Bills of Lading Act, but not fully conforming to its replacement under state law, Article 7 of the Uniform Commercial Code. 39 Stat. 538 (1916); 49 U.S.C. §§ 81-124 (to be codified as subtitle V of 49 U.S.C.). *See Chesapeake & O. Ry. v. Martin,* 283 U.S. 209 (1931).

Bill of sale: Instrument that evidences the sale or transfer of personal property.

Biomass property: Property and equipment for the burning or conversion of energy sources other than oil and gas, for which a special tax credit is available under section 48(l) and related sections of the Internal Revenue Code. I.R.C. § 48(l)(15).

BIS: Bank for International Settlements.

Blanket bond: Bond secured by a blanket mortgage.

Blanket mortgage: General mortgage; a mortgage on all of the property of the mortgagor.

Blank indorsement: Under Article 3 of the Uniform Commercial Code –Commercial Paper, an indorsement in blank "specifies no particular indorsee and may consist of a mere signature. An instrument payable to order and indorsed in blank becomes payable to bearer and may be negotiated by delivery alone until specially indorsed." UCC Section 3-204(b). A blank indorsement may be converted to a special indorsement; UCC Section 3-204(c). See also special indorsement.

Blockage discount: Reduction in price or valuation (from the quoted market price) of a large block of stock, because liquidation of the block would be expected to depress the price of the stock. *See* Treas. Reg. § 20.2031-2(e).

Blocking: Action by the United States Department of the Treasury prohibiting any transaction with respect to any property subject to United States jurisdiction in which a particular foreign country or national has an interest. *See* 31 C.F.R. §§ 500.201–202, 515.201–202, 520.101. *See* Sommerfield, *Treasury Regulation of Foreign Assets and Trade,* in I. W. Surrey & D. Wallace, Jr., ed., *A Lawyer's Guide to International Business Transactions* 265 (2d ed. 1977).

Blue-sky cases: Supreme court cases holding that state regulation of securities does not constitute an undue burden on interstate commerce, and blue-sky laws are thus valid: *Hall v. Geiger-Jones Co.,* 242 U.S. 539 (1917); *Caldwell v. Sioux Falls Stock Yards Co.,* 242 U.S. 559 (1917); *Merrick v. N.W. Halsey & Co.,* 242 U.S. 568 (1917). *See* L. Loss & E. Cowett, *Blue Sky Laws* 13 (1958).

Blue-sky laws: State laws regulating the sale of securities. *E.g.,* New York Gen. Bus. Law §§ 352–359h; Cal.

Corp. Code §§ 25000–25705. *See generally* L. Loss & E. Cowett, *Blue Sky Laws* (1958). For the origination of the term, see Mulvey, *Blue Sky Law,* 36 Can. L. T. 37 (1916). See also Uniform Securities Act; blue-sky cases.

Board of directors: Governing body of a corporation, composed of all of the directors. *See* Securities and Exchange Commission, *Staff Report on Corporate Accountability* F1 (1980); *Corporate Director's Guidebook,* 33 Bus. Law. 1591 (1978).

Boilerplate: Provisions of a contract included in all contracts of that type, usually lengthy and sometimes printed in fine print.

Bona fide purchaser: Purchaser for value in good faith without notice of defects in title. In connection with the sale of securities, Article 8 of the Uniform Commercial Code—Investment Securities, provides that a "bona fide purchaser" is a "purchaser for value in good faith and without notice of any adverse claim who takes delivery of a security in bearer form or of one in registered form issued to him or indorsed to him or in blank." UCC Section 8-302. A "bona fide purchaser" acquires a security free of any adverse claim. UCC Section 8-301(2). *See also* UCC Section 8-304; Del. Code Ann. tit. 8 § 162(c).

Bond: That which binds; an instrument evidencing an obligation, usually for the payment of money. In the narrowest sense, a bond is a long-term debt instrument, secured by a mortgage on real property or by some other form of security. Shorter-term instruments would be called notes, and unsecured obligations would be called debentures. However, in a broader sense, the term "bond" may be used to mean any and all fixed-income debt securities, including notes and debentures, as opposed to stocks. *See* Treas. Reg. § 1.171-4(a); N.Y. Bus. Corp. Law § 102(a)(1).

Bond anticipation note: Note issued by a state or municipality to cover short-term cash needs pending the issue of long-term bonds. Bond anticipation notes are short-term, intended to be retired out of the proceeds of a long-term bond issue.

Bond-equivalent yield: Yield to maturity of a discounted instrument using a 365-day year, based on the amount of the investment (the discounted amount) rather than the face amount of the instrument. The bond-equivalent yield is higher than the bank discount rate for a given price.

Bond interest coverage: Annual income or earnings of an entity, before deduction of interest and taxes, divided by the annual interest on its bonds.

Bond power: Power of attorney for the transfer of registered bonds.

Bond ratio: Proportion of bonds in total capitalization, obtained by dividing the face value of bonds outstanding by the capitalization, the total value of bonds, preferred stock, common stock (par value), capital surplus, and accumulated retained earnings.

Bond resolution: Resolution of the board of directors of a corporation, or the governing body of a government entity, authorizing the issue of a series of bonds. The obligations of the issuing entity, and any limitations thereon, are usually set forth in some detail in the bond resolution, particularly in the case of municipal bonds.

Book value: Value of an asset or entire enterprise as shown on the balance sheet of that enterprise. Book value is the original cost less depreciation, and at any time may be more or less than actual value, or market value. In the case of common stock, the "book value" is the book value of the issuer of the stock, divided by the number of outstanding shares.

Boot: Additional consideration for a transfer or exchange. In connection with an exchange of property of like kind (for which gain or loss would not be recognized for federal income tax purposes), gain would be recognized to the extent of any cash or other property received "to boot." Such cash or other property is called "boot." I.R.C. § 1031(b). *See* D. Mellinkoff, *The Language of the Law* 47 (1963). In connection with a nontaxable exchange in a corporate organization, "boot" is money or property other than stock or securities, and is taxable; *see* I.R.C. §§ 354(a), 356.

Bootstrap sale: Device to convert ordinary income to capital gains by selling a business or income-producing property to an exempt organization in an installment sale, the sale price to be paid entirely out of the earnings from the business or property. Section 514 of the Internal Revenue Code restricts the use of "bootstrap" sales by imposing a tax on the income received by the exempt organization in proportion to the debt existing on the income-producing property. *See Commissioner v. Brown,* 325 F. 2d 313 (9th Cir. 1963); Lanning, *Tax Erosion and the "Bootstrap Sale" of a Business,* 108 U. of Pa. L. Rev. 623, 943 (1960).

Borden: *United States v. Borden Co.,* 370 U.S. 460 (1962), a significant case on the defense of cost justification to charges of price discrimination.

Bottleneck monopoly: See essential facility doctrine.

Bottom-line method: Method of reporting the consolidated taxable income of an affiliated group in which the taxable income of each component member of the group is determined, and then combined. *See* I.R.C. § 818(f); compare **phase-by-phase method.**

Bottomry bond: Device for securing a loan by an interest in a vessel, occasionally used before ship mortgages were sanctioned by statute. Bottomry bonds were of only limited value, because if the vessel sank, the loan was discharged. *See The Grapeshot,* 76 U.S. (9 Wall.) 129, 135 (1870).

Boycott: Group or collective forbearance from purchasing from or doing business with an entity. Sometimes used as a tactic in labor organization; *see* section 8(b)(4) of the National Labor Relations Act, 29 U.S.C. 158(b)(4). As an antitrust matter, see **collective refusal to deal.** *See* Saltoun, *Regulation of Foreign Boycotts,* 33 Bus. Law. 559 (1978).

Bracket: Grouping of underwriters in a syndicate for an issue of securities. The underwriters are organized, and shown in publications describing the issue, into brackets depending on their role in the offering. In the top bracket are the managers of the offering, perhaps with the lead manager on top. Lower brackets list underwriters with lesser participations in the offering, and the last bracket will usually consist of regional houses in the selling group. Within brackets, the underwriters usually are listed alphabetically.

Branch: Under the Uniform Commercial Code, branch includes "a separately incorporated foreign branch of a bank." UCC Section 1-201(7).

"B" reorganization: Corporate acquisition by exchange of stock. See **reorganization.**

Bridge loan: Loan for a short period of time, pending receipt of anticipated funds, such as from the sale of property.

Broadcast Bureau: Bureau of the Federal Communications Commission responsible for licensing and regulation of radio and television broadcasting, including international shortwave broadcasting, on commercial frequencies. Other radio communications, including amateur radio operations, are regulated by the Private Radio Bureau.

Broker: Person who arranges or effects transactions, usually sales transactions, for the account of others, for compensation. For the purpose of the Securities Exchange Act of 1934, a "broker" is "any person engaged in the business of effecting transactions in securities for the account of others, but does not include a bank." Securities Exchange Act of 1934, section 3(a)(4); 15 U.S.C. § 78c(a)(4). *See* II L. Loss, *Securities Regulation* 1295 (2d ed. 1961). See also **dealer.** For the purpose of Article 8 of the Uniform Commercial Code–Investment Securities, a "broker" is a person "engaged for all or part of his time in the business of buying and selling securities, who in the transaction concerned acts for, or buys a security from or sells a security to a customer." UCC Section 8-303. The term "broker" can be distinguished from "dealer" in that a broker effects transactions for the account of others, whereas a dealer effects transactions for his own account, and may keep securities in inventory for resale.

Brokerage: Fee paid a broker for arranging or effecting a transaction.

Brokerage provision: Section 2(c) of the Robinson-Patman Act, prohibiting the parties to a sales transaction from granting or receiving a "commission, brokerage, or other compensation, or any allowance or discount in lieu thereof, except for services rendered in connection with the sale or purchase of goods, wares, or merchandise ... ." 15 U.S.C. § 13(c). *See FTC v. Henry Broch & Co.,* 363 U.S. 166 (1960). *See generally* American Bar Association, Section of Antitrust Law, *Antitrust Law Developments* 149 (1975).

Broker-dealer: With respect to securities, a person engaged in the business of effecting transactions in securities for the account of others (broker) or for his own account (dealer); an entity fitting the definition of both "broker" and "dealer" under the Securities Exchange Act of 1934. *See* Cal. Corp. Code § 25004.

Brother-sister controlled group: For the purpose of the Internal Revenue Code provisions on the filing of consolidated tax returns by a "controlled group of corporations," brother-sister controlled group means two or more corporations in which five or fewer persons who are individuals, estates, or trusts own stock possessing:

(A) at least 80 percent of the total combined voting power of all classes of stock entitled to vote or at least 80 percent of the total value of shares of all classes of the stock of each corporation, and

(B) more than 50 percent of the total combined voting power of all classes of stock entitled to vote or more than 50 percent of the total value of shares of all classes of stock of each corporation, taking into account the stock ownership of each such person only to the extent such stock ownership is identical with respect to each such corporation.

I.R.C. § 1563(a)(2). *See also* I.R.C. § 179(d)(7).

Brown Shoe: *Brown Shoe Co. v. United States,* 370 U.S. 294 (1962), a significant case regarding the definition of relevant markets for establishing the competitive impact of mergers. *See generally* American Bar Association, Section of Antitrust Law, *Antitrust Law Developments* 65 (1975).

Bubble Act: 6 Geo. I. c. 18 (1719); the first securities regulation law, passed in England after the "South Sea bubble" burst in 1719. *See* I. L. Loss, *Securities Regulation* 4 (2d ed. 1961).

Bubble policy: Enforcement policy of the Environmental Protection Agency under the Clean Air Act in which emissions of air pollutants are permitted if offsetting reductions are made in emissions at another plant in the area, so that there is not any net increase in air pollution.

Bucketing: Contracting for sales and purchases of securities or commodities at the prices quoted in the market, without actually executing the orders, but making settlements as if the securities or commodities had been purchased and sold. Cal. Corp. Code § 29008; N.Y. Gen. Bus. Law § 351. *See* Smith, *The Commodity Futures Trading Commission and the Return of the Bucketeers: A Lesson in Regulatory Failures,* 57 N.D. L. Rev. 7 (1981).

Bucket shop: Place where bucketing is conducted. *See* Cal. Corp. Code § 29006; N.Y. Gen. Bus. Law § 351-d.

Bulk sale: See bulk transfer.

Bulk transfer: Sale or transfer, not in the ordinary course of business, of a major part of the materials, supplies, merchandise, or other inventory of a business. UCC Section 6-102. *See* Article 6 of the Uniform Commercial Code—Bulk Transfers. A bulk transfer covered by Article 6 of the Uniform Commercial Code is ineffective against creditors of the transferor unless notice is given to creditors in the manner provided in Section 6-107 of the UCC. UCC Section 6-105. *See* UCC Section 9-111.

Bullet loan: Loan requiring regular payments of interest, but without any reduction or amortization of principal until maturity. The entire principal amount will then be due in one payment, called a "bullet" payment.

B-unit: Unit of currency consisting of equal proportions of United States dollars, German marks, French francs, Swiss francs, and British pounds.

Burden: Under the Uniform Commercial Code, the burden of establishing a fact means "the burden of persuading the triers of fact that the existence of the fact is more probable than its nonexistence." UCC Section 1-201(8).

Burn-up contract: Lease of nuclear fuel. *See* Financial Accounting Standards Board, Statement of Financial Accounting Standards No. 13, *Accounting for Leases,* paragraph 1 (1976).

Business corporation: Corporation organized for profit under the business corporation law of a state. The term usually does not include banking corporations, insurance companies, nonprofit corporations, and professional corporations, all of which usually are organized pursuant to special statutes.

Business corporation law: State statute providing for the creation and regulation of corporations formed for profit. Thirty-five states use a version of the Model Business Corporation Act promulgated by the Committee on Corporate Laws, Section of Corporate, Banking and Business Law of the American Bar Association. Other states, such as New York, use a unique statute incorporating elements of the Model Business Corporation Act; *see* N.Y. Bus. Corp. Law. Delaware, known for its hospitality to corporations, has a statute reflecting that view; Del. Code Ann. tit. 8. *See also* Cal. Corp. Code.

Business day: Any day except one on which banks are authorized to be closed. Usually Monday through Friday, excluding federal holidays, in the case of national banks, and excluding official state holidays, in the case of state-chartered banks.

Business development company. Company that has elected to be regulated as a business development company under sections 55 through 65 of the Investment Company Act of 1940. Small Business Incentive Act of 1980, Pub. L. No. 96-477, 94 Stat. 2275 (1980); 15 U.S.C. §§ 80a-53–64. *See* 17 C.F.R. 230.405; 47 Fed. Reg. 11380 (1982); Miller, *Small Business Investment Companies: Licensing, Tax and Securities Considerations,* 36 Bus. Law. 1679, 1689 (1981).

Business judgment rule: Rule that a corporate director acting in "good faith and with reasonable care and diligence" will not be held personally liable for a mistake in judgment. *Hodges v. New England Screw Co.,* 3 R.I. 9, 18 (1853). *See also Johnson v. Trueblood,* 629 F. 2d 287, 292 (3d Cir. 1980); *Panter v. Marshall Field & Co.,* 486 F. Supp. 1168 (N.D. Ill. 1980), *aff'd* 646 F. 2d 271 (7th Cir. 1981). The rule is incorporated in some business corporation laws: Model Business Corporation Act § 35 (1979); N.Y. Bus. Corp. Law § 717. A precise proposed formulation of the rule is set forth in Arsht, *The Business Judgment Rule Revisited,* 8 Hofstra L. Rev. 93 (1979). *See generally* Veasey, *Seeking a Safe Harbor from Judicial Scru-*

tiny of Directors' Business Decisions—An Analytical Framework for Litigation Strategy and Counseling Directors, 37 Bus. Law. 1247 (1982); Block & Prussin, *The Business Judgment Rule and Shareholder Derivative Actions: Viva Zapata?* 37 Bus. Law. 27 (1981).

Business purpose rule: Rule of tax law that the tax attributes of a transaction will be denied if the transaction is "an operation having no business or corporate purpose ... ." *Gregory v. Helvering,* 293 U.S. 465, 469 (1935). The requirement for a business purpose may be imposed on other types of transactions; *e.g.,* a corporate acquisition of its own stock in an effort to "go private" should be motivated by a business purpose of the corporation, not a personal objective of a shareholder. *Bryan v. Brock & Blevins Co.,* 490 F. 2d 563 (5th Cir.), *cert. denied,* 419 U.S. 844 (1974); *see Guidelines on Going Private,* 37 Bus. Law. 313 (1981).

Business review letter: See business review procedure.

Business review procedure: Procedure whereby the Department of Justice may issue a statement of enforcement intention with respect to a specific pending transaction upon application by the parties in cases presenting difficult antitrust questions. 28 C.F.R. § 50.6.

Business trust: Business organization using a trust relationship to provide continuity of life and limited liability. The business property is conveyed to the trustees, the trustees run the business, and the interests of the beneficiaries are transferable. A business trust is often called a Massachusetts trust. *See* Cook, *The Mysterious Massachusetts Trusts,* 9 A.B.A. J. 763 (1893).

Buy American Act: Federal statute requiring supplies and materials acquired for public use to be manufactured, mined, or produced in the United States, except under certain circumstances. Pub. L. No. 428, ch. 212, 47 Stat. 1489, 1520 (1933), 41 U.S.C. § 10a-d. *See* Trainor, *The Buy American Act: Examination, Analysis and Comparison,* 64 Mil. L. Rev. 101 (1974); Freiberg & Dunn, *The Buy American Act and Other Buy National Programs,* in I W. Surrey & D. Wallace, Jr., ed., *A Lawyer's Guide to International Business Transactions* 291 (2d ed. 1977).

Buy-back: Repurchase agreement.

Buyer: In Article 2 of the Uniform Commercial Code–Sales a buyer means "a person who buys or contracts to buy goods." UCC Section 2-103(1)(a).

Buyer in ordinary course of business: Under the Uniform Commercial Code:

a person who in good faith and without knowledge that the sale to him is in violation of the ownership rights or security interest of a third party in the goods buys in ordinary course from a person in the business of selling goods of that kind but does not include a pawnbroker. All persons who sell minerals or the like (including oil and gas) at wellhead or minehead shall be deemed to be persons in the business of selling goods of that kind. "Buying" may be for cash or by exchange of other property or on secured or unsecured credit and includes receiving goods or documents of title under a pre-existing contract for sale but does not include a transfer in bulk or as security for or in total or partial satisfaction of a money debt.

UCC Section 1-201(9). A "buyer in ordinary course of business," except in certain transactions involving farm products, takes free of a security interest created by the seller even though the security interest is perfected and even though the buyer knows of its existence. UCC Section 9-307.

Buyer provision: Section 2(f) of the Robinson-Patman Act, prohibiting the knowing inducement or receipt of a price discrimination that is illegal under section 2(a) of that act. 15 U.S.C. § 13(f). *See Automatic Canteen Co. of America v. FTC,* 346 U.S. 61 (1953). *See generally* American Bar Association, Section of Antitrust Law, *Antitrust Law Developments* 159 (1975).

Buy-out agreement: Agreement among the stockholders of a close corporation (and sometimes the corporation) for the purchase by the stockholders (or the corporation) of the shares of a stockholder upon his death or in other specified circumstances, so as to maintain control of the corporation and to provide a means of liquidating a stockholder's interest upon death. *See generally* Matsen, *A New Look at Business Buy-Out Agreements,* Prac. Law., July 15, 1979, at 43.

Buy-sell agreement: Buy-out agreement.

BV: *Besloten Vennootschap,* limited liability company organized under the laws of The Netherlands.

By-laws: Regulations or rules adopted by an organization for its management. As to corporate by-laws, *see* Model Business Corporation Act § 27 (1979); N.Y. Bus. Corp. Law § 601; Del. Code Ann. tit. 8 § 109; Cal. Corp. Code § 212.

C

C. & F.: Cost and freight; term of delivery for a transaction for the sale of goods to be shipped overseas. A selling price C. & F. means that the price includes the cost of the goods and the freight charges to the named destination. The risk of loss passes to the buyer upon delivery to the carrier, and if the goods are lost the buyer must seek his remedy against the carrier. A C. & F. contract may specify that the seller will procure insurance and charge the buyer for the premium. The term C. & F. in a contract imposes the same obligations on the seller as the term C.I.F., except as to insurance. UCC Section 2-320. Compare **C.I.F.**

CAB: Civil Aeronautics Board.

Cable Television Bureau: Bureau of the Federal Communications Commission responsible for such federal regulation of cable television as is authorized by law.

C.A.F.: French equivalent of C.I.F.

Call: Option to purchase a security at a specified price. In the case of a debt instrument, a call is a right of the debtor to redeem or prepay the debt prior to maturity.

Callable: Subject to call, or redemption, by the issuer before maturity.

Call date: Earliest date on which a debt instrument may be redeemed by the issuer (if the instrument provides for redemption before maturity).

Calvo clause: Clause in the constitutions of several Latin American countries adopting the Calvo doctrine.

Calvo doctrine: Principle that collection of debts and private claims does not justify armed intervention by governments, first enunciated by Carlos Calvo of Argentina in 1868. 3 C. Calvo, *Le Droit International Theoretique et Practique,* paragraphs 1280, 1297.

Cancellation: In Article 2 of the Uniform Commercial Code–Sales, cancellation occurs "when either party puts an end to the contract for breach by the other and its effect is the same as that of 'termination' except that the cancelling party also retains any remedy for breach of the whole contract or any unperformed balance." UCC Section 2-106(4). See termination.

Capital: Under the Delaware Corporation Law, the capital of a corporation is that part of the consideration received for shares of capital stock determined by the board of directors to be capital. The excess of net assets of the corporation over capital is surplus. Del. Code Ann. tit. 8. § 154. See also stated capital.

Capital asset: Asset for which the gain or loss in a sale or exchange receives capital gain treatment under the Internal Revenue Code. Under the Code, the term "capital asset" means "property," but does not include stock in trade and inventory, depreciable business property, real property used in a trade or business, copyrights held by the creator of the work or the person for whom the work was created, notes or accounts receivable acquired from the sale of stock in trade or inventory, and publications of the United States government acquired by means other than purchase at the price offered to the public. I.R.C. § 1221.

Capital contributed in excess of par: Capital surplus.

Capital contribution: See investment by owners.

Capital distribution: See distribution to owners.

Capital gain (or loss): Profit (or loss) on the sale of capital assets. Capital gains are taxed at a lower rate than other types of income if the assets have been held for a certain minimum period—one year under current tax law. I.R.C. §§ 1201–1256. See long-term capital gain, short-term capital gain.

Capital gain dividend: Dividend of a regulated investment company designated by that company as a capital gain dividend, so long as the aggregate of such dividends does not exceed the capital gain of the investment company for that period. I.R.C. § 852(b)(3).

Capital gain net income: Excess of the gains from sales or exchanges of capital assets over the losses from such sales or exchanges. I.R.C. § 1222(9).

Capital lease: Lease that must be shown on the balance sheet in accordance with Standard No. 13 of the Financial Accounting Standards Board. A lease should be classified as a capital lease by a lessee if one or more of the following criteria are met:

• the lease transfers ownership of the property to the lessee at the end of the lease term;

• the lease contains a bargain purchase option, permitting the lessee to acquire the property for less than the fair value;

• the lease term is equal to 75% or more of the estimated useful life of the property (except in certain cases involving used property);

• the present value of the lease payments equals or exceeds 90% of the fair value of the property (less the amount of investment tax credit retained by the lessor) at the beginning of the lease.

Financial Accounting Standards Board, Statement of Financial Accounting Standards No. 13, *Accounting for Leases,* paragraph 7 (1976).

Capital stock: All of the stock of a corporation, preferred and common.

Capital surplus: Amount paid in by shareholders in excess of the par value of the shares; entire surplus of a corporation other than its earned surplus. Model Business Corporation Act § 2(m) (1979); N.Y. Bus. Corp. Law § 102(a)(2); *see also* Del. Code Ann. tit. 8 § 154. See **surplus.**

Capital surplus rule:

Capital surplus, however created, should not be used to relieve the income account of the current or future years of charges which would otherwise fall to be made thereagainst. This rule might be subject to the exception that where, upon reorganization, a reorganized company would be relieved of charges which would require to be made against income if the existing corporation were continued, it might be regarded as permissible to accomplish the same result without reorganization provided the facts were as fully revealed to and the action as formally approved by the shareholders as in reorganization.

American Institute of Certified Public Accountants, Accounting Research Bulletin No. 43, Ch. 1A, paragraph 2 (1934). See **quasi-reorganization.**

Capitalization: The total of the book value of bonds, preferred stock, common stock and capital surplus, and accumulated retained earnings.

Capitalization ratios: Ratios representing the proportions of bonds (bond ratio), preferred stock (preferred stock ratio), and common stock, capital surplus, and accumulated retained earnings (common stock ratio) to total capitalization.

Capper-Volstead exemption: Legislation providing antitrust immunity to agricultural cooperatives for certain cooperative marketing activities. Cooperative Marketing Associations Act, Pub. L. No. 146, ch. 57, 42 Stat. 388 (1922), 7 U.S.C. §§ 291, 292; *see United States v. Borden Co.,* 308 U.S. 188 (1939); *Maryland & Virginia Milk Producers Association, Inc., v. United States,* 362 U.S. 458 (1960); *see generally* American Bar Association, Section of Antitrust Law, *Antitrust Law Developments* 392 (1975).

Cardinal change: Change order, issued by the government in connection with a procurement or acquisition contract, outside of the general scope of the contract. Under federal procurement regulations the government can require changes in contract work if such change is "within the general scope of the contract." A change order outside of that scope, or "cardinal change," is a breach of contract by the government. *Freund v. United States,* 260 U.S. 60 (1922); *see Air-A-Plane Corp. v. United States,* 187 Ct.Cl. 269, 408 F. 2d 1030 (1969); DAR §§ 7-103.2, 7-602.3, 7–1909.2; FPR §§ 1-7.102-2, 1-7.602-3.

Carriage of Goods By Sea Act: Federal statute covering certain aspects of ocean shipping. Pub. L. No. 521, ch. 229, 49 Stat. 1207 (1936); 46 U.S.C. §§ 1300–15.

Carrier: Provider of transportation for compensation. See **common carrier, contract carrier.** Definitions of various types of carriers are set forth in 49 U.S.C. § 10102. For the purpose of ICC regulation of securities, see 49

U.S.C. § 11301. *See also* I.R.C. § 3231(g).

Carrier's lien: Security interest of a carrier in goods covered by a bill of lading for charges for storage, transportation, or preservation of the goods. *See* UCC Section 7-307.

Carry: The interest cost of money borrowed to make an investment.

Carryback: Losses and tax credits that cannot be utilized to reduce income tax liability in the year incurred and that can be "carried back" for application against income in earlier years. I.R.C. §§ 46(b), 172, 1212.

Carry forward: Carryover.

Carryover: Losses and tax credits that cannot be utilized to reduce income tax liability in the year incurred and that can be "carried over" for application against income in later years. I.R.C. §§ 46(b), 172, 381, 1212.

CARS: Cable television and associated microwave radio relay service.

Case law: Law developed from written and reported decisions in individual controversies, as compared to the law expressed in statutes.

Cash basis: System of accounting that treats income as having occurred when actually received (rather than when earned or accrued), and expenses as having occurred when paid (rather than when the liability therefor arises). See accrual accounting.

Cash collateral: Under section 363 of the Bankruptcy Code, covering the use of the property of a bankrupt estate by the trustee, limitations are set forth on the use of "cash collateral." 11 U.S.C. 363(c)(2). The term means "cash, negotiable instruments, documents of title, securities, deposit accounts, or other cash equivalents in which the estate and an entity other than the estate have an interest." 11 U.S.C. § 363(a); *see* S. Rep. No. 95-989, 95th Cong., 2d Sess. 55 (1978); 124 Cong. Rec. H11093 (1978) (remarks of Rep. Edwards).

Cash dividend: Dividend paid in cash (or check), as compared to a stock dividend.

Cash equivalent: Short-term investments readily converted to cash, such as Treasury bills and certificates of deposit. See **cash collateral;** 11 U.S.C. 363(a).

Cash flow: Net income, depreciation, and amortization for a given period; surplus of cash receipts over cash disbursements. *See* SEC Accounting Series Release No. 142, 38 Fed. Reg. 9159 (1973).

Cashier's check: Check issued by a bank as its own obligation.

Cash letter of credit: Letter from a bank to a correspondent bank directing the correspondent bank to make available to the holder a certain amount of funds within a certain period.

Cash management bills: Very short-term Treasury bills, usually with a maturity of less than one month, designed to meet the cash needs of the Treasury pending receipt of tax revenues; sometimes called "short-dated" bills.

Cash-out merger: Freeze-out or squeeze-out merger. *See Roland International Corp. v. Najjar,* 407 A. 2d 1032, 1033 (Del. S. Ca. 1979).

Cash sale: In the case of a sale of securities, delivery of and payment for the security on the same day. Compare **regular way.**

Catch-up adjustment: Adjustment for the cumulative effect of an accounting change. *See* Financial Accounting Standards Board, Statement of Financial Accounting Standards No. 3, *Reporting Accounting Changes in Interim Financial Statements,* paragraphs 6, 7 (1974).

CATS: Certificate of Accrual of Treasury Securities, an interest in a fund of interest payments (coupon CATS) or principal payments (principal CATS) of a certain maturity of United States Treasury obligations. See also **TIGR.**

C.B.: Cumulative Bulletin.

CBI: Certificate of beneficial interest.

CBO: 1. Congressional Budget Office. 2. Certificate of beneficial ownership. See **certificate of beneficial interest.**

CBOE: Chicago Board Options Exchange.

CBOT: Chicago Board of Trade.

CCC: 1. Commodity Credit Corporation. 2. *Cwmni cyfyngedig cyhoeddus* (public limited company)—Welsh corporation whose stock is publicly traded.

CD: Certificate of deposit.

CDR: Collateralized depositary receipt.

Cease and desist order: Order issued by a federal bank regulatory agency pursuant to the Financial Institutions Supervisory Act requiring a bank, a bank holding company, or a bank official to terminate unlawful, unsafe, or unsound banking practices. Cease and desist orders can be enforced directly by the courts. A form of cease and desist order is also issued by the Federal Trade Commission.

Cedel: Clearing system for Eurobonds, owned by several European banks.

Central bank: Official, or government-sponsored bank of a given nation. The central bank of the United States is the Federal Reserve System.

Central Bank for Cooperatives: Central bank for the district Banks for Cooperatives, owned by the district banks, providing credit services to them and participating in the larger loans. See **Bank for Cooperatives, Farm Credit Administration.**

CEQ: Council on Environmental Quality.

CEO: Chief executive officer.

Certainty: Under the Restatement of Contracts, an offer cannot be accepted to form a contract unless the terms of the contract are "reasonably certain." "The terms of a contract are reasonably certain if they provide a basis for determining the existence of a breach and for giving an appropriate remedy." *Restatement, Second, Contracts* § 33 (1981).

Certificate of beneficial interest; certificate of beneficial ownership: Evidence of participation in a portfolio of loans or securities.

Certificate of deposit: Receipt for an interest-bearing time deposit at a bank or savings institution that cannot be withdrawn before a specified maturity date without being subject to an interest penalty. Large CDs of $100,000 or more are usually negotiable and can be sold or transferred. Certificates of deposit are not usually subject to the deposit interest rate ceilings of Federal Reserve Regulation Q, and thus carry higher rates of interest than demand deposits. *See* Nelson, *Negotiable Certificates of Deposit,* in T. Cook, ed., *Instruments of the Money Market* 57 (4th ed., 1977). For the purpose of Article 3—Commercial Paper and Article 4—Bank Deposits and Collections of the Uniform Commercial Code, a broader definition is used: "an acknowledgment by a bank of receipt of money with an engagement to repay it ..." in writing and otherwise in compliance with the requirements for form of negotiable instruments. UCC Section 3-104.

Certificate of incorporation: 1. Instrument filed with the appropriate state authorities in Delaware and certain other states to create a corporation. 2. Document evidencing the filing of articles of incorporation in states with a business corporation law based on the Model Business Corporation Act. 3. Special act of the legislature or charter creating a corporation. The term usually includes all amendments. Del. Code Ann. tit. 8. § 104; N.Y. Bus. Corp. Law § 102(a)(3). For the requirements for contents of a certificate of incorporation, see Del. Code Ann. tit. 8 § 102; N.Y. Bus. Corp. Law § 402. See also **articles of incorporation.**

Certificate of interest: Evidence of participation in a portfolio of loans or securities; in railroad equipment financing, evidence of participation in conditional sale indebtedness.

Certificate of participation: Evidence of an interest in a pool of loans or mortgages held by a federal agency. The federal agency makes the loans or takes the mortgages and issues certificates of participation to investors. The principal and interest payments on the loans or mortgages are used to service the certificates, but the United States in effect guarantees the certificates because the issuing agency has the right to draw on the United States Treasury to service the certificates. The use of certificates of participation by federal agencies has declined in favor of financing by the Federal Financing Bank. *See* Nelson, *Federal Agency Securities,* in T. Cook, ed., *Instruments of the Money Market* 85 (4th ed., 1977).

Certificate of title: Certificate issued by a state agency providing evidence of ownership of motor vehicles and certain other types of personal property. In the case of motor vehicles, notation on the certificate of title is the exclusive means of perfecting a security interest in that vehicle in most states. *See* UCC Section 9-103(2).

Certification mark: Type of mark "used upon or in connection with the products or services of one or more persons, other than the owner of the mark, to certify regional or other origin, material, mode of manufacture, quality, accuracy or other characteristics of such goods or services or that the work or labor on the goods or services was performed by members of a union or other organization." 15 U.S.C. § 1127. See **trademark.**

Certified: When used with respect to financial statements, means "examined and reported upon with an opinion expressed by an independent public or certified public accountant." Regulation S-X, 17 C.F.R. § 210.1-02(f); 17 C.F.R. § 230.405, 47 Fed. Reg. 11380 (1982).

Certified check: Check accepted by the bank on which it is drawn. *See* UCC Section 3-411.

CETA: Comprehensive Employment and Training Act of 1973.

C.F.: Cost, freight. See **C.& F.**

C.F.A.: Certified Financial Analyst.

C.F.R.: Code of Federal Regulations.

CFTC: Commodity Futures Trading Commission.

Chandler Act: Federal legislation substantially revising the Bankruptcy Act. Pub. L. No. 696, ch. 575, 52 Stat.

840 (1938). The Bankruptcy Act has since been superseded by the Bankruptcy Code.

Change in Bank Control Act: Federal statute requiring notice to the appropriate federal banking agen cy before a disposition of voting stock. 12 U.S.C. § 1817(j).

Changes in financial position: Flows or changes in assets or claims to assets over time. Financial Accounting Standards Board, Statement of Financial Accounting Concepts No. 3, *Elements of Financial Statements of Business Enterprises,* paragraph 14, n.6 (1980). See also **financial position.**

Charge-back: Revocation of credit given for a check or other item by a collecting bank that has made provisional settlement on that item if the bank fails to receive final settlement for the item. *See* UCC Section 4-212.

Charter: 1. To hire or lease a vessel. 2. In the case of corporations, the act of a state in authorizing and creating a corporation. See **certificate of incorporation; articles of incorporation.** In the case of other organizations, the declaration of trust, articles of association or partnership, or similar instrument creating the organization. As to the nature of a corporate charter, see *Trustees of Dartmouth College v. Woodward,* 17 U.S. (4 Wheat.) 518 (1819).

Charterer: Party who hires or charters a vessel from the owner.

Charter party: Contract for the use or hire of a vessel. Charter parties may be for a single voyage (voyage charter) or for a fixed period of time (time charter). A time charter in which the charterer furnishes the crew, operates the vessel, and pays all expenses is called a bareboat charter.

Chattel: Article of personal property. See **personal property**.

Chattel mortgage: Mortgage of personal property; grant of a right in or a lien on personal property to secure payment of an obligation. Since the adoption of the Uniform Commercial Code, an instrument styled a chattel mortgage would be regarded as a security interest, except in the case of vessels. *See generally* I. G. Gilmore, *Security Interests in Personal Property* 24 (1965); L. Jones, *Chattel Mortgages and Conditional Sales* (6th ed., Bowers, 1933).

Chattel paper: Under the Uniform Commercial Code, "a writing or writings which evidence both a monetary obligation and a security interest in or a lease of specific goods, ..." UCC Section 9-105(1)(b). The Uniform Commercial Code usage of the term excludes vessel charters.

Check: As defined in Article 3—Commercial Paper and Article 4—Bank Deposits and Collections of the Uniform Commercial Code, a check is "a draft drawn on a bank and payable on demand," in writing and otherwise in compliance with the requirements for form of negotiable instruments. UCC Section 3-104.

Check clearing: Movement of checks from the banks where they are deposited back to those on which they are written, and the movement of funds in

the opposite direction, resulting in appropriate credits to the accounts of banks of deposit and debits to the accounts of the paying bank. Checks may be cleared through the Federal Reserve System or through a private clearing arrangement among banks.

Check-off: Deduction of union dues from wages and forwarding to the union by the employer.

Chicago Board Options Exchange: Exchange market, sponsored by the Chicago Board of Trade, for the trading of certain stock options.

Chinese wall: Communication barrier between parts of an organization to avoid disclosure of confidential information by one part of the organization to others or to avoid conflict of interest arising from sharing information among the functions of a multi-function organization. For example, an investment banking firm would erect a "Chinese wall" around the merger group to prevent confidential information concerning pending mergers from reaching the trading staff. *See* Herzel & Colling, *The Chinese Wall and Conflict of Interest in Banks*, 34 Bus. Law. 73 (1978); Lipton & Mazur, *The Chinese Wall Solution to the Conflict Problems of Securities Firms*, 50 N.Y.U. L. Rev. 459 (1975).

CHIPS: Clearing House Interbank Payments System, a computerized clearing system of the New York Clearing House.

Choateness: Federal rule, applicable to tax liens, that a security interest in rights to future payments does not become "choate" until the property subject to the lien is identified and its amount known. *Glass City Bank v. United States*, 326 U.S. 265 (1945); *see United States v. City of New Britain*, 347 U.S. 81 (1954). (The word "choate" is used in these decisions as the opposite of "inchoate," although, like "inept" and "inane," "choate" normally does not appear in the English language without the prefix "in.") The "choateness" rule has led to conflicts between security interests in future payments perfected under state law (the Uniform Commercial Code) and subsequent federal tax liens. *See also United States v. Kimbell Foods, Inc.*, 440 U.S. 715 (1979); Burke, *Secured Transactions*, 34 Bus. Law. 1547 (1979); Schimberg, *Secured Transactions*, 35 Bus. Law. 1165 (1980).

CID: 1. Civil investigative demand. 2. Commercial item description.

CIDA: Canadian International Development Agency.

C.I.F.: Cost, insurance, freight; a term of delivery for a transaction for the sale of goods to be shipped overseas. A selling price C.I.F. means that the price includes the cost of the goods and the insurance and freight to the named destination. The risk of loss passes to the buyer upon delivery to the carrier, and if the goods are lost the buyer must seek his remedy against the carrier. Upon presentation of the carrier's bill of lading by the seller, the buyer must pay the price without waiting for delivery of the goods. Under Article 2 of the Uniform Commercial Code–Sales, the term C.I.F. destination requires the seller to:

(a) put the goods into the possession of a carrier at the port for shipment and obtain a negotiable bill or bills of lading covering the entire transportation to the named destination; and

(b) load the goods and obtain a receipt from the carrier (which may be contained in the bill of lading) showing that the freight has been paid or provided for; and

(c) obtain a policy or certificate of insurance, including any war risk, of a kind and on terms then current at the port of shipment in the usual amount, in the currency of the contract, shown to cover the same goods covered by the bill of lading and providing for payment of loss to the order of the buyer or for the account of whom it may concern; but the seller may add the price of the premium for any such war risk insurance; and

(d) prepare an invoice of the goods and procure any other documents required to effect shipment or to comply with the contract; and

(e) forward and tender with commercial promptness all the documents in due form and with any indorsement necessary to perfect the buyer's rights.

UCC Section 2-320.

Circumstances: In accounting terminology:

Circumstances are a condition or set of conditions that develop from an event or a series of events, which may occur almost imperceptibly and may converge in random or unexpected ways to create situations that might otherwise not have occurred and might not have been anticipated. To see the circumstance may be fairly easy, but to discern specifically when the event or events that caused it occurred may be difficult or impossible. For example, a debtor's going bankrupt or a thief's stealing gasoline may be an event, but a creditor's facing the situation that its debtor is bankrupt or a warehouse's facing the fact that its tank is empty may be a circumstance.

Financial Accounting Standards Board, Statement of Financial Accounting Concepts No. 3, *Elements of Financial Statements for Business Enterprises,* paragraph 76 (1980). Compare **event.**

CIS: Competitive impact statement.

Citizen: For the purpose of the privileges and immunities section of the United States Constitution, a corporation is not a citizen; *Paul v. Virginia,* 75 U.S. (8 Wall.) 168 (1868). See *Western Turf Ass'n v. Greenberg,* 204 U.S. 359 (1907). A corporation is a citizen of the state of its incorporation and the state of its principal place of business for the purpose of obtaining diversity in the federal courts; 28 U.S.C. § 1332(c).

Civil Aeronautics Board: Independent federal regulatory agency responsible for the promotion and the economic regulation of interstate air carriage. *See* Federal Aviation Act of 1958, Pub. L. No. 85-726, 72 Stat. 731 (1958), 49 U.S.C. §§ 1301–1551. The Airline Deregulation Act of 1978 substantially reduced the regulatory powers of the CAB, and provided for the abolition of the CAB by January 1, 1985. Pub. L. No. 95-504, 92 Stat. 1705 (1978). *See* 14 C.F.R. § 384.

Civil Division: Division of the United States Department of Justice responsible for litigation on behalf of the United States and its agencies.

Civil investigative demand: Demand for documentary material issued by the Attorney General of the United States or the Assistant Attorney General in charge of the Antitrust Division in connection with an antitrust investigation. See **Antitrust Civil Process Act.**

Civil law: System of jurisprudence used in those countries of continental Europe that derived their legal system from the Romans, generally based on a collection of comprehensive codes of laws, rather than an accretion of cases, as is the situation in the English-speaking, common-law countries. The legal systems of Quebec Province and the State of Louisiana are based on the French civil law.

Claim: For the purpose of the Bankruptcy Code, the broadest possible definition of "claim" is used:

(A) right to payment, whether or not such right is reduced to judgment, liquidated, unliquidated, fixed, contingent, matured, unmatured, disputed, undisputed, legal, equitable, secured, or unsecured; or

(B) right to an equitable remedy for breach of performance if such breach gives rise to a right to payment, whether or not such right to an equitable remedy is reduced to judgment, fixed, contingent, matured, unmatured, disputed, undisputed, secured, or unsecured.

11 U.S.C. § 101(4); *see* H.R. Rep. No. 95-595, 95th Cong., 1st Sess. 309 (1977).

Claim-of-right doctrine: Principle that payments must be included in gross income if the taxpayer receives them under a claim of right. If it is later discovered that the taxpayer was not entitled to such payments and they are returned, a deduction is available for the repayment. *See* I.R.C. § 1341; Wootton, *The Claim of Right Doctrine and Section 1341*, 34 Tax Law. 297 (1981).

Class action: Court action by one or more members of a class as representatives of all members of a class. A class action is permitted in federal district courts only if:

(1) the class is so numerous that joinder of all members is impracticable, (2) there are questions of law or fact common to the class, (3) the claims or defenses of the representative parties are typical of the claims or defenses of the class, and (4) the representative parties will fairly and adequately protect the interests of the class.

Fed. R. Civ. Proc. 23. *See Zahn v. International Paper Co.*, 469 F. 2d 1033 (2d Cir. 1972); *Eisen v. Carlisle & Jacqueline*, 417 U.S. 156 (1974). *See generally Newberg on Class Actions: A Manual for Group Litigation at the Federal and State Levels* (1977); Scher, *Opening State Courts to Class Actions: The Uniform Class Actions Act*, 32 Bus. Law. 75 (1976). For antitrust class actions, see American Bar Association, Section of Antitrust Law, *Antitrust Law Developments* 302 (1975). For securities class actions, *see* Block & Warren, *New Battles in the "Class Struggle"—The Federal Courts Reexamine the Securities Class Action*, 34 Bus. Law. 455 (1979).

Class I railroad: Railroad company having annual carrier operating revenues in excess of $50,000,000. 49 C.F.R. § 1240.1.

Class life: See asset depreciation range and class life system.

Clausula compromisoria: In Latin America, an agreement to submit future disputes to arbitration.

Clawback: Recapture; term used in the United Kingdom to describe the tax provision that recovered previously granted tax benefits related to stock relief (a deduction for increases in the carrying amount of inventory).

Clayton Act: Federal antitrust law prohibiting price discrimination and certain other anticompetitive activities, anticompetitive mergers and acquisitions, interlocking directorates between banks and between competitive businesses, and dealings by common carriers with suppliers with whom there exists an interlock, except by competitive bidding. Pub. L. No. 212, ch. 323, 38 Stat. 730 (1914); 15 U.S.C. §§ 12–27. *See generally* American Bar Association, Section of Antitrust Law, *Antitrust Law Developments* 37, 64 (1975).

Clean Air Act: Federal statute to control air pollution. Pub. L. No. 88-206, 77 Stat. 392 (1963); 42 U.S.C. §§ 7401–7626.

Clean credit; clean letter of credit: Letter of credit that will be honored upon presentation of a draft without supporting documents. Compare documentary credit.

Clean draft: Draft the honor of which is not conditioned upon the presentation of other documents. Compare documentary draft.

Clean Water Act of 1977: Amendment to the Federal Water Pollution Control Act, Pub. L. No. 95-217, 91 Stat. 1566 (1977).

Clearing: In the case of a check, presentation by the bank in which the check is deposited to the bank on which it is written, and payment from the account of the writer to the account of the holder. In the case of a security, transfer of the certificate and payment therefor in settlement of accounts after a trading transaction.

Clearing agency: With respect to securities, "any person who acts as an intermediary in making payments or deliveries or both in connection with transactions in securities or who provides facilities for comparison of data respecting the terms of settlement of securities transactions, to reduce the number of settlements of securities transactions, or for the allocation of securities settlement responsibilities." Securities Exchange Act of 1934, section 3(a)(23); 15 U.S.C. § 78c(a)(23). The term includes an entity that acts as custodian of securities in connection with a system of central handling of transactions in a given security without transfer of the certificates, but excludes banks, brokers, and dealers under certain circumstances, life insurance companies, and open-end investment companies.

Clearing corporation: For the purpose of Article 8 of the Uniform Commercial Code–Investment Securities, a "clearing corporation" is a corporation "all of the capital stock of which is held by or for a national securities exchange or association registered under a statute of the United States such as the Securities Exchange Act of 1934." UCC Section 8-102(3).

Clearing house: Association of banks or other financial institutions through which checks or other instruments for the payment of money are cleared, or settled and paid. *See* UCC Section 4-104(d).

Clearing house funds: Funds available when the check has cleared through the clearing house in the city in question. Usually this means funds are available the next day, if the clearing house clears checks overnight. Some clearing houses clear checks late in the same day received by a certain deadline, however. Compare **federal funds; immediately available funds.**

Close corporation: Under Delaware law, a close corporation is a corporation whose certificate of incorporation provides that the stock may be held by not more than 30 persons, shall have certain restrictions on transfer, and shall not be offered in a "public offering." Del. Code Ann. tit. 8 § 342. In California, a close corporation cannot have more than ten shareholders; Cal. Corp. Code § 158. In those states that recognize close corporations as a special type, some relief is provided from the formalities of corporate governance, and shareholders' agreements restricting share transfer are given effect. Del. Code Ann. tit. 8 §§ 341–356; Cal. Corp. Code § 300(b). The Model Business Corporation Act does not contemplate "close corporations" as a special type, but changes have been proposed: *Proposed Statutory Close Corporation Supplement to the Model Busi-*

ness Corporation Act, 37 Bus. Law. 269 (1981). In the absence of such statutory sanction, the term "closely-held corporation" might be more appropriate. *See generally* F. O'Neal, *Close Corporations* (2d ed. 1971); O'Neal, *Close Corporations: Existing Legislation and Recommended Reform,* 33 Bus. Law. 873 (1978).

Closed-end fund: Closed-end investment company.

Closed-end investment company: Investment company with a limited number of shares outstanding, and whose shares are not redeemable. Investors in a closed-end fund must purchase and sell the shares on the open market. The value of the shares of a closed-end fund is determined by the market in those shares, not the value of the securities held by the fund. Compare open-end investment company. The difference between an open-end investment company and a closed-end investment company is that the shares of the former are redeemable. Investment Company Act of 1940, section 5(a)(2), 15 U.S.C. § 80a-5(a)(2). See investment company.

Closed-end lease: Lease, usually of vehicles or equipment, in which the lessee has no further obligation at the end of the lease term other than the return of the leased equipment to the lessor. Compare open-end lease.

Closed mortgage: Mortgage bond issue in which all bonds authorized have been issued and delivered.

Closed shop: Place of employment where employees are required to be members of the particular union representing those employees as a condition precedent to employment.

Closely held corporation: Corporation with a limited number of shareholders and with restrictions on transfer of shares; See close corporation.

Closing agreement: Agreement between a taxpayer and the Commissioner of the Internal Revenue Service (or his designee) conclusively determining liability in respect of any tax for a specific period ending prior to the agreement. I.R.C. § 7121; Treas. Reg. § 301.7121.

Closing price: The price at which the last transaction in a security took place before the close of business of the exchange on which the security is traded on a given day.

Closing transaction: Transaction in which the writer of an option discharges his obligation thereunder.

Coast Guard, United States: Federal marine enforcement and safety service. The Coast Guard is a branch of the Armed Services; during peace time it operates within the United States Department of Transportation, but at time of war or when the President directs, it operates as part of the United States Navy. The Coast Guard is responsible for enforcement of maritime laws on the high seas and in navigable inland waters, suppression of smuggling, commercial vessel and private boat safety, protection of the marine environment, maintenance of aids to navigation, and port safety. *See* 14 U.S.C. §§ 1-894.

COCOM: Consultive Group Coordinating Committee, an informal organization of the United States, Japan, and certain European countries to coordinate controls on exports of certain strategic commodities.

Code of Federal Regulations: Codification of general and permanent rules published in the Federal Register by the executive departments and agencies of the federal government. The code is divided into fifty titles representing broad subject areas subject to federal regulation, and each title is reissued annually.

Co-determination: Election of labor representatives to the board of directors of a corporation. *See* Gruson & Meilicke, *The New Co-Determination Law in Germany*, 32 Bus. Law. 571 (1977).

COFC: Container on flat car.

COGSA: Carriage of Goods by Sea Act.

Cogeneration: Production of electricity and heat energy in the same process, for example, by using steam to drive turbines to generate electricity, and then using the waste steam for heat. *See* section 210 of the Public Utility Regulatory Policies Act of 1978. As to the definition of cogeneration equipment for the energy tax credit, see I.R.C. § 48(l)(14).

Coinsurance: Sharing of the risk of insurance between insurance companies, usually by one company insuring losses below a given amount, and the other insuring greater losses; or sharing of the risk of loss between an insurance company and the insured by the use of deductible provisions whereby the insurance company only covers losses over a given, "deductible," amount.

COLA: Cost-of-living adjustment.

Cold comfort: That which is derived from accountants' "comfort letters" in securities underwritings, in respect of the financial data in the prospectus. See comfort letter.

Collapsible corporation: Corporation used as device to convert ordinary income from corporate operations into capital gain from the sale of stock or distribution of assets, by making such a sale or distribution before the income is realized. Such gain would be treated as ordinary income, however, by section 341 of the Internal Revenue Code. The Code definition of a "collapsible corporation" is:

a corporation formed or availed of principally for the manufacture, construction, or production of property, for the purchase of property which (in the hands of the corporation) is property described in paragraph (3) (of I.R.C. § 341(b)), or for the holding of stock in a corporation so formed or availed of, with a view to—

(A) the sale or exchange of stock by its shareholders (whether in liquidation or otherwise), or a distribution to its shareholders, before the realization by the corporation manufacturing, constructing, producing, or purchasing the property of a substantial part of the taxable income to be derived from such property, and

(B) the realization by such shareholders of gain attributable to such property.

I.R.C. § 341(b). *See* Rev. Rul. 72-48, 1972-1 C.B. 102; Ginsburg, *Collapsible*

Corporations–Revisiting an Old Misfortune, 33 Tax L. Rev. 307 (1978).

Collateral: Property used to secure a loan and subject to seizure by the lender upon default; property subject to a security interest. UCC Section 9-105(1)(c). For the purpose of Article 9 of the Uniform Commercial Code –Secured Transactions, the term "collateral" includes accounts and chattel paper that have been sold.

Collateral estoppel: Judgment on a given set of facts between parties that operates as a bar to litigation of the same factual issue in a second action between the same parties on a different claim. *See Cromwell v. County of Sac,* 94 U.S. 351 (1876); *Lawlor v. National Screen Service Corp.,* 349 U.S. 322, 326 (1955).

Collateral trust bond: Bond secured by other securities, usually by deposit with the indenture trustee.

Collecting bank: For the purpose of Article 3–Commercial Paper, and Article 4–Bank Deposits and Collections, of the Uniform Commercial Code, collecting bank means "any bank handling the item for collection except the payor bank." UCC Section 4-105(d).

Collection guaranteed: Under Article 3 of the Uniform Commercial Code –Commercial Paper, such words or equivalent words added to a signature on an instrument mean that "the signer engages that if the instrument is not paid when due he will pay it according to its tenor, but only after the holder has reduced his claim against the maker or acceptor to judgment and execution has

been returned unsatisfied, or after the maker or acceptor has become insolvent or it is otherwise apparent that it is useless to proceed against him." UCC Section 3-416(2). See also **payment guaranteed.**

Collective bargaining: Under section 8 of the National Labor Relations Act:

to bargain collectively is the performance of the mutual obligation of the employer and the representative of the employees to meet at reasonable times and confer in good faith with respect to wages, hours, and other terms and conditions of employment, or the negotiation of an agreement, or any question arising thereunder, and the execution of a written contract incorporating any agreement reached if requested by either party, but such obligation does not compel either party to agree to a proposal or require the making of a concession...

29 U.S.C. §§ 158(d).

Collective investment fund: See common trust fund.

Collective mark: Type of mark used by members of a cooperative, an association, or other collective group or organization, including marks used to indicate membership in a union, an association, or other organization. 15 U.S.C. 1054. See **trademark.**

Collective refusal to deal: Boycott, or refusal on the part of a group of sellers to sell to an entity or group, or concerted action on the part of business entities to deprive others of access to merchandise to sell to the public. Collective refusals to deal (also called concerted refusals to deal) are usually regarded as "per se" violations of section 1 of the Sherman Act. *See, e.g, United States v. General Motors Corp.*, 384 U.S. 127 (1965); *see generally* American Bar Association, Section of Antitrust Law, *Antitrust Law Developments* 17, 344 (1975). See also boycott.

Co-maker: Co-signer.

Co-manager: Investment banking firm participating in an underwriting of the issuance of securities, ranking just below the lead manager.

Combination in restraint of trade: See restraint of trade.

COMEX: Commodity Exchange, Inc.

Comfort letter: Letter furnished by independent accountants for the issuer of securities to the underwriters regarding the financial data included in the registration statement. *See* American Institute of Certified Public Accountants, Statement on Auditing Standards No. 38, *Letters for Underwriters* (1981). *See generally* Resnik, *Understanding Comfort Letters for Underwriters*, 34 Bus. Law. 1725 (1979). See also **negative assurance.**

Comity: The voluntary recognition of the laws of one jurisdiction by another.

Commerce: The term "commerce" is used in federal statutes to impart federal jurisdiction under the commerce clause of the Constitution, and is traditionally given broad construction. It is not limited to the buying and selling of goods, but includes "intercourse." *Gibbons v. Ogden*, 22 U.S. (9

Wheat.) 1, 189 (1824). *See Swift & Co. v. United States*, 196 U.S. 375, 398 (1905). As used in the Clayton Act, the term "commerce" means "trade or commerce among the several states and with foreign nations. . . ." The term includes trade or commerce involving the District of Columbia, territories, and insular possessions and other places under the jurisdiction of the United States. 15 U.S.C. § 12. *See* section 4 of the Federal Trade Commission Act, 15 U.S.C. § 44; section 2(6) of the National Labor Relations Act, 29 U.S.C. § 152(b). See also **affecting commerce; commerce clause.**

Commerce, United States Department of: Cabinet-level department of the administrative branch of the United States Government, responsible for a large variety of programs to promote the economic development and technological advancement of the United States. *See* Pub. L. No. 426, ch. 141, 37 Stat. 736 (1913); 15 U.S.C. § 1501–1527. Operating units of the Department of Commerce include the International Trade Administration, the Economic Development Administration, the Minority Business Development Agency, the National Bureau of Standards, the National Oceanic and Atmospheric Administration, the National Technical Information Service, the Patent and Trademark Office, the Bureau of the Census, the Bureau of Economic Analysis, the Bureau of Industrial Economics, the National Telecommunications and Information Administration, the United States Travel Service, the Office of Product Standards Policy, and the Regional Action Planning Commissions.

Commerce Business Daily: Publication of the United States Department of Commerce having synopses of government procurements, sales, and contract awards.

Commerce clause: Clause 3 of section 8 of Article I of the United States Constitution, granting Congress the power "To regulate Commerce with foreign Nations, and among the several States, and with the Indian Tribes." The commerce clause is the basis for a significant proportion of federal legislation. *See, e.g., Dahnke-Walker Milling Co. v. Bondurant,* 257 U.S. 282 (1921). See also **commerce; affecting commerce.**

Commercial bank: Bank owned by stockholders and operated for profit, which is permitted by state and federal law to engage in more varied lending activities and offer more financial services than other depositary institutions, such as savings banks. Usually a commercial bank emphasizes the use of demand deposits and short-term loans, whereas a savings bank emphasizes time deposits and long-term loans, but the activities of both types of institutions overlap to a considerable extent. In connection with the definition of "commercial banking" for determining the relevant market in bank merger cases, *see United States v. Connecticut National Bank,* 418 U.S. 656 (1974), in which the servicing of commercial enterprises was held to be the unique feature of commercial banks.

Commercial item description: Specification for acquisition by the Federal Supply Service of commercial off-the-shelf or commercial-type products.

Commercial letter of credit: See standby letter of credit.

Commercial paper: 1. Short-term unsecured promissory notes sold by large, credit-worthy corporations at a discount to dealers, institutional investors, and other corporations. The maturity of these notes is nine months or less, in order to take advantage of the exemption from registration afforded by section 3(a)(3) of the Securities Act of 1933. *See* SEC Release No. 33-4412, 26 Fed. Reg. 9158 (1961); *Sanders v. John Nuveen & Co.,* 463 F. 2d 1075 (7th Cir.), *cert. denied,* 409 U.S. 1009 (1972). *See generally* Lowenstein, *The Commercial Paper Market and the Federal Securities Laws,* 4 Corp. L. Rev. 128 (1981); Hicks, *Commercial Paper: An Exempted Security Under Section 3(a)(3) of the Securities Act of 1933,* 24 U.C.L.A. L. Rev. 227 (1976); Joines & Nelson, *Commercial Paper,* in T. Cook, ed., *Instruments of the Money Market* 66 (4th ed. 1977). 2. Instruments covered by Article 3 of the Uniform Commercial Code, including drafts, checks, certificates of deposit, and notes, but not instruments covered by Article 8–Securities. *See* UCC Section 3-103, Official Comment; UCC Section 8-102(1)(b).

Commercial unit: In Article 2 of the Uniform Commercial Code–Sales, "commercial unit" means

such a unit of goods as by commercial usage is a single whole for the purposes of sale and division of which materially impairs its character or value on the market or in use. A commercial unit may be a single article (as a machine) or a set of articles (as a suite of furniture or an assortment of sizes) or a quantity (as a bale, gross, or carload) or any other unit treated in use or in the relevant market as a single whole.

UCC Section 2-105(6). *See also* UCC Section 2-601 regarding buyer's rights on improper delivery.

Commitment fee: Fee charged by a lending institution for entering into a commitment to lend funds within a certain period.

Commodities clause: Clause 8 of section 1 of the Interstate Commerce Act, prohibiting a railroad company from transporting commodities (other than timber) owned by it or in which it has an interest. The commodities clause is now codified at 49 U.S.C. 10746.

Commodity: 1. For the purpose of the Commodity Exchange Act:

The word "commodity" shall mean wheat, cotton, rice, corn, oats, barley, rye, flaxseed, grain sorghums, mill feeds, butter, eggs, Solanum tuberosum (Irish potatoes), wool, wool tops, fats and oils (including lard tallow, cottonseed oil, peanut oil, soybean oil and all other fats and oils), cottonseed meal, cottonseed, peanuts, soybeans, soybean meal, livestock, livestock products, and frozen concentrated orange juice, and all other goods and articles, except onions as provided in Public Law 85-839 (7 U.S.C. § 13-1), and all services, rights, and interests in which contracts for future delivery are presently or in the future dealt in. . . .

7 U.S.C. § 2. *See* H.R. Rep. No. 975, 93d Cong., 2d Sess. 61, 76 (1974); 120 Cong. Rec. 34736 (1974) (remarks of Rep. Poage). 2. For the purpose of section 2(a) of the Clayton Act, prohibiting price discrimination between purchasers of commodities, the term is usually regarded as being confined to tangible goods and articles of commerce, and excludes rights under licenses and patents, leases, and other intangibles. *See* American Bar Association, Section of Antitrust Law, *Antitrust Law Developments* 112 (1975).

Commodity broker: As defined in the Bankruptcy Code, a "futures commission merchant, foreign futures commission merchant, clearing organization, leverage transaction merchant, or commodity options dealer ... with respect to which there is a customer ... ." 11 U.S.C. § 101(5).

Commodity clause: Clause in a contract providing for future payment in commodities or in currency equivalents of commodities (at the then prevailing price). *See generally* Rosenn, *Protecting Contracts from Inflation*, 33 Bus. Law. 729 (1978).

Commodity Control List: List of all commodities over which export licensing authority is exercised pursuant to the Export Administration Act of 1969, Pub. L. No. 91-184, 83 Stat. 841 (1969), 50 U.S.C. App. §§ 2401–13.

Commodity Credit Corporation: Agency of the United States, operating within the Department of Agriculture, chartered to stabilize and protect farm income and prices, to assist in maintaining balanced and adequate supplies of agricultural commodities, and to facilitate the orderly distribution of commodities. The CCC purchases agricultural commodities to stabilize prices, selling and disposing of those commodities in domestic and foreign markets, and using them in foreign assistance programs. The CCC offers financial assistance for agricultural storage facilities, and makes loans against grains held in storage pursuant to the grain reserve program. *See* Commodity Credit Corporation Charter Act, Pub. L. No. 806, ch. 704, 62 Stat. 1070 (1948); 15 U.S.C. § 714.

Commodity Exchange Act: Federal statute providing for the regulation of commodities exchanges. Pub. L. No. 675, ch. 545, 49 Stat. 1491 (1936). In 1974 the act was substantially revised to create the Commodity Futures Trading Commission. Pub. L. No. 93-463, 88 Stat. 1389 (1974).

Commodity future: Agreement to buy or sell a given amount of a commodity at a future date, at a fixed price.

Commodity Futures Trading Commission: Independent agency of the United States government formed to regulate trading in agricultural and other commodities futures on commodities exchanges. *See* the Commodity Futures Trading Commission Act of 1974, Pub. L. No. 93-463, 88 Stat. 1389 (1974), 7 U.S.C. § 4a; H.R. Rep. No. 975, 93d Cong., 2d Sess. (1974); S. Rep. No. 1131, 93d Cong., 2d Sess. (1974); 17 C.F.R. § 140. *See generally* P. Johnson, *Commodities Regulation* (1981); Schneider & Santo, *Commodities Future Trading Commission: A Review of the 1978 Legislation,* 34 Bus. Law. 1755 (1979); Schief & Markham, *The Nation's "Commodity Cops"—Efforts by the Commodity Futures Trading Commission to Enforce the Commodity Exchange Act,* 34 Bus. Law. 19 (1978); Greenstone, *The CFTC and Government Reor-*

ganization: Preserving Regulatory Independence, 33 Bus. Law. 163 (1977).

Commodity pool operator: As set forth in the Commodities Exchange Act:

The term "commodity pool operator" shall mean any person engaged in a business which is of the nature of an investment trust, syndicate, or similar form of enterprise and who, in connection therewith, solicits, accepts, or receives from others, funds, securities, or property, either directly or through capital contributions, the sale of stock or other forms of securities, or otherwise, for the purpose of trading in any commodity for future delivery on or subject to the rules of any contract market, but does not include such persons not within the intent of this definition as the Commission may specify by rule or regulation or by order.

Section 2(a)(1), 7 U.S.C. § 2.

Commodity trading advisor: "Person who, for compensation or profit, engages in the business of advising others, either directly or through publications or writings, as to the value of commodities or as to the advisability of trading in any commodity for future delivery ... ; or who for compensation or profit, and as part of a regular business, issues or promulgates analyses or reports concerning commodities; ... ." Section 2(a)(1) of the Commodity Exchange Act, 7 U.S.C. § 2.

Common carrier: One who undertakes to furnish transportation of persons or property, or communications service, for compensation, to all who would use the service. *See United States v. Queen,* 445 F. 2d 358 (10th Cir.), *cert. denied,* 404 U.S. 1003 (1971); *Ellis v. ICC,* 237 U.S. 434 (1915); *General American Tank Car Corp. v. El Dorado*

Terminal Co., 308 U.S. 422 (1940). For the purpose of regulation by the Interstate Commerce Commission, *see* 49 U.S.C. § 10102(4). See **carrier;** contract carrier.

Common Carrier Bureau: Bureau of the Federal Communications Commission responsible for the federal regulation of common carrier telephone, telegraph, radio, and satellite communications.

Common law: The system of jurisprudence prevailing in English-speaking countries, based on customs and usages, as interpreted by the courts and memorialized in written decisions.

Common market: The European Economic Community, the European Coal and Steel Community, and the European Atomic Energy Community.

Common stock: Stock not entitled to a preference in the distribution of dividends or assets. N.Y. Bus. Corp. Law § 501(b); Cal. Corp. Code § 159.

Common stock equivalent: Securities other than common stock that should be dealt with as common stock in determining earnings per share. *See* American Institute of Certified Public Accountants, Accounting Principles Board Opinion No. 15, Appendix D, paragraph 5 (1968). Certain warrants and convertible securities are common stock equivalents. *See* id., paragraphs 30–39.

Common stock ratio: Proportion of common stock and surplus in total capitalization, determined by dividing the total value of common stock (book value), capital surplus, and accumulated retained earnings by total capitalization.

Common trust fund: Fund maintained by a bank for the collective investment of funds held by the bank in its capacity as trustee, executor, administrator, or guardian, or as custodian of accounts maintained in a similar capacity. *See* I.R.C. § 584; SEC Rule 132, 17 C.F.R. § 230.132. *See generally* Wade, *Bank-Sponsored Collective Investment Funds: An Analysis of Applicable Federal Banking and Securities Laws,* 35 Bus. Law. 361 (1980).

Community Reinvestment Act: Federal law designed to encourage federally insured commercial banks, mutual savings banks, and savings and loan associations to help meet the credit needs of the communities in which they are chartered. Title VIII of the Housing and Community Development Act of 1977, Pub. L. No. 95-128, 91 Stat. 1111, 1147 (1977); 12 U.S.C. §§ 2901–2905. *See* Regulation BB of the Federal Reserve System, 12 C.F.R. § 228; Canner & Cleaver, *The Community Reinvestment Act: A Progress Report,* 66 Fed. Res. Bull. 87 (1980).

Commuter air carrier: Air carrier providing regularly scheduled service using passenger aircraft with a maximum capacity of 56 passengers, or cargo aircraft having a maximum payload of 18,000 pounds. Commuter air carriers are exempt from economic regulation by the Civil Aeronautics Board. *See* section 416(b) of the Federal Aviation Act, 49 U.S.C. § 1386(b).

Companies Act: Name usually given the law regulating corporate organization and powers in England and other British Commonwealth countries.

Company: Organization or association of persons for the joint conduct of business. A "company" need not be a corporation. *See* section 2(a)(8) of the Investment Company Act; *Prudential Insurance Co. v. SEC,* 326 F. 2d 383 (3d Cir.), *cert. denied,* 377 U.S. 953 (1964).

Comparability: In accounting terminology, "The quality of information that enables users to identify similarities in and differences between two sets of economic phenomena." Financial Accounting Standards Board, Statement of Financial Accounting Concepts No. 2, *Qualitative Characteristics of Accounting Information,* paragraph 171 (1980).

Compensating balances: Amounts required to be kept on deposit with a bank making a loan for the duration of the loan or the commitment therefor. Such amounts are usually in demand accounts, not bearing interest.

Competent evidence: Evidence that is admissible in a jury trial.

Competition, Bureau of: Unit of the Federal Trade Commission responsible for FTC antitrust activities.

Competitive bidding: Procedure for purchase or sale whereby bids are solicited from the public at large or from selected bidders and the purchase or sale is awarded to the bidder furnishing the most favorable price or combination of price, terms, and commodity or service. For the rules for competitive bidding for the purpose of section 10 of the Clayton Act (15 U.S.C. § 20), see 49 C.F.R. § 1010. For the requirement for competitive bidding in the issuance of carrier securities, see Ex Parte 158, *In re Competitive Bidding in the Sale of Securities,* 257 ICC 129 (1944), 307 ICC 1 (1952).

Competitive impact statement: Statement prepared by the Department of Justice pursuant to the Antitrust Procedures and Penalties Act (15 U.S.C. 16(b)–(h)) describing and explaining a proposed consent decree in settlement of a civil antitrust suit.

Competitive injury: Economic injury sufficient to justify a charge of price discrimination under the Robinson-Patman Act. *See American Oil Co. v. FTC,* 325 F. 2d 101 (7th Cir. 1963), *cert. denied,* 377 U.S. 954 (1964); *see also Beatrice Foods Co.,* 76 F.T.C. 719 (1969), *aff'd sub nom. Kroger Co. v. FTC,* 438 F. 2d 1372 (6th Cir.), *cert. denied,* 404 U.S. 871 (1971). *See generally* American Bar Association, Section of Antitrust Law, *Antitrust Law Developments* 116 (1975).

Completed-contract method: Method of accounting for long-term construction contracts that recognizes income only when the contract is completed, or substantially so. *See* American Institute of Certified Public Accountants, Accounting Research Bulletin No. 45, *Long-Term Construction-Type Contracts,* paragraph 9 (1955); International Accounting Standards Committee, Statement of International Accounting Standards 11, paragraph 9 (1979). *See also* section 229 of the Tax Equity and Fiscal Responsibility Act of 1982.

Completeness: In accounting terminology, "The inclusion in reported information of everything material that is necessary for faithful representation of the relevant phenomena." Financial Accounting Standards Board, Statement of Financial Accounting Concepts No. 2, *Qualitative Characteristics of Accounting Information,* paragraph 171 (1980). See also **material.**

Composition: Voluntary insolvency proceeding whereby the creditors of the insolvent debtor agree to a plan for the discharge of obligations in a lump sum or over a period of time. Compositions are common-law devices, and have been largely superseded by proceedings under the Bankruptcy Code.

Compound interest: Interest calculated by adding simple interest to the principal at regular periods, and using the sum as the principal for calculating the interest for the next period. The formula for the amount that will result from payment of compound interest at an annual rate i on an amount A for y years, compounded n times per year, is

$$A (1 + i/n)^{ny}$$

Compound-interest bond: Debt security on which interest accrued is not paid to the holder, but itself earns interest, compounded, until the entire amount, principal plus accrued and compounded interest, is payable at maturity. Effectively, the interest is rein-

vested at the "coupon" rate. See also zero-coupon bond.

Comprehensive Employment and Training Act of 1973: Federal statute, administered by the Department of Labor, that provides grants and assistance for a broad range of employment services. Pub. L. No. 93-203, 87 Stat. 839 (1973).

Comprehensive Environmental Response, Compensation, and Liability Act of 1980: Federal statute establishing a "superfund" for compensation for damage due to spillage of hazardous substances. Pub. L. No. 96-510, 94 Stat. 2767 (1980), 42 U.S.C. §§ 9601–9657.

Comprehensive income: In accounting terminology:

Comprehensive income is the change in equity (net assets) of an entity during a period from transactions and other events and circumstances from non-owner sources. It includes all changes in equity during a period except those resulting from investments by owners and distributions to owners.

Comprehensive income has four basic elements: revenues, expenses, gains, and losses. Financial Accounting Standards Board, Statement of Financial Accounting Concepts No. 3, *Elements of Financial Statements of Business Enterprises,* paragraphs 56, 147(1980).

Compromiso: In Latin America, a submission agreement, or agreement to submit an existing controversy to arbitration.

Comptroller of the Currency: The officer of the United States Treasury Department who is responsible for chartering and supervising the activities of national banks. *See* Act of Feb. 25, 1863, ch. 58, 12 Stat. 665; 12 U.S.C. §§ 1–15; 12 C.F.R. § 4.

Concentration: Share of the relevant market enjoyed by a firm contemplating merger, or the combined market share of the merger partners. In *United States v. Philadelphia National Bank*, 374 U.S. 321 (1963), the Supreme Court set standards of concentration, stating that a merger that resulted in a 30% market share by the merged entity and an increase in concentration of 33% were presumptively unlawful. Later cases have held lower concentrations to be sufficient to prohibit a merger. *E.g., United States v. Von's Grocery*, 384 U.S. 270 (1966); *United States v. Pabst Brewing Co.*, 384 U.S. 546 (1966). *See generally* American Bar Association, Section of Antitrust Law, *Antitrust Law Developments* 74 (1975). See also **Herfindahl-Hirschman index.**

Concerted refusal to deal: See collective refusal to deal.

Concession: Discount to underwriter of a securities issue.

Condemnation: 1. Taking of private property by a government entity, with compensation to the owner. 2. Disposition of a vessel by an admiralty court.

Condition: "Event, not certain to occur, which must occur, unless its non-occurrence is excused, before performance under a contract becomes due." *Restatement, Second, Contracts,* § 224 (1981).

Conditional check: Check tendered with conditions noted thereon, usually to the effect that negotiation of the check constitutes acceptance of certain terms. *See* UCC Section 1-207; Hawkland, *The Effect of UCC § 1-207 on the Doctrine of Accord and Satisfaction by Conditional Check,* 74 Com. L. J. 329 (1969).

Conditional delivery: Tender of delivery of goods by a seller conditioned upon payment therefor. *See* UCC Section 2-507(2).

Conditional sale: Sale of property subject to the condition that the purchase price is paid. Payment would be deferred, and interest would be paid on the outstanding unpaid balance. Originally, the vendor would retain title to the property until the purchase price was fully paid, but under the Uniform Commercial Code, the vendor's interest is described as a security interest. Modern forms of security agreements under the Uniform Commercial Code have largely replaced conditional sales as a form of security for the purchase price of property, but the form is still used for the financing of railroad equipment and some motor carrier equipment, because of a loophole in the laws regulating the issuance of securities by carriers. *See Association of Am. Railroads v. United States,* 603 F. 2d 953 (D.C. Cir. 1979). See also **New York plan.** For a complete treatment of conditional sales before the advent of the Uniform Commercial Code, *see* 3 L. Jones, *Chattel Mortgages and Conditional Sales* (6th ed., Bowers, 1933). *See also* I G. Gilmore, *Security Interests in Personal Property* 62 (1965).

Condition precedent: Condition that must be satisfied in order for an obligation under a contract to arise. As to presupposed conditions in a contract for the sale of goods, *see* UCC Section 2-615.

Condition subsequent: Condition that is to be satisfied after performance by the other party to the contract, the failure of which will permit the other party to rescind his performance. *See Restatement, Second, Contracts* § 230 (1981). The term has been eliminated in the Restatement of Contracts Second. *Restatement, Second, Contracts* § 224, comment e (1981).

Conference agreement: As defined by the Federal Maritime Commission, an agreement among ocean carriers that will or could reasonably be expected to cause the parties to become a dominant force in the trade. Attributes of conference agreements are collective establishment of uniform rates, charges, and practices relating to the receipt, carriage, and delivery of cargo; the filing of a common tariff; and the designation of a conference administration. 46 C.F.R. § 522.2(a)(1).

Confidential business information: For the purpose of the Freedom of Information Act exemption for "commercial or financial information obtained from a person and privileged or confidential" (5 U.S.C. § 552(b)(4)), a commercial or financial matter is "confidential" if "disclosure of the information is likely to have either of the following effects: (1) to impair the Government's ability to obtain necessary information in the future; or (2) to cause substantial harm to the competi-

tive position of the person from whom the information was obtained." *National Parks & Conservation Association v. Morton*, 498 F. 2d 765, 770 (D.C. Cir. 1974). *See McCarthy & Kornmeier, Maintaining the Confidentiality of Confidential Business Information Submitted to the Federal Government*, 36 Bus. Law. 57 (1980).

Confidential employee: Employee who assists and acts in a confidential capacity to persons who exercise managerial functions in labor relations, or who otherwise has access to an employer's sensitive labor relations information. A confidential employee does not have the right of collective bargaining under the National Labor Relations Act as a matter of National Labor Relations Board policy, but may have other protections under that law. *See NLRB v. Hendricks County Rural Electric Membership Corp.*, 45A U.S. 170, (1981); *Pullman Standard Div., Pullman Inc.*, 214 NLRB 762 (1974); *Ford Motor Co.*, 66 NLRB 1317, 1322 (1946).

Confirmed credit: Letter of credit in which a party (the "confirmer" or "confirming bank") other than the issuer has engaged that the obligations of the letter of credit will be performed. UCC Section 5-107, Official Comment, point 2. In Article 2 of the Uniform Commercial Code–Sales, with respect to a letter of credit or a banker's credit, confirmed credit means that "the credit must also carry the direct obligation of such an (financing) agency which does business in the seller's financial market." UCC Section 2-325. See **letter of credit; financing agency; confirming bank.**

Confirmer: Bank or other person that engages that it will honor a letter of credit issued by another, or that the issuer will perform its obligations thereunder. The Uniform Commercial Code term is "confirming bank."

Confirming bank: With respect to a letter of credit, a confirming bank is a bank "which engages either that it will itself honor a credit already issued by another bank or that such a credit will be honored by the issuer or a third bank." UCC Section 5-103(1)(f). Despite the use of the word "bank" in the term, a confirmer of a letter of credit does not have to be a bank; *Barclays Bank v. Mercantile Nat'l Bank,* 339 F. Supp. 457 (N.D. Ga. 1972), *aff'd,* 481 F. 2d 1224 (5th Cir. 1973).

Conformed copy: Copy of a document conformed to the original executed counterpart by printing or typing in the signatures and other marks appearing on the execution counterpart. Conformed copies are prepared for use by the parties in administering the contract, while the executed counterparts are kept in safekeeping.

Conforming: In Article 2 of the Uniform Commercial Code–Sales, "goods or conduct including any part of a performance are 'conforming' or conform to the contract when they are in accordance with the obligations under the contract." UCC Section 2-106. *See also* UCC Sections 2-601–16. regarding breach, repudiation, and excuse when nonconforming goods are involved.

Conglomerate merger: Merger that is not horizontal or vertical; merger in which there are "no discernible relationships in the nature of business between the acquiring firm and the acquired firm." H.R. Rep. No. 1191, 81st Cong., 1st Sess. 11 (1949); *see FTC v. Proctor & Gamble Co.,* 386 U.S. 568, 577 n. 2 (1967); *see generally* American Bar Association, Section of Antitrust Law, *Antitrust Law Developments* 79 (1975).

Congressional Budget Office: Unit of the legislative branch of the United States government formed to provide Congress basic budget data and analyses of alternative fiscal, budgetary, and program policy issues. The CBO does economic forecasting and cost projections on a regular basis, analyzes the budget and budget proposals, and conducts special studies. *See* Congressional Budget Office Act of 1974, Pub. L. No. 93-344, 88 Stat. 297, 302 (1974); 2 U.S.C. §§ 601–04.

Conscious parallelism: Interdependent consciously parallel action among competitors sufficient to justify a charge of price fixing or other concerted anticompetitive activity under the Sherman Act; acceptance of a plan of price fixing or other anticompetitive activity without simultaneous action or agreement. *See Interstate Circuit, Inc., v. United States,* 306 U.S. 208 (1939); *see generally* American Bar Association, Section of Antitrust Law, *Antitrust Law Developments* 34 (1975); Blechman, *Conscious Parallelism, Signalling and Facilitating Devices: The Problem of Tacit Collusion under the Antitrust Laws,* 24 N.Y.L.S. L. Rev. 881 (1979).

Consent decree: Court order confirming a settlement between litigants, usually the Antitrust Division of the

Department of Justice and the defendant or prospective defendant in an antitrust action. *See* American Bar Association, Section of Antitrust Law, *Antitrust Law Developments* 237 (1975). See also **Antitrust Procedures and Penalties Act;** compare **consent order.**

Consent dividend: Amount for which the deduction for dividends paid can be taken, even though not actually paid, if the stockholder consents. Such a dividend is considered as a dividend in money to the stockholder and a simultaneous contribution to capital of the corporation by the stockholder. I.R.C. §§ 561, 565. See **consent stock.**

Consent judgment: See consent decree.

Consent order: Agreement between the Federal Trade Commission and a potential respondent in an FTC administrative proceeding, whereby an issue is settled by negotiation before the commencement of a formal FTC adjudicative proceeding. 16 C.F.R. §§2.31 –34. *See* American Bar Association, Section of Antitrust Law, *Antitrust Law Developments* 211 (1975). Compare **consent decree.**

Consent stock: Stock in respect of which the holder agrees in a consent filed with the corporation's income tax return to have an amount treated as dividends under the dividends paid deduction, and a simultaneous contribution to capital. "Consent stock" is defined in the Internal Revenue Code to mean "the class or classes of stock entitled, after the payment of preferred divi-

dends, to a share in the distribution (other than in complete or partial liquidation) within the taxable year of all the remaining earnings and profits, which share constitutes the same proportion of such distribution regardless of the amount of such distribution." I.R.C. § 565(f). See **consent dividend;** I.R.C. §§ 561–65.

Consequential damages: Damages due to breach of contract other than loss in value, such as injury to persons or property resulting from defective performance. *See Restatement, Second, Contracts* § 347 (1981). Under the Uniform Commercial Code provisions for the sale of goods, consequential damages resulting from a seller's breach include:

(a) any loss resulting from general or particular requirements and needs of which the seller at the time of contracting had reason to know and which could not reasonably be prevented by cover or otherwise; and
(b) injury to person or property proximately resulting from any breach of warranty.

UCC Section 2-715. Consequential damages may be limited by contract, unless such limitation is unconscionable. UCC Section 2-719. See also **damages; incidental damages; proximate cause.**

Conservatism: In accounting terminology, "A prudent reaction to uncertainty to try to ensure that uncertainty and risks inherent in business situations are adequately considered." Financial Accounting Standards Board, Statement of Financial Accounting Concepts No. 2, *Qualitative Characteristics of Accounting Information,* paragraph 171 (1980).

Consideration: Performance or a return promise sought by a promisor and given by a promisee in exchange for the promisor's promise. Performance may consist of

(a) an act other than a promise, or

(b) a forbearance, or

(c) the creation, modification, or destruction of a legal relation.

Restatement, Second, Contracts § 71 (1981). "Consideration" is an essential element of an enforceable contract, except in those jurisdictions that give effect to contracts under seal. For the requirements for consideration for an obligation under a negotiable instrument, *see* UCC Section 3-408. *See* D. Melinkoff, *The Language of the Law* 180 (1963).

Consignee: 1. Person to whom goods are consigned. 2. Person to whom goods are shipped. In the case of a bill of lading or other document of title, consignee means "the person named in a bill to whom or to whose order the bill promises delivery." UCC Section 7-102(1)(b).

Consignment: 1. Delivery of goods to a person for sale. Under Article 2 of the Uniform Commercial Code–Sales, a consignment to a person maintaining a place of business at which he deals with goods of the kind involved is deemed a "sale or return" with respect to the rights of creditors of such person, unless certain precautions are taken to protect the interest of the consignor in the goods. UCC Section 2-326(3). *See* UCC Section 9-114; *see generally* Harrington, *The Law of Consignments: Antitrust and Commercial Pitfalls*, 34 Bus. Law. 431 (1979). 2. Shipment of goods under a bill of lading or other document of title.

Consignor: 1. Person delivering goods under a consignment. 2. Shipper. In the case of a bill of lading or other document of title, consignor means "the person named in a bill as the person from whom the goods have been received for shipment." UCC Section 7-102(1)(b).

Consistency: In accounting terminology, "Conformity from period to period with unchanging policies and procedures." Financial Accounting Standards Board, Statement of Financial Accounting Concepts No. 2, *Qualitative Characteristics of Accounting Information*, paragraph 171 (1980).

Consolidated financial statements: Financial statements that present the assets, liabilities, shareholders' accounts, revenue, and expenses of a parent company and its subsidiaries as those of a single enterprise. International Accounting Standards Committee, Statement of International Accounting Standards 3, *Consolidated Financial Statements*, paragraph 4 (1976). *See* SEC Regulation S-X, Art. 3A, 17 C.F.R. § 210.3A; *see generally* Fiflis, *Accounting for Mergers, Acquisitions and Investments, in a Nutshell: The Interrelationships of, and Criteria for, Purchase or Pooling, the Equity Method, and Parent-Company-Only and Consolidated Statements*, 37 Bus. Law. 89 (1981).

Consolidation: Combination of two or more corporations into a new corporation, or transfer of substantially all the assets of two or more corporations to a new corporation. *See* Treas. Reg. §

1.368-2. See reorganization; statutory consolidation.

Consortium bank: International bank formed by a group or consortium of commercial banks for the pooling of international business.

Conspicuous: For the purpose of the Uniform Commercial Code:

A term or clause is conspicuous when it is so written that a reasonable person against whom it is to operate ought to have noticed it. A printed heading in capitals (as: NON-NEGOTIABLE BILL OF LADING) is conspicuous. Language in the body of a form is "conspicuous" if it is in larger or other contrasting type or color. But in a telegram any stated term is "conspicuous". Whether a term or clause is "conspicuous" or not is for decision by the court.

UCC Section 1-210(10). *See Rudy's Glass Constr. Co. v. E. F. Johnson Co.,* 404 So. 2d 1987 (Fla. App. 1981).

Constant-dollar accounting: Method of reporting financial statement elements in dollars, each of which has the same (i.e., constant) general purchasing power. This method of accounting can be described as accounting in units of general purchasing power or as accounting in units of current purchasing power. Financial Accounting Standards Board, Statement of Financial Accounting Standards No. 33, *Financial Reporting and Changing Prices,* paragraph 22 (1979).

Construction: Ascertainment of legal operation or effect. *See* Patterson, *The Interpretation and Construction of Contracts,* 64 Colum. L. Rev. 833 (1964). Compare interpretation.

Construction-differential subsidy: Subsidy paid by the Maritime Subsidy Board to help equalize the difference in cost between having a vessel constructed or reconstructed in a representative foreign shipyard and having the same vessel constructed or reconstructed in the United States, under Title V of the Merchant Marine Act, 1936, 46 U.S.C. §§ 1151–61. *See* Caras, *U.S. Maritime Administration Financing Procedures Available for New Ship Construction,* 36 Bus. Law. 1887 (1981).

Construction financing: Financing during the period of construction of a project, intended to be repaid out of proceeds of a long-term financing at the completion of the project, or the proceeds of the sale of the project.

Construction industry proviso: Proviso to section 8(e) of the National Labor Relations Act, which provides a limited exception from otherwise illegal secondary boycott activity for certain construction industry practices. 29 U.S.C. § 158(e).

Construction mortgage: For the purpose of Article 9 of the Uniform Commercial Code–Secured Transactions, a mortgage is a construction mortgage to the extent that "it secures an obligation incurred for the construction of an improvement on land including the acquisition cost of the land, if the recorded writing so indicates." UCC Section 9-313(1)(c).

Constructive: Established by a legal conclusion.

Constructive dividend: Payment by a corporation to a stockholder, such as a redemption of stock, that is treated by the Internal Revenue Service as a dividend and taxed as such. *See* Rev. Rul. 58-614, 1958-2 C.B. 920; Rev. Rul. 59-286, 1959-2 C.B. 103.

Constructive notice: Information imputed by law to a person, whether or not he has it, because he could have discovered it by diligent inquiry, and his situation puts upon him the duty to make such inquiry. A filing of a financing statement in the proper place constitutes constructive notice of a security interest in the property described in the statement to anyone considering acquiring an interest in that property.

Constructive ownership: Ownership imputed by law. As to constructive ownership of stock, *see* I.R.C. § 318.

Constructive receipt: Treatment of deferred compensation or other income that is not actually received, as received for tax purposes. *See* Metzer, *Constructive Receipt, Economic Benefit and Assignment of Income: A Case Study in Deferred Compensation,* 29 Tax L. Rev. 525 (1974).

Constructive trust: Trust imposed on property by operation of law, in order to preserve property held by one party (the "constructive trustee") for the benefit of another. *See Restatement, Second, Contracts* § 340 (1981); *Restatement of Security* §§ 29–34 (1941).

Consumer: As defined in the Magnuson-Moss Warranty–Federal Trade Commission Improvement Act, a consumer is

a buyer (other than for purposes of resale) of any consumer product, any person to whom such product is transferred during the duration of an implied or written warranty (or service contract) applicable to the product, and any other person who is entitled by the terms of such warranty (or service contract) or under applicable State law to enforce against the warrantor (or service contractor) the obligations of the warranty (or service contract).

Section 101(3), 15 U.S.C. § 2301(3).

Consumer goods: For the purpose of Article 9 of the Uniform Commercial Code–Secured Transactions, goods are consumer goods if they "are used or bought primarily for personal, family or household purposes; ... ." UCC Section 9-109. Consumer goods are one of several classes of goods established under Article 9 that are subject to different rules regarding rights of purchasers from the debtor, priority of claims, place of filing, and rights after default. See also **consumer product.**

Consumer product: As defined in the Magnuson-Moss Warranty–Federal Trade Commission Improvement Act, a consumer product is "any tangible personal property which is distributed in commerce and which is normally used for personal, family, or household purposes (including any property intended to be attached to or installed in any real property without regard to whether it is so attached or installed)." Section 101(1), 15 U.S.C. § 2301(1). *See generally* Popper, *The New Federal Warranty Law: Guide to Compliance,* 32 Bus. Law. 399 (1977). *See also* the definition in section 3 of the Consumer Product Safety Act, 15 U.S.C. § 2052(1).

Consumer Product Safety Commission: Independent agency of the United States government with primary responsibility for establishing mandatory product safety standards to reduce the unreasonable risk of injury from consumer products. The CPSC has the authority to ban hazardous consumer products and engages in consumer and industry information and education programs. See the Consumer Product Safety Act, Pub. L. No. 92-573, 86 Stat. 1207 (1972); 15 U.S.C. §2051n–2081; The CPSC administers the Flammable Fabrics Act, Pub. L. No. 88, ch. 164, 67 Stat. 111 (1953), 15 U.S.C. §§ 1191–1204; the Poison Prevention Packaging Act of 1970, Pub. L. No. 91-601, 84 Stat. 1670 (1970), the Federal Hazardous Substances Labeling Act, Pub. L. No. 86-613, 74 Stat. 372 (1960), 15 U.S.C. §§ 1261–74, and related laws.

Contingency: In accounting terminology, "A contingency is a condition or situation, the ultimate outcome of which, gain or loss, will be confirmed only on the occurrence, or non-occurrence, of one or more uncertain future events." International Accounting Standards Committee, Statement of International Accounting Standards, Statement 10, *Contingencies and Events Occurring After the Balance Sheet Date,* paragraph 3 (1978). Another definition is provided in Financial Accounting Standards Board, Statement of Financial Accounting Principles No. 5, *Accounting for Contingencies,* paragraph 1 (1975): "a contingency is defined as an existing condition, situation, or set of circumstances involving uncertainty as to possible gain ... or loss ... to an enterprise that will ultimately be resolved when one or more future events occur or fail to occur."

Contingent liability: Liability that may or may not arise in the future, depending on a factor other than the passage of time. A guaranty of the indebtedness of another would be a contingent liability. See contingency.

Contingent rentals: Increases or decreases in lease payments that result from changes occurring subsequent to the inception of the lease in the factors (other than the passage of time) on which lease payments are based, except as are related to increases in the construction or acquisition cost of the leased property. Financial Accounting Standards Board, Statement of Financial Accounting Standards No. 29, *Determining Contingent Rentals, an Amendment of Statement No. 13,* paragraph 11 (1979); Statement of Financial Accounting Principles No. 13, *Accounting for Leases,* paragraph 5n (1976) (as amended).

Continuation statement: Statement filed to continue the effectiveness of a financing statement filed to perfect a security interest in personal property under Article 9 of the Uniform Commercial Code–Secured Transactions. Such a financing statement will lapse after five years, except in the case of a "transmitting utility"; a continuation statement may be filed within six months prior to the expiration of the financing statement to continue the effectiveness of the financing statement for another five years. UCC Section 9-403(3).

Continuous disclosure: See integrated disclosure.

Contract: "A promise or set of promises for the breach of which the law gives a remedy, or the performance of which the law in some way recognizes as a duty." *Restatement, Second, Contracts,* § 1 (1981). In order for a promise or set of promises to be enforceable as a contract, a number of elements are necessary, including a promisor and a promisee with legal capacity, a manifestation of assent (in writing, in many cases), and sufficient consideration. *See generally, Restatement, Second, Contracts,* (1981). Under the Uniform Commercial Code, a contract means "the total legal obligation which results from the parties' agreement as affected by this Act and any other applicable rules of law." UCC Section 1-201(11). As to the formation of a contract under the Uniform Commercial Code, see UCC Section 2-201–10. Compare **agreement; bargain.**

Contract-bar rule: Policy of the National Labor Relations Board that a valid union contract for three years or more will bar for three years another union's petition for certification.

Contract carrier: Carrier providing transportation for compensation under continuing agreements, rather than on the basis of individual shipments. For definitions for the purpose of Interstate Commerce Commission regulation of motor contract carriers and water contract carriers, *see* 49 U.S.C. §§ 10102(5), (12), (28).

Contract for sale: In Article 2 of the Uniform Commercial Code–Sales, a "contract for sale" includes "both a present sale of goods and a contract to sell goods at a future time." UCC Section 2-106.

Contract of adhesion: Contract in which the terms are dictated by one party, and freedom of contract is generally lacking. *See* Kessler, *Contracts of Adhesion–Some Thoughts about Freedom of Contract,* 43 Colum. L. Rev. 629 (1943). The term was introduced to American law in Patterson, *The Delivery of a Life Insurance Policy,* 33 Harv. L. Rev. 198, 222 (1919).

Contract of sale: For the purpose of the Commodity Exchange Act, the term "contract of sale" includes "sales, agreements of sale, and agreements to sell." 7 U.S.C. § 2.

Contract not to sue: "Contract under which the obligee of a duty promises never to sue the obligor or a third person to enforce the duty or not to do so for a limited time." *Restatement, Second, Contracts,* § 285 (1981).

Contract rights: Under the 1962 version of the Uniform Commercial Code, contract rights, for the purpose of Article 9–Secured Transactions meant "any right to payment under a contract not yet earned by performance and not evidenced by an instrument or chattel paper." The term has been absorbed into the term "accounts" in the 1972 version of the Uniform Commercial Code, which prevails in most states. UCC Section 9-106.

Contribution: Doctrine that losses are to be distributed among persons who are jointly and severally liable either pro rata or apportioned by considering fault, unjust enrichment, or degree of participation in the wrongful conduct. *Restatement of Restitution* § 81 (1937).

Contribution to capital: Amounts received by a corporation from its shareholders, not included in gross income. *See* I.R.C. § 118.

Contributory infringement: Selling "a component of a patented machine, manufacture, combination or composition, or a material or apparatus for use in practicing a patented process, constituting a material part of the invention, knowing the same to be especially made or especially adapted for use in an infringement of such patent, and not a staple article or commodity of commerce suitable for substantial non-infringing use, ..." 35 U.S.C. § 271(c). *See Aro Manufacturing Co. v. Convertible Top Replacement Co.,* 377 U.S. 476 (1964); *see generally* American Bar Association, Section of Antitrust Law, *Antitrust Law Developments* 339 (1975); Samuels & Samuels, *Contributory Infringement: Relief for the Patent Owner,* 4 Corp. L. Rev. 332 (1981).

Control: In the case of corporations, the percentage of stock ownership that constitutes "control" varies substantially, depending on the legislative context. For the purpose of income tax treatment of corporate reorganizations, control means "the ownership of stock possessing at least 80 percent of the total combined voting power of all classes of stock entitled to vote and at least 80 percent of the total number of shares of all other classes of stock of the corporation." I.R.C. § 368(c). A regulated investment company "controls" an issuer of securities if it owns 20 percent or more of the total combined voting power of all classes of stock entitled to vote. I.R.C. § 851(c)(2). In certain circumstances, five percent holding

has been considered to be effective control; *United States v. Citizens & Southern National Bank,* 422 U.S. 86 (1975). *See* Change in Bank Control Act, 12 U.S.C. § 1817(j); section 2(a)(9) of the Investment Company Act of 1940, 15 U.S.C. § 80a-2(a)(9). For accounting purposes, "control" usually means ownership of a majority of the outstanding voting stock. American Institute of Certified Public Accountants, Accounting Principles Board Opinion No. 18, *The Equity Method of Accounting for Investments in Common Stock,* paragraph 3c (1971); International Accounting Standards Committee, Statement of International Accounting Standards 3, *Consolidated Financial Statements,* paragraph 4 (1976). Some tests do not depend on a percentage; in SEC regulations, the term means "the possession, direct or indirect, of the power to direct or cause the direction of the management and policies of a person, whether through the ownership of voting securities, by contract, or otherwise; ...." Regulation S-X, 17 C.F.R. § 210.102(g); 17 C.F.R. § 230.405, 47 Fed. Reg. 11380, 11435 (1982). *See* Sommer, *Who's "In Control"?—S.E.C.,* 21 Bus. Law. 559 (1966). *See also* Cal. Corp. Code § 160. As to "control group," *see United States v. Upjohn,* 449 U.S. 383 (1981).

Controlled foreign corporation: For the purpose of subpart F of the Internal Revenue Code, a controlled foreign corporation is a "foreign corporation of which more than 50 percent of the total combined voting power of all classes of stock entitled to vote is owned (within the meaning of section 958(a)), or is considered as owned by applying the rules of ownership of section

958(b), by United States shareholders on any day during the taxable year of such foreign corporation." I.R.C. § 957(a). *See generally* Liebman, *Note on the Tax Treatment of Joint Venture Income Under Subpart F: An Addendum,* 32 Bus. Law. 1819 (1977); Liebman, *The Tax Treatment of Joint Venture Income Under Subpart F: Some Issues and Alternatives,* 32 Bus. Law. 341 (1977).

Controlled group of corporations: Group of corporations that must share the $25,000 income tax bracket amount subject to a lower rate of tax than amounts over $25,000; that is, corporations in a controlled group cannot each use the lower rate applicable to income up to $25,000. Control may be through parent-subsidiary relationships or common control (brother-sister controlled group). Control, in most cases, means ownership of 80% of the total combined voting power of all classes of voting stock or 80% of the total value of shares. I.R.C. § 1563. *See also* I.R.C. § 851(c)(3).

Convention for the Unification of Certain Rules Relating to International Transportation by Air, with Additional Protocol: International agreement adopted in Warsaw on October 12, 1929, relating to various matters of commercial air transportation, including the limitation of liability of carriers to passengers. The Warsaw Convention entered into force in the United States on October 29, 1934, subject to a reservation. 49 Stat. 3000; Treaties in Force 248 (1979).

Convention on the International Recognition of Rights in Aircraft: International agreement, regarding security interests in aircraft, recommended by the International Civil Aviation Conference in Chicago in 1944, and adopted in Geneva on June 19, 1948. This convention entered into force for the United States on September 17, 1953 (4 U.S.T. 1830) and has been adopted by 38 other countries. Treaties in Force 252 (1979).

Convention on the Recognition and Enforcement of Foreign Arbitral Awards: International agreement, done at New York on June 10, 1958, covering international commercial arbitration. The convention, called the New York Convention, has been adopted by the United States (21 U.S.T. 2517) and 52 other countries. Treaties in Force 240 (1979).

Convention on the Settlement of Investment Disputes between States and Nationals of other States: International agreement, sponsored by the World Bank, providing for arbitration of certain commercial disputes. This convention was done at Washington on March 18, 1965, and entered into force for the United States on October 14, 1966. 17 U.S.T. 1270; Treaties in Force 275 (1979).

Conversion: 1. The exchange of one type of security of an issuer (usually debt securities or preferred stock) into another type of security of that issuer (usually common stock), in the exercise of specific conversion rights. 2. The exchange of one currency for another. Financial Accounting Standards Board, Statement of Financial Accounting Principles No. 8, *Accounting for the Translation of Foreign Currency Transactions and Foreign Currency Financial*

Statements, paragraph 243 (1975). 3. Wrongful interference with the possession of control of the personal property of another. The remedy for conversion is not usually return of the property, but payment by the convertor to the owner of the full value of the property. *See Restatement, Second, Torts* § 222A (1965). With respect to conversion of instruments covered by Article 3 of the Uniform Commercial Code, *see* UCC Section 3-419.

Conversion parity: In the case of a bond or other debt security with conversion rights to stock, the price of that stock that will equal the value of the convertible security. Conversion rights ordinarily would not be exercised until the market price of the stock reached or exceeded conversion parity.

Conversion price: The price assigned to common stock that determines the number of shares of common stock into which a security is convertible.

Conversion rate; conversion ratio: In connection with convertible securities, the number of shares of the security (usually common stock) into which each share of the convertible security can be converted.

Conversion value: Current market value of the securities obtainable upon conversion of a convertible security, less any payment required for conversion.

Convertible: When used in connection with preferred stock or debt securities, meaning convertible into another security of the same issuer, usually common stock, at the option of the holder at a fixed "conversion" price,

usually within a fixed period. *See* American Institute of Certified Public Accountants, Accounting Principles Board Opinion No. 14, *Accounting for Convertible Debt and Debt Issued with Stock Purchase Warrants* (1966).

Conveyance: Sale or transfer. For certain purposes, the term may include a grant of security interest or mortgage; *e.g.,* under the Federal Aviation Act, the term "conveyance" means "a bill of sale, contract of conditional sale, mortgage, assignment of mortgage, or other instrument affecting title to, or interest in, property." Section 101(20), 49 U.S.C. § 1301(20). *See* 14 C.F.R. § 49.17.

Cooperative: Association of producers or consumers, organized for collective effort in production, marketing, or purchasing, with the earnings, savings, or benefits distributed among the shareholders or members in proportion to their respective share of production, transactions, or patronage. *See* Cal. Corp. Code § 12201; I.R.C. §§ 1381 –88; Selden, *An Analysis of Cooperative Buying Associations–Including New Concerns for Franchise Systems,* 37 Bus. Law. 1569 (1982).

Cooperative bank: For the purposes of the Internal Revenue Code, a "cooperative bank" is "an institution without capital stock organized and operated for mutual purposes and without profit," eligible for federal deposit insurance, subject to banking regulations, and meeting certain requirements of the definition of a domestic building and loan association under the Code. I.R.C. § 7701(a)(32).

Copyright: Right under federal law in a work of authorship fixed in a tangible medium. *See* 17 U.S.C. § 102. *See generally* 17 U.S.C. §§ 101–810, M. Nimmer, *Nimmer on Copyright* (1981).

Copyright Office: Unit of the Library of Congress responsible for administering the system of copyright protection for books, periodicals, musical compositions, dramatic compositions, motion pictures, recordings, and similar works. *See* 17 U.S.C. §§ 701–10.

Copyright Royalty Tribunal: Unit of the legislative branch of the United States government that makes determinations concerning the adjustment of royalty rates for records, jukeboxes, and certain cable television transmissions, and the use by public broadcasting stations of certain graphic works. *See* 17 U.S.C. §§ 801–10.

Corner: Ownership or control of such a large portion of a particular security or commodity available in the market that the price can be manipulated. If a trader has a corner, traders with short positions will be forced to cover at the price set by the holder of the corner. *See Great Western Food Distributors, Inc., v. Brannan,* 201 F. 2d 476 (7th Cir.), *cert. denied,* 345 U.S. 997 (1953).

Corporation: Artificial and immortal entity, created pursuant to statute or act of legislature, with liability of its owners for its debts and misdeeds limited to their investment therein. In the words of Justice Marshall:

A corporation is an artificial being, invisible, intangible, and existing only in contemplation of law. Being the mere creature of law, it possesses only those properties which the charter of its creation confers upon it, either expressly, or as incidental to its very existence. These are such as are supposed best calculated to effect the object for which it was created. Among the most important are immortality, and, if the expression may be allowed, individuality; properties, by which a perpetual succession of many persons are considered the same, and may act as a single individual. They enable a corporation to manage its own affairs, and to hold property without the perplexing intricacies, the hazardous and endless necessity, of perpetual conveyances for the purpose of transmitting it from hand to hand. It is chiefly for the purpose of clothing bodies of men, in succession, with these qualities and capacities, that corporations were invented, and are in use. By these means, a perpetual succession of individuals are capable of acting for the promotion of a particular object, like one immortal being.

Trustees of Dartmouth College v. Woodward, 17 U.S. (4 Wheat.) 518, 636 (1819). *See Lawson v. Household Finance Corp.,* 17 Del. Ch. 343, 152 A. 723 (1930). State corporation laws usually define the term as a corporation organized pursuant to such laws; Del. Code Ann. tit. 8. § 101; N.Y. Bus. Corp. Law § 102(a)(4); Model Business Corporation Act § 2(a) (1979). Most federal statutes relating to corporations construe the term broadly. For example, under the Federal Trade Commission Act, the term includes:

any company, trust, so-called Massachusetts trust, or association, incorporated or unincorporated, which is organized to carry on business for its own profit or that of its members, and has shares of capital or capital stock or certificates of interest, and any company, trust, so-called Massachusetts trust, or association, incorporated or unincorporated, without shares of capital or capital stock or certificates of interest, except partnerships, which is organized to carry on business for its own profit or that of its members.

15 U.S.C. § 44. The Bankruptcy Code definition includes unincorporated associations of limited liability, but not limited partnerships; 11 U.S.C. § 101(8). The legislative history of the Bankruptcy Code states that labor unions are intended to be covered; H.R. Rep. No. 95-595, 95th Cong., 1st Sess. 309 (1977). For the purpose of the Internal Revenue Code, the term "corporation" includes "associations, joint-stock companies, and insurance companies." I.R.C. § 7701(a)(3). An "association" may be taxed as a corporation if it more nearly resembles a corporation than a partnership or trust, by reference to certain "corporate" attributes: associates, an objective to carry on a business and divide the profits, continuity of life, centralization of management, liability for corporate debts limited to corporate property, and free transferability of interests. Treas. Reg. § 301.7701-2; *Morrisey v. Commissioner,* 296 U.S. 344 (1935). A corporation validly existing under state laws may be disregarded for tax purposes; *e.g. Gregory v. Helvering,* 293 U.S. 465 (1935).

Corps of Engineers: Unit of the United States Army that administers the Army's Civil Works Program, a program of construction of dams and waterway improvements. See **pork barrel.**

Corpus: Principal of a fund or bond, as distinguished from income or interest.

The plural form, corpora, is usually encountered in reference to the elements of a debt security representing the obligation to pay principal at maturity (perhaps in serial maturities), after the interest coupons have been stripped away.

Corrective advertising: Disclosure in a portion of advertising, pursuant to an order of the Federal Trade Commission, either that the FTC has challenged previous advertising for a product, or that the product does not have the particular characteristic claimed for it. *See* American Bar Association, Section of Antitrust Law, *Antitrust Law Developments* 205 (1975).

Correspondent bank: Bank that accepts deposits of and performs banking services for another bank, usually located in another city.

Co-sale agreement: Agreement among shareholders of a corporation that one shareholder may not sell his shares unless other shareholders are given the option to sell on the same terms.

Co-signer: Person who, in addition to the original maker or signer, signs a note or other financial obligation and thus assumes liability therefor.

Cosmetic: For the purpose of the Federal Trade Commission Act, the term "cosmetic" means "(1) articles to be rubbed, poured, sprinkled, or sprayed on, introduced into, or otherwise applied to the human body or any part thereof intended for cleansing, beautifying, promoting attractiveness, or altering the appearance, and (2) articles intended for use as a component for any such article; except that such term shall not include soap." Section 15, 15 U.S.C. § 55(e).

Cost: As defined by the Financial Accounting Standards Board:

"Cost" is the sacrifice incurred in economic activities–that which is given up or foregone to consume, to save, to exchange, to produce, etc. For example, the value of cash or other resources given up (or the present value of an obligation incurred) in exchange for a resource is the cost of the resource acquired. Similarly, the expiration of future benefits caused by using a resource in production is the cost of using it.

Financial Accounting Standards Board, Statement of Financial Accounting Concepts No. 1, *Objectives of Financial Reporting by Business Enterprises,* paragraph 45, n. 11 (1978). *See also* American Institute of Certified Public Accountants, Accounting Principles Board Statement No. 4, Ch. 6, *Generally Accepted Accounting Principles –Pervasive Principles,* paragraph 28 (1970).

Cost Accounting Standards Board: Agency of Congress that promulgates cost accounting standards for defense contractors and subcontractors. *See* Pub. L. No. 91-379, 84 Stat. 796 (1970); 50 U.S.C. App. § 2168; 4 C.F.R. §§ 301–5.

Cost-benefit analysis: Method of analysis of large engineering and public works projects whereby costs and benefits are determined, quantified, and compared. If benefits exceed costs (the benefit/cost ratio exceeding one), the project is justified by this method. The method should be used with care and its results viewed with suspicion because hard data, usually on the cost side, is often mixed with soft, speculative data, usually on the benefit side.

Cost company: Corporation with nominal capital that holds title to a mineral interest and production facilities, whose shareholders agree to take the products of such facilities in proportion to their ownership interests. The cost company is not separately taxable, but files an information tax return; the shareholders report their pro-rata shares of income and expenses on their own returns. *See* Rev. Rul. 56-542, 1956-2 C.B. 327.

Cost depletion: Method of determining depletion deductions by reference to the cost of the property. The cost of the property is divided by an estimate of the number of units that can be extracted from the property, and the cost depletion deduction for each year is that per-unit cost times the number of units extracted in that year. I.R.C. §§ 611, 612. See also **percentage depletion.**

Cost justification: Defense to a charge of price discrimination, based on section 2(a) of the Robinson-Patman Act, which permits price "differentials which make only due allowance for differences in the cost of manufacture, sale, or delivery resulting from the differing methods or quantities in which such commodities are to such purchasers sold or delivered ... ." 15 U.S.C. § 13(a). *See United States v. Borden Co.,* 370 U.S. 460 (1962). *See generally* American Bar Association, Section of Antitrust Law, *Antitrust Law Developments* 136 (1975).

Cost method: Method of accounting for investments in common stock in which the investor records the investment at cost, and recognizes as income dividends received out of earnings accumulated since the date of the acquisition. American Institute of Certified Public Accountants, Accounting Principles Board Opinion No. 18, *The Equity Method of Accounting for Investments in Common Stock,* paragraph 6a (1971). *See* Fiflis, *Accounting for Mergers, Acquisitions and Investments, in a Nutshell: The Interrelationships of, and Criteria for, Purchase or Pooling, the Equity Method, and Parent-Company-Only and Consolidated Statements,* 37 Bus. Law. 89 (1981). Compare **equity method.**

Cost of sales: Costs associated with manufacturing or sales, including all direct labor and material costs, and plant overhead and depreciation.

Cost of service: Method of rate regulation whereby the cost of providing the service is used as the basis for determining the rate to be paid for the service. Compare **value of service.**

Cost or market, whichever is lower: See lower of cost or market.

Cost-plus contract: Contract for a construction or development project in which costs are difficult to estimate in advance, whereby the party performing the service is reimbursed for allowable or otherwise defined cost, plus a fee. *See* International Accounting Standards Committee, Statement of International Accounting Standards 11, *Accounting for Construction Contracts,* paragraph 6 (1979).

Cost-plus-fixed-fee contract: Type of cost-plus contract in which the fee is a fixed amount, rather than determined as a percentage of costs or an incentive fee.

Cost-plus-incentive-fee contract: Type of cost-plus contract in which the fee is calculated on a formula to increase compensation for holding costs below a target figure, or for performance in excess of agreed-upon standards.

Cost recovery index: Index published quarterly by the Interstate Commerce Commission for use by railroad companies as a basis for rate adjustments.

Council of Economic Advisers: Unit of the Executive Office of the President that advises the President on economic matters and recommends economic policy. *See* Employment Act of 1946, Pub. L. No. 304, ch. 33, 60 Stat. 23, 24 (1946); 15 U.S.C. § 1023.

Council on Environmental Quality: Unit of the Executive Office of the President established to formulate and recommend national policies to promote the improvement of the quality of the environment. *See* National Environmental Policy Act of 1969, Pub. L. No. 91-190, 83 Stat. 852 (1969); Environmental Quality Improvement Act of 1970, Pub. L. No. 91-224, 84 Stat. 91, 114 (1970), 42 U.S.C. §§ 4371–74. An important function of the CEQ is the review of environmental impact statements after the final statement has been prepared but before the action contemplated by the statement is taken. *See* 40 C.F.R. § 1500–17.

Council on Wage and Price Stability: Unit of the Executive Office of the President, now disbanded, established to monitor the economy as a whole, with the emphasis on productivity, prices, and profits, and to administer voluntary wage and price standards. *See* Council on Wage and Price Stability Act, Pub. L. No. 93-387, 88 Stat. 750 (1974).

Counterclaim: Claim by the defendant in a court proceeding against the plaintiff. Fed R. Civ. Proc. 13. In federal court, a counterclaim is compulsory if it arises out of the same "transaction or occurrence" that is the subject matter of the opposing party's claim, and does not involve a third party over which the court cannot acquire jurisdiction; "permissive counterclaims" involving claims not arising out of the transaction or occurrence are also permitted. *See Moore v. New York Cotton Exchange*, 273 U.S. 593 (1926). *See generally* Kennedy, *Counterclaims under Federal Rule 13*, 11 Houston L. Rev. 255 (1974).

Counter-offer: "Offer made by an offeree to his offeror relating to the same matter as the original offer and proposing a substituted bargain differing from that proposed by the original offer." *Restatement, Second, Contracts,* § 39 (1981). A counter-offer extinguishes an offeree's power of acceptance of an offer, unless a contrary intention is manifested by the offeror or the offeree.

Countervailing duty: Special duty imposed on foreign merchandise equal to the amount of any "bounty or grant" paid or bestowed by a foreign government or other entity with respect to the manufacture, production, or exportation of such merchandise. Section 303 of the Tariff Act of 1930, Pub. L. No. 361, ch. 497, 46 Stat. 590, 19 U.S.C. § 1303. *See* Feller, *Countervailing Duties,* in I. W. Surrey & D. Wallace, Jr., ed., *A Lawyer's Guide to International Business Transactions* 119 (2d ed. 1977); Butler, *Countervailing Duties and Export Subsidization; A Re-emerging Issue in International Trade,* 9 Va. J. Int'l L. 82 (1969).

Coupon: Part of a bond, representing a single payment of interest, which can be detached, or "clipped," and presented by the holder to the issuer or the paying agent for the payment of that interest. The term "coupon" is often used to mean the rate of interest on a bond.

Coupon bond: Bond, usually a bearer bond, with coupons for interest payments.

Coupon rate: Rate of interest stated for a debt security; not necessarily the same as the yield.

Course of dealing: Under the Uniform Commercial Code, agreements are to be interpreted by reference to the course of dealing between the parties and usage of trade, not by a layman's interpretation or a strict legal construction. A "course of dealing" is "a sequence of previous conduct between the parties to a particular transaction which is fairly to be regarded as establishing a common basis of understanding for interpreting their expressions and other conduct." UCC Section 1-205; *see Restatement, Second, Contracts,* § 223 (1981). See also **usage of trade.**

Course of performance: Under Article 2 of the Uniform Commercial Code–Sales, a "course of performance" accepted or acquiesced in without objection is relevant in determining the meaning of an agreement, and may be relevant to show a modification of any term of an agreement for the sale of goods inconsistent with such term. UCC Section 2-208.

Court of Claims: United States federal court responsible for hearing cases involving claims against the United States, including claims for the refund of federal income and excise taxes. *See* Act of Feb. 24, 1855, ch. 122, 10 Stat. 612; 28 U.S.C. § 171–75; 28 U.S.C. §§ 1491–1506.

Court of Customs and Patent Appeals, United States: United States federal court responsible for hearing appeals from the decisions of the Customs Court, the Patent and Trademark Office, the United States International Trade Commission, and certain other administrative decisions. 28 U.S.C. §§ 1541—1545. The Court also hears petitions for extraordinary writs under the All Writs Act, Pub. L. No. 475, ch. 231, 36 Stat. 1087, 1156 (1911); 28 U.S.C. § 1651(a). *See* Pub. L. No. 914, ch. 488, 45 Stat. 1475 (1929), 28 U.S.C. §§ 211–16.

Covenant: Agreement; promise.

Cover: 1. Procurement of substitute goods. Under Article 2 of the Uniform Commercial Code–Sales, if a buyer's sales contract has been breached by the seller by a failure to make conforming delivery or repudiation, the buyer may "cover" by "making in good faith and without unreasonable delay any reasonable purchase of or contract to purchase goods in substitution for those due from the seller." Damages are then measured by the difference between the cost of cover and the contract price, together with incidental and consequential damages. UCC Section 2-712; *see also* UCC Section 2-711. 2. Sale of securities on behalf of another to disguise the identity of the true seller. 3. Purchase of securities to meet an existing obligation to sell securities that were not owned at the time of the agreement to sell (short sale). 4. In respect of coverage of losses in foreign exchange due to strengthening of a foreign currency and a net liability position, "cover" is the amount by which the foreign currency cost of assets carried at cost in foreign currency, translated at the current rate, exceeds their cost translated at historical rates (their cost in dollars). Financial Accounting Standards Board, Statement of Financial Accounting Standards No. 8, *Accounting for the Translation of Foreign Currency Transactions and Foreign Currency Financial Statements,* paragraph 174 (1975).

Coverage: Ratio of the earnings of an entity, before deduction of interest and other fixed charges, to fixed charges (fixed-charge coverage), interest (interest coverage), or preferred stock dividends (preferred dividend coverage). *See* SEC Accounting Series Releases No. 119, 122, 36 Fed. Reg. 11918, 15527 (1971).

Coverage test: Provision in legal investment laws requiring a certain minimum earnings "coverage" of fixed charges, by earnings being available in some multiple of fixed charges, for the securities of a issuer to be a legal investment for savings banks or insurance companies. *See, e.g.,* Mass. Gen. Laws Ann., ch. 168, § 44.

Covered call: 1. Call whose writer owns the security for which the call is written (or holds a call at an equal or lower price). 2. Call whose holder has sold the security for which the call is written short.

Covered put: 1. Put whose writer holds a put on the security for which the put is written at an equal or greater price. 2. Put whose holder owns the security for which the put is written. See put.

Cover note: Certificate of insurance issued by an insurance broker.

CPA: Certified Public Accountant.

CPM: Critical path method. See pert.

CPO: Commodity pool operator.

CPSC: Consumer Product Safety Commission.

Cram-down: Confirmation of a plan of reorganization over the objections of a class of creditors if the plan "does not discriminate unfairly, and is fair and equitable." 11 U.S.C. 1129(b). *See generally* Lake, *Representing Secured Creditors under the Bankruptcy Code,* 37 Bus. Law. 1153 (1982).

Credit: 1. Amount due a person or business. 2. Accounting entry that decreases assets and increases liability, net worth, or profits. 3. To add to an account. 4. Loan. 5. Letter of credit.

Credit line: Undertaking on the part of a financial institution to lend in the future, usually with a set limit of loans outstanding at any given time.

Credit memo: Document evidencing the existence of a credit to an account.

Creditor: Person to whom a debt is owed. Under the Uniform Commercial Code, the term "creditor" includes "a general creditor, a secured creditor, a lien creditor and any representative of creditors, including an assignee for the benefit of creditors, a trustee in bankruptcy, a receiver in equity and an executor or administrator of an insolvent debtor's or assignor's estate." UCC Section 1-201(12). Under the Bankruptcy Code, the term means parties with claims that arose before the filing of the petition; 11 U.S.C. § 101(9); H.R. Rep. No. 95-595, 95th Cong., 1st Sess. 309 (1977).

Credit union: Financial cooperative organization of individuals with a common affiliation, such as employment or membership in a labor union. Credit unions accept deposits from members, make loans to members, and pay interest to depositors out of the earnings.

Creeping tender offer: Acquisition of shares of a corporation by open market purchases followed by a formal tender offer. Under certain circumstances, the open market purchases will be integrated with the formal tender offer, requiring disclosure under the Williams Act. *See Kennecott Copper Corp. v. Curtiss-Wright Corp.*, 584 F. 2d 1195 (2d Cir. 1978); Einhorn & Blackburn, *The Developing Concept of "Tender Offer": An Analysis of the Judicial and Administrative Interpretations of the Term*, 23 N.Y.L.S. L. Rev. 379 (1978); Lipton, *Open Market Purchases*, 32 Bus. Law. 1321 (1977).

"C" reorganization: Corporate acquisition by exchange of stock for assets. See **reorganization.**

CRI: Cost recovery index.

Criminal Division: Division of the United States Department of Justice responsible for enforcement of federal criminal statutes (except those assigned to the Antitrust, Civil Rights, and Tax Divisions, and certain other divisions.) The Criminal Division provides support for the U.S. Attorneys' offices, sets policy, and participates in the larger cases.

Cross-acceleration clause: Clause in a debt instrument that provides that the debt is accelerated if other specified debts of the debtor are accelerated.

Cross-claim: Claim by a party to court proceeding "against a co-party arising out of the transaction or occurrence that is the subject matter either of the original action or of a counterclaim therein or relating to any property that is the subject matter of the original action." Fed. R. Civ. Proc. 13(g). Co-parties are parties on the same side of an action, so a cross-claim would be by one defendant against another, or by one

plaintiff against another in respect of a counterclaim.

Cross-default clause: Clause in a debt instrument or other obligation that provides that a default on another debt or obligation of the debtor or obligor will be treated as a default under the instrument in question.

Crude Oil Windfall Profit Tax Act of 1980: Federal tax legislation with special provisions for taxing oil company profits. Pub. L. No. 96-223, 94. Stat. 229 (1980).

CTA: Commodity trading advisor.

Cumulative Bulletin: Semi-annual publication of the Internal Revenue Service that consolidates the Internal Revenue Bulletins.

Cumulative dividends: Dividends on cumulative preferred stock.

Cumulative preferred stock: Preferred stock on which all past dividends must be paid before any dividends are paid on common stock. *See* Del. Code Ann. tit. 8 § 151(c). *See Bank of America v. West End Chemical Co.*, 37 Cal. App. 2d 685, 100P. 2d 318 (1940).

Cumulative rate of return: Rate of return for more than one year, compounded.

Cumulative voting: Method of election of directors of a corporation in which all directors to be elected on that occasion are elected in a single balloting; each share is entitled to the same number of votes as there are directors to be elected, and votes may be cumulated by a shareholder by giving one candidate as many votes as the number of directors to be elected times the number of shares held (or by distributing such votes on the same principle among a number of candidates). If directors are to be elected by cumulative voting, the certificate or articles of incorporation must so provide. Model Business Corporation Act § 33 (1979); N.Y. Bus. Corp. Law § 618; Del. Code Ann. tit. 8 § 214. A minority shareholder could not obtain representation on the board of directors in individual elections of directors, but if directors are to be elected by cumulative voting, such a shareholder may be able to elect one or more directors by accumulating its votes and casting them for such directors. *See* Campbell, *The Origin and Growth of Cumulative Voting for Directors*, 10 Bus. Law. 3 (1955).

Cure right: Right to cure defaults on an obligation. Cure rights are often used in the debt instrument of a leveraged lease, giving the owner and lessor of the property under lease the right to cure defaults of the lessee, to avoid the exercise of remedies by the debt participant against the property.

Currency: Under Article 3 of the Uniform Commercial Code–Commercial Paper, an instrument payable in "currency" is payable in money. UCC Section 3-107. See **money;** UCC Section 1-201(24).

Currency option clause: Clause in a debt obligation permitting the holder to take payment of principal and interest in a currency other than the currency in which the obligation is issued.

Current account balance: The difference between a nation's exports and imports of goods, services, and transfers, excluding transactions in financial assets and liabilities.

Current assets: Assets in cash or convertible into cash, or otherwise available to pay debts. As stated by the American Institute of Certified Public Accountants:

For accounting purposes, the term current assets is used to designate cash and other assets or resources commonly identified as those which are reasonably expected to be realized in cash or sold or consumed during the normal operating cycle of the business. Thus the term comprehends in general such resources as (a) cash available for current operations and items which are the equivalent of cash; (b) inventories of merchandise, raw materials, goods in process, finished goods, operating supplies, and ordinary maintenance material and parts; (c) trade accounts, notes, and acceptances receivable; (d) receivables from officers, employees, affiliates, and others, if collectible in the ordinary course of business within a year; (e) instalment or deferred accounts and notes receivable if they conform generally to normal trade practices and terms within the business; (f) marketable securities representing the investment of cash available for current operations; and (g) prepaid expenses such as insurance, interest, rents, taxes, unused royalties, current paid advertising service not yet received, and operating supplies. Prepaid expenses are not current assets in the sense that they will be converted into cash but in the sense that, if not paid in advance, they would require the use of current assets during the operating cycle.

American Institute of Certified Public Accountants, Accounting Research

Bulletin 43, Ch. 3A, *Current Assets and Current Liabilities*, paragraph 4 (1953).

Current cost accounting: Method of measuring and reporting assets and expenses associated with the use or sale of assets, at their current cost or lower recoverable amount at the balance sheet date or at the date of use or sale. Financial Accounting Standards Board, Statement of Financial Accounting Standards No. 33, *Financial Reporting and Changing Prices*, paragraph 22b (1979).

Current cost/constant dollar accounting: Method of accounting based on measures of current cost or lower recoverable amount in terms of dollars, each of which has the same general purchasing power. Financial Accounting Standards Board, Statement of Financial Accounting Standards No. 33, *Financial Reporting and Changing Prices*, paragraph 22c (1979).

Current cost/nominal dollar accounting: Method of accounting based on measures of current cost or lower recoverable amount without restatement into units, each of which has the same general purchasing power. Financial Accounting Standards Board, Statement of Financial Accounting Standards No. 33, *Financial Reporting and Changing Prices*, paragraph 22d (1979).

Current dollars: Dollars as of the current time, without any adjustment for purchasing power.

Current funds: Under Article 3 of the Uniform Commercial Code—Commercial Paper, an instrument payable in current funds is payable in money. UCC Section 3-107. See money; UCC Section 1-201(24).

Current liabilities: Liabilities for money owed, usually within one year. As stated by the American Institute of Certified Public Accountants:

The term current liabilities is used principally to designate obligations whose liquidation is reasonably expected to require the use of existing resources properly classifiable as current assets, or the creation of other current liabilities. As a balance-sheet category, the classification is intended to include obligations for items which have entered into the operating cycle, such as payables incurred in the acquisition of materials and supplies to be used in the production of goods or in providing services to be offered for sale; collections received in advance of the delivery of goods or performance of services; and debts which arise from operations directly related to the operating cycle, such as accruals for wages, salaries, commissions, rentals, royalties, and income and other taxes. Other liabilities whose regular and ordinary liquidation is expected to occur within a relatively short period of time, usually twelve months, are also intended for inclusion, such as short-term debts arising from the acquisition of capital assets, serial maturities of long-term obligations, amounts required to be expended within one year under sinking fund provisions, and agency obligations arising from the collection or acceptance of cash or other assets for the account of third persons.

American Institute of Certified Public Accountants, Accounting Research Bulletin 43, Ch. 3A, *Current Assets and Current Liabilities*, paragraph 7 (1953).

Current-noncurrent method: Method of translating assets and liabilities measured in foreign currency that translates current assets and liabilities at the current rate and noncurrent assets and liabilities at the applicable historical rates. Financial Accounting Standards Board, Statement of Financial Accounting Standards No. 8, *Accounting for the Translation of Foreign Currency Transactions and Foreign Currency Financial Statements,* paragraphs 121, 129–32 (1975).

Current operating performance: Concept of accounting for extraordinary or nonrecurring items whereby such items are not included in reported net income. *See* American Institute of Certified Public Accountants, Accounting Principles Board Opinion No. 9, *Reporting the Results of Operations,* paragraph 9 (1966); International Accounting Standards Committee, Statement of International Accounting Standards 8, *Unusual and Prior Period Items and Changes in Accounting Policies,* paragraph 5 (1978). Compare all-inclusive.

Current rate: In accounting for foreign exchange transactions, the "current rate" is the rate of exchange at the balance sheet date. Financial Accounting Standards Board, Statement of Financial Accounting Standards No. 8, *Accounting for the Translation of Foreign Currency Transactions and Foreign Currency Financial Statements,* paragraph 30 (1975).

Current rate method: Method of translating assets and liabilities measured in foreign currency that translates all assets and liabilities at the current rate. Financial Accounting Standards Board, Statement of Financial Accounting Standards No. 8, *Accounting for the Translation of Foreign Currency Transactions and Foreign Currency Financial Statements,* paragraphs 121, 133–39 (1975).

Current ratio: Ratio of current assets to current liabilities. See acid-test ratio.

Current transaction: Section 3(a)(3) of the Securities Act of 1933 provides an exemption for registration for "any note, draft, bill of exchange, or banker's acceptance which arises out of a current transaction or the proceeds of which have been or are to be used for current transactions, and which has a maturity at the time of issuance of not exceeding nine months, ..." 15 U.S.C. § 77c(a)(3). This exemption for commercial paper has been narrowly construed on the basis of the phrase "current transaction," the SEC staff taking the position that the proceeds of commercial paper offerings must be used for current operating expenses, and not for application to plant or permanent uses, for the exemption to be available.

Current yield: Ratio of annual interest or earnings to the current market price of a security, usually expressed as a percentage.

Cursory review: Review by the Securities and Exchange Commission staff of a registration statement that is apparently well prepared or is based on an earlier registration statement, in which written or oral comments are not provided and the review process is handled expeditiously. SEC Release No. 33-5231 (1972). Compare **summary review**.

Custodian: Person appointed by a court to manage a corporation in case of deadlock or other cause preventing management of the corporation by its board of directors. A custodian has the powers of a receiver, except that a custodian is charged with continuation of the business, and cannot liquidate and distribute the corporate assets. Del. Code Ann. tit. 8 § 226. The term is given a broader definition under the Bankruptcy Code:

(A) receiver or trustee of any property of the debtor, appointed in a case or proceeding not under this title;

(B) assignee under a general assignment for the benefit of debtor's creditors; or

(C) trustee, receiver, or agent under applicable law, or under a contract, that is appointed or authorized to take charge of property of the debtor for the purpose of enforcing a lien against such property, or for the purpose of general administration of such property for the benefit of the debtor's creditors.

11 U.S.C. § 101(10); *see* H.R. Rep. No. 95-595, 95th Cong., 1st Sess. 310 (1977).

Custodian bank: As defined in Article 8 of the Uniform Commercial Code–Investment Securities, a custodian bank is "any bank or trust company which is supervised and examined by state or federal authority having supervision over banks and which is acting as custodian for a clearing corporation." UCC Section 8-102(4).

Customer: 1. For the purpose of Article 3–Commercial Paper, and Article 4–Bank Deposits and Collections, of the Uniform Commercial Code, a customer is "any person having an account with a bank or for whom a bank has agreed to collect items and includes a bank carrying an account with another bank." UCC Section 4-104(1)(e). 2. For the purpose of Article 5 of the Uniform Commercial Code–Letters of Credit, a customer is "a buyer or other person who causes an issuer to issue a credit," including "a bank which procures issuance or confirmation on behalf of that bank's customer." UCC Section 5-103(1)(g).

Customer limitation: See **vertical restraint**.

Customs Court, United States: United States federal court responsible for hearing cases involving the tariff laws. *See* Pub. L. No. 703, ch. 589, 70 Stat. 532 (1956), 28 U.S.C. §§ 251–57.

Customs Service, United States: Unit of the United States Department of the Treasury charged with collecting duties on goods imported to the United States, interdicting contraband, and administering laws relating to copyright, patent and trademark, quota, and marking requirements for imported goods. See Pub. L. No. 751, ch. 348, 44 Stat. 1381 (1927).

Customs union: Group of countries that have eliminated duties and other trade restrictions among themselves, but apply substantially the same duties and other regulations of commerce to trade with nonmembers. *See* General Agreement on Tariff and Trade, Article XXIV. Compare **free trade area**.

D

D/A draft: Documents against acceptance draft.

Damages: Compensation for loss due to the unlawful act or omission of another, or for the breach of a contract. In contracts for the sale of goods, the Uniform Commercial Code provides that the damages of the seller for nonacceptance or repudiation by the buyer "is the difference between the market price at the time and place of tender and the unpaid contract price together with any incidental damages provided in this Article (Section 2-710), but less expenses saved in consequence of the buyer's breach." If this measure of damages "is inadequate to put the seller in as good a position as performance would have done then the measure of damages is the profit (including reasonable overhead) which the seller would have made from full performance by the buyer, together with any incidental damages provided by this Article (Section 2-710), due allowance for costs reasonably incurred and due credit for payments or proceeds of resale." UCC Section 2-708. If the seller breaches the contract for the sale of goods by nonde-

livery or repudiation, the buyer's damages are "the difference between the market price at the time when the buyer learned of the breach and the contract price together with any incidental and consequential damages provided in this Article (Section 2-715), but less expenses saved in consequence of the seller's breach." UCC Section 2-713. If the goods are accepted but are nonconforming, the buyer may recover as damages "the loss resulting in the ordinary course of events from the seller's breach as determined in any manner which is reasonable." The measure of damages for breach of warranty by the seller is "the difference at the time and place of acceptance between the value of the goods accepted and the value they would have had if they had been as warranted, unless special circumstances show proximate damages of a different amount." Incidental and consequential damages are also available to a buyer. UCC Section 2-714. *See also* UCC Section 2-712; consequential damages; expectation interest; incidental damages; liquidated damages; market price; reliance interest; restitution interest.

Daniel: *International Brotherhood of Teamsters v. Daniel,* 439 U.S. 551 (1979); a significant case on the breadth of the term "security" and the availability of remedies under the securities laws.

DAR: Defense Acquisition Regulation. These regulations regarding the purchase of materials and supplies by the United States Department of Defense are set forth at 32 C.F.R. parts 1–39.

Day order: Order for the purchase or sale of securities that must be executed, if at all, on the same day it is given.

DCAA: Defense Contract Audit Agency.

DCO: Delayed Compliance Order.

Deadlock: State of corporate inaction or indecision brought about by equal votes or voting strength on opposite sides of the issue. An irreconcilable deadlock can result in dissolution of a corporation; see Model Business Corporation Act § 97 (1979); Del. Code Ann. tit. 8 § 226; Cal. Corp. Code §§ 1800–9; *Ringling Bros. v. Ringling,* 29 Del. Ch. 610, 53 A. 2d 441 (1947).

Deadweight tonnage: Measure of the capacity of a tank vessel; the weight of cargo, fuel, stores, and ballast that a vessel can carry when submerged to the load line. See also **gross tonnage**.

Dealer: For the purpose of the Securities Act of 1933, the term "dealer" means "any person who engages either for all or part of his time, directly or indirectly, as agent, broker, or principal, in the business of offering, buying, sell-ing, or otherwise dealing or trading in securities issued by another person." Section 2(12); 15 U.S.C. § 77b(12). For the purpose of the Securities Exchange Act of 1934, a distinction is drawn between dealer and broker, a dealer being one who buys and sells for his own account: "The term 'dealer' means any person engaged in the business of buying and selling securities for his own account, through a broker or otherwise, but does not include a bank, or any person insofar as he buys or sells securities for his own account, either individually or in some fiduciary capacity, but not as part of a regular business." Section 3(a)(5); 15 U.S.C. § 78c(a)(5). As to the difference in definition between the two acts, see II L. Loss, *Securities Regulation* 1295 (2d ed. 1961), V L. Loss, *Securities Regulation* 3355 (supp. 1969). See also **broker**.

Debenture: Long-term debt instrument that is not secured by an interest in specific property, but is a general obligation of the issuer. See **bond**.

Debt: "The classic debt is an unqualified obligation to pay a sum certain at a reasonably close fixed maturity date along with a fixed percentage in interest payable regardless of the debtor's income or lack thereof." *Gilbert v. Commissioner of Internal Revenue,* 248 F. 2d 399, 402 (2d Cir. 1957). As to the difference between debt and equity for federal income tax purposes, *see* I.R.C. § 385; 47 Fed. Reg. 164 (1982). *See* Plumb, Jr., *The Federal Income Tax Significance of Corporate Debt: A Critical Analysis and a Proposal,* 26 Tax L. Rev. 369 (1971). Under the Bankruptcy Code, a debt is a "liability on a claim." 11 U.S.C. § 101(11); *See* H.R. Rep.

No. 95-595, 95th Cong., 1st Sess. 310 (1977).

Debt limit: Maximum amount of debt that a government entity can enter into.

Debtor: Person who owes payment. For the purpose of Article 9 of the Uniform Commercial Code–Secured Transactions, the term "debtor" can mean either the person who owes an obligation or the owner of collateral:

"Debtor" means the person who owes payment or other performance of the obligation secured, whether or not he owns or has rights in the collateral, and includes the seller of accounts or chattel paper. Where the debtor and the owner of the collateral are not the same person, the term "debtor" means the owner of the collateral in any provision of the Article dealing with the collateral, the obligor in any provision dealing with the obligation, and may include both where the context so requires; ....

UCC Section 9-105(1)(d). Under the Bankruptcy Code, the term "debtor" means a person or municipality concerning which a case under that Code has been commenced. 11 U.S.C. § 101(12); see H.R. Rep. No. 95-595, 95th Cong., 1st Sess. 310 (1977).

Debtor in possession: In a reorganization proceeding under Chapter 11 of the Bankruptcy Code, the "debtor in possession" is the "debtor," except when a trustee is serving in the case. 11 U.S.C. § 1101(1); see H.R. Rep. No. 95-595, 95th Cong., 1st Sess. 401 (1977).

Debt ratio: Ratio of total debt to net worth of a business entity.

Declaration date: Date on which the payment of a dividend is declared by the board of directors of a corporation.

Declaratory judgment: Declaration by a court of the "rights and other legal relations of any interested party seeking such declaration, whether not further relief is or could be sought." 28 U.S.C. § 2201; Fed. R. Civ. Proc. 57.

Declining balance: Method of depreciation whereby a percentage, calculated by applying a certain multiplier to 100% divided by the useful life of the property, is applied in each year to the depreciated cost of the property at the beginning of the year (the balance in the asset account as it has declined each year). For double-declining balance depreciation, the multiplier is two; for 150% declining balance, the multiplier would be one and one-half. Double-declining balance depreciation of property with a life of five years would be two times 20%, or 40%, applied to 100% of the cost in the first year, applied to 60% of the cost in the second year, then to 36%, then to 21.6%, and finally to 12.96% in the final year. Since property depreciated by the declining-balance method will never reach a balance of zero, salvage value can be ignored in this method. In order to depreciate to zero salvage value, the remaining balance should be depreciated in the last year, in effect switching to the straight-line method. Treas. Reg. § 1-167(b)-2. Deductions under the accelerated cost recovery system, as set forth in the statute, are calculated by the 150% declining-balance method, with a switch to the straight-line method in the final year to reach a balance of zero. (The statutory method assumes that the property was placed in service at the midpoint of the taxable year, so the first year's deduction is only half of the figure expected for the 150% declining-balance method.) I.R.C. § 168(b). *See* American Institute of Certified Public Accountants, Accounting Research Bulletin No. 44, *Declining-Balance Depreciation* (1958). Compare **sum-of-the-years' digits.**

Deed of trust: Instrument, similar to a mortgage, for securing a loan by an interest in real property. The property is conveyed by the borrower to a trustee, for the benefit of the lender, to be held in trust and reconveyed upon satisfaction of the debt obligation.

Deep-discount bonds: Bonds that are offered with a coupon interest rate lower than the current market rate, and thus are sold at a substantial discount to provide yield to maturity equal to the current market for bonds of equivalent grade. If the bonds are sold at a discount at the original offering, the appreciation in value as the bonds approach maturity would be treated as ordinary income, not capital gains. Deep-discount bonds provide call protection, because they can be redeemed only at par. Sometimes bonds sold in the secondary market at a much lower price than par, because of low coupon rate or poor quality, are called deep-discount bonds.

Deep Rock doctrine: Doctrine that debt claims of a common stockholder parent corporation should be subordinated to the equity claims of preferred stockholders in the case of bankruptcy of a corporation that is insufficiently capitalized. *Taylor v. Standard Gas &*

Electric Co., 306 U.S. 307 (1939); the name comes from Deep Rock Oil Corporation, the subsidiary of Standard Gas & Electric Company. See **thin capitalization.**

De facto corporation: Association that has corporate attributes, but is defective in meeting the requirements of law for the creation of a corporation. If certain tests are met, including good faith, colorable compliance with corporate laws, and use of corporate powers, such an association may be regarded as a corporation in fact, if not in law. *See, e.g., Inter-Ocean Newspaper Co. v. Robertson,* 296 Ill. 92, 129 N.E. 523 (1921); Berle, Jr., *The Theory of Enterprise Entity,* 47 Colum. L. Rev. 343 (1947).

De facto merger: Corporate reorganization by sale or acquisition of assets or exchange of stock, treated as a statutory merger for the purpose of employing safeguards such as requirements for stockholder approval and dissenters' appraisal rights. *See Perl v. IU International Corp.,* 61 Haw. 622, 607 P. 2d 1036, 1043 (1980); *Applestein v. United Bd. & Carton Corp.,* 60 N.J. Super. 333, 159 A. 2d 146, *aff'd,* 33 N.J. 72, 161 A. 2d. 474 (1960); *Orzeck v. Engelhart,* 41 Del. Ch. 361, 195A. 2d 375 (1963).

Default: 1. Failure to perform an obligation. The term is not defined in the Uniform Commercial Code, but debt instruments and finance leases are usually very specific in identifying certain breaches of obligation as "events of default." *See* UCC Sections 9-503–7. 2. Failure to plead or otherwise defend an action, resulting in a judgment by default. Fed. R. Civ. Proc. 55.

Defendant: Party against whom an action is brought. Under the Uniform Commercial Code, the term "defendant" includes "a person in the position of defendant in a cross-action or counterclaim." UCC Section 1-201(13).

Defense Contract Audit Agency: Unit of the Department of Defense, reporting to the Assistant Secretary of Defense (Comptroller), formed to audit contracts and subcontracts for the Department of Defense. The DCAA from time to time performs audits for other government agencies.

Deferral method: Method of accounting for the investment tax credit in which credits are deferred and amortized over the life of the acquired property. Compare flow-through method.

Deferred taxes: Tax effects that are deferred for allocation to income tax expense of future periods. American Institute of Certified Public Accountants, Accounting Principles Board Opinion No. 11, *Accounting for Income Taxes,* paragraph 12h (1967).

Deficiency dividends: If a deficiency in federal income tax of a personal holding company is determined, the company may reduce or eliminate the deficiency by distributing "deficiency dividends" within 90 days of the determination and taking a deduction therefor. I.R.C. § 547.

Deficiency letter: Letter of comment supplied by the staff of the Securities and Exchange Commission with respect to a registration statement filed with the Commission. *See* SEC Release No. 33-5231 (1972).

Defined-benefit pension plan: Pension plan with specified benefits, or a specified formula for benefits, not related to contributions. The employer's contributions are determined actuarially on the basis of the benefits expected to become payable. American Institute of Certified Public Accountants, Accounting Principles Board Opinion No. 8, *Accounting for the Cost of Pension Plans,* Appendix B, paragraph 18 (1966); *see* Financial Accounting Standards Board, Statement of Financial Accounting Standards No. 35, *Accounting and Reporting by Defined Benefit Pension Plans* (1980).

Defined-contribution pension plan: Pension plan in which the amount of contribution by the employer is specified or determined in accordance with a formula. The benefits are also specified, but if the amounts contributed are inadequate or excessive to fund the stated benefits, either the benefits or the contributions are adjusted. American Institute of Certified Public Accountants, Accounting Principles Board Opinion No. 8, *Accounting for the Cost of Pension Plans,* Appendix B, paragraph 19 (1966). See also money-purchase pension plan.

Definite time: Under Article 3—Commercial Paper of the Uniform Commercial Code, an instrument, to be treated as a negotiable instrument, must be payable on demand or at a "definite time." UCC Section 3-104(1)(c). An instrument is payable at a "definite time" if by its terms it is payable

(a) on or before a stated date or at a fixed period after a stated date; or

(b) at a fixed period after sight; or

(c) at a definite time subject to any acceleration; or

(d) at a definite time subject to extension at the option of the holder, or to extension to a further definite time at the option of the maker or acceptor or automatically upon or after a specified act or event.

UCC Section 3-109.

Delegation of duty: Authorization to another to perform duty under a contract. Unless a contract specifies otherwise, a party may delegate its duty of performance to another, but such delegation does not relieve the party delegating the duty of liability for breach. UCC Section 2-210; *Restatement, Contracts, Second,* § 318. See assignment.

Delivered pricing: Method of pricing in which the price to the purchaser is effective at the point of delivery and is determined by a formula reflecting transportation costs, but is independent of all or part of actual transportation costs. Delivered prices may be based on the most favorably located supply point or may be the same for a given geographic zone. Delivered pricing has been attacked as anticompetitive; *e.g. F.T.C. v. Cement Institute,* 333 U.S. 683 (1948); *see* American Bar Association, Section of Antitrust Law, *Antitrust Law Developments* 130 (1975).

Delivered weight: Term in a contract for the sale of goods C.I.F. or C. & F., which means that the seller will reasonably estimate the weight and the payment due on tender of the documents called for by the contract will be based on such estimate, but the buyer and seller will adjust the final price based on the actual weight. UCC Section 2-321.

Delivery: Under the Uniform Commercial Code, delivery "with respect to instruments, documents of title, chattel paper or securities means voluntary transfer of possession." UCC Section 1-201(14). As to when delivery of investment securities occurs, see UCC Section 8-313.

Delivery on condition: Tender of delivery of goods by a seller conditioned upon payment therefor. *See* UCC Section 2-507(2).

Delivery order: Under Article 7 of the Uniform Commercial Code—Documents of Title, a delivery order is "a written order to deliver goods directed to a warehouseman, carrier or other person who in the ordinary course of business issues warehouse receipts or bills of lading." UCC Section 7-102(1)(d).

Delivery vs. payment: Delivery of a security against payment therefor.

Delivery vs. receipt: Delivery of a security for a receipt, rather than payment.

Demand deposit: Bank deposit that can be withdrawn on demand, without prior notice, such as a checking account.

Demand note: Promissory note payable, not on a set date, but on demand. See on demand.

Demise charter: Nautical equivalent of a finance lease. See bare-boat charter.

Demurrage: Compensation to the owner of a vessel, rail car, or container for use or detention beyond a fixed period for use or unloading.

De novo review: Review or new examination by an appellate tribunal of the findings of fact of an administrative agency or lower court. *See Citizens to Preserve Overton Park, Inc., v. Volpe,* 401 U.S. 402 (1971). Compare **substantial evidence test.**

Depletion: Accounting entry to reflect the use or consumption of a natural resource, such as coal or petroleum. *See* I.R.C. §§ 611–14. See also **cost depletion; percentage depletion.**

Deponent: Person who gives testimony in a deposition.

Deposit account: For the purpose of Article 9 of the Uniform Commercial Code–Secured Transactions, the term "deposit account" means "a demand, time, savings, passbook or like account maintained with a bank, savings and loan association, credit union or like organization, other than an account evidenced by a certificate of deposit." UCC Section 9-105(1)(e).

Depositary bank: For the purpose of Article 3–Commercial Paper, and Article 4–Bank Deposits and Collections, of the Uniform Commercial Code, "depositary bank" means "the first bank to which an item is transferred for collection even though it is also the payor bank; ... ." UCC Section 4-105.

Depositary Institutions Deregulation and Monetary Control Act of 1980: Federal statute revising certain banking laws. Pub. L. No. 96-221, 94 Stat. 132 (1980). Title V provides for federal preemption of state usury laws for certain credit transactions.

Deposit ceiling rate of interest: Maximum interest rate that can be paid on savings and time deposits at federally insured commercial banks, mutual savings banks, savings and loan associations, and credit unions. Such ceilings are established by the Federal Reserve Board, the Federal Deposit Insurance Corporation, the Federal Home Loan Bank Board, and the National Credit Union Administration. *See* Regulation Q of the Federal Reserve System, 12 C.F.R. § 217.

Deposition: The taking of testimony, under oath, of witnesses to an action as a means of preserving testimony that would be presented at trial. Fed. R. Civ. Proc. 27–32.

Deposit rate ceiling: See **deposit ceiling rate of interest.**

Depreciable assets: Assets that are expected to be used during more than one accounting period, have a limited useful life, and are held by an enterprise for use in the production or supply of goods and services, for rental to others, or for administrative purposes. International Accounting Standards Committee, Statement of International Accounting Standards 4, *Depreciation Accounting,* paragraph 2 (1976).

Depreciated cost: Cost less accumulated depreciation; book value.

Depreciation: Accounting entry that adjusts the book value of an asset downward to reflect reduction in value due to wear and tear and obsolescence, and which reduces income by an equivalent amount. For depreciation deductions available under the Internal Revenue Code, see I.R.C. § 167; see also **accelerated cost recovery system** ; I.R.C. § 168; International Accounting Standards Committee, Statement of International Accounting Standards 4, *Depreciation Accounting* (1976).

Deputization: Designation by a lender or investor of an employee or other person as director to represent its interests on the board of corporation, resulting in treatment of that lender or investor as an "insider" for the purpose of the short-swing profits provision of section 16(b) of the Securities and Exchange Act of 1934. *Rottner v. Lehman*, 193 F. 2d 564, 566 (2d Cir. 1952). *See* Knepper, *Liability of Officer-Directors*, 40 Ohio St. L. J. 341, 355 (1979).

Derivative action: Action by a shareholder or member to enforce a right of a corporation or unincorporated association. The action is one that should be brought by the corporation or association itself, but if it fails to do so, shareholders have the right to assert the action, such right being derived from the corporation or association. Fed. R. Civ. Proc. 23.1. *See Zapata Corp. v. Maldonado,* 430 A. 2d 779 (Del. Supr. 1981); *Maldonado v. Flynn,* 485 F. Supp. 274 (S.D. N.Y. 1980); Block & Prussin, *The Business Judgment Rule and Shareholder Derivative Actions: Viva Zapata?* 37 Bus. Law. 27 (1981); Coffee, Jr., & Schwartz, *The Survival of the Derivative Suit: An Evaluation and a Proposal for Legislative Reform,* 81 Colum. L. Rev. 261(1981). See **class action.**

Design patent: Patent for a "new, original and ornamental design for an article of manufacture... ." 35 U.S.C. § 171.

Desk, The: Trading desk at the New York Federal Reserve Bank, through which open market purchases and sales of government securities are made.

Destination bill of lading: Bill of lading issued at the destination, rather than at the place of shipment. A destination bill may be issued by the carrier at the request of the consignor, or issued in substitution for an outstanding bill of lading or receipt for the goods. *See* UCC Section 7-305.

Destination contract: Contract for the sale of goods under which the seller bears the risk of loss and the expense of delivery to a given destination. See **F.O.B.; ex-ship;** compare **shipment contract.**

Determination: For certain purposes of the Internal Revenue Code, a determination is a decision of the Tax Court or other court of competent jurisdiction, a closing agreement or other agreement of the Secretary of the Treasury in respect of tax liability. I.R.C. §§ 547(c), 1313(a).

Development: As defined by the Financial Accounting Standards Board:

Development is the translation of research findings or other knowledge into a plan or design for a new product or process or for a significant improvement to an existing product or process whether intended for sale or use. It includes the conceptual formulation, design, and testing of product alternatives, construction of prototypes, and operation of pilot plants. It does not include routine or periodic·alterations to existing products, production lines, manufacturing processes, and other on-going operations even though those alterations may represent improvements and it does not include market research or market testing activities. (The term "product" includes service and the term "process" includes technique.)

Financial Accounting Standards Board, Statement of Financial Accounting Standards No. 2, *Accounting for Research and Development Costs,* paragraphs 8, 24–30 (1974); see Financial Accounting Standards Board, Interpretation No. 6, *Applicability of FASB Statement No. 2 to Computer Software: An Interpretation of FASB Statement No. 2* (1975); International Accounting Standards Committee, Statement of International Accounting Standards 9, *Accounting for Research and Development Activities* (1978). Compare **research.**

Development stage enterprise: Enterprise that is devoting substantially all of its efforts to establishing a new business and planned principal operations have not commenced or have not generated significant revenue. *See* Financial Accounting Standards Board, Statement of Financial Accounting Standards No. 7, *Accounting and Reporting by Development Stage Enterprises* (1975).

Development well: Well drilled within the proved area of an oil or gas reservoir to the depth of a stratigraphic horizon known to be productive. Financial Accounting Standards Board, Statement of Financial Accounting Standards No. 19, *Financial Accounting and Reporting by Oil and Gas Producing Companies,* Appendix C (1977).

DIDC: Depository Institutions Deregulation Committee.

Dilution: 1. With respect to common stock, the effect on the rights thereof and earnings thereon from the issuance of additional shares or rights thereto; in accounting for earnings per share, dilution is "A reduction in earnings per share resulting from the assumption that convertible securities have been converted or that options and warrants have been exercised or other shares have been issued upon the fulfillment of certain conditions." American Institute of Certified Public Accountants, Accounting Principles Board Opinion No. 15, *Earnings per Share,* Appendix D, paragraph 10 (1968). See also **dilutive security.** 2. In connection with an issue of common stock, the effect on the interests of purchasers thereof from the issuance of shares to officers, directors, and promoters for cash consideration that is substantially less than the offering price.

Dilutive security: Security that results in a decrease in the amount reported as earnings per share. *See* American Institute of Certified Public Accountants, *Computing Earnings per Share: Accounting Interpretations of APB Opinion No. 15, Earnings per Share,* paragraphs 56, 57 (1970). See also **dilution.**

Director: Member of the governing board of a corporation. N.Y. Bus.

Corp. Law § 102(a)(5). *See* Securities Exchange Act of 1934, section 3(a)(7); 15 U.S.C. § 78c(a)(7); Cal. Corp. Code § 164.

Direct placement: Placement of an issue of securities by an issuer directly with an investor or group of investors, without the involvement of a broker or underwriter.

Disappearing corporation: Corporation that is merged into another corporation, where the other corporation is the survivor. Cal. Corp. Code §§ 161, 165.

DISC: Type of domestic corporation that derives 95% of its income from export sales, and that may defer paying tax on a portion of that income. The deferred income is taxed to the shareholders when distributed, when the shareholder sells his shares, or when the corporation ceases to qualify as a DISC. *See* I.R.C. §§ 291(a)(4), 991—995. The acronym means "Domestic International Sales Corporation," but the term "DISC" is used in the Internal Revenue Code. *See* Bardack & Wright, *Corporate and Tax Aspects of European Sales Subsidiaries: A Primer,* 33 Bus. Law. 49, 66 (1977).

Discharge: Release from obligation. As to discharge of parties under instruments covered by Article 3 of the Uniform Commercial Code, see UCC Section 3-601.

Disclaimer: Denial or repudiation of a right or interest. Sometimes used to deny responsibility, as "disclaimer of warranty." As to warranties, *see* UCC Section 2-316.

Disclosure: Reporting of material information to a government agency in documents available to the public. The underlying principle of the federal securities laws is the "full and fair disclosure of the character of securities … ." Securities Act of 1933. "Sunlight is said to be the best of disinfectants, electric light the most efficient policeman." L. Brandeis, *Other People's Money and How the Bankers Use It* (1914). *See generally* I. L. Loss, *Securities Regulation* 121 (2d. ed. 1961). *See SEC v. Texas Gulf Sulphur Co.,* 401 F. 2d 833 (2d Cir. 1968) *(en banc), cert. denied sub nom. Coates v. SEC,* 394 U.S. 976 (1969); Bauman, *Rule 10b-5 and the Corporation's Affirmative Duty to Disclose,* 67 Georgetown L.J. 935 (1979); B. Creed, *ERISA Compliance: Reporting and Disclosure* (1981); Hewitt, *Developing Concepts of Materiality and Disclosure,* 32 Bus. Law. 887 (1977). See also **material.**

Discount: 1. Deduction from a gross, or nominal amount; difference between the published price and the actual sale price. 2. Difference, expressed as a percentage, between the par value and the sales, or offering price, of a bond or other fixed-income security, if such price is lower than the par value. See premium. 3. Difference between a value at a future time and the present value, giving effect to the time value of money, by reducing the future value by an interest, or "discount" rate.

Discounted cash flow: Present value of a future cash flow, obtained by discounting the future item to the present at a given rate, compounded.

Discount window: Facility of the Federal Reserve System for extending credit directly to member banks. *See* Regulation A of the Federal Reserve System, 12 C.F.R. 201; Parthemos, *The Discount Window,* in T. Cook, ed., *Instruments of the Money Market* 28 (4th ed., 1977).

Discovery: Process of discovering and developing information in the possession of the adverse party to a court proceeding that is "relevant to the subject matter involved in the pending action." Fed. R. Civ. Proc. 26. Discovery may be by oral examinations by depositions, written interrogatories, production of documents, inspection of land, property, and things, and physical and mental examination. *See* Underwood, *A Guide to Federal Discovery Rules* (1979); *see generally* L. Jaworski, *The Right and the Power* (1975).

Discretionary funds: Funds held by a financial institution for investment in the name and for the account of the owner of the funds; such investment, however, being made at the discretion of the financial institution. Compare advisory funds.

Dishonor: Refusal to accept, or honor, an instrument. Under Article 3–Commercial Paper of the Uniform Commercial Code, an instrument is "dishonored" when:

(a) a necessary or optional presentment is duly made and due acceptance or payment is refused or cannot be obtained within the prescribed time or in case of bank collections the instrument is seasonably returned by the midnight deadline (Section 4-301); or

(b) presentment is excused and the instrument is not duly accepted or paid.

UCC Section 3-507. *See* UCC Section 3-508.

Disinterested person: For the purpose of the Bankruptcy Code, a person who is not a creditor, an equity security holder, an "insider," an investment banker for securities outstanding or issued in the three years preceding the filing of the petition, an attorney for such an investment banker, a director, officer, or employee of such an investment banker in the preceding two years, or a person who has "an interest materially adverse to the interest of the estate or of any class of creditors or equity security holders, by reason of any direct or indirect relationship to, connection with, or interest in, the debtor ... " or such an investment banker. 11 U.S.C. § 101(13); *see* H.R. Rep. No. 95-595, 95th Cong., 1st Sess. 310 (1977).

Disintermediation: Movement of funds by small investors out of depositary institutions directly into financial assets, such as money market instruments.

Dissenter; dissenting shareholder; dissident shareholder: Shareholder of a corporation who objects to a statutory merger (and in some states, certain other corporate actions) and who has asserted rights to be paid the fair value of his shares. *See* Model Business Corporation Act §§ 80, 81 (1979); New York Bus. Corp. Law § 623; Del. Code Ann. tit. 8 § 262; Cal. Corp. Code §§ 1300–12.

Dissolution: Termination of a corporation's existence. *See* Model Business Corporation Act §§ 82–96 (1979); N. Y. Bus. Corp. Law §§ 1001–9, 1101–18;

Del. Code Ann. tit. 8 §§ 271–84; Cal. Corp. Code §§ 1800–2011. See also judicial dissolution.

Distribution to owners: Capital distribution; decrease in the net assets of an enterprise resulting from transferring assets, rendering services, or incurring liabilities by the enterprise to the owners. Distributions to owners decrease equity. Financial Accounting Standards Board, Statement of Financial Accounting Concepts No. 3, *Elements of Financial Statements of Business Enterprises,* paragraph 53 (1980).

Divestiture: Remedy in the case of mergers held to be in violation of section 7 of the Clayton Act, requiring disposition of the acquired company or its stock over a given period. *E.g. United States v. E. I. duPont de Nemours & Co.,* 366 U.S. 316 (1961); *International Telephone & Telegraph Corp. v. General Telephone & Electronics Corp.,* 351 F. Supp. 1153 (D. Hawaii 1972), *aff'd in part and rev'd in part,* 518 F. 2d 913 (9th Cir. 1975); *see* American Bar Association, Section of Antitrust Law, *Antitrust Law Developments* 98, 295 (1975).

Dividend: Amount to be divided among several persons in accordance with a fixed scheme, for example, dividends of corporate profits to the shareholders. *Pennington v. Commonwealth Hotel Const. Corp.,* 17 Del. Ch. 394, 155 A. 514 (1931). *See* Del. Code Ann. tit. 8. § 170; N.Y. Bus. Corp. Law § 510; Model Business Corporation Act § 45 (1979); Cal. Corp. Code §§ 500–7. Under the Internal Revenue Code, a dividend is any distribution of property

made by a corporation to its shareholders out of its earnings and profits. I.R.C. § 316(a); *see also* I.R.C. §§ 312, 317, 6042 (b). As to the distinction between dividends and interest, see I.R.C. § 385 and regulations thereunder, 47 Fed. Reg. 164 (1982). *See also* Kingson, *The Deep Structure of Taxation: Dividend Distributions,* 85 Yale L. J. 861 (1976).

Dividends-paid deduction: Deduction against "accumulated taxable income," for the purpose of the accumulated earnings tax, available for dividends paid under sections 561–5 of the Internal Revenue Code. Payment of dividends is not ordinarily deductible from corporate taxable income.

Dividends-received deduction: Deduction against taxable income for federal income tax available to corporations for dividends received from other corporations. The dividends received deduction applies to 100% of dividends received from certain affiliates and 85% of other dividends. Small business investment companies operating under the Small Business Investment Act of 1958 may deduct 100% of dividends received. I.R.C. §§ 241–6.

Dividend yield: Ratio, expressed as a percentage, of the current dividend of a security to the current market price.

Dock warrant: Form of receipt issued by a shipping company upon delivery of goods to its dock. A dock warrant is not usually negotiable, but it entitles the holder to have issued to him a bill of lading, which may be negotiable. UCC Section 1-201, Official Comment, Point 15.

Document: For the purpose of Article 7 of the Uniform Commercial Code–Documents of Title, "document" means document of title. UCC Section 7-102(1)(e). For the purpose of Article 9 of the Uniform Commercial Code–Secured Transactions, the term "document" also includes receipts for goods stored under bond. UCC Section 9-105(1)(f). For the purpose of Article 5 of the Uniform Commercial Code–Letters of Credit, "document" is a broader term, and means "any paper including document of title, security, invoice, certificate, notice of default and the like." UCC Section 5-103(1)(b).

Documentary credit; documentary letter of credit: Letter of credit that can be drawn upon by presentation of specified documents. Compare clean credit; clean letter of credit.

Documentary draft: Draft the honor of which is conditioned upon presentation of other documents, such as documents of title or invoices. UCC Sections 4-104(1)(f), 5-103(1)(b). *See* UCC Sections 4-501–4. Compare clean draft.

Document of title: Instrument evidencing ownership. Under the Uniform Commercial Code, the term includes:

bill of lading, dock warrant, dock receipt, warehouse receipt or order for the delivery of goods, and also any other document which in the regular course of business or financing is treated as adequately evidencing that the person in possession of it is entitled to receive, hold and dispose of the document and the goods it covers. To be a document of title a document must purport to be issued by or addressed to a bailee and purport to cover goods in the bailee's possession which are either identified or are fungible portions of an identified mass.

UCC Section 1-201(15). The Official Comments add that the definition is written in terms of function so that new forms of document of title can be added as they are invented. *See generally* R. Riegert & R. Braucher, *Documents of Title* (3d ed. 1978).

Documents against acceptance draft: Documentary draft in which the documents are surrendered to the drawee when the drawee accepts the draft. The acceptance obliges the drawee to honor the draft at a later date.

Documents against payment draft: Documentary draft in which the documents are surrendered to the drawee upon payment.

Doing business: Conduct of business activities by a corporation in a foreign state (i.e., a state other than that in which it has been incorporated) to such an extent that the corporation is subject to the foreign state's taxing jurisdiction, is subject to the process of that state's courts, and is subject to that state's regulatory and qualification statutes. The extent of business activities that constitute "doing business," and thus subjects a corporation to the jurisdiction of the courts of a particular state, varies from state to state, depending on local statutes and court interpretations. Model Business Corporation Act § 106 (1979); Del. Code Ann. tit. 8 § 373; N.Y. Bus. Corp. Law § 1301; Cal. Corp. Code § 191. *See Liq-*

uid Carriers Corp. v. American Marine Corp., 375 F. 2d 951 (2d Cir. 1967); *Northwestern States Portland Cement Co. v. Minnesota,* 358 U.S. 450 (1959); *Eli Lilly & Co. v. Sav-on-Drugs, Inc.*, 366 U.S. 276 (1961); Note, *Sanctions for Failure to Comply with Corporate Qualification Statutes: An Evaluation,* 63 Colum. L. Rev. 117 (1963); *see generally,* CT Corporation System, *What Constitutes Doing Business* (1976). The concept of "doing business" is also relevant to the availability of the exemption from registration for intrastate transactions under section 3(a)(11) of the Securities Act of 1933, which is limited to securities issued to "persons resident within a single State or Territory, where the issuer is a person resident and doing business within ... such State or Territory." 15 U.S.C. § 77c(a)(11). *See* SEC Rule 147, 17 C.F.R. § 230.147.

DOL: United States Department of Labor.

Domestic: For the purpose of state business corporation laws, a "domestic" corporation is one organized under the laws of that state. Model Business Corporation Act § 2(a) (1979); Cal. Corp. Code § 167. For the purpose of the Internal Revenue Code, "domestic" when applied to a corporation or partnership means "created or organized in the United States or under the laws of the United States or of any State." I.R.C. § 7701(a)(4).

Domestic International Sales Corporation: See DISC.

DOT: Department of Transportation. Usually this means the United States Department of Transportation, but it may mean the department of transportation of a state.

Double call: Right of an issuer of debt obligations with sinking fund or principal amortization provisions to redeem or prepay the principal in amounts double the regular sinking fund or principal amortization payment on any given date for such payment.

Double-declining balance: See declining balance.

Double-dip lease: Lease financing transaction enabling both the lessor and the lessee to obtain the tax benefits of equipment ownership because of different interpretations of the structure of the transaction by tax authorities in the United States and in the United Kingdom. A double-dip lease is a net, or finance lease, with the lessee in the United States and the lessor in the United Kingdom. The lease will have a fixed-price purchase option at a nominal price or a price lower than the estimated value of the asset being leased at the time of exercise of the option (called a "peppercorn" option). United States tax authorities look upon such a transaction as in substance a conditional sale, the lessee being regarded as the owner and thus entitled to such investment credit and accelerated depreciation deductions as are available for the asset under lease. British tax authorities give effect to the form and regard the British lessor as the owner, entitled to such tax benefits of ownership as are available under British law. Thus the tax benefits of equipment ownership are available to both the lessee and the lessor. *See generally* Park, *Tax Characteris-*

tics of International Leases, The Contour of Ownership, 67 Cornell L. Rev. 103 (1981).

Double-entry system: System of accounting in which each recorded event affects at least two items in the financial accounting records. Generally accepted accounting principles are based on the double-entry system. American Institute of Certified Public Accountants, Accounting Principles Board Statement No. 4, Ch. 7, *Generally Accepted Accounting Principles–Broad Operating Principles,* paragraph 13 (1970); *see generally,* Financial Accounting Standards Board, Statement of Financial Accounting Concepts No. 3, *Elements of Financial Statements of Business Enterprises* (1980).

Double tax-exempt: In referring to municipal bonds, this term means that the interest is exempt from both federal and state income taxes. Some bonds are triple-exempt, being also exempt from city taxes.

Downstream merger: Merger between a parent corporation and a subsidiary in which the surviving corporation is the subsidiary. *See* Del. Code Ann. tit. 8 § 253. Compare **upstream merger.**

D/P draft: Documents against payment draft.

Draft: Order or direction by one party (the drawer) to another party (the drawee) to pay a specified sum to a third party (the payee). *See* UCC Section 3-104.

Drawee: Party on whom a draft is drawn, and who has the obligation to make payment in accordance with the terms of the draft.

Drawer: Party who makes or draws a draft.

Dribble: Sale of unregistered securities under Rule 144 of the Securities and Exchange Commission.

Drug: For the purpose of the Federal Trade Commission Act, the term "drug" means:

(1) articles recognized in the official United States Pharmacopoeia, official Homoeopathic Pharmacopoeia of the United States, or official National Formulary, or any supplement to any of them; and (2) articles intended for use in the diagnosis, cure, mitigation, treatment, or prevention of disease in man or other animals; and (3) articles (other than food) intended to affect the structure or any function of the body of man or other animals; and (4) articles intended for use as a component of any article specified in clauses (1), (2), or (3); but does not include devices or their components, parts, or accessories.

Section 15(c), 15 U.S.C. § 55(c). "Device" is defined in section 15(d), 15 U.S.C. § 55(d).

Dual presentation: Presentation with equal prominence on the face of the income statement of primary earnings per share and fully diluted earnings per share. American Institute of Certified Public Accountants, Accounting Principles Board Opinion No. 15, *Earnings per Share,* Appendix D, paragraph 11 (1968).

Dual-rate contract: Agreement of an ocean shipper to use carriers that are members of a conference agreement exclusively in return for rates substantially lower than those charged shippers who do not enter into such contracts. The shipper would be penalized for using nonconference carriers.

Due diligence: Investigation conducted to discharge one's obligation under section 11(b) of the Securities Act of 1933, which excuses liability for false or misleading statements in registration statements if a person had, "after reasonable investigation, reasonable ground to believe ... that the statements therein were true and that there was no omission to state a material fact required to be stated therein or necessary to make the statements therein not misleading ... ." 15 U.S.C. § 77k(b). *See* 17 C.F.R. § 230.176, SEC Release No. 33-6383, 47 Fed. Reg. 11380, 11433 (1982); *Escott v. BarChris Construction Corp.*, 283 F. Supp. 643 (S.D. N.Y. 1968); *Feit v. Leasco Data Processing Equip. Corp.*, 332 F. Supp. 544 (E.D.N.Y. 1971).

Due negotiation: Under Article 7 of the Uniform Commercial Code–Documents of Title:

A negotiable document of title is "duly negotiated" when it is negotiated in the manner stated in this section to a holder who purchases it in good faith without notice of any defense against or claim to it on the part of any person and for value, unless it is established that the negotiation is not in the regular course of business of financing or involves receiving the document in settlement or payment of a money obligation.

UCC Section 7-501. The holder of a document of title that has been duly negotiated acquires title to the document, title to the goods, and rights to the obligation of the issuer to hold or deliver the goods. *See* UCC Section 7-502.

Due-on-sale clause: Clause in a mortgage of real property providing that the principal amount of the mortgage is immediately due and payable if the property is sold by the mortgagor. *See* Squires, *A Comprehensible Due-on-Sale Clause (with Form),* The Practical Lawyer, April 15, 1981, at 67.

Duly authorized: When applied to stock in an opinion of counsel, the term "duly authorized" means that under applicable law and the certificate of incorporation and by-laws of a corporation, that corporation had the power to issue the stock and and took all corporate action necessary to authorize such issuance. *See Legal Opinions to Third Parties: An Easier Path,* 34 Bus. Law. 1891, 1909 (1979).

Dummy corporation: Inactive corporation organized to hold record title to property or otherwise to conceal the actual owners or operators of property or business.

Dumping: Selling a product in an export market at a price lower than that charged in the domestic market. See antidumping law.

Dutch auction: Method of offering securities by auction, in which the amount of securities offered is expected to be greater than that for which bids would be received from any single purchaser or syndicate. Bids received are ranked from the highest to the lowest price; then these bids are accepted, starting with the highest price, until the aggregate amount of the offered securities is reached. The lowest price accepted in order to sell the entire offering is used as the sale price for all securities offered at the auction.

E

Earned surplus: Corporate profits, not distributed to shareholders or transferred to capital or capital surplus. As defined in section 2 of the Model Business Corporation Act:

"Earned surplus" means the portion of the surplus of a corporation equal to the balance of its net profits, income, gains and losses from the date of incorporation, or from the latest date when a deficit was eliminated by an application of its capital surplus or stated capital or otherwise, after deducting subsequent distributions to shareholders and transfers to stated capital and capital surplus to the extent such distributions and transfers are made out of earned surplus. Earned surplus shall include also any portion of surplus allocated to earned surplus in mergers, consolidations or acquisitions of all or substantially all of the outstanding shares or of the property and assets of another corporation, domestic or foreign.

New York law has a less complex definition:

"Earned surplus" means the portion of the surplus that represents the net earnings, gains or profits, after deduction of all losses, that have not been distributed to the shareholders as dividends, or transferred to stated capital or capital surplus, or applied to other purposes permitted by law. Unrealized appreciation of assets is not included in earned surplus.

N. Y. Bus. Corp. Law § 102(a)(6). See surplus.

Earned surplus rule: "Earned surplus of a subsidiary company created prior to acquisition does not form a part of the consolidated earned surplus of the parent company and subsidiaries; nor can any dividend declared out of such surplus properly be credited to the income account of the parent company." American Institute of Certified Public Accountants, Accounting Research Bulletin No. 43, Ch. 1A, paragraph 3 (1934); see American Institute of Certified Public Accountants, Accounting Research Bulletin No. 51, *Consolidated Financial Statements* (1959).

Earnings: Net profit. For the purpose of calculating the ratio of earnings to fixed charges used in a prospectus, "earnings" means "pretax income from continuing operations" plus the fixed charges, with certain other adjustments. 17 C.F.R. § 229.503(d)(3); 47 Fed. Reg. 11380, 11424 (1982). The Financial Accounting Standards Board has adopted the term "comprehensive income" in place of the traditional accounting term "earnings." Financial Accounting Standards Board, Statement of Financial Accounting Concepts No. 3, *Elements of Financial Statements of Business Enterprises,* paragraph 1, n. 1 (1980).

Earnings and profits: The Internal Revenue Code defines "dividends" as distributions of property made by a corporation out of "earnings and profits." I.R.C. § 316. Such "earnings and profits" are determined in accordance with special rules, and thus are not always equal to earned surplus or taxable income. I.R.C. § 312.

Earnings per share: The amount of earnings attributable to each share of common stock. *See* American Institute of Certified Public Accountants, Accounting Principles Board Opinion No. 15, *Earnings per Share* (1968). See fully diluted earnings per share.

Earnings report: Statement of income.

Easement: Right to use land, owned by another, for a particular purpose, such as access to another parcel of land.

ECLA: Economic Commission for Latin America.

Economic Analysis, Bureau of: Unit of the United States Department of Commerce that develops information on the economy and prepares analyses and projections. The Bureau publishes monthly the Survey of Current Business and the Business Conditions Digest.

Economic Development Administration: Unit of the United States Department of Commerce established to administer the Public Works and Economic Development Act of 1965, Pub. L. No. 89-136, 79 Stat. 552 (1965), 42 U.S.C §§ 3121–3266. The programs of the EDA include grants, loans, and loan guaranties for projects in areas with severe unemployment and low family income. *See* 13 C.F.R. §§ 301–18.

Economic Recovery Tax Act of 1981: Amendment to the Internal Revenue Code providing for income tax reduction, business investment incentives, and certain reforms. Pub. L. No. 97-34, 95 Stat 172 (1981). *See* S. Rep. No. 97-144, 97-176, H.R. Rep. No. 97-201, 97-215, 97th Cong., 1st Sess. (1981).

Economic Regulatory Administration: Unit of the United States Department of Energy that administers those regulatory programs not assigned to the Federal Energy Regulatory Commission. The ERA programs relate generally to the pricing and distribution of oil. The ERA also intervenes in proceedings before the Federal Energy Regulatory Commission and other federal and state regulatory bodies.

ECSC: European Coal and Steel Community.

ECU: European Currency Unit.

EDA: Economic Development Administration.

Edge Act corporation; Edge corporation: Corporation formed by a United States bank to engage in foreign banking and financing. The name comes from the law permitting such activities, section 25(a) of the Federal Reserve Act, called the Edge Act for its sponsor, Senator Walter Edge of New Jersey. Pub. L. No. 106, ch. 18, 41 Stat. 378 (1919); 12 U.S.C. §§ 611–31. *See* Regulation K of the Federal Reserve System, 12 C.F.R. § 211; J. Houpt, *Performance and Characteristics of Edge Corporations* (Federal Reserve System Staff Study, 1981); J. Baker & G. Bradford, *American Banks Abroad: Edge Act Companies and Multinational Banking* (1974); McPheters, *Formation of Edge Act Corporations by Foreign Banks,* 37 Bus. Law. 593 (1982). See also agreement corporation.

Education, United States Department of: Cabinet-level department of the executive branch of the United States government established to administer federal programs for aid to education. *See* Department of Education Organization Act, Pub. L. No. 96-88, 93 Stat. 668 (1979), 20 U.S.C. §§ 3401–3510.

EEC: European Economic Community.

EEOC: Equal Employment Opportunity Commission.

Effective annual yield: Yield on an investment, taking into effect compounding, but expressed as the equivalent simple interest rate. See effective rate.

Effective date: Date on which a registration statement filed with the Securities and Exchange Commission under the Securities Act of 1933 becomes effective; usually the twentieth day after filing. Securities Act of 1933, section 8, 15 U.S.C. § 77h.

Effective rate: 1. The simple annual interest rate on a debt security that will provide an amount of interest equal to the nominal interest rate, compounded at the intervals at which interest payments are made. The effective rate for an annual interest rate i compounded n times per year is equal to

$$(1 + i/n)^n - 1$$

2. In the case of a finance lease, the interest rate implicit in the lease rental rate, including any period of "interim" rent before the commencement of the term of the lease that involves the full, regular payments, and giving effect to end-of-term provisions at fixed amounts, such as a fixed-price purchase option or a put.

Effects doctrine: As expressed by Judge Learned Hand, "any state may impose liabilities, even upon persons not within its allegiance, for conduct outside its borders that has consequences within its borders which the state reprehends; ... ." *United States v. Aluminum Co. of America,* 148 F. 2d 416, 443 (1945).

EFT: Electronic funds transfer.

EFTA: European Free Trade Association.

EIS: Environmental Impact Statement.

Ejusdem generis: Of the same kind or class; rule of construction used where general words follow an enumeration of specific things, to limit the construction of the general words to things only of the kind or class specifically mentioned. This rule received the disapproval of the Supreme Court in *S.E.C. v. C. M. Joiner Leasing Corp.*, 320 U.S. 344 (1943), but was followed in *Association of Am. Railroads v. United States*, 603 F. 2d 953 (D.C. Cir. 1979).

Electronic funds transfer: Transfer of funds that is initiated through an electronic terminal, telephone, or computer or magnetic tape, other than one originated by paper instrument, or unless specifically exempted, and that authorizes a financial institution to debit or credit a customer's asset account. Section 903(6) of the Electronic Fund Transfer Act, 15 U.S.C. 1693a(6); 12 C.F.R. § 205.2(g). See Electronic Fund Transfer Act.

Electronic Fund Transfer Act: Title XX of the Financial Institutions Regulatory and Interest Rate Control Act of 1978, Pub. L. No. 95-630, 92 Stat. 3641, 3728 (1978), 15 U.S.C. §§ 1693–1693r. *See* Regulation E of the Federal Reserve System, 12 C.F.R. § 205; Brandel & Schellie, *Electronic Fund Transfer Act*, 35 Bus. Law. 1275 (1980); Schellie, *Electronic Fund Transfer Act*, 34 Bus. Law. 1441 (1979); *EFT Symposium*, 13 U. San Francisco L. Rev. 225 (1979). See also electronic funds transfer.

Eminent domain: Power of a government entity to take private property for public use. The power may be used to convey property to the government entity, or if sanctioned by statute, to condemn property for use by a private entity engaged in an activity of public benefit, such as a railroad or utility company.

Employee: One who is employed, or is acting in the interests of an employer. Under the National Labor Relations Act the term "employee" includes "any individual whose work has ceased as a consequence of, or in connection with, any current labor dispute or because of any unfair labor practice, and who has not obtained any other regular and substantially equivalent employment, ..." The term as used therein does not include agricultural laborers, domestic servants, the children and spouse of an employer, independent contractors, supervisors, employees of employers subject to the Railway Labor Act, and employees of any entity not treated as an "employer" under the Act. Section 2(3) of the National Labor Relations Act, 29 U.S.C. § 152(3). See employer; confidential employee. In many situations, the term "employee" does not include officers and directors; *e.g.* 17 C.F.R. 230.405, 47 Fed. Reg. 11380, 11435 (1982); Del. Code Ann. tit. 8. § 300. For other purposes the term "employee" is quite broad and includes officers (but not directors) of corporations; Model Business Corporation Act § 2(o). For purposes of certain wage deduction provisions of the Internal Revenue Code, the term includes officers and any individuals who have the status of employees at common law; agent-drivers and commission-drivers for meat, vegetables, bakery products, beverages (except milk), or laundry or dry-cleaning service; full-time life insurance salespeople; home workers performing work on goods supplied by the employer; and traveling or city salespeople. I.R.C. § 3121(d); *see also* I.R.C. §§ 1402(d), 3231(b), 3306(i), 3401(c), 7701(a)(20).

Employee Retirement Income Security Act of 1974: Federal legislation covering employee pension plans, administered jointly by the Departments of Labor and Treasury. Pub. L. No. 93-406, 88 Stat. 829 (1974). Part of ERISA is codified at 29 U.S.C. §1001 et seq.; other parts are incorporated in the Internal Revenue Code. *See* B. Creed, *ERISA Compliance: Reporting and Disclosure* (1981); *ERISA and the Investment Management and Brokerage Industries: Five Years Later,* 35 Bus. Law. 189 (1979).

Employee Stock Ownership Plan: Qualified stock bonus plan (which may have provisions for money purchase) under which employees may receive as bonus or purchase securities of their employer. *See* I.R.C. §§ 415(c)(6)(B), 4975(e)(7); *see generally* I.R.C. §§ 401–25; H. Weyher & H. Knott, *The Employee Stock Ownership Plan* (1982); Givner, *ESOPs and the Federal Securities Laws,* 31 Bus. Law. 1889 (1976); Reder & Gresham, *Federal and State Securities Aspects of Employee Stock Ownership Plans,* 31 Bus. Law. 1459 (1976); Bushman, *Employee Stock Ownership Plan: A Unique Method of Corporate Financing,* 113 Trusts & Est. 580 (1974).

Employer: One who hires or engages the services of others. For the purpose of the National Labor Relations Act, the term "employer" includes "any person acting as an agent of an employer, directly or indirectly," but does not include the United States government, government corporations, Federal Reserve Banks, State and local governments, employers subject to the Railway Labor Act, labor organizations (except when acting as an employer) and officers and agents of labor organizations. Section 2(2) of the National Labor Relations Act, 29 U.S.C. § 152(2). *See also* section 3(e) of the Labor-Management Reporting and Disclosure Act of 1959, 29 U.S.C. § 402(e); I.R.C. §§ 3231(a), 3306(a), 3401(d). See also **employee.**

Employment and Training Administration: Branch of the United States Department of Labor that includes the offices and services that administer federal employment service and work-training programs. Units of the ETA include the United States Employment Service, the Office of Comprehensive Employment Development, and the Unemployment Insurance Service. Programs include grants under the Comprehensive Employment and Training Act (CETA), the Work Incentive Program (WIN), Help through Industry Retraining (HIRE), the Vocational Exploration Program (VEP), the Job Corps, the Senior Community Service Employment Program, the Targeted Outreach Program (TOP), and the National On-the-Job Training Program (OJT).

Employment Service, United States: Unit of the Employment and Training Administration of the United States Department of Labor charged with the administration of the Wagner-Peyser Act of 1933 (Pub. L. No. 30, ch. 49, 48 Stat. 113 (1933), 29 U.S.C.

§ 49), providing assistance to the states in maintaining local public employment offices.

Employment Standards Administration: Unit of the United States Department of Labor, charged with the administration of wage and hour provisions of the Fair Labor Standards Act, the federal contract compliance programs, workers' compensation programs under the Federal Employees Compensation Act and the Longshoremen's and Harbor Workers' Compensation Act, and the "Black Lung" benefit provisions of the Federal Coal Mine Health and Safety Act of 1969.

Encumbrance: Lien or claim against property, or an interest in property other than the primary ownership interest. "Encumbrance" usually refers to a lien or claim on real property, but the term may also apply to a claim on personal property, no other term being available. *See* UCC Section 9-105(1)(g).

Endorse: To sign on the back. The Uniform Commercial Code uses the spelling "indorse."

Endorsement: Signature on the back of an instrument by the payee, denoting transfer of the instrument.

Energy, United States Department of: Cabinet-level department of the executive branch of the United States government formed to consolidate major federal energy functions in one agency. DOE has many of the responsibilities formerly allocated to the Energy Research and Development Administration, the Federal Energy Administration, the Federal Power Commission, and certain regional power administrations, and has taken over certain energy-related functions of the Interstate Commerce Commission and the Departments of Interior, Housing and Urban Development, Commerce, and Navy. DOE has research and development programs, programs of assistance for energy projects, and regulatory functions. A major component of DOE is the Federal Energy Regulatory Commission, an independent agency within the Department. *See* Department of Energy Organization Act, Pub. L. No. 95-91, 91 Stat. 565 (1977), 42 U.S.C. §§ 7101–7298.

Energy Information Administration: Unit of the United States Department of Energy established to collect and publish data on energy reserves, the financial status of energy companies, and production, demand, and consumption of energy and energy resources.

Energy property: Type of property for which a special federal tax credit of up to 15% is available. I.R.C. §§ 46(a)(2)(C), 46(a)(7). The term includes solar or wind energy facilities, recycling equipment, shale oil equipment, certain hydroelectric generating facilities, cogeneration equipment, and equipment for generating power from other than oil and gas. I.R.C. § 48(l).

Energy Tax Act of 1978: Amendment to the Internal Revenue Code providing for residential energy credits, the gas guzzler tax, and other energy-related tax measures. Pub. L. No. 95-618, 92 Stat. 3174 (1978).

Engaged in commerce: The merger restrictions of section 7 of the Clayton Act (15 U.S.C. § 18) relate to corporations "engaged in commerce." That phrase has been held to be less broad than the phrase "affecting commerce," which would have the full reach of the commerce clause of the Constitution. To "engage in commerce" means to engage in the production, distribution, or acquisition of goods or services in commerce among the United States or between the United States and a foreign country. *United States v. American Building Maintenance Industries*, 422 U.S. 271 (1975).

Enjoin: To require, by action of a court of equity, a party to perform or to refrain from performing a specified act.

Enterprise entity doctrine: Doctrine permitting service of process in antitrust suits against foreign corporations. *See* Section 12 of the Clayton Act, 15 U.S.C. § 22.

Entire fairness test: Test applied in "going private" transactions relating to the fairness of the transaction to shareholders, requiring the court to consider the purpose of the transaction, the adequacy of disclosure, the fiduciary duties of the directors, the adequacy of the merger price, and the significance of the approval voting requirements. *See Weinberger v. UOP, Inc.*, 426 A. 2d 1333 (Del. Ch. 1981).

Entity: In accounting terminology, a specific business enterprise. American Institute of Certified Public Accountants, Accounting Principles Board Statement No. 4, Ch. 5, *Basic Features and Basic Elements of Financial Accounting*, paragraph 3 (1970).

Entrusting: Under Article 2 of the Uniform Commercial Code–Sales, when goods are entrusted to a merchant who deals in goods of that kind, the merchant has the power to transfer all rights to those goods to a buyer in the ordinary course of business. "'Entrusting' includes any delivery and any acquiescence in retention of possession regardless of any condition expressed between the parties to the delivery or acquiescence and regardless of whether the procurement of the entrusting or the possessor's disposition of the goods have been such as to be larcenous under the criminal law." UCC Section 2-403. This provision reflects a policy favoring buyers in the ordinary course of business, and protecting such buyers from hidden interests in goods.

Environmental Impact Statement: Comprehensive description of the environmental effects of a major federal action, prepared pursuant to the National Environmental Policy Act.

Environmental Protection Agency: Independent agency in the executive branch of the United States government that administers federal laws relating to the control of environmentally hazardous activities and substances. *See* 40 C.F.R. §§ 1–51.

EPA: EPA: Environmental Protection Agency.

EPS: Earnings per share.

Equal Employment Opportunity Act of 1972: Federal statute amending the Civil Rights Act of 1964 to promote equal employment opportunities for American workers. Pub. L. No. 92-261, 86 Stat. 103 (1972).

Equal Employment Opportunity Commission: Independent agency of the United States government that administers and enforces federal laws relating to employment discrimination, including the Civil Rights Act of 1964, Pub. L. No. 88-352, 78 Stat. 241(1964), 42 U.S.C. §§ 2000a–h, the Equal Employment Opportunity Act of 1972, and related statutes.

Equipment: For the purpose of Article 9 of the Uniform Commercial Code–Secured Transactions, goods are "equipment" if "they are used or bought for use primarily in business (including farming or a profession) or by a debtor who is a non-profit organization or a governmental subdivision or agency or if the goods are not included in the definitions of inventory, farm products or consumer goods; . . . ." UCC Section 9-109(2).

Equipment trust: Form of secured financing, often used for railroad equipment and occasionally used for other equipment, particularly aircraft. A corporate trustee acquires the equipment for the benefit of the financing parties, and leases the equipment to the user, the party requiring the financing. The lease rents are calculated to repay to the financing parties the principal amount of their investment, together with interest, during the term of the lease. At the end of the lease term, when all amounts have been paid, the ownership of the equipment passes to the lessee. Such a lease is not a true lease, but a "lease for security" under the Uniform Commercial Code. See **Philadelphia plan.** More modern forms of financing, using the corporate trustee acting for the financing parties but employing a simplified security agreement rather than the sham lease, may also be called "equipment trusts." An exemption for registration of an "interest in a railroad equipment trust" in section 3(a)(6) of the Securities Act of 1933 employs a broad definition that takes in other types of railroad equipment financing, such as conditional sales and leases, but is limited to obligations of common carriers.

Equipment trust certificate: Evidence of participation in an equipment trust financing.

Equitable: Available only in equity. Equitable remedies are remedies traditionally available only in courts of equity, and are different from and more flexible than legal remedies (remedies available in courts of law). Equitable remedies include specific performance and injunctive relief, whereas legal remedies are usually limited to money damages. Most modern courts in the United States have both legal and equitable jurisdiction.

Equitable subordination: Use by a bankruptcy court of its equitable powers to subordinate certain claims of a class that would otherwise be treated as equal under the bankruptcy statutes. *See Pepper v. Litton,* 308 U.S. 295 (1939); 11 U.S.C. §510(c); H.R. Rep. No. 95-595, 95th Cong., 1st Sess. 359 (1977); S. Rep. No. 989, 95th Cong., 2d Sess. 74 (1978); 124 Cong. Rec.

H11113, H11095, S17430, S17412 (1978). *See generally* Herzog & Zweibel, *The Equitable Subordination of Claims in Bankruptcy,* 15 Vand. L. Rev. 83 (1961).

Equity: 1. Ownership interest. An equity holder is "an adventurer in the corporate business; he takes the risk, and profits from success." *Commissioner of Internal Revenue v. O.P.P. Holding Corp.,* 76 F. 2d 11, 12 (2d Cir. 1935). Compare **debt.** As to the difference between equity and debt for tax purposes, *see* I.R.C. § 385; Treas. Reg. § 1-385, 47 Fed. Reg. 164 (1982). 2. Net worth of a business, or the value belonging to the owners less debt; as defined by the Financial Accounting Standards Board, "Equity is the residual interest in the assets of an entity that remains after deducting its liabilities." Financial Accounting Standards Board, Statement of Financial Accounting Concepts No. 3, paragraph 43 (1980). See **equity security.** 3. System of jurisprudence apart from, and collateral to, the law, the object of which is to render justice by permitting relief of types not contemplated by law. Equitable relief may include such remedies as an injunction or specific performance, where legal relief could only be money damages. Actions in equity once required the use of separate, special courts, but now most American courts have both equitable and legal jurisdiction.

Equity capital: As defined by the International Accounting Standards Committee, "Equity capital is the issued share capital of a company which is neither limited nor preferred in its participation in distributions of the profits of a company or in the ultimate distribution of its assets." International Accounting Standards Committee, Statement of International Accounting Standards 3, *Consolidated Financial Statements,* paragraph 4 (1976).

Equity financing: The raising of capital for an enterprise by the issue and sale of stock.

Equity kicker: Ownership share, or an option for an ownership share, in a project taken by a lending institution in consideration for making a loan for the project.

Equity method: Method of accounting by a corporate investor for certain types of long-term investments in associated companies and for certain unconsolidated subsidiaries, under which the investment account of the investor is adjusted in the consolidated financial statements for the change in the investor's share of the net assets of the investee. The income statement reflects the investor's share of the results of operations of the investee. *See* American Institute of Certified Public Accountants, Accounting Principles Board Opinion No. 18, *The Equity Method of Accounting for Investments in Common Stock,* paragraph 6b (1971); Fiflis, *Accounting for Mergers, Acquisitions and Investments, in a Nutshell: The Interrelationships of, and Criteria for, Purchase or Pooling, the Equity Method, and Parent-Company-Only and Consolidated Statements,* 37 Bus. Law. 89 (1981). Compare **cost method.**

Equity of redemption: Right of a borrower to redeem property taken by a creditor in satisfaction of a debt.

Equity participation: Investment in a project or lease transaction that involves acquisition of an ownership interest in the project or equipment, compared to the debt participation, a loan.

Equity receivership: System of reorganization, often used for railroad companies before the passage of amendments to the Bankruptcy Act in 1933, whereby a court of equity took jurisdiction of an insolvent entity and appointed a receiver to arrange for disposition of the assets and to settle creditors' claims.

Equity risk premium: Difference between the rate of return on equity securities such as common stocks, and the rate of return on the least risky investments, such as United States Treasury bills.

Equity security: For the purpose of the Securities Exchange Act of 1934:

The term "equity security" means any stock or similar security; or any security convertible, with or without consideration, into such a security, or carrying any warrant or right to subscribe to or purchase such a security; or any such warrant or right; or any other security which the Commission shall deem to be of similar nature and consider necessary or appropriate, by such rules and regulations as it may prescribe in the public interest or for the protection of investors, to treat as an equity security.

Section 3(a)(11), 15 U.S.C. § 78c(a)(ii). *See* Regulation S-X, 17 C.F.R. § 210.1-02(i). Regulation C of the Securities and Exchange Commission embellishes the definition to include any

certificate of interest or participation in any profit sharing agreement, preorganization certificate or subscription, transferable share, voting trust certificate or certificate of deposit for an equity security, limited partnership interest, interest in a joint venture, or certificate of interest in a business trust; ... or any put, call, straddle, or other option or privilege of buying such a security from or selling such a security to another without being bound to do so.

17 C.F.R. § 230.405, 47 Fed. Reg. 11380, 11435 (1982). *See also* Cal. Corp. Code § 168. Under the Bankruptcy Code, an "equity security" is defined as a:

(A) share in a corporation, whether or not transferable or denominated "stock," or similar security;

(B) interest of a limited partner in a limited partnership; or

(C) warrant or right, other than a right to convert, to purchase, sell, or subscribe to a share, security, or interest of a kind specified in subparagraph (A) or (B) of this paragraph;

11 U.S.C. § 101(15); *see* H.R. Rep. No. 95-595, 95th Cong., 1st Sess. 311 (1977). The Financial Accounting Standards Board offers another definition:

Equity security encompasses any instrument representing ownership shares (e.g., common, preferred, and other capital stock), or the right to acquire (e.g., warrants, rights, and call options) or dispose of (e.g., put options) ownership shares in an enterprise at fixed or determinable prices. The term does not encompass preferred stock that by its terms either must be redeemed by the issuing enterprise or is redeemable at the option of the investor, nor does it include treasury stock or convertible bonds.

Financial Accounting Standards Board, Statement of Financial Accounting Standards No. 12, *Accounting for Certain*

Marketable Securities, paragraph 7a (1975).

Equivalent bond yield: Annual yield on a short-term, noninterest-bearing security (sold at a discount) that is comparable to the yield customarily quoted on interest-bearing securities, that is, the yield based on the annual coupon rate without considering the compounding effect of semiannual payments of interest. *See* M. Stigum, *Money Market Calculations: Yields, Break-Evens, and Arbitrage,* 33 (1981).

ERA: Economic Regulatory Administration.

ERISA: Employee Retirement Income Security Act of 1974.

ERTA: Economic Recovery Tax Act of 1981.

Escalation clause: Clause in a contract that permits the rate for payments to be increased in accordance with a formula based on an index, such as the producer price index, or the cost of materials or labor or other item subject to unpredictable increases.

Escape clause: Article XIX of the General Agreement on Tariff and Trade, which allows a country to impose temporary import restrictions and tariffs in certain circumstances, usually when injury to domestic producers is threatened. *See* Jackson, *The General Agreement on Tariffs and Trade,* in I W. Surrey & D. Wallace, Jr., ed., *A Lawyer's Guide to International Business Transactions* 37, 65 (2d ed. 1977); Metzger, *Escape Clause and Adjustment Assistance: Proposals and Assessments,* 2 Law & Pol. Int'l Bus. 353 (1970).

Escheat: Process by which property held by fiduciaries is deemed abandoned after a certain period of inactivity in the account or lack of communication, and is paid to the state. *E.g.,* N. Y. Aband. Prop. Law.

ESOP: Employee Stock Ownership Plan.

ESOT: Employee Stock Ownership Trust.

Essential facility doctrine: Doctrine that a single firm or joint venture controlling an "essential facility" must grant access to that facility to competitors if the facility is important to the ability of the competitors to compete with the control group or person, and cannot be reasonably duplicated. Also called the "bottleneck monopoly" doctrine. *See United States v. Terminal R. R. Assn. of St. Louis,* 224 U.S. 383 (1912); *Associated Press v. United States,* 326 U.S. 1 (1945); *Silver v. New York Stock Exchange,* 373 U.S. 341 (1963).

Estate tax bonds: Government bonds that are acceptable at par plus accrued interest when paying estate taxes, even though the market value may be less than par; often called "flower" bonds.

ETA: Employment and Training Administration.

ETC: Export Trade Corporation.

EUA: European unit of account.

EURCO: European Composite Unit.

Eurobill of exchange: Bill of exchange expressed in a European currency.

Eurobond: Debt obligation issued and sold in a jurisdiction outside of the country in whose currency the obligation is denominated. Eurobonds are usually denominated in United States or Canadian dollars, and are usually sold in Europe. *See generally* M. Mendelsohn, *Money on the Move* (1980). See also Eurodollar.

Euroclear: System for the clearing of Eurobonds, owned by a group of banks and operated by Morgan Guaranty Trust Company of New York.

Eurocredit: Medium-term international credit provided by banks or bank syndicates denominated in currencies that need not be those of the banks or the borrower.

Eurocurrency: Deposit in a bank of one country denominated in the currency of another, as marks deposited in London, or pounds in Paris. Eurocurrency denominated in dollars is referred to as Eurodollars.

Eurodollar: Deposits denominated in United States dollars held at banks and other financial institutions outside of the United States. The name originated because of the large amounts of such deposits in Western Europe, but similar deposits in other parts of the world are also called Eurodollars. *See* M. Mendelsohn, *Money on the Move* (1980); Snellings, *The Euro-Dollar Market,* in T. Cook, ed., *Instruments of the Money Market* 94 (4th ed., 1977); Newburg, *Financing in the Euromarket by U.S. Companies: A Survey of the Legal and Regulatory Framework,* 33 Bus. Law. 2171 (1978); Calhoun, Jr., *Eurodollar Loan Agreements: An Introduction and*

Discussion of Some Special Problems, 32 Bus. Law. 1785 (1977).

Eurodollar CD: Certificate of deposit issued by a foreign branch of a United States bank or by a foreign commercial bank, denominated in dollars.

Eurodollar rate: London Interbank offered rate of interest for dollars.

European Composite Unit: Unit of value consisting of a mix of European currencies.

European Currency Unit: Unit of value consisting of a mix of currencies of the original six members of the European Economic Community.

European unit of account: Unit incorporating a mix of currencies. *See* Blondeel, *A New Form of International Financing: Loans in European Units of Account,* 64 Colum. L. Rev. 995 (1964); Note, *The Unit of Account: Enforceability Under American Law of Maintenance-of-Value Provisions in International Bonds,* 71 Yale L. J. 1294 (1962).

Event: In accounting terminology, "a happening of consequence to an entity." Financial Accounting Standards Board, Statement of Financial Accounting Concepts No. 3, *Elements of Financial Statements of Business Enterprises,* paragraph 75 (1980). Compare circumstances.

Exchange offer: Offer involving the acquisition of securities of a corporation in exchange for securities of the acquiring corporation; similar to a tender offer, but the offer involves payment for the tendered securities with securities instead of cash. *See* McAtee, *Exchange Offers,* 10 Inst. Sec. Reg. 113 (1979).

Exchange rate: Ratio between a unit of one currency and the amount of another currency for which that unit can be exchanged at a particular time. Financial Accounting Standards Board, Statement of Financial Accounting Standards No. 8, *Accounting for the Translation of Foreign Currency Transactions and Foreign Currency Financial Statements,* paragraph 30 (1975).

Excise tax: "A hateful tax levied upon commodities, and adjudged not by the common judges of property, but wretches hired by those to whom excise is paid." S. Johnson, *Dictionary of the English Language* (1755).

Exclusive agency jurisdiction: Doctrine that the jurisdiction of an administrative agency over a given matter is exclusive, preempting application of antitrust laws. *See Hughes Tool Co. v. Trans World Airlines, Inc.,* 409 U.S. 363 (1973); *United States v. National Ass'n of Securities Dealers, Inc.,* 422 U.S. 694 (1975). *See generally* American Bar Association, Section of Antitrust Law, *Antitrust Law Developments* 412 (1975). See also primary jurisdiction.

Exclusive dealing arrangement: Agreement whereby a purchaser agrees to make purchases of a given commodity for a given period of time from one supplier, to the exclusion of others. An exclusive dealing arrangement may be a violation of section 1 of the Sherman Act, section 3 of the Clayton Act, or section 5 of the Federal Trade Commission Act. *See, e.g., Standard Oil Co. of*

Calif. v. United States, 337 U.S. 293 (1949); *Tampa Electric Co. v. Nashville Coal Co.,* 365 U.S. 320 (1961); *see generally* American Bar Association, Section of Antitrust Law, *Antitrust Law Developments* 43 (1975). Under Article 2 of the Uniform Commercial Code–Sales, a lawful exclusive dealing arrangement between a buyer and a seller of goods imposes "an obligation by the seller to use best efforts to supply the goods and by the buyer to use best efforts to promote their sale." UCC Section 2-306. See **requirements contract.**

Exclusive license: Grant of rights by an owner of a patent, trade secret, trademark, or copyright in which legal title is retained by the grantor/licensor, and the rights acquired by the licensee are comparable to those of an assignment. *See Waterman v. Mackenzie,* 138 U.S. 252 (1891).

Excuse: Under Section 2-615 of the Uniform Commercial Code, a seller of goods may be excused from performance by failure of presupposed conditions. *See also* UCC Section 2-616.

Ex-dividend: Without the dividend; used to describe a stock sale in which the seller retains the right to a recently declared dividend.

Executive officer: For the purpose of the Trust Indenture Act of 1939, the term "executive officer" means "the president, every vice president, every trust officer, the cashier, the secretary, and the treasurer of a corporation, and any individual customarily performing similar functions with respect to any organization whether incorporated or unincorporated, but shall not include the chairman of the board of directors." Section 303(6), 15 U.S.C. § 77ccc(6). For the purpose of registration statements, SEC Regulation C includes within the term the "president, any vice president of the registrant in charge of a principal business unit, division or function (such as sales, administration or finance), any other officer who performs a policy making function or any other person who performs similar policy making functions for the registrant. Executive officers of subsidiaries may be deemed executive officers of the registrant if they perform such policy making functions for the registrant." 17 C.F.R. § 230.405, 47 Fed. Reg. 11380, 11436 (1982).

Executory contract: Contract in which some performance obligation remains to be fulfilled. Executory contracts are not defined in the Bankruptcy Code, but the legislative history suggests that the term "generally includes contracts on which performance remains due to some extent on both sides." H.R. Rep. No. 95-595, 95th Cong., 1st Sess. 347 (1977); *see* 11 U.S.C. 365; Countryman, *Executory Contracts in Bankruptcy,* Part 1, 57 Minn. L. Rev. 439 (1973), Part II, 58 Minn. L. Rev. 479 (1974); Fogel, *Executory Contracts and Unexpired Leases in the Bankruptcy Code,* 64 Minn. L. Rev. 341 (1980).

Exempted security: 1. Security exempt from the registration requirements of the Securities Act of 1933 (but not the section 12 rescission remedies and the section 17 prohibition against fraud). Exempted securities include securities issued or guaranteed by government agencies, securities of banks, interests in common trust funds, industrial development bonds, interests in qualified pension and profit sharing plans, notes maturing in nine months or less, securities of nonprofit organizations, securities of savings and loan associations and certain farmers' cooperatives, securities of regulated motor carriers, railroad equipment obligations, certificates issued by a trustee or a debtor in a case under the Bankruptcy Code, insurance policies, securities issued in intrastate transactions, and such other securities as the SEC may decide to exempt. Securities Act of 1933, section 3, 15 U.S.C. § 77c. See **Regulation A.** 2. For the purpose of the Securities Exchange Act of 1934, an "exempted security" is a security that is a direct obligation of the United States or guaranteed by the United States. Section 3(a)(12), 15 U.S.C. § 78c(a)(12).

Exempted transaction: Issuance of securities in a transaction exempt from the registration requirements of the Securities Act of 1933. Exempted transactions include transactions "by any person other than an issuer, underwriter, or dealer," transactions "not involving a public offering" (the "private placement" exemption), transactions by a dealer, transactions by a broker upon customers' unsolicited orders, and certain real estate transactions. Securities Act of 1933, section 4, 15 U.S.C. § 77d. *See generally* J. Hicks, *Exempted Transactions under the Securities Act of 1933* (1979).

Exempt organization: Organization exempt from the payment of federal income taxes. I.R.C. § 501(c); *see generally* I.R.C. §§ 501-28.

Exercise price: Price at which an option, such as a put or call, is or can be exercised.

Eximbank: Export-Import Bank of the United States.

Ex parte communication: The Administrative Procedure Act defines an "ex parte communication" as "an oral or written communication not on the public record with respect to which reasonable prior notice to all parties is not given, but it shall not include requests for status reports on any matter or proceeding covered by this subchapter." 5 U.S.C. § 551(14).

Expectation interest: In connection with a contract, the "expectation interest" is the interest of a promisee "in having the benefit of his bargain by being put in as good a position as he would have been in had the contract been performed." *Restatement, Second, Contracts*, § 344 (1981). The purpose of judicial remedies for breach of contract is the protection of the expectation interest, the reliance interest, and the restitution interest. *See* UCC Section 1-106.

Expenses: As defined by the Financial Accounting Standards Board, "Expenses are outflows or other using up of assets or incurrences of liabilities (or a combination of both) during a period from delivering or producing goods, rendering services, or carrying out other activities that constitute the entity's ongoing major or central operations." Financial Accounting Standards Board, Statement of Financial Accounting Concepts No. 3, *Elements of Financial Statements of Business Enterprises,* paragraph 65 (1980).

Experimental use doctrine: Doctrine permitting public use of an invention prior to filing an application for patent if such use is conducted for the purpose of testing rather than exploitation, without violating the "public use" bar against patenting. *See* Welch, *Patent Law's Ephemeral Experimental Use Doctrine: Judicial Lip Service to a Judicial Misnomer or the Experimental Stage Doctrine,* 11 U. Tol. L. Rev. 865 (1980).

Expertise: Financial and accounting data are "expertized" when they are "covered by a report of independent accountants, who consent to be named as experts, based on an examination made in accordance with generally accepted auditing standards." American Institute of Certified Public Accountants, Statement on Auditing Standards No. 38, *Letters for Underwriters,* paragraph 2 (1981).

Exploratory well: For the purpose of accounting by oil and gas companies, an exploratory well is "a well that is not a development well, a service well, or a stratigraphic test well, ..." as such terms are defined in Appendix C to Financial Accounting Standards Board Statement of Financial Accounting Standards No. 19, *Financial Accounting and Reporting by Oil and Gas Producing Companies* (1977).

Export Administration Act of 1969: Federal statute providing for controls on the export of strategic goods. Pub. L. No. 91-184, 83 Stat. 841 (1969); 50

U.S.C. App. §§ 2401–13. *See* Stein, *Export Controls,* in I W. Surrey & D. Wallace, Jr., ed., *A Lawyer's Guide to International Business Transactions* 147 (2d ed. 1977).

Export-Import Bank of the United States: Independent agency of the United States government formed to facilitate exports by extending loans, guaranties, and export credit insurance. The Eximbank finances its credit operations by borrowing from the Federal Financing Bank, by issuing debentures, and by selling certificates of beneficial interest and participation certificates in its loan portfolio. Export-Import Bank Act of 1945, Pub. L. No. 173, ch. 341, 59 Stat. 526 (1945), 12 U.S.C. § 635. *See* Corette, *Export-Import Bank of the United States,* in II W. Surrey & D. Wallace, Jr., ed., *A Lawyer's Guide to International Business Transactions* 369 (2d ed. 1979); Rendell, *Export Financing and the Role of the Export-Import Bank of the United States,* 11 J. Int'l L. & Econ. 91 (1976).

Export trade corporation: Foreign corporation, controlled by United States shareholders, that is engaged principally in export trade and 90% of whose income is derived from sources outside the United States. Export trade corporations are entitled to special treatment under the Internal Revenue Code. I.R.C. §§ 970–71.

Exposed net asset position: In connection with accounting for foreign exchange transactions, "The excess of assets that are measured or denominated in foreign currency and translated at the current rate over liabilities that are measured or denominated in foreign currency and translated at the current rate." Financial Accounting Standards Board, Statement of Financial Accounting Standards No. 8, *Accounting for the Translation of Foreign Currency Transactions and Foreign Currency Financial Statements,* Appendix E (1975).

Exposed net liability position: In connection with accounting for foreign exchange transactions, "The excess of liabilities that are measured or denominated in foreign currency and translated at the current rate over assets that are measured or denominated in foreign currency and translated at the current rate." Financial Accounting Standards Board, Statement of Financial Accounting Standards No. 8, *Accounting for the Translation of Foreign Currency Transactions and Foreign Currency Financial Statements,* Appendix E (1975).

Ex-rights: Used to describe a security that is offered or sold without warrants or other rights that may have accompanied the security when issued.

Ex-ship: From the carrying vessel; a term in a contract for the sale of goods under which the seller bears the expense of shipment and the risk of loss until the goods are unloaded from the vessel. UCC Section 2-322.

Extension agreement: Agreement of creditors to extend the due date of debts.

External bond: Bond issued by a country in another country, and payable in the currency of the host country.

Extraordinary item: In accounting terminology, an event or transaction that is distinguished by its unusual nature and the infrequency of its occurrence. American Institute of Certified Public Accountants, Accounting Principles Board Opinion No. 30, *Reporting the Results of Operations—Reporting the Effects of Disposal of a Segment of Business, and Extraordinary, Unusual and Infrequently Occurring Events and Transactions,* paragraph 20 (1973).

F

FAA: 1. Federal Aviation Administration. 2. Foreign Assistance Act.

Face value: Value that appears on the face of a security.

Facility fee: Fee charged by a financial institution for a credit commitment not drawn upon.

Factor: Entity that provides business financing by purchasing accounts receivable at a discount. The factor usually assumes the risk of collection.

Failing company doctrine: Defense to a charge of violation of section 7 of the Clayton Act (prohibiting anti-competitive mergers and acquisitions) based on the impending failure of the acquired company, and the assertion that the acquiring company is the only available purchaser. *See Citizens Publishing Co. v. United States,* 394 U.S. 131 (1969). *See generally* United States Department of Justice, *Merger Guidelines* (1982); American Bar Association, Section of Antitrust Law, *Antitrust Law Developments* 72 (1975);

Laurenza, *Section 7 of the Clayton Act and the Failing Company: An Updated Perspective,* 65 Va. L. Rev. 947 (1979).

Fair Credit Reporting Act: Federal legislation regulating certain activities of consumer credit reporting agencies. Pub. L. No. 91-508, 84 Stat. 1128 (1970); 15 U.S.C. §§ 1681–81t. *See generally* Feldman & Gordin, Jr., *Privacy and Personal Information Reporting: The Legislative Boom,* 35 Bus. Law. 1259 (1980).

Fair inference rule: Rule to ease the burden of demonstrating compliance with the United States citizenship requirements for vessel registration by widely held corporations. 51% ownership by citizens can be established by an affidavit of an appropriate corporate officer to the effect that at least 65% of the stockholders of the corporation have addresses within the United States; 75% ownership by citizens can be fairly inferred by a showing of 90% domestic addresses. 46 C.F.R. § 221.11. *See* Shipping Act, 1916, section 2, 46 U.S.C. § 802.

Fair Labor Standards Act: Federal legislation regulating minimum wages and other labor conditions. Pub. L. No. 718, ch. 676, 52 Stat. 1060 (1938); 29 U.S.C. §§ 201–19.

Fairness doctrine: Doctrine that the dominant party in a merger where the merging corporations are under common control and do not bargain at arm's length must establish the "full fairness" of the proposed exchange, *i.e.,* that the value of what the stockholders receive in the merger is equivalent to the value of what is surrendered. *See Singer v. The Magnavox Co.,* 380 A. 2d 969 (Del. Supr. 1977); *Sterling v. Mayflower Hotel Corp.,* 93 A. 2d 107 (Del. Supr. 1952); *see generally* E. Folk III, *The Delaware General Corporation Law* 333 (1972); McBride, *Delaware Corporate Law: Judicial Scrutiny of Mergers—The Aftermath of Singer v. The Magnavox Company,* 33 Bus. Law. 2231 (1978). See also entire fairness test.

Fairness opinion: Opinion given by an investment banking firm as to the financial fairness of an acquisition. *See* Chazen, *Fairness from a Financial Point of View in Acquisitions of Public Companies: Is "Third-Party Sale Value" the Appropriate Standard?* 36 Bus. Law. 1439 (1981); Feuerstein, *Valuation and Fairness Opinions,* 32 Bus. Law. 1337 (1977).

Fair Packaging and Labeling Act: Federal statute requiring the disclosure of accurate product quality information to consumers, administered by the Federal Trade Commission. Pub. L. No. 89-755, 80 Stat. 1256 (1966); 15 U.S.C. §§ 1451–61

Fair use: Justifiable use of copyrighted materials, not constituting an infringement. 17 U.S.C. § 107; *see Folsom v. Marsh,* 9 F. Cas. 342 (C.C.D. Mass. 1841). As to "fair use" in photocopying, see *Williams & Wilkins Co. v. United States,* 487 F. 2d 1345 (Ct. Cl. 1973); Pegram, *Photocopying in Profit-Oriented Organizations Under the Copyright Revision Act of 1976,* 34 Bus. Law. 1251 (1979).

False advertisement: As defined in the Federal Trade Commission Act, "false advertisement" means:

an advertisement, other than labeling, which is misleading in a material respect; and in determining whether any advertisement is misleading, there shall be taken into account (among other things) not only representations made or suggested by statement, word, design, device, sound, or any combination thereof, but also the extent to which the advertisement fails to reveal facts material in the light of such representations or material with respect to the consequences which may result from the use of the commodity to which the advertisement relates under the conditions prescribed in such advertisement, or under such conditions as are customary or usual. No advertisement of a drug shall be deemed to be false if it is disseminated only to members of the medical profession, contains no false representation of a material fact, and includes, or is accompanied in each instance by truthful disclosure of, the formula showing quantitatively each ingredient of such drug.

Section 15(a)(1), 15 U.S.C. § 55(a)(1). With respect to oleomargarine, *see* 15 U.S.C. § 55(a)(2). The New York General Business Law uses a similar definition, without the references to drugs. N.Y. Gen. Bus. L. § 350-a.

Fannie Mae: Federal National Mortgage Association.

Farm Credit Act of 1971: Federal statute authorizing the federal land banks and the farm credit system; Pub. L. No. 92-181, 85 Stat. 583 (1971), 12 U.S.C. §§ 2001–2259; 12 C.F.R. §§ 600–19.

Farm Credit Administration: Independent agency of the United States government that supervises the Farm Credit System. See **Farm Credit Act of 1971.**

Farm Credit Consolidated System-wide Discount Notes: Short-term notes of the Farm Credit Banks. These notes are the joint and several obligations of the Farm Credit Banks.

Farm Credit System: Federally sponsored system of credit and credit-related services for farmers, ranchers, commercial fishermen, rural homeowners, and certain farm-related businesses. The Farm Credit System is made up of the Federal Land Banks, the Federal Land Bank Association, Federal Intermediate Credit Banks and Production Credit Associations, and Banks for Cooperatives. See **Farm Credit Act of 1971.**

Farmers Home Administration: Agency of the United States Department of Agriculture that makes loans in rural areas for farms, homes, and community facilities. The FmHA currently obtains its funds by borrowing from the Federal Financing Bank, but it has in the past issued certificates of beneficial ownership in its loan portfolio. The authority of the FmHA is derived from the Consolidated Farm and Rural Development Act, Pub. L. No. 87-128, 75 Stat. 307 (1961), and Title V of the Housing Act of 1948, Pub. L. No. 901, ch. 832, 62 Stat. 1268, 1283 (1948). *See* 42 U.S.C. § 1471; 7 C.F.R. §§ 1804–90t.

Farmout agreement: Agreement whereby an oil or gas lease is assigned, or "farmed out," by the holder of the lease, the "farmor," to another operator, the "farmee." The farmee undertakes to drill on the lease at its own risk, and agrees to share part of the royalties with the farmor. The expression is derived from baseball: players for whom there is no room on the roster and who need development are assigned to minor-league "farm" teams, or "farmed out." *See* Scott, *How to Prepare an Oil and Gas Farmout Agreement,* 33 Baylor L. Rev. 63 (1981).

Farm products: For the purpose of Article 9 of the Uniform Commercial Code–Secured Transactions, goods are "farm products" if "they are crops or livestock or supplies used or produced in farming operations or if they are products of crops or livestock in their unmanufactured states (such as ginned cotton, wool-clip, maple syrup, milk and eggs), and if they are in the possession of a debtor engaged in raising, fattening, grazing or other farming operations. If goods are farm products they are neither equipment nor inventory." UCC Section 9-109(3).

F.A.S.: Free alongside; term of delivery used in transactions for the sale of goods to be shipped by vessel. Delivery F.A.S. means the seller must at his own expense and risk deliver the goods alongside a vessel or on a dock designated by the buyer. UCC Section 2-319.

FASB: Financial Accounting Standards Board.

Fault: Under the Uniform Commercial Code, fault means wrongful act, omission, or breach. UCC Section 1-201 (16).

FBI: Federal Bureau of Investigation.

FCC: Federal Communications Commission.

FCIA: Foreign Credit Insurance Association.

FCM: Futures commission merchant.

FCPA: Foreign Corrupt Practices Act.

FCRA: Fair Credit Reporting Act.

FDA: Food and Drug Administration.

FDIC: Federal Deposit Insurance Corporation.

Featherbedding: Establishment or maintenance of jobs not necessary for efficient operations.

Fed, The: Federal Reserve System.

Federal Advisory Committee Act: Legislation providing for appointment and utilization of advisory committees for the executive branch of the federal government. Pub. L. No. 92-463, 86 Stat. 770 (1972).

Federal Arbitration Act: Federal statute covering arbitration of maritime and commercial disputes. Pub. L. No. 401, ch. 213, 43 Stat. 883 (1925); 9 U.S.C. §§ 1–14, 201–8.

Federal Aviation Act of 1958: Statute providing for federal regulation of the airline industry, and covering other matters related to civil aviation. Pub. L. No. 85-726, 72 Stat. 731 (1958); 49 U.S.C. §§ 1301–1542.

Federal Aviation Administration: Branch of the United States Department of Transportation. The primary responsibility of the FAA is aviation safety; the FAA maintains air navigation facilities and the air traffic control system, and regulates the design, construction, and maintenance of civil aircraft. The FAA also administers a program of aircraft loan guaranties. *See* 14 C.F.R. §§ 1–49.

Federal Bill of Lading Act: See Bill of Lading Act.

Federal Bureau of Investigation: Investigative arm of the United States Department of Justice.

Federal Communications Commission: Independent agency of the United States government that regulates interstate and foreign communications by wire and radio. The jurisdiction of the FCC includes cable television, commercial broadcasting, private radio communications, and common carrier radio and wire communications, including satellite communications. *See* Communications Act of 1934, Pub. L. No. 416, ch. 652, 48 Stat. 1064 (1934), 15 U.S.C. § 21, 47 U.S.C. §§ 35, 151–609; Communications Satellite Act of 1962, Pub. L. No. 87-624, 76 Stat. 419 (1962), 47 U.S.C. §§ 701–44; 47 C.F.R. §§ 0–19.

Federal Contract Compliance Programs, Office of: Unit of the Employment Standards Administration of the United States Department of Labor responsible for coordination of government programs to achieve nondiscrimination in employment by government contractors and subcontractors and in federally assisted programs. *See* D. Copus & L. Rosenzweig, ed., *OFCCP and Federal Contract Compliance* (1981).

Federal Crop Insurance Corporation: Corporation within the United States Department of Agriculture that provides insurance against loss of crops from unavoidable causes such as weather, insects, and disease. *See* Federal Crop Insurance Act, Pub. L. No. 439, ch. 30, 52 Stat. 31, 72 (1938); 7 U.S.C. §§ 1501–18.

Federal Deposit Insurance Act: Act establishing the program of insurance for deposits in national banks and certain state banks administered by the Federal Deposit Insurance Corporation; former section 12B of the Federal Reserve Act, Pub. L. No. 66, ch. 89, 48 Stat. 162 (1933), now separately stated by Pub. L. No. 797, ch. 967, 64 Stat. 873 (1950); 12 U.S.C. §§ 1811–31.

Federal Deposit Insurance Corporation: Independent agency within the executive branch of the United States government that insures deposits at most commercial banks and mutual savings banks. The FDIC has primary federal supervisory authority over insured state banks that are not members of the Federal Reserve System. See Federal Deposit Insurance Act.

Federal Discount Rate: Rate of interest charged on federal funds, on a discount basis.

Federal Emergency Management Agency: Independent agency in the executive branch of the United States government that administers federal programs for emergency preparedness and disaster relief.

Federal Energy Regulatory Commission: Independent agency within the United States Department of Energy that performs economic regulation of the transportation and sale of natural gas, the transmission of electric power, and the transportation of oil by pipeline. *See* Department of Energy Organization Act, Pub. L. No. 95-91, 91 Stat. 565 (1977).

Federal Executive Boards: Boards composed of the heads of the field offices of federal agencies in a given major metropolitan area, established to coordinate local federal activities.

Federal Farm Credit Banks Consolidated Systemwide Bonds: Bonds issued as joint and several obligations of the Farm Credit Banks, used to finance the credit activities of the Farm Credit System. Such bonds are not obligations of nor are they guaranteed by the United States government.

Federal Farm Credit Board: Policy making body for the Farm Credit Administration. The Board appoints the Governor, the chief executive officer of the Farm Credit Administration.

Federal Financing Bank: Agency of the United States Treasury formed to permit other government agencies to obtain financing at the most favorable rates. The Federal Financing Bank lends to other agencies of the federal government, using funds borrowed from the Treasury. The rate charged by the Federal Financing Bank is usually 1/8% over the Treasury's borrowing rate for equivalent maturities. The Federal Financing bank also purchases securities guaranteed by other federal agencies. *See* Federal Financing Bank Act of 1973, Pub. L. No. 93-224, 87 Stat. 937 (1973), 12 U.S.C. §§ 24, 2281–94; Nelson, *Federal Agency Securities,* in T. Cook, ed., *Instruments of the Money Market* 85 (4th ed., 1977).

Federal funds: Funds that are immediately available and not subject to reserve requirements. Historically, federal funds meant bank balances with the Federal Reserve System that member banks lend each other, usually on an overnight basis. Federal funds now include repurchase agreements and certain other kinds of borrowing by commercial banks from other types of depositary institutions and federal agencies. *See* Monhollon, *Federal Funds,* in T. Cook, ed., *Instruments of the Money Market* 38 (4th ed., 1977).

Federal funds check: Check drawn by a bank on its account with a Federal Reserve Bank. Federal funds checks provide immediately available funds.

Federal Highway Administration: Branch of the United States Department of Transportation that is responsible for federal programs of aid for highway construction, certain highway safety programs, and enforcement of safety standards for commercial motor carriers.

Federal Home Loan Bank: One of the twelve regional banks organized under the Federal Home Loan Bank Act to provide a flexible credit reserve to member thrift institutions. The Federal Home Loan Banks finance their credit activities by participating in the issue of consolidated bonds, the joint and several obligations of all such banks. *See* Federal Home Loan Bank Act, Pub. L. No. 304, ch. 522, 47 Stat. 725 (1932), 12 U.S.C. §§ 1421–49.

Federal Home Loan Bank Board: Independent agency in the executive branch of the United States government that supervises all federal savings and loan associations, federally chartered mutual savings banks, and federally insured state-chartered savings and loan associations. The FHLBB also operates the Federal Savings and Loan Insurance Corporation, the Federal Home Loan Bank System, and the Federal Home Loan Mortgage Corporation. *See* Federal Home Loan Bank Act, Pub. L. No. 304, ch. 522, 47 Stat. 725 (1932), 12 U.S.C. §§ 1421–49; Home Owners' Loan Act of 1933, Pub. L. No. 43, ch. 64, 48 Stat. 128 (1933), 12 U.S.C. §§ 1461–68; Financial Institutions Regulatory and Interest Rate Control Act of

1978, Pub. L. No. 95-630, 92 Stat. 3641 (1978).

Federal Home Loan Bank System: Federal agency operated by the Federal Home Loan Bank Board that provides credit for member savings institutions to promote the availability of home financing.

Federal Home Loan Mortgage Corporation: Federal agency operated by the Federal Home Loan Bank Board chartered to promote secondary markets for conventional residential mortgages. This agency, called "Freddie Mac," purchases such mortgages, raising the funds to do so by selling mortgage-related instruments and issuing guaranteed mortgage certificates and mortgage participation certificates. *See* Federal Home Loan Mortgage Corporation Act, Title III of the Emergency Home Finance Act of 1970, Pub. L. No. 91-351, 88 Stat. 450 (1970).

Federal Insurance Administration: Unit of the Federal Emergency Management Agency that administers programs of insurance and reinsurance against losses due to floods and civil disturbances.

Federal Intermediate Credit Bank: Bank authorized by Title II of the Farm Credit Act of 1971 to make loans to, and discount agricultural paper for, production credit associations, state and national banks, livestock loan companies, agricultural credit corporations, and similar organizations in connection with the Farm Credit System. The Federal Intermediate Credit Banks finance their

credit activities by participating in the issue of joint and several obligations of all such banks, called consolidated bonds.

Federal Labor Relations Authority: Independent agency of the United States government that supervises labor-management relations for employees of the federal government. *See* Title VII of the Civil Service Reform Act of 1978, Pub. L. No. 95-454, 92 Stat. 1111, 1191 (1978), 5 U.S.C. §§ 7101–35.

Federal Land Bank: Bank authorized by Title I of the Farm Credit Act of 1971 to make loans to farmers and ranchers for agricultural purposes or other needs, and to finance rural housing. Federal Land Banks are owned by their member-borrowers and finance their credit activities by participating in the issue of joint and several obligations of all such banks, called consolidated bonds. See **Farm Credit Administration.**

Federal Maritime Commission: Independent agency of the United States government that performs economic regulation of domestic and foreign waterborne offshore commerce. The authority of the FMC is found in the Shipping Act, 1916, Pub. L. No. 260, ch. 451, 39 Stat. 728 (1916), 46 U.S.C. §§ 801–42, the Merchant Marine Act, 1920, Pub. L. No. 261, ch. 250, 41 Stat. 988 (1920), 46 U.S.C. §§ 861–89, the Intercoastal Shipping Act, 1933, Pub. L. No. 415, ch. 199, 47 Stat. 1425 (1933), 46 U.S.C. §§ 843–48, the Merchant Marine Act, 1936, Pub. L. No. 835, ch. 858, 49 Stat. 1985 (1936), 46 U.S.C. §§

1101–1295, and certain provisions of other statutes.

Federal Mediation and Conciliation Service: Independent agency of the United States government established to provide mediation services to resolve labor-management disputes. *See* section 202 of the Labor Management Relations Act, 1947.

Federal National Mortgage Association: Government-sponsored but privately owned corporation that assists the secondary market in mortgages, both conventional and government insured and guaranteed, by purchasing and lending on the security of such mortgages. The FNMA (Fannie Mae) finances these activities by the sale of debentures and short-term notes in the private market and, in certain cases, to the Treasury of the United States.

Federal Open Market Committee: Committee of the seven members of the Board of Governors of the Federal Reserve System and five of the twelve Federal Reserve Bank presidents. The Committee sets Federal Reserve guidelines regarding the purchase and sale of government securities in the open market as a means of influencing the volume of bank credit and money, and establishes policy relating to Federal Reserve System operations in the foreign exchange markets.

Federal Procurement Policy, Office of: Unit of the Office of Management and Budget that sets policy for procurement by federal agencies and recipients of federal grants and assistance. *See* Office of Federal Procurement Policy Act, Pub. L. No.93-400, 88 Stat. 796 (1974), 41 U.S.C. §§ 401–12.

Federal Railroad Administration: Branch of the United States Department of Transportation, established to give balance within the Department of Transportation to the established aviation and highway activities. The FRA administers aid programs, enforces rail safety legislation, sponsors research, development, and rail transportation improvement projects, and operates The Alaska Railroad.

Federal Register: Publication issued by the Office of the Federal Register, National Archives and Records Service of the General Services Administration on every federal working day containing presidential documents, documents of general applicability and legal effect, and documents and notices required to be published by statute. Publication in the Federal Register of notices, proposed regulations, and final regulations is an essential part of the federal rule-making process. *See* Federal Register Act, Pub. L. No. 220, ch. 417, 49 Stat. 500 (1935), 44 U.S.C. §§ 1501–11. *See generally* Office of the Federal Register, National Archives and Records Service, General Services Administration, *The Federal Register: What It Is and How to Use It* (1980).

Federal Reserve Bank: One of the twelve banks of the Federal Reserve System.

Federal Reserve discount rate: Interest rate at which member banks of the Federal Reserve System borrow funds for short periods directly from

Federal Reserve banks. The board of directors of each Federal Reserve Bank must establish the discount rate every fourteen days, subject to the approval of the Board of Governors of the Federal Reserve System.

Federal Reserve notes: Obligations of the United States government, put into circulation by the Federal Reserve System, that serve as the circulating paper currency in the United States.

Federal Reserve System: The central bank of the United States, chartered by Congress, and consisting of a seven-member Board of Governors in Washington, D.C., 12 regional reserve banks, and about 5600 commercial banks that are members of the system. All national banks are members of the system; state-chartered banks may elect to become members. Approximately 40% of all banks are member banks, accounting for over 70% of all bank deposits. State bank members are supervised by the Board of Governors and the Reserve Banks; national bank members are supervised by the Comptroller of the Currency. The Federal Reserve establishes and administers monetary and credit policy. *See* Federal Reserve Act, Pub. L. No. 43, ch. 6, 38 Stat. 251 (1913), 12 U.S.C. §§ 221–522.

Federal Savings and Loan Association: Savings institution chartered and supervised by the Federal Home Loan Bank Board pursuant to section 5 of the Home Owners' Loan Act of 1933, Pub. L. No. 43, ch. 64, 48 Stat. 128, 132 (1933), 12 U.S.C. §§ 1461–68.

Federal Savings and Loan Insurance Corporation: Federal agency operated by the Federal Home Loan Bank Board that insures deposits at federal savings and loan associations and those state-chartered associations that apply and are accepted. *See* Title IV of the National Housing Act, Pub. L. No. 479, ch. 847, 48 Stat. 1246, 1255 (1934), 12 U.S.C. §§ 1724–30.

Federal Securities Code: Code proposed by the American Law Institute to replace seven principal federal securities laws: the Securities Act of 1933, the Securities Exchange Act of 1934, the Public Utility Holding Company Act of 1935, the Trust Indenture Act of 1939, the Investment Company Act of 1940, the Investment Advisors Act of 1940, and the Securities Investor Protection Act of 1970 (for citations see **securities laws**). The reporter for the project was Professor Louis Loss of Harvard University Law School. *See* Finn, *The Impact of the Proposed Federal Securities Code Upon the Banking Industry*, 36 Bus. Law. 397 (1981).

Federal Supply Service: Unit of the General Services Administration that procures supplies and materials for the agencies of the federal government.

Federal tax lien: Lien in favor of the United States for claims relating to failure to pay taxes. *See* Federal Tax Lien Act of 1966, I.R.C. §§ 6321–26; H.R. Rep. No. 1884, 89th Cong., 2d Sess. (1966); 817 C.B. 1966-2; W. Plumb, Jr., *Federal Tax Liens* (3d ed. 1972); Plumb, Jr., *The New Federal Tax Lien Law*, 22 Bus. L. 271 (1967).

Federal Trade Commission: Independent agency of the United States government created to prevent unfair trade practices and unfair methods of competition. The FTC has antitrust jurisdiction under the Federal Trade Commission Act and the Clayton Act, exercised by the Bureau of Competition, has the authority to prohibit deceptive advertising and marking, and administers certain provisions of the Truth in Lending Act and the Fair Credit Reporting Act.

Federal Trade Commission Act: Act prohibiting "unfair methods of competition" and "unfair or deceptive acts or practices," creating the Federal Trade Commission, and giving that agency certain authority to prevent such methods and acts. Pub. L. No. 203, ch. 311, 38 Stat. 717 (1914), 15 U.S.C. §§ 41–58. *See generally* American Bar Association, Section of Antitrust Law, *Antitrust Law Developments* 165 (1975).

Federal Trade Commission Improvement Act of 1975: Federal statute amending the Federal Trade Commission Act and providing other measures of consumer protection. Pub. L. No. 93-637, 88 Stat. 2193 (1975). *See* H.R. Rep. No. 93-1606, 93d Cong., 2d Sess. (1974).

Federal Water Pollution Control Act: Legislation providing for water pollution control activities by certain federal agencies and establishing programs of assistance for waste treatment. Pub. L. No. 845, ch. 758, 62 Stat. 1155, 33 U.S.C. §§ 1151–1376. *See* Federal Water Pollution Control Act Amendments of 1972, Pub. L. No. 92-500, 86 Stat. 816 (1972).

Fed. Reg.: Federal Register.

Fed wire: Federal Reserve Communications System, an electronic communications system interconnecting Federal Reserve offices, the Federal Reserve Board, member banks, the United States Treasury, and other government agencies. The Fed wire is used for transferring member bank reserve balances and government securities.

Fee; fee simple: With respect to real property, the highest interest or estate in that property; ownership with unconditional power of disposition; in the case of an individual, a fee simple estate will descend to his heirs.

FEI: Financial Executives Institute.

FERC: Federal Energy Regulatory Commission.

FFB: Federal Financing Bank.

FHWA: Federal Highway Administration.

Fictitious name: Name, other than the name of the owner of the business, under which business is done; in the case of partnerships, a name other than the name of a partner. The use of a fictitious name usually requires registration of that name in a public office to identify the actual owner of the business.

Fiduciary: For the purpose of the Internal Revenue Code, "fiduciary" means a "guardian, trustee, executor, administrator, receiver, conservator, or any person acting in any fiduciary capacity for any person." I.R.C. § 7701(a)(6). A person is a fiduciary under ERISA with respect to a plan to the extent (i) he exercises any discretionary authority or discretionary control respecting management of such plan or exercises any authority or control respecting management or disposition of its assets, (ii) he renders investment advice for a fee or other compensation, direct or indirect, with respect to any moneys or other property of such plan, or has authority or responsibility to do so, or (iii) he has discretionary authority or discretionary responsibility in the administration of such plan.

ERISA § 3(21), 29 U.S.C. § 1002(21). *See ERISA and the Investment Management and Brokerage Industries: Five Years Later,* 35 Bus. Law. 189, 199 (1979).

Fiduciary funds: Funds held for investment by a financial institution for the account of another, but invested at the discretion of the institution and in its own name.

Field: For the purpose of accounting by oil and gas companies, a "field" is

An area consisting of a single reservoir or multiple reservoirs all grouped on or related to the same individual geological structural feature and/or stratigraphic condition. There may be two or more reservoirs in a field which are separated vertically by intervening impervious strata, or laterally by local geologic barriers, or by both. Reservoirs that are associated by being in overlapping or adjacent fields may be treated as a single or common operational field. The geological terms "structural feature" and "stratigraphic condition" are intended to identify localized geological features as opposed to the broader terms of basins, trends, provinces, plays, areas-of-interest, etc.

Financial Accounting Standards Board, Statement of Financial Accounting Standards No. 19, *Financial Accounting and Reporting by Oil and Gas Producing Companies,* Appendix C (1977).

Field-of-use limitation: Limitation in a patent license to a certain field of use by the licensee. *See General Talking Pictures Corp. v. Western Electric Co.,* 305 U.S. 124 (1938).

Field warehousing: Arrangement for secured financing of business inventory whereby a "warehouse" is established and operated on the business premises of the party requiring financing, the inventory is stored in the warehouse, and the financing party advances funds against warehouse receipts. The practice was made obsolete by the Uniform Commercial Code provisions for security interests in shifting stock in the borrower's possession. *See* Friedman, *Field Warehousing,* 42 Colum. L. Rev. 991 (1942).

FIFO: First in, first out.

FIFRA: Federal Insecticide, Fungicide and Rodenticide Act.

Fill or kill: Exercise or release an option.

Finance lease: Lease intended as a financing device rather than as a contract for the use of equipment or possession of property. The lessor in a finance lease is usually a financing party who expects a fixed return for a given period, and thus a finance lease usually is noncancellable and places all burden of maintenance and risk of loss on the lessee. Usually the term of a finance lease approaches the useful life of the asset being leased, and the lease rents are sufficient to recover to the lessor the cost of the asset. See also capital lease; net lease. Section 209(a) of the Tax Equity and Fiscal Responsibility Act of 1982 introduced the term into the Internal Revenue Code; in the case of a lease entered into after December 31, 1983, covering equipment meeting the definition of "finance lease property," the fact that the lessee has the right to purchase the leased property at a fixed price that is not less than ten percent of the original cost thereof or that the property is of a type not readily usable by other than the lessee ("limited use property") shall not be taken into account in determining whether such agreement is a lease. I.R.C. § 168(f)(8)(A). See finance lease property.

Finance lease property: Amendments to the Internal Revenue Code made by the Tax Equity and Fiscal Responsibility Act of 1982 provide for special treatment of leases of "finance lease property." See finance lease. In general, "finance lease property" is new section 38 property leased within three months after having been placed in service. I.R.C. § 168(f)(8)(B); *see also* I.R.C. § 168(f)(8)(C).

Financial Accounting Standards Board:

The Financial Accounting Standards Board (the "Standards Board" or the "Board" or the "FASB") is an independent body created within the private sector to serve an important public interest. Its principal purpose is to issue Statements of Financial Accounting Standards designed to establish or improve standards of financial accounting and reporting for the guidance and education of the public, including issuers, attestors and users of financial information, investors, creditors, educators, and government. Financial Accounting Standards Board *Rules of Procedure.*

Financial futures: Contracts for future delivery of money market instruments. *See generally* M. Stigum, *Money Market Calculations: Yields, Break-Evens, and Arbitrage* 151 (1981).

Financial institution: Institution that uses its funds chiefly to purchase financial assets, such as deposits, loans, bonds, and other securities, as opposed to tangible property. Financial institutions may be depositary institutions, such as commercial banks, savings banks, and credit unions, or nondepository institutions, such as insurance companies and pension funds.

Financial Institutions Regulatory and Interest Rate Control Act of 1978: Federal legislation involving a variety of banking matters, including electronic fund transfer and federal charters for state mutual savings banks. Pub. L. No. 95-630, 92 Stat. 3641 (1978).

Financial position: State or status of assets or claims to assets at a given time. Financial Accounting Standards Board, Statement of Financial Accounting Concepts No. 3, *Elements of Financial Statements of Business Enterprises,* paragraph 14, n. 6 (1980). Compare changes in financial position.

Financial statements: Balance sheets, income statements or profit and loss accounts, statements of changes in financial position, notes, and other statements and explanatory materials that are identified as being part of the financial statements. International Accounting Standards Committee, *Preface to Statements of International Accounting Standards,* paragraph 5 (1978).

Financing agency: Under Article 2 of the Uniform Commercial Code–Sales, a financing agency is a bank or other financial institution that participates in sales transactions as a financing entity or intermediary in respect of devices used to facilitate sales transactions, such as bills of lading:

"Financing agency" means a bank, finance company or other person who in the ordinary course of business makes advances against goods or documents of title or who by arrangements with either the seller or the buyer intervenes in ordinary course to make or collect payment due or claimed under the contract for sale, as by purchasing or paying the seller's draft or making advances against it or merely by taking it for collection whether or not documents of title accompany the draft. "Financing agency" includes also a bank or other person who similarly intervenes between persons who are in the position of buyer and seller in respect to the goods (Section 2-707).

UCC Section 2-104.

Financing statement: Document filed in a public office in order to perfect a security interest in certain kinds of personal property under Article 9 of the Uniform Commercial Code–Secured Transactions. A security agreement may be filed as a financing statement, but the usual financing statement is a special printed form, approved by the secretary of state of the state in question, which when properly filled in will have the names and addresses of the debtor,

the secured party, and any assignee of the secured party, and a description of the collateral, and is signed by the debtor (and by the secured party, in states that still use the 1962 version of Article 9). *See* UCC Section 9-402.

FIRICA: Financial Institutions Regulatory and Interest Rate Control Act of 1978.

Firm commitment underwriting: Arrangement for the underwriting of an issue of securities whereby the underwriter or underwriting group agrees to purchase the entire issue, thus bearing the risk of resale. Compare **best-efforts underwriting.**

FIRPA: Foreign Investment in United States Real Property Act of 1980.

First deed of trust: First mortgage; see trust deed.

First in, first out: Accounting rule that presumes that merchandise or inventory is used or sold in the order that it was acquired. Compare **last in, first out.**

First mortgage: Mortgage with priority over other mortgages on a given piece of property.

FISC: Foreign international sales corporation. *See* I.R.C. § 993(e). See also **DISC.**

Fiscal agent: Agent of a corporation or municipality authorized to handle payments under a given issue of securities.

Fiscal policy: Government policy regarding taxation and spending, executed by Congress and the executive branch. Compare **monetary policy.**

Fiscal year: Twelve-month period designated as a year for accounting purposes. A fiscal year need not correspond to a calendar year; the term is sometimes used to denote a twelve-month period that does not correspond to a calendar year. Under the Internal Revenue Code the term "fiscal year" means "an accounting period of twelve months ending on the last day of any month other than December." I.R.C. § 7701(a)(24). *See also* Regulation S-X, 17 C.F.R. § 210.1-02(k).

Fisher effect: Effect of anticipated inflation on interest rates, identified by Irving Fisher in the book *Appreciation and Interest* in 1898.

Fishing expedition: Unwarranted use by the Federal Trade Commission of the right of access to the records of a corporation under section 9 of the Federal Trade Commission Act, 15 U.S.C. § 49. "Anyone who respects the spirit as well as the letter of Fourth Amendment would be loath to believe that Congress intended to authorize one of its subordinate agencies to sweep all our traditions into the fire ... and to direct fishing expeditions into private papers on the possibility that they may disclose evidence of crime." Justice Holmes in *FTC v. American Tobacco Co.,* 264 U.S. 298, 307 (1924). *See United States v. Morton Salt Co.,* 338 U.S. 632 (1950); American Bar Association, Section of Antitrust Law, *Antitrust Law Developments* 217 (1975). The term is also used to describe other types of random searches without specificity as to matters being investigated; *e.g., Nodana Petroleum Corp. v. State ex rel Brennan,* 123 A. 2d 243 (Del. Supr. 1956).

Fixed assets: Property, plant, and equipment.

Fixed charges: Expenses occurring on a regular basis. Fixed charges always include interest payments on long-term debt, and may include lease rents and depreciation charges. For the purpose of calculating the ratio of earnings to fixed charges in a prospectus:

The term "fixed charges" shall mean the total of (A) interest, whether expensed or capitalized; (B) amortization of debt expense and discount or premium relating to any indebtedness, whether expensed or capitalized; (C) such portion of rental expenses can be demonstrated to be representative of the interest factor in the particular case; and (D) preferred stock dividend requirements of majority-owned subsidiaries, excluding in all cases items which would be or are eliminated in consolidation.

SEC Regulation S-K, Item 503(d)(4).

Fixed-income: 1. When used to describe securities, bearing a fixed rate of interest or dividends. 2. When used to describe people, depending on investments in fixed-income securities or pension plans with benefits fixed at a dollar rate, and thus subject to erosion of income by inflation.

Fixture: Item of personal property that becomes attached or related to real property in such a way as to become subject to interests in the real property. *See* UCC Section 9-313; Kripke, *Fix-*

tures under the Uniform Commercial Code, 64 Colum. L. Rev. 44 (1964). *See also Holt v. Henley,* 232 U.S. 637 (1914).

Fixture filing: The filing of a financing statement pursuant to Article 9 of the Uniform Commercial Code —Secured Transactions, in respect of goods that are or are to become fixtures, in the office where interests in real property would be filed or recorded. *See* UCC Section 9-313.

Flat: 1. With respect to the price of a bond or other debt security, not including accrued interest. 2. With respect to interest, calculated for the duration of the loan and then added to principal, with periodic payments being calculated by dividing the total of principal and interest by the number of payments. This method disregards the repayment or amortization of principal. Also called add-on.

Fleet mortgage: Preferred mortgage on a fleet of vessels. *See* Ship Mortgage Act, 1920, subsection D, subdivision (f), 46 U.S.C. § 922(f). *See The Emma Giles,* 15 F. Supp. 502 (D. Md. 1936).

Float: Money that is represented by a check that has been negotiated, before that check clears. For a period of time, until clearance, that amount may appear on the books of both the check writer and the check receiver, due to the lag in the check collection process.

Floating lien: Lien or security interest that attaches to property as it comes into the possession of the debtor. *See* UCC Section 9-204.

Floating rate: Interest rate on a debt instrument that is changed from time to time to conform to the prevailing market rate.

Floating rate CD: Term certificate of deposit bearing an interest rate that is subject to periodic adjustment by the issuer, usually every six months.

Floating-rate note: Note bearing an interest rate that is subject to adjustment by the issuer, usually every six months. Floating-rate notes are issued in the Eurocurrency markets, bearing interest at an agreed level above the London Interbank Offered Rate (LIBOR).

Floor broker: Broker conducting business at a stock or commodities exchange. Section 2 of the Commodity Exchange Act defines a floor broker as "any person who, in or surrounding any 'pit', 'ring', 'post', or other place provided by a contract market for the meeting of persons similarly engaged, shall purchase or sell for any other person any commodity for future delivery on or subject to the rules of any contract market." 7 U.S.C. § 2.

Flooring contract: Security interest in a dealer's inventory, pursuant to a "floor plan" financing arrangement.

Floor plan: Financing arrangement for a dealer's inventory whereby the financing agency takes a security interest in that inventory, but the interest is released, item by item, as the inventory is sold. The term was coined for use in financing automobile dealers' inventories—the automobiles on the showroom floor—but now is used for inventory financing arrangements for other types of businesses.

Flower bond: Estate tax bond.

Flow-through method: Method of accounting for the investment tax credit by treating it as an increase in net income in the year that it arises, instead of reflecting the credit in net income over the productive life of the property. *See* American Institute of Certified Public Accountants, Accounting Principles Board Opinion No. 4, *Accounting for the Investment Credit* (1964).

FMC: Federal Maritime Commission.

FmHA: Farmers Home Administration.

F.O.B.: Free on board; delivery term for contracts for the sale of goods, establishing the point at which the risk of loss is transferred. Under Article 2 of the Uniform Commercial Code–Sales:

(a) when the term is F.O.B. the place of shipment, the seller must at that place ship the goods in the manner provided in this Article (Section 2-504) and bear the expense and risk of putting them into the hands of the carrier; or

(b) when the term is F.O.B. the place of destination, the seller must at his own expense and risk transport the goods to that place and there tender delivery of them in the manner provided in this Article (Section 2-503);

(c) when under either (a) or (b) the term is also F.O.B. vessel, car or other vehicle, the seller must in addition at his own expense and risk load the goods on board. If the term is F.O.B. vessel the buyer must name the vessel and in an appropriate case the seller must comply with the pro-

visions of this Article on the form of bill of lading (Section 2-323).

UCC Section 2-319.

FOIA: Freedom of Information Act.

Food and Drug Administration: Branch of the United States Department of Health and Human Services responsible for enforcing the Federal Food, Drug, and Cosmetic Act, regulating the sale and labeling of foods, drugs, and cosmetics. *See* 21 U.S.C. §§ 301–92, 451–70, 601–95, 1031–56.

Foods, Bureau of: Unit of the Food and Drug Administration responsible for FDA activities with respect to food and cosmetics.

Footing error: Error in the addition of a column of figures or other calculation in a document, usually in favor of the party preparing the document and not accidental. When and if the error is discovered, the defense of the party preparing the document to a charge of fraud is that the figures used to make the calculation, shown in the document, are accurate and the incorrect total is only a "footing error." See **mathematical or clerical error.**

Force majeure: Superior or irresistible force that in some circumstances excuses delay in performance of a contract. A force majeure clause might enumerate such forces, such as riots, strikes, civil commotion, flood, fire, acts of God, etc. *See Restatement, Second, Contracts* § 261 (1981); UCC Section 2-615; Squillante & Congalton, *Force Majeure,* 80 Comm. L. J. 4 (1975). In connection with delays in bank collections, *see* UCC Section 4-108. See also impracticable.

Foreclose: To divest a debtor of possession of property subject to a mortgage, security interest, or lien.

Foreign: For the purpose of the Internal Revenue Code, "foreign," when applied to a corporation or partnership, means a "corporation or partnership which is not domestic." I.R.C. § 7701(a)(5). See domestic.

Foreign Assistance Act of 1973: Federal legislation providing for foreign aid. Pub. L. No. 93-189, 87 Stat. 714 (1973); 22 U.S.C. §§ 2151–2784. *See* Grant, *The Foreign Economic Assistance Program,* in II W. Surrey & D. Wallace, Jr., ed., *A Lawyer's Guide to International Business Transactions* 195 (2d ed. 1979).

Foreign bonds: Debt obligations issued and denominated in the currency of the country of issue by a nonresident issuer. Foreign bonds are different from Eurobonds in that foreign bonds are regulated by the country in which they are issued, whereas Eurobonds, denominated in another currency, are not.

Foreign Claims Settlement Commission of the United States: Separate agency within the United States Department of Justice that determines claims of United States nationals against foreign governments. *See* the International Claims Settlement Act of 1949, Pub. L. No. 454, ch. 53, 64 Stat. 12 (1949), 22 U.S.C. §§ 1621–44; the War Claims Act of 1948, Pub. L. No. 896, ch. 826, 62 Stat.

1240 (1948), 50 U.S.C. App. §§ 2001–16.

Foreign corporation: Corporation organized under the laws of another jurisdiction. Del. Code Ann. tit. 8 § 371(a); N.Y. Bus. Corp. Law. § 102(a)(7); Model Business Corporation Act § 2(b); Cal. Corp. Code § 171.

Foreign Corrupt Practices Act: Federal statute amending the Securities Exchange Act of 1934 to prohibit corporations subject to that act from making certain payments to foreign officials and other foreign persons, and making certain changes in record-keeping requirements. Pub. L. No. 95-213, 91 Stat. 1494 (1977); *see* S. Rep. No. 95-114, 95th Cong., 1st Sess. (1977); H.R. Rep. No. 95-640, 95th Cong., 1st Sess. (1977); 17 C.F.R. § 674; Gareis, *The Corrupt Practices Act,* 14 Int'l Law. 377 (1980); Baker, *Accounting and Accountability: Overview of the Accounting Provisions of the Foreign Corrupt Practices Act of 1977,* 36 Wash. & Lee L. Rev. 809 (1979); *A Guide to the New Section 13(b)(2) Accounting Requirements of the Securities Exchange Act of 1934 (Section 102 of the Foreign Corrupt Practices Act of 1977),* 34 Bus. Law. 307 (1978).

Foreign Credit Insurance Association: Association of commercial insurance companies formed by the Eximbank and the insurance industry to provide credit protection for United States exporters. Policies issued by the FCIA insure repayment in the event of default by a foreign buyer. *See* Linzmeyer, *Eximbank Exporter Assistance Programs,* 60 Marq. L. Rev. 825 (1977).

Foreign currency translation: Process of expressing amounts denominated or measured in one currency in terms of another currency by use of the exchange rate. *See* Financial Accounting Standards Board, Statement of Financial Accounting Standards No. 8, *Accounting for the Translation of Foreign Currency Transactions and Foreign Currency Financial Statements* (1975).

Foreign Exchange Desk: Foreign currency trading desk at the New York Federal Reserve Bank. This desk trades in the foreign currency market for the account of the Federal Open Market Committee as agent for the United States Treasury; and as agent for foreign central banks.

Foreign exchange rate: Number of units of one currency needed to purchase a unit of another currency; the value of one currency in terms of another.

Foreign exchange transaction: Purchase or sale of one currency with another, or trading in currencies.

Foreign personal holding company: Foreign corporation, of which 50% of the stock is owned by not more than five United States citizens, that derives at least 60% (50% after the first taxable year) of its income from "foreign personal holding company income," which consists of dividends, gains from securities and commodities transactions, estates and trusts, personal service contracts, use of corporate property by shareholders, and rents. I.R.C. §§ 552, 553. United States shareholders are subject to tax in undistributed as well as distributed income from a foreign personal holding company. I.R.C. §§ 551–58.

Foreign tax credit: Credit to United States income taxes for foreign taxes paid. I.R.C. §§ 33, 901–8.

Foreign trade: As defined in the Merchant Marine Act, 1936, "foreign trade" means trade between the United States and a foreign country, but in the case of liquid and dry bulk cargo vessels, for the purpose of the Title XI financing guaranties, Title V construction-differential subsidies, and the use of capital construction funds under the Title VI operating-differential subsidy program, "foreign trade" includes trade between foreign ports, without any requirement for a connection with the United States. Section 905, 46 U.S.C. § 1244; section 1104, 46 U.S.C. § 1274.

Foreign trade organization: Organization established in the Soviet Union and Eastern European countries with exclusive authority to handle export-import transactions involving specified groups of commodities.

Forest Service: Unit of the United States Department of Agriculture responsible for the management of the forest reserves of the United States.

Form 1-A: Form of offering statement filed with the Securities and Exchange Commission in connection with an offering of securities in a transaction exempt from registration under Regulation A. 17 C.F.R. §§ 230.251–64.

Form 8-A: Form for registration of certain classes of securities with the Securities and Exchange Commission pursuant to section 12(b) or 12(g) of the Securities Exchange Act of 1934. 17 C.F.R. § 249.208a.

Form 8-B: Form for registration of securities of certain successor issuers with the Securities and Exchange Commission pursuant to section 12(b) or 12(g) of the Securities Exchange Act of 1934. 17 C.F.R. § 249.208b.

Form 8-K: Form of report required to be filed with the Securities and Exchange Commission pursuant to the Securities Exchange Act of 1934 upon the occurrence of change of control, acquisition or disposition of significant amount of assets, bankruptcy, change in certifying accountant, or other materially important event. 17 C.F.R. § 249.308. *See* SEC Release 34-18524, 47 Fed. Reg. 11380, 11471 (1982). *See also* 17 C.F.R. § 240.13a-11, 17 C.F.R. § 240.15d-11.

Form 10: Form of registration statement filed with the Securities and Exchange Commission pursuant to section 12(b) or 12(g) of the Securities Exchange Act of 1934, for which no other form is prescribed. 17 C.F.R. § 249.210. See **Form 8-A; Form 8-B.**

Form 10-K: Form of annual report required to be filed with the Securities and Exchange Commission pursuant to the Securities Exchange Act of 1934. 17 C.F.R. § 249.308a. *See* SEC Release 34-18524, 47 Fed. Reg. 11380, 11472 (1982).

Form 10-Q: Form of quarterly report required to be filed with the Securities and Exchange Commission pursuant to

the Securities Exchange Act of 1934. 17 C.F.R. § 249.308a. *See* SEC Release 34-18524, 47 Fed. Reg. 11380, 11472 (1982); SEC Release No. 33-6288, 46 Fed. Reg. 12480 (1981). *See also* 17 C.F.R. § 240.13a-13, 17 C.F.R. § 240.15d-13.

Form 11-K: Form of annual report of employee stock purchase, savings, and similar plans required to be filed with the Securities and Exchange Commission pursuant to section 15(d) of the Securities Exchange Act of 1934. 17 C.F.R. § 249.311, 249.15d-21. *See* SEC Release 34-17117 (1980).

Form N-1: Form of registration statement under the Securities Act of 1933 under section 8(b) of the Investment Company Act of 1940 for open-end management investment companies. 17 C.F.R. § 274.11.

Form N-2: Form of registration statement under the Securities Act of 1933 under section 8(b) of the Investment Company Act of 1940 for closed-end management investment companies. 17 C.F.R. § 274.11a.

Form S-1: Form of registration statement under the Securities Act of 1933 requiring the most complete disclosure, and permitting no incorporation by reference of other materials. This form must be used by registrants that have been reporting under the Securities Exchange Act of 1934 for less than three years, and may be used by others. 17 C.F.R. § 239.11, SEC Release No. 33-6383, 47 Fed. Reg. 11380, 11449 (1982).

Form S-2: Form of registration statement under the Securities Act of 1933 which combines reliance on incorporating reports under the Securities Exchange Act of 1934 by reference with delivery to investors of streamlined information of the type included in form 10-K. The use of this form is available to registrants that have been reporting under the Securities Exchange Act of 1934 for three years or more. 17 C.F.R. § 239.12, SEC Release No. 33-6383, 47 Fed. Reg. 11380, 11451 (1982).

Form S-3: Form of registration statement under the Securities Act of 1933 that allows maximum use of incorporation by reference of reports under the Securities Exchange Act of 1934. 17 C.F.R. § 239.13, SEC Release No. 33-6383, 47 Fed. Reg. 11380, 11453 (1982).

Form S-6: Form of registration statement under the Securities Act of 1933 for unit investment trusts registered under the Investment Company Act of 1940 on form N-8B-2. 17 C.F.R. § 239.16.

Form S-8: Form of registration statement under the Securities Act of 1933 for securities to be offered to employees pursuant to certain plans. 17 C.F.R. 239.16b. *See* SEC Release No. 33-5767, 41 Fed. Reg. 52662 (1976).

Form S-11: Form of registration statement under the Securities Act of 1933 for securities of certain real estate companies. 17 C.F.R. § 239.18

Form S-14: Form of simplified registration statement under the Securities Act of 1933 for securities issued in certain transactions under Rules 133 and 145, 17 C.F.R. §§ 230.133, 230.145. 17 C.F.R. § 239.23

Form S-15: Optional form of registration statement under the Securities Act of 1933 for securities offered in certain mergers and exchange offers. 17 C.F.R. § 239.29.

Form S-18: Form of registration statement under the Securities Act of 1933 for securities offered by certain issuers in an aggregate offering price of $5,000,000 or less. 17 C.F.R. § 239.28. *See* SEC Release Nos. 33-6287 (1981), 33-6299 (1981).

Form T-1: Statement as to eligibility and qualification of a corporate trustee under the Trust Indenture Act of 1939.

Forsham: *Forsham v. Harris,* 445 U.S. 169 (1980), significant case on the limits of availability of materials under the Freedom of Information Act.

Forward: At a future time.

Forward contract: Contract for delivery or execution at a future time. Forward contracts are similar to futures contracts, but are transactions between two parties rather than standardized contracts traded in the futures markets. Because of their commercial rather than investment nature, forward contracts are not subject to regulation under the Commodity Exchange Act. *See* Financial Accounting Standards Board, Technical Bulletin re APB Opinion No. 22, *Disclosure of Interest Rate Futures Contracts and Forward and Standby Contracts* (1981).

Forward exchange contract: Agreement to exchange at a specified future date currencies of different countries at a specified rate. A forward exchange contract may be used to hedge a foreign currency commitment. Financial Accounting Standards Board, Statement of Financial Accounting Standards No. 8, *Accounting for the Translation of Foreign Currency Transactions and Foreign Currency Financial Statements,* paragraph 22 (1975).

Forward rate: Exchange rate specified in a forward exchange contract.

Four R Act: Railroad Revitalization and Regulatory Reform Act of 1976.

FPR: Federal Procurement Regulation. 41 C.F.R. §§ 1-1–1-30.

FRA: Federal Railroad Administration.

Fractional share: Interest in a corporation that is less than a whole share. *See* Model Business Corporation Act § 24 (1979).

Franchise: Freedom from a restriction; thus a privilege of doing business in a particular jurisdiction or privilege of engaging in a certain type of business granted by an entity in a position to prohibit or restrict that business. A government agency may grant a franchise for a certain type of business in its jurisdiction, or a corporation may grant a franchise to another corporation or individual to use its name and business practices. California has a Franchise Investment Law, which defines a franchise as a contract by which:

(a) A franchisee is granted the right to engage in the business of offering, selling, or distributing goods or services under a marketing plan or system prescribed in substantial part by a franchisor; and

(b) The operation of the franchisee's business pursuant to such plan or system is substantially associated with the franchisor's trademark, service mark, trade name, logotype, advertising or other commercial symbol designating the franchisor or its affiliate; and

(c) The franchisee is required to pay, directly or indirectly, a franchise fee.

Cal. Corp. Code § 31005; see §§ 31000–420. See Financial Accounting Standards Board, Statement of Financial Accounting Standards No. 45, *Accounting for Franchise Fee Revenue,* Appendix A (1981); Fern, *The Overboard Scope of Franchise Regulation: A Definitional Dilemma,* 34 Bus. Law. 1387 (1979). See also **franchise disclosure rule.**

Franchise disclosure rule: Regulation of the Federal Trade Commission imposing disclosure requirements on offerors of franchise situations. Final Guides to the Franchising and Business Opportunity Ventures Trade Regulation Rule, 44 Fed. Reg. 49966 (1979). *See generally* Black, *New Federal Trade Commission Franchise Disclosure Rule: Application to Distributorship Arrangements,* 35 Bus. Law. 409 (1980).

Franchisee: Person to whom a franchise is granted. Cal. Corp. Code § 31006.

Franchise tax: Tax payable in respect of the right to do business in a jurisdiction. *See* Model Business Corporation Act §§ 132, 133 (1979).

Franchisor: Person who grants a franchise. Cal. Corp. Code § 31007.

Fraudulent: In connection with contracts, a misrepresentation is "fraudulent"

if the maker intends his assertion to induce a party to manifest his assent and the maker

(a) knows or believes that the assertion is not in accord with the facts, or

(b) does not have the confidence that he states or implies in the truth of the assertion, or

(c) knows that he does not have the basis that he states or implies for the assertion.

Restatement, Second, Contracts § 162 (1981). *See Restatement, Second, Torts* § 526 (1977). See also material.

Fraudulent conveyance: A conveyance or transfer of property against the interests of a third party with a claim against that property. *See Twyne's case,* 3 Co. Rep. 80b, 76 Eng. Rep. 809 (Star Chamber, 1601); Statute of 13 Elizabeth, ch. 5 (1570). A conveyance of personal property without transfer of possession is regarded as a fraudulent conveyance in some jurisdictions, unless a notice is filed in a public office. *See, e.g.,* Cal. Civ. Code § 3440. See fraudulent transfer.

Fraudulent transfer: Under the Bankruptcy Code a fraudulent transfer or obligation is one that was made or incurred on or within one year before the filing of the petition in bankruptcy, if the debtor:

(1) made such transfer or incurred such obligation with actual intent to hinder, delay, or defraud any entity to which the debtor was or became, on or after the date that such transfer occurred or such obligation was incurred, indebted; or

(2) (A) received less than a reasonably equivalent value in exchange for such transfer or obligation; and

(B) (i) was insolvent on the date that such transfer was made or such obligation was incurred, or became insolvent as a result of such transfer or obligation; (ii) was engaged in business, or was about to engage in business or a transaction, for which any property remaining with the debtor was unreasonably small capital; or (iii) intended to incur, or believed that the debtor would incur, debt that would be beyond the debtor's ability to pay as such debts matured.

11 U.S.C. § 548(a). The trustee in bankruptcy may avoid any such transfer or obligation. *See* H.R. Rep. No. 95-595, 95th Cong., 1st Sess. 375 (1977); Cook, *Fraudulent Transfer Liability Under the Bankruptcy Code,* 17 Hous. L. Rev. 263 (1980). See also fraudulent conveyance.

FRCD: Floating rate certificate of deposit. See floating rate CD.

Freddie Mac: Federal Home Loan Mortgage Corporation, or a mortgage-backed security of that agency.

Freedom of Information Act: Federal law requiring agencies of the United States government to make certain information available to the public. Pub. L. No. 89-554, 80 Stat. 378, 383 (1966), 5 U.S.C. § 552. *See A Citizen's Guide on How to Use the Freedom of Information Act and the Privacy Act in Re-*

questing Government Documents, H.R. Rep. No. 95-793, 95th Cong., 1st Sess. (1977).

Free trade area: Group of countries that have eliminated duties and other trade restrictions among themselves, but retain individual tariffs and restrictions for trade with nonmembers. *See* General Agreement on Tariff and Trade, Article XXIV. Compare customs union.

Freeze-out: Statutory merger, sale of assets to an affiliated corporation, or share consolidation, with the intention (or result) of eliminating the interests of certain minority shareholders. Also called squeeze-out and cash-out merger. *See* F. O'Neal, *"Squeeze-outs" of Minority Shareholders: Expulsion or Oppression of Business Associates* (1975); Brudney & Chirelstein, *A Restatement of Corporate Freezeouts,* 87 Yale L. J. 1354 (1978); Elfin, *Changing Standards and the Future Course of Freezeout Mergers,* 5 J. Corporation L. 261 (1980).

Freezing: See blocking.

Freight conference agreement: See conference agreement.

"F" reorganization: Change in identity, form, or place of reorganization of one corporation. I.R.C. § 368(a); section 225 of the Tax Equity and Fiscal Responsibility Act of 1982. See reorganization.

FRN: Floating-rate note.

FSLIC: Federal Savings and Loan Insurance Corporation.

FSS: Federal Supply Service.

FTC: Federal Trade Commission.

FTO: Foreign trade organization

Full-cost method: Method of accounting for oil and gas activities in which costs that cannot be directly related to the discovery of specific oil and gas reserves are carried forward to future periods as costs of oil and gas reserves generally, instead of being charged to expense. Financial Accounting Standards Board, Statement of Financial Accounting Standards No. 19, *Financial Accounting and Reporting by Oil and Gas Producing Companies,* paragraphs 102, 104–10 (1977). *See* SEC Regulation S-X, 17 C.F.R. § 210.4-10(i); SEC Accounting Series Release No. 253, 43 Fed. Reg. 40688 (1978). Compare **successful efforts method.**

Full faith and credit: Phrase denoting the undertaking of any entity to honor an obligation fully; state statutes and municipal bond resolutions often use this phrase to signify that the state or municipal agency is fully bound on a particular obligation, and federal statutes providing for government guaranties use the phrase to signify the highest obligation of the United States. *E.g.,* section 1103(d) of the Merchant Marine Act, 1936, 46 U.S.C. § 1273(d). *See Seward v. Bowers,* 37 N.M. 385, 391 (1933). The phrase also appears in the United States Constitution (Art. IV, section 1) in connection with the obligation of the states to honor the acts of other states. *See* D. Melinkoff, *The Language of the Law* 348 (1963).

Full-payout lease: As defined by the Comptroller of the Currency, a "full-payout lease" is one in which the lessor expects to realize the return of its full investment in the property plus the cost of financing over the term of the lease from the rentals, the tax benefits, and the estimated residual value at the end of the lease term (not exceeding 25% of the original cost). 12 C.F.R. § 7.3400.

Full recourse: In connection with the assignment of an account or obligation, meaning that the assignee has recourse against the assignor for full payment of the obligation if the obligor defaults.

Full warranty: Under the Magnuson-Moss Warranty–Federal Trade Commission Improvement Act, a warranty designated as "full" must be a written warranty meeting the standards of section 104 of the Act, i.e., such warranty must provide a remedy for a product defect, may not limit the duration of implied warranties, must show conspicuously any limitations on consequential damages, and must provide for a replacement or refund if the product cannot be repaired after a reasonable number of attempts. 15 U.S.C. §§ 2303, 2304. *See generally* Popper, *The New Federal Warranty Law: A Guide to Compliance*, 32 Bus. Law. 399 (1977).

Fully diluted earnings per share: As defined by the Accounting Principles Board of the American Institute of Certified Public Accountants:

The amount of current earnings per share reflecting the maximum dilution that would have resulted from conversions, exercises, and other contingent issuances that individually would have decreased earnings per share and in the aggregate would have a dilutive effect. All such issuances are assumed to have taken place at the beginning of the period (or at the time the contingency arose, if later).

American Institute of Certified Public Accountants, Accounting Principles Board Opinion No. 15, *Earnings per Share,* Appendix D, paragraph 14 (1968).

Fully paid: As used in opinions of counsel with respect to stock, "fully paid" means that the consideration established by the corporate action authorizing the issuance of the stock and the corporate agreements in connection therewith was sufficient under law and the certificate of incorporation, and has been paid in full. *Legal Opinions to Third Parties: An Easier Path,* 34 Bus. Law. 1891, 1911 (1979).

Functional discount: Discount or price reduction given a customer in exchange for the customer's assumption of certain functions related to distribution. As to the antitrust aspects of functional discounts, *see, e.g., National Parts Warehouse,* 63 F.T.C. 1692 (1963), *aff'd sub nom. General Auto Supplies, Inc. v. FTC,* 346 F. 2d 311 (7th Cir.), *petition for cert. dismissed,* 382 U.S. 923 (1965); *see generally* American Bar Association, Section of Antitrust Law, *Antitrust Law Developments* 125 (1975); Calvani, *Functional Discounts under the Robinson-Patman Act,* 17 B.C. Ind. & Com. L. Rev. 543 (1976).

Funded debt: Long-term debt of a corporation or municipality. The term usually excludes debt falling due within one year.

Funds statement: Statement of source and application of funds.

Fungible: Consisting of indistinguishable units, so that one may be used to discharge an obligation for another, as grain of a given grade, or oil of a given type. Fungible goods are dealt with by weight or other measure, rather than by identification of specific units or items. Under the Uniform Commercial Code, fungible "with respect to goods or securities means goods or securities of which any unit is, by nature or usage of trade, the equivalent of any other like unit. Goods which are not fungible shall be deemed fungible for the purpose of this Act to the extent that under a particular agreement or document unlike units are treated as equivalents." UCC Section 1-201(17).

FUTA: Federal Unemployment Tax.

Future goods: Under Article 2 of the Uniform Commercial Code–Sales, goods must be both existing and identified before any interest in them can pass. Goods that are not both existing and identified are "future goods"; a purported present sale of future goods is regarded as a contract to sell. UCC Section 2-105.

Futures commission merchant: As defined in section 2 of the Commodity Exchange Act, the term "futures commission merchant" includes "individuals, associations, partnerships, corporations, and trusts engaged in soliciting or in accepting orders for the purchase or sale of any commodity for future delivery on or subject to the rules of any contract market and that, in or in connection with such solicitation or acceptance of orders, accepts any money, securities, or property (or extends credit in lieu thereof) to margin, guarantee, or secure any trades or contracts that result or may result therefrom." 7 U.S.C. § 2.

Futures contract: Contract for the future delivery of a commodity. *See* H.R. Rep. No. 93-975, 93d Cong., 2d Sess. 130 (1974). See also **Commodity Futures Trading Commission.**

G

GAAP: Generally accepted accounting principles.

GAAS: Generally accepted auditing standards.

Gain: Increase in value, as distinguished from income. As defined by the Financial Accounting Standards Board, "Gains are increases in equity (net assets) from peripheral or incidental transactions of an entity and from all other transactions and other events and circumstances affecting the entity during a period except those that result from revenues or investments by owners." Financial Accounting Standards Board, Statement of Financial Accounting Concepts No. 3, *Elements of Financial Statements of Business Enterprises,* paragraph 67 (1980).

GAO: General Accounting Office.

GATT: General Agreement on Tariffs and Trade.

GCM: General Counsel's Memorandum, an internal document of the Internal Revenue Service.

G-DEST license: License for the export of any commodity to any country for which a validated license is not required. 15 C.F.R. § 371.3.

GEM: Growing equity mortgage.

General Accounting Office: Independent agency in the legislative branch of the United States government with responsibility for legal, accounting, auditing, and claims settlement functions with respect to federal government programs and operations. The GAO was created by the Budget and Accounting Act, 1921 (31 U.S.C. §§ 41–46), and its duties have been extended by the Government Corporation Control Act (31 U.S.C. § 841–69), the Legislative Reorganization Act of 1946 (31 U.S.C. § 60), the Accounting and Auditing Act of 1950 (31 U.S.C. § 65–67), the Legislative Reorganization Act of 1970 (31 U.S.C. § 1151–57), the Congressional Budget and Impoundment Control Act of 1974 (31 U.S.C. § 1301–53), and the General Accounting Act of 1974 (31 U.S.C.§ 52c). The Office is headed by the

Comptroller General of the United States.

General Agreement on Tariffs and Trade: International agreement establishing a general code of conduct for trade and providing a mechanism for resolving disputes. *See* Jackson, *The General Agreement on Tariffs and Trade,* in I. W. Surrey & D. Wallace, Jr., ed., *A Lawyer's Guide to International Business Transactions* 37 (1977).

General average: System of compensating the owners of cargo that was jettisoned at sea to save the vessel, out of the value of the cargo that was saved. *See* G. Gilmore & C. Black, Jr., *The Law of Admiralty* 244 (2d ed. 1975).

General intangible: Under Article 9 of the Uniform Commercial Code—Secured Transactions, "general intangibles" are "any personal property (including things in action) other than goods, accounts, chattel paper, documents, instruments, and money." UCC Section 9-106.

Generalized preferences: System of providing trade preferences to developing countries, modifying the most-favored-nation concept of trade equality. *See* Trade Act of 1974, 19 U.S.C. §§ 2461–65.

Generally accepted accounting principles: As defined by the Accounting Principles Board of the American Institute of Certified Public Accountants:

Generally accepted accounting principles incorporate the consensus at a particular time as to which economic resources and obligations should be recorded as assets and liabilities by financial accounting, which changes in assets and liabilities should be recorded, when these changes should be recorded, how the assets and liabilities and changes in them should be measured, what information should be disclosed and how it should be disclosed, and which financial statements should be prepared.

American Institute of Certified Public Accountants, Accounting Principles Board Statement No. 4, Ch. 6, *Generally Accepted Accounting Principles—Pervasive Principles,* paragraph 1 (1970). The American Institute of Certified Public Accountants Special Committee on Opinions of the Accounting Principles Board has defined "generally accepted accounting principles" as those having "substantial authoritative support"; the latter term has definitional problems of its own: *see* Armstrong, *Some Thoughts on Substantial Authoritative Support,* J. of Accountancy, April 1969, at 44. *See also* SEC Accounting Series Release No. 4, 11 Fed. Reg. 10913 (1938).

Generally accepted auditing standards: As set forth by the American Institute of Certified Public Accountants:

General Standards

1. The examination is to be performed by a person or persons having adequate technical training and proficiency as an auditor.

2. In all matters relating to the assignment, an independence in mental attitude is to be maintained by the auditor or auditors.

3. Due professional care is to be exercised in the performance of the examination and the preparation of the report.

Standards of Field Work

1. The work is to be adequately planned and assistants, if any, are to be properly supervised.

2. There is to be a proper study and evaluation of the existing internal control as a basis for reliance thereon and for the determination of the resultant extent of the tests to which auditing procedures are to be restricted.

3. Sufficient competent evidential matter is to be obtained through inspection, observation, inquiries, and confirmations to afford a reasonable basis for an opinion regarding the financial statements under examination.

Standards of Reporting

1. The report shall state whether the financial statements are presented in accordance with generally accepted accounting principles.

2. The report shall state whether such principles have been consistently observed in the current period in relation to the preceding period.

3. Informative disclosures in the financial statements are to be regarded as reasonably adequate unless otherwise stated in the report.

4. The report shall either contain an expression of opinion regarding the financial statements, taken as a whole, or an assertion to the effect that an opinion cannot be expressed. When an overall opinion cannot be expressed, the reasons therefor should be stated. In all cases where an auditor's name is associated with financial statements, the report should contain a clear-cut indication of the character of the auditor's examination, if any, and the degree of responsibility he is taking.

American Institute of Certified Public Accountants, Statement on Auditing Standards No. 1, Codification of Auditing Standards and Procedures, section 150, *Generally Accepted Auditing Standards*, paragraph 2 (1972).

General mortgage: Mortgage on substantially all of the property of an entity. Railroads and utilities often have general mortgages to secure bond issues.

General obligation bond: Bond issued by a business or government entity that constitutes a general obligation of that entity, not limited to specific sources of revenue. A general obligation bond of a government entity usually is supported by an undertaking to exercise taxing power to discharge the obligation of the bond. Compare **revenue bond; moral obligation bond.**

General partner: Partner with all of the rights and obligations of a partner in a partnership, including liability for the debts of the partnership. Every partnership must have at least one general partner. See limited partner.

General Services Administration: Independent agency of the United States government established by section 101 of the Federal Property and Administrative Services Act of 1949 (Pub. L. No. 52, ch. 288, 63 Stat. 377, 379) to manage the property, records, supplies, facilities, and materials of the federal government.

General stock ownership corporation: Corporation chartered by an act of a state legislature or referendum after December 31, 1978, and before January 1, 1984, that is owned by residents of the state. A GSOC may elect not to be subject to federal income tax, and in such case the taxable income and credits are allocated to the shareholders. I.R.C. §§ 1391–97.

Genuine: Under the Uniform Commercial Code, "free of forgery or counterfeiting." UCC Section 1-201(18).

Geographic restrictions: See territorial restrictions.

GIGO: Garbage in, garbage out; a reference to the dependence of the results of analysis on the data used.

Ginnie Mae: Government National Mortgage Association, or an obligation issued thereby.

Glass-Steagall Banking Act of 1933: Federal statute prohibiting commercial banks from investment banking activities. Pub. L. No. 66, ch. 89, 48 Stat. 162 (1933) (codified in various sections of 12 U.S.C.). *See Investment Co. Inst. v. Camp,* 401 U.S. 617 (1971). *See generally* Perkins, *The Divorce of Commercial and Investment Banking: A History,* 88 Banking L. J. 483 (1971).

Globe doctrine: Practice of the National Labor Relations Board of withholding designation of bargaining units until elections have been held to determine the preferences of the employees. *See Globe Machine & Stamping Co.,* 3 N.L.R.B. 294 (1937).

GmbH: *Gesellschaft mit beschrankter Haftung;* company with limited liability; German corporate form used where the stock is not publicly traded. Compare **AG.**

GMC: Guaranteed mortgage certificate.

GNMA: Government National Mortgage Association.

GNP: Gross national product.

GO bond: General obligation bond.

Going concern value: Value of an established enterprise taking into account its history of and prospects for profits, rather than merely the value of its assets and liabilities.

Going private: Reduction in public shareholdings of a corporation by the purchase of its shares by a controlling shareholder or the corporation itself in the public market or otherwise with the intention of restoring the corporation to status as privately, rather than publicly, held, and terminating registration under the Securities and Exchange Act of 1934, thus providing some relief from the disclosure requirements of that act. *See* SEC Rule 13e-3, 17 C.F.R. § 240.13e-3. The term may also include transactions that eliminate minority shareholders. *See* A. Borden, *Going Private* (1982); *Guidelines on Going Private,* 37 Bus. Law. 313 (1981).

Going public: The issue and sale of stock of a corporation to the public, involving registration of the issue with the Securities and Exchange Commission and otherwise complying with the disclosure requirements of the securities laws. *See generally* Schneider, Manko & Kant, *Going Public: Practice, Procedure, and Consequences,* 27 Vill. L. R. 1 (1981).

Good cause exemption: Section 553(b)(B) of the Administrative Procedure Act provides an exemption from the notice and hearing requirements of rule-making "when the agency for good cause finds ... that notice and public procedure thereon are impracticable, unnecessary, or contrary to the public interest." 5 U.S.C. § 553(b)(B); *see also* 5 U.S.C. § 553(d)(3).

Good delivery: In the case of the sale of a security, satisfaction of the requirements for delivery of the security imposed by the exchange on which it is sold.

Good faith: Under the Uniform Commercial Code, "honesty in fact in the conduct or transaction concerned." UCC Section 1-201(19). *See also* Section 1-203. Certain sections of the Uniform Commercial Code add requirements for good faith: in Article 2 of the Uniform Commercial Code–Sales, good faith in the case of a merchant means "honesty in fact and the observance of reasonable commercial standards of fair dealing in the trade." UCC Section 2-103(1)(b). In Article 7 of the Uniform Commercial Code–Documents of Title, the requirement of observance of reasonable commercial standards is added. UCC Section 7-404. *See Restatement, Second, Contracts* § 205 (1981); Summers, *"Good Faith" in General Contract Law and the Sales Provisions of the Uniform Commercial Code,* 54 Va. L. Rev. 195 (1968). *See also* 11 U.S.C. § 1325(a)(3).

Goods: 1. Article 2 of the Uniform Commercial Code–Sales applies only to "transactions in goods." UCC Section 2-102. Goods are defined as follows:

"Goods" means all things (including specially manufactured goods) which are movable at the time of identification to the contract for sale other than the money in which the price is to be paid, investment securities (Article 8) and things in action. "Goods" also includes the unborn young of animals and growing crops and other identified things attached to realty as described in the section on goods to be severed from realty (Section 2-107).

UCC Section 2-105(1). For the purpose of Article 7 of the Uniform Commercial Code–Documents of Title, goods are more narrowly defined as "all things which are treated as movable for the purposes of a contract of storage or transportation." UCC Section 7-102(1)(f). Article 9 of the Uniform Commercial Code–Secured Transactions, uses still another definition:

"Goods" includes all things which are movable at the time the security interest attaches or which are fixtures (Section 9-313), but does not include money, documents, instruments, accounts, chattel paper, general intangibles, or minerals or the like (including oil and gas) before extraction. "Goods" also includes standing timber which is to be cut and removed under a conveyance or contract for sale, the unborn young of animals, and growing crops.

UCC Section 9-105(1)(h).

Good until canceled: In describing an order to buy or sell securities, meaning effective until executed or canceled; open order.

Good will: Expectation of continued business due to established relations with customers or a favorable reputation; the present value of future income attributable to the good will of a business. *See* I.R.C. § 263(b). See also **goodwill.**

Goodwill: Excess of the cost of an acquired company over the sum of identifiable net assets. American Institute of Certified Public Accountants, Accounting Principles Board Opinion No. 17, *Accounting for Intangible Assets,* paragraph 1 (1970). See also **good will.**

Government Corporation Control Act: Federal statute regarding corporations owned by the United States government. Pub. L. No. 248, ch. 577, 59 Stat. 597 (1945), 31 U.S.C. §§ 841–69.

Government Financial Operations, Bureau of: Unit of the United States Department of the Treasury responsible for accounting, cash management, deposits, and disbursements of the United States Treasury.

Government in the Sunshine Act: Federal statute requiring meetings of government agencies to be open to the public, except under certain circumstances. Pub. L. No. 94-409, 90 Stat. 1241 (1976), 5 U.S.C. § 552b.

Government National Mortgage Association: Agency of the United States Department of Housing and Urban Development charged with the administration of Title III of the National Housing Act, the provision of special assistance in the financing of eligible types of federally underwritten mortgages, the provision of mortgage credit through the Emergency Home Purchase Assistance Act of 1974, the mortgage-backed security program, the management and liquidation of the portfolio of mortgages held by GNMA, the management of the Government Mortgage Liquidation Trust, the Federal Assets Liquidation Trust, the Federal Assets Financing Trust, and the guaranty of trust certificates and such other securities as shall be backed by trusts or pools composed of mortgages insured by HUD or guaranteed by the Veterans Administration. GNMA (Ginnie Mae) finances its operations by issuing a variety of obligations, such as debentures, participation certificates, mortgage-backed bonds, and pass-through securities, all being obligations of the United States government. The pass-through securities represent interests in pools of mortgages, have maturities matching the underlying mortgages, and are subject to prepayment when and as the underlying mortgages are prepaid.

GPM: Graduated payment mortgage.

Grace period: Period allowed for the payment of a debt, insurance premium, or other contractual obligation that is permitted to elapse before the obligation is deemed in default and the other party to the contract is entitled to avoid its obligations or to exercise remedies.

Graduated payment mortgage: Loan secured by a mortgage in which the payments (combined principal and interest) increase, usually in steps, during the life of the loan.

Grandfather clause: Clause of a law granting grandfather rights.

Grandfather right: Right to continue to engage in an activity prohibited by statute because that activity predates the statute. Grandfather rights may be specifically addressed in a "grandfather clause" in the statute. An example is nonbank activities of bank holding companies that may be continued in certain cases under the grandfather clause of the Bank Holding Company Act.

Grantback: Provision in a patent licensing agreement that requires the licensee to license or assign improvement patents to the licensor. As to the antitrust aspects of grantbacks, *see Transparent-Wrap Machine Corp. v. Stokes & Smith Co.,* 329 U.S. 637 (1947); *United States v. Associated Patents, Inc.,* 134 F. Supp. 74 (E.D. Mich. 1955), *aff'd per curiam sub nom. Mac Investment Co. v. United States,* 350 U.S. 960 (1956); *see generally* American Bar Association, Section of Antitrust Law, *Antitrust Law Developments* 336 (1975).

Grantee: The party that conveys or transfers property to another.

Grantor: The party that receives property transferred or conveyed by another.

Grantor trust: Trust used in leveraged leasing transactions and certain other circumstances, designed to permit the tax aspects of the trust activities to pass through to the grantor. The grantor is the party creating the trust and contributing money or property to the trust. *See* I.R.C. §§ 671–79.

Gratuitous assignment: Assignment that is not given or taken in exchange for a performance or return promise that would be consideration for a promise, or as security for or in total or partial satisfaction of a preexisting debt or other obligation. *Restatement, Second, Contracts,* § 332(5) (1981).

Grease: Amounts paid to government officials to facilitate routine, nondiscretionary, administrative actions. "Grease" payments are deductible as a business expense, but illegal bribes and kickbacks are not. I.R.C. § 162(c)(1); section 288(a) of the Tax Equity and Fiscal Responsibility Act of 1982.

Green Shoe option: Option granted to underwriters of an offer of securities entitling them to purchase a specified number of additional securities within a certain period at the same price as the original issue to cover overallotments.

Gross book value: Value of an asset on the books of an entity, without giving effect to depreciation.

Gross income: For federal income tax purposes, "all income from whatever source derived … ." I.R.C. § 61(a).

Gross national product: The aggregate of a nation's expenditures on goods and services.

Gross operating margin: Ratio of gross profit to sales.

Gross tonnage: Measure of the capacity of a vessel obtained by measurement of the size rather than actually determining the weight of the vessel and possible cargo; a gross ton is equal to one hundred cubic feet of enclosed space. See **deadweight tonnage.**

Growing equity mortgage: Loan, secured by a mortgage, that has a scheduled annual increase in the monthly payments through the term of the loan. A growing equity mortgage would be fully repaid in a much shorter period than a conventional level-payment mortgage with the same initial payment obligation.

GSA: General Services Administration.

GSOC: General stock ownership corporation.

GTDA license: License for the export of data generally available to the public, scientific and educational data not related to design, production, or utilization of industrial processes, and data contained in foreign patent applications. 15 C.F.R. § 379.3.

Guarantee, guaranty: Undertaking to perform the obligations of another. Traditionally, the noun form is "guaranty" and the verb form is "guarantee," but the latter spelling is commonly used for both forms. "Guarantee" may also mean the person to whom the guaranty is made. As to guaranties on negotiable instruments, *see* UCC Section 3-416. *See Restatement, Second, Contracts* § 88 (1981); Financial Accounting Standards Board, Statement of Financial Accounting Standards No. 5, *Accounting for Contingencies* (1975); Financial Accounting Standards Board, Interpretation No. 34, *Disclosure of Indirect Guarantees of Indebtedness of Others: An Interpretation of Statement No. 5* (1981); Cherin, Ash & Burlingame, *Enforceability of Guarantees and Other Credit Support Provided Among Members of a Corporate Group: A Bibliography,* 34 Bus. Law. 2029 (1979). See also **collection guaranteed; contingency; payment guaranteed.**

Guaranteed benefit policy: Under the Employee Retirement Income Security Act of 1974, a "guaranteed benefit policy" means an insurance policy or contract that provides for specific benefits which are guaranteed by the insurer, rather than depending on the amount in a fund. ERISA, section 401(b)(2)(B). As to the assets of an insurance company supporting a guaranteed benefit policy being regarded as "assets of the plan," *see* American Bar Association National Institute, *Fiduciary Responsibilities under the Pension Reform Act,* 31 Bus. Law. 1, 257 (1975).

Guaranteed mortgage certificate: Debt instrument representing an undivided interest in a group of conventional residential mortgages issued by the Federal Home Loan Mortgage Corporation. Interest is payable semiannually; principal installments are payable once a year regardless of the status of the underlying mortgages. The usual term of a GMC is thirty years, but the holder may require the Federal Home Loan Mortgage Corporation to redeem the certificate at par on certain earlier dates.

Guarantee of the signature: Under Article 8 of the Uniform Commercial Code—Investment Securities, the issuer of securities may require certain assurances that an indorsement of a security is genuine, including a "guarantee of the signature" of the person indorsing. Such a guaranty means "a guarantee signed by or on behalf of a person reasonably believed by the issuer to be responsible." The issuer may adopt standards for such responsibility if such standards are not "manifestly unreasonable." Usually a commercial bank will be specified. UCC Section 8-402(2). For the effect of the guaranty, *see* UCC Section 8-312.

Guideline period: See asset depreciation range and class life system.

Guidelines: Guidelines used by the Internal Revenue Service to determine, for the purpose of issuing an advance ruling, whether certain transactions purporting to be leases are, in fact, leases for federal income tax purposes.

Rev. Proc. 75-21, 1975-1 C.B. 715. *See generally* Macan, *Tax Aspects of Equipment Leasing,* in B. Fritch & A. Reisman, ed., *Equipment Leasing— Leveraged Leasing* 377 (2d ed. 1980). See also **merger guidelines.**

Gun jumping: Publicity about a company or its products prior to registration of an offer of securities designed to stimulate interest in such securities, and thus constituting an offer in violation of section 5(c) of the Securities Act of 1933. *See Chris Craft Ind. v. Bangor-Punta Corp.,* 426 F.2d 569 (2d Cir. 1970); SEC Release Nos. 33-5927 (1978), 33-5009 (1969), 33-4697 (1964), 33-3844 (1957). As to permitted publicity, *see* SEC Rule 135, 17 C.F.R. § 230.135,

H

Half-year convention: Special convention for establishing the date equipment will be deemed first put into service when the asset depreciation range system is used to determine useful life for depreciation under section 167 of the Internal Revenue Code. The half-year convention treats all property put into service in a given tax year as having been placed in service on the first day of the second half of the tax year. The modified half-year convention treats all property placed in service in the first half-year as having been placed in service on the first day of the tax year, and all property placed in service in the second half-year as having been placed in service on the first day of the next tax year. *See* Treas. Reg. § 1.167(a)-11(c)(2). The accelerated cost recovery system, adopted as a substitute for depreciation for property placed in service during 1981 or later by the Economic Recovery Tax Act of 1981, adopts the half-year convention for all property subject to that system in the statutory cost recovery allowances. I.R.C. § 168.

Harter Act: Federal statute regarding ocean bills of lading. Act of Feb. 13, 1899, ch. 105, 27 Stat. 445; 46 U.S.C. 190–95.

Hart-Scott-Rodino Antitrust Improvements Act of 1976: Federal legislation amending the Antitrust Civil Process Act and amending section 7 of the Clayton Act to require notification to antitrust agencies prior to merger. Pub. L. No. 94-435, 90 Stat. 1383 (1976); 15 U.S.C. 18a. *See* 16 C.F.R. §§ 801–3; *see generally* S. Axinn, B. Fogg, & N. Stoll, *Acquisitions under the Hart-Scott-Rodino Antitrust Improvements Act* (1979); Goolrick, *The End of the "Midnight Merger": an Overview of the New FTC Premerger Notice Rules,* 34 Bus. Law. 63 (1978); Kintner, Griffin, & Goldston, *The Hart-Scott-Rodino Antitrust Improvements Act of 1976: An Analysis,* 46 Geo. Wash. L. Rev. 1 (1977).

Hazardous waste: Under the Resource Conservation and Recovery Act, a "hazardous waste" is a solid waste, or combination of solid wastes, which because of its quantity, concentration, or physical, chemical, or infectious characteristics may:

(A) cause, or significantly contribute to an increase in mortality or an increase in serious irreversible, or incapacitating irreversible, illness; or

(B) pose a substantial present or potential hazard to human health or the environment when improperly treated, stored, transported, or disposed of, or otherwise managed.

Section 1004(5); 42 U.S.C. § 6903(5). *See* 40 C.F.R. § 262.11. "Solid waste" is defined in section 1004(27) of the Resource Conservation and Recovery Act, 42 U.S.C. § 6903(27). *See* 40 C.F.R. §§ 260.10, 261.2. *See generally* Rosbe, *RCRA and Regulation of Hazardous and Nonhazardous Solid Wastes— Closing the Circle of Environmental Control,* 35 Bus. Law. 1519 (1980).

HCFA: Health Care Financing Administration.

Health and Human Services, United States Department of: Cabinet-level department of the executive branch of the United States government responsible for the administration of federal health and welfare services. HHS includes the Social Security Administration, the Food and Drug Administration, the Public Health Service, and the Health Care Financing Administration. HHS is what remained of the Department of Health, Education, and Welfare when the Department of Education was carved out in 1979. *See* Department of Education Organization Act, Pub. L. No. 96-88, 93 Stat. 669, 695 (1979); 20 U.S.C. § 3508.

Health Care Financing Administration: Unit of the United States Department of Health and Human Services responsible for the administration of Medicare, Medicaid, and related federal programs.

Hearing: Oral proceeding before a tribunal. *See* K. Davis, *Administrative Law Text* 157 (3d ed. 1972). See also **after notice and a hearing.**

Heat supply contract: Finance lease of nuclear fuel.

Hedge: To enter into a transaction intended to protect against losses in another transaction for the purchase or sale of a commodity or security. An outright purchase or sale would be "hedged" by the purchase of an option or futures contract in the same commodity or security, but of opposite tenor. For example, a long position in a security could be protected against price declines by purchasing a put option for that security, and a short position protected against price increase by a call option. In connection with an export sale, an exporter can hedge against changes in foreign exchange rates by selling forward the currency the exporter expects to receive. *See* M. Stigum, *Money Market Calculations: Yields, Break-Evens, and Arbitrage* 152 (1981); 17 C.F.R. § 1.3(z). As to federal income tax aspects of hedging transactions, *see* I.R.C. § 1256(e); S. Rep. No. 97-144, 97th Cong., 1st Sess. 159 (1981); Lee, *The Taxation of Commodity Straddles under the Economic Recovery Tax Act of 1981,* Prac. Law., Jan. 15, 1982, at 11, 20.

Hell-or-high-water clause: Section in finance lease or take-or-pay type of contract providing that the lessee or obligor must make all rental and other payments under the lease or contract "come hell or high water," unconditionally, without setoff for any claim against the lessor or other party to the contract. The hell-or-high-water clause is an essential feature of a lease or take-or-pay type of contract that will be used to support a debt obligation.

Herfindahl-Hirschman index: The sum of the squares of the market shares of each firm in a given market. The Herfindahl-Hirschman index provides a measure of the concentration level in a given market, which can be used to show the increase in concentration due to mergers. As used by the Antitrust Division, total concentration, a single-firm monopoly, has an index of 10,000 (100% × 100%); the index for a market with a firm with a 60% share and a firm with a 40% share would be 5200 (60 × 60 = 3600, 40 × 40 = 1600). United States Department of Justice, *Merger Guidelines* (1982).

HHS: United States Department of Health and Human Services.

Hire-purchase agreement: In British parlance, a conditional sale agreement, or a lease in which the lessee may acquire the leased asset by making regular payments for the term of the lease or hire contract, and then making a final, fixed payment to acquire full ownership.

Historical cost/constant dollar accounting: Method of accounting based on measures of historical prices in dollars, each of which has the same general purchasing power. Financial Accounting Standards Board, Statement of Financial Accounting Standards No. 33, *Financial Reporting and Changing Prices,* paragraph 22e (1979).

Historical cost/nominal dollar accounting: The generally accepted method of accounting, used in primary financial statements, based on measures of historical prices in dollars without restatement into units, each of which has the same general purchasing power. Financial Accounting Standards Board, Statement of Financial Accounting Standards No. 33, *Financial Reporting and Changing Prices,* paragraph 22f (1979).

Historical rate: In connection with foreign-exchange transactions, the rate of exchange in effect on the date the specific transaction occurred. Financial Accounting Standards Board, Statement of Financial Accounting Standards No. 8, *Accounting for the Translation of Foreign Currency Transactions and Foreign Currency Financial Statements,* paragraph 30 (1975).

Hochfelder: *Ernst & Ernst v. Hochfelder,* 425 U.S. 185 (1976), a significant case in connection with SEC rule 10b-5.

Holder: 1. Under the Uniform Commercial Code, "a person who is in possession of a document of title or an instrument or an investment security drawn, issued or indorsed to him or to his order or to bearer or in blank." UCC 1-201(20). 2. With respect to patents, under the Internal Revenue Code a "holder" is any individual whose efforts created the patent or any individual who has acquired the rights thereto, except employers and relatives. I.R.C. § 1235(b).

Holder in due course: Under Article 3—Commercial Paper and Article 4—Bank Deposits and Collections of the Uniform Commercial Code, a holder in due course is a holder who takes an instrument:

(a) for value; and

(b) in good faith; and

(c) without notice that it is overdue or has been dishonored or of any defense against or claim to it on the part of any person.

UCC Section 3-302. A holder in due course has special rights under the Uniform Commercial Code, taking the instrument free from claims of any person and defenses of any party to the instrument, with certain exceptions. UCC Section 3-305.

Holder of record: Holder of a security shown on the issuer's records or the records of the indenture trustee.

Hold harmless: To indemnify.

Holding company: Corporation whose primary business is owning the stock, perhaps all of the stock, of another or other corporations. Holding companies are often used to own and control regulated enterprises so that the holding company will not be affected by the regulatory mechanism. *See* section 2(7) of the Public Utility Holding Company Act of 1935, 15 U.S.C. § 79b(a)(7).

Holding company system: Holding company and its subsidiaries. *See* section 2(9) of the Public Utility Holding Company Act of 1935, 15 U.S.C. § 79b(a)(9); I.R.C. § 1083(b).

Holding period: The period for which property must be held in order to receive capital gains treatment on the gain or loss from the sale or exchange. *See* I.R.C. §§ 1222, 1250(e).

Home port: Port where the documents and records relating to a vessel are kept; port of documentation. *See* Home Port Act, Pub. L. No. 420, ch. 235, 43 Stat. 947 (1925), 46 U.S.C. §§ 18, 1011–14; 46 C.F.R. § 67.19.

Honor: Under the Uniform Commercial Code, "to pay or to accept and pay, or where a credit so engages to purchase or discount a draft complying with the terms of the credit." UCC Section 1-201(21).

Horizontal merger: Merger between companies that compete in the same line of business. As to the antitrust aspects of horizontal mergers, see *Brown Shoe Co. v. United States,* 370 U.S. 294 (1962); *see generally,* American Bar Association, Section of Antitrust Law, *Antitrust Law Developments* 74 (1975); Kintner & Postol, *A Review of the Law of Horizontal Mergers,* 66 Geo. L. J. 1405 (1978).

Horizontal price fixing: Agreement among competitors to fix or control prices. Horizontal price fixing is a "per se" violation of section 1 of the Sherman Act. *See, e.g., United States v. Trenton Potteries Co.,* 273 U.S. 392 (1927). *See generally* American Bar Association, Section of Antitrust Law, *Antitrust Law Developments* 2 (1975).

Hot cargo agreement: Agreement whereby an employer "ceases or refrains or agrees to cease or refrain from handling, using, selling, transporting or otherwise dealing in any of the products of any other employer, or cease doing business with any other person, ..." National Labor Relations Act, section 8(e); 29 U.S.C. § 158(e). Hot cargo agreements are unenforceable and void, except in the construction and garment industries.

Hot issue: Issue of securities that increase in price rapidly after the initial offering.

Housing and Urban Development, United States Department of: Cabinet-level department of the executive branch of the United States government responsible for federal programs related to housing and community development. Programs include urban planning assistance, grants under variety of urban assistance programs, and mortgage insurance and credit assistance for housing.

H.R.: House of Representatives.

HSR: Hart-Scott-Rodino Antitrust Improvements Act of 1976.

HUD: United States Department of Housing and Urban Development.

Hulk: Old railroad car requiring rebuilding or heavy repair for further use.

Hybrid rule-making: Rule-making proceeding involving contested factual issues that combines some of the characteristics of the formal adjudicative processes of sections 556 and 557 of the Administrative Procedure Act with the informal rule-making procedure under section 553. *See Vermont Yankee Nuclear Power Corp. v. Natural Resources Defense Council, Inc.*, 435 U.S. 519 (1978).

Hypothecation: Grant of security interest, lien, or other interest in property without surrender of possession.

I

IACAC: Inter-American Commercial Arbitration Commission.

IASC: International Accounting Standards Committee.

IATA: International Air Transport Association.

IBRD: International Bank for Reconstruction and Development.

ICAO: International Civil Aviation Organization.

ICC: 1. Interstate Commerce Commission. 2. International Chamber of Commerce.

ICI: Investment Company Institute.

ICSID: International Centre for the Settlement of Investment Disputes.

ICSID Convention: International Convention on the Settlement of Investment Disputes between States and Nationals of Other States.

IDA: International Development Association.

IDB: 1. Industrial Development Bond. 2. Inter-American Development Bank.

IDC: Intangible drilling costs.

Identification: Under Article 2 of the Uniform Commercial Code–Sales, a buyer obtains rights in specific goods under a contract by "identification" of existing goods as goods to which the contract refers. Identification can be by agreement of the parties, or in the absence of such agreement, identification occurs:

(a) when the contract is made if it is for the sale of goods already existing and identified;

(b) if the contract is for the sale of future goods other than those described in paragraph (c), when goods are shipped, marked or otherwise designated by the seller as goods to which the contract refers;

(c) when the crops are planted or otherwise become growing crops or the young are conceived if the contract is for the sale of unborn young to be born within twelve months after contracting or for the sale of crops to be harvested within twelve months or the next normal harvest season after contracting whichever is longer.

UCC Section 2-501. The buyer has a right to goods so identified upon the seller's insolvency. UCC Section 2-502.

IDR: International depositary receipt, a European analog of the American depositary receipt.

IFAC: International Federation of Accountants.

IFC: International Finance Corporation.

If-converted method: Method of calculating earnings per share data that assumes conversion of convertible securities as of the beginning of the earliest period reported, or time of issuance, if later. American Institute of Certified Public Accountants, Accounting Principles Board Opinion No. 15, *Earnings per share,* Appendix D, paragraph 15 (1968).

IMCO: Intergovernmental Maritime Consultive Organization.

IMF: International Monetary Fund:

Immediately available funds: Funds available the same day as received, such as federal funds. Compare **clearing house funds.**

Impleader: Action by a defendant (or by the plaintiff in the case of a counterclaim by the defendant) to bring into the case a third party who is or may be liable for all or part of the plaintiff's claim against the defendant (or defendant's claim against the plaintiff, in the case of a counterclaim). The party impleading a third-party defendant is called a third-party plaintiff. *See* Fed. R. Civ. Proc. 14.

Implicit rate: When used to consider lease rentals, the rate of interest that would yield combined "level" payments of principal and interest equal to the lease rentals for the same recovery of principal contemplated by those lease rentals. Thus the lease rentals are considered as debt payments, with each payment consisting of some principal recovery and interest at the "implicit" rate. As used in Standard No. 13 of the Financial Accounting Standards Board, the discount rate that, when applied to the lease payments and unguaranteed residual value, causes the aggregate present value at the beginning of the lease term to be equal to the cost of the equipment, less any investment tax credit retained by the lessor.

Implied contract: Contract implied from the conduct of the parties, rather than oral or written manifestations of assent. *See Restatement, Second, Contracts* § 4, comment a (1981).

Implied warranty: Under Article 2 of the Uniform Commercial Code–Sales, a sale of goods by a merchant in goods of that kind carries with it an implied warranty as to merchantability and other warranties that may arise from course of dealing or usage of trade. UCC Section 2-314. See **merchantability.** Where the seller has reason to know the particular purpose for which the goods are required and the buyer relies on the seller's skill in selecting the goods, there is implied a warranty that the goods shall be fit for such purpose. UCC Section 2-315. Implied warranties can be modified or excluded by conspicuous language, expressions such as "as is" or "with all faults," an inspection that ought to reveal defects, and the course of dealing, the course of performance, and the usage of trade. UCC Section 2-316.

Impracticable: Not feasible. In connection with the discharge of contracts for impracticability, "impracticable" is something less than impossible but more than impractical. *See Restatement, Second, Contracts* § 261, UCC Section 2-615; *Florida Power & Light v. Westinghouse Electric Corp.*, 517 F. Supp. 440 (E.D. Va. 1981); Comment, *Contractual Flexibility in a Volatile Economy: Saving U.C.C. Section 2-615 from the Common Law,* 72 Nw. U. L. Rev. 1032 (1978); Duesenberg, *Contract Impracticability: Courts Begin to Shape* § 2-615, 32 Bus. Law. 1089 (1977).

Improvement of position test: Principle that a floating lien on inventory or receivables is valid and may not be avoided in bankruptcy to the extent that the secured creditor has not improved its position. 11 U.S.C. 547(c)(5).

Improvements: Addition or enhancement; with respect to real property, the term includes buildings and other structures erected thereon. With respect to tax treatment of improvements to leased property, *see* Rev. Proc. 79-48, 1979-2 C.B. 529; Stern, *The Tax Impact on the Lessor of the Lessee's Improvements to Real Estate,* 8 J. Real Est. Tax. 99 (1981); Bartlett, *Tax Treatment of Replacements of Leased Property and of Leasehold Improvements Made by a Lessee,* 30 Tax Law. 105 (1976).

Inadvertent investment company: Corporation that fits the definition of an investment company under section 3(a)(3) of the Investment Company Act of 1940, even though it does not intend to be an investment company. *See* 15 U.S.C. § 80a-3(a)(3); Mendelsohn, Goldfus & Mackey, *Status Seeking: Resolving the Status of Inadvertent Investment Companies,* 38 Bus. Law. 193 (1982).

Incentive stock option: Option granted by an employer on its stock as part of the employee's compensation. Under I.R.C. § 422A, added by the Economic Recovery Tax Act of 1981, an incentive stock option, meeting certain requirements, may be received and exercised by the employee without recognizing gross income; any gain from the sale of the stock would be treated as a long-term capital gain if the requirements for the minimum holding period are met. *See* Temporary Regulations, § 14a.422A-1, T.D. 7799, 46 Fed. Reg. 61839 (1981).

Inception of the lease: Date of the lease agreement or the commitment, if a commitment is made earlier. Such a commitment, to be regarded as the "inception of the lease," must be in writing, signed by the parties, and specific as to the principal provisions of the transaction. Financial Accounting Standards Board, Statement of Financial Accounting Standards No. 13, *Accounting for Leases,* paragraph 5b (1976); *see* Financial Accounting Standards Board, Statement of Financial Accounting Standards No. 23, *Inception of the Lease* (1978).

Incidental beneficiary: An incidental beneficiary of a promise in a contract is "a beneficiary who is not an intended beneficiary." *Restatement, Second, Contracts* § 302 (1981).

Incidental damages: Damages for breach of contract, other than loss of value, incurred in a reasonable effort to avoid loss. *See Restatement, Second, Contracts* § 347 (1981). Under the Uniform Commercial Code provisions for the sale of goods, incidental damages for a buyer's breach "include any commercially reasonable charges, expenses or commissions incurred in stopping delivery, in the transportation, care and custody of goods after the buyer's breach, in connection with the return or resale of the goods or otherwise resulting from the breach." UCC Section 2-710. Incidental damages for a seller's breach "include expenses reasonably incurred in inspection, receipt, transportation and care and custody of goods rightfully rejected, any commercially reasonable charges, expenses or commissions in connection with effecting cover and any other reasonable expense incident to the delay or other breach." UCC Section 2-715. These UCC definitions are intended to be illustrative, not exhaustive. UCC Section 2-715, Official Comment, Point 1. See also **damages; consequential damages.**

Includible corporation: Corporation that can be included in the affiliated group that files a consolidated income tax return. I.R.C. § 1504(b). See **affiliated group.**

Income: Produce of work, business, lands, or investments. The use of the term "income" with respect to taxes thereon in the sixteenth amendment to the Constitution has been held to mean "gains, profits, and income derived from sales," although the term is sometimes used to refer to revenues of operations, dividends, and interest, as distinguished from appreciation in value, called gain. *Merchant's Loan & Trust Co. v. Smietanka,* 255 U.S. 509 (1921). *See also Eisner v. Macomber,* 252 U.S. 189 (1920); *Bingham v. Long,* 249 Mass. 79, 144 N.E. 77 (1924); *Trefry v. Putnam,* 227 Mass. 522, 116 N.E. 904 (1917).

Income bond: Bond on which interest is paid only when earned.

Income determination: Process of identifying, measuring, and relating revenue and expenses of an enterprise for an accounting period. American Institute of Certified Public Accountants, Accounting Principles Board Statement No. 4, Ch. 6, *Generally Accepted Accounting Principles—Pervasive Principles,* paragraph 11 (1970).

Income from continuing operations: Income after applicable income taxes but excluding the results of discontinued operations, extraordinary items, and the cumulative effect of accounting changes. Financial Accounting Standards Board, Statement of Financial Accounting Standards No. 33, *Financial Reporting and Changing Prices,* paragraph 22g (1979).

Income statement: Statement of revenue, expenses, gains, losses, and net income recognized during an accounting period. See **statement of income.**

Income taxes: Taxes based on income. *See* American Institute of Certified Public Accountants, Accounting Principles Board Opinion No. 11, *Accounting for Income Taxes* (1967); American Institute of Certified Public Accountants, *Accounting for Income Taxes: Accounting Interpretations of APB Opinion No. 11* (1969).

Incorporator: Person who signs and delivers the articles of incorporation for a new corporation to the secretary of state or other appropriate entity. Model Business Corporation Act § 53 (1979); Del. Code Ann. tit. 8 § 101(a).

Incremental borrowing rate: The interest rate that a party would have to pay for a new loan. In connection with a lease financing, the lessee's incremental borrowing rate is the interest rate that the lessee would have to pay to borrow the funds necessary to purchase the property being leased. The incremental borrowing rate is the interest rate that should be used by a lessee in determining the present value of the lease rentals (unless it is able to learn the lessor's implicit rate), for the purpose of establishing whether a lease is a capital lease. *See* Financial Accounting Standards Board, Statement of Financial Accounting Standards No. 13, *Accounting for Leases,* paragraph 5 (1976); *see also* Financial Accounting Standards Board, Statement of Financial Accounting Standards No. 47, *Disclosure of Long-Term Obligations,* Appendix B (1981).

Indemnity: 1. Obligation to compensate another for a loss, arising out of equitable principles as to who should bear such loss. *See Restatement of Restitution* § 76 (1937). 2. Contractual undertaking or obligation to compensate a person for loss or damage resulting from a given range of circumstances or events.

Indenture: 1. Contract between two or more parties, prepared with a counterpart for each party. The term is derived from the old practice of identifying the counterparts as being of the same instrument by identical indentations at the top or sides, made by placing one counterpart on top of the other and cutting the indentations together. 2. Trust indenture. The Trust Indenture Act of 1939 defines an "indenture" as "any mortgage, deed of trust, trust or other indenture, or similar instrument or agreement (including any supplement or amendment to any of the foregoing), under which securities are outstanding or are to be issued, whether or not any property, real or personal, is, or is to be, pledged, mortgaged, assigned, or conveyed thereunder." Section 303(7), 15 U.S.C. § 77ccc(7). The Bankruptcy Code uses a similar definition at 11 U.S.C. § 101(22); *see* H.R. Rep. No. 95-595, 95th Cong., 1st Sess. 311 (1977).

Indenture trustee: Trustee for the bondholders in a bond issue, or for the debt participants in a lease or loan transaction, with duties set forth in a trust indenture. The indenture trustee usually handles the payments, holds the interests in the collateral, and is empowered to exercise remedies. *See* section 303(10) of the Trust Indenture Act of 1939, 15 U.S.C. § 77ccc(10); 11 U.S.C. § 101(23). See also **trust indenture**. *See generally* J. Kennedy & R. Landau, *Corporate Trust Administration and Management* (1975).

Independent: Not subject to control. This term is difficult to define in objective standards to an extent greater than this English language meaning found in conventional dictionaries. The term is instead usually construed subjectively by a court or administrative agency deciding if a certain person in certain circumstances is "independent" in the legislative context. As to whether a public accountant would be considered "independent" by the Securities and Exchange Commission, *see* Regulation S-X, 17 C.F.R. § 210.2-01; SEC Accounting Series Release No. 234, 42 Fed. Reg. 64304 (1977); SEC Accounting Series Release No. 126, 37 Fed. Reg. 14294 (1972); *see also* Cal. Corp. Code § 115.

Independent agency: Agency of the United States government that is not part of the administrative branch. The principal regulatory agencies, such as the Interstate Commerce Commission and the Federal Trade Commission, are independent agencies.

Independent director: Member of the board of directors of a corporation who is not an officer of the corporation, is not related to its officers, and does not represent concentrated or family holdings.

Index clause: Clause in a contract linking the value of future payments to a published price index, such as the producer price index. *See generally* Rosenn, *Protecting Contracts from Inflation,* 33 Bus. Law. 729 (1978).

Indirect guarantee of indebtedness: As stated by the Financial Accounting Standards Board:

An indirect guarantee of the indebtedness of another arises under an agree-ment that obligates one entity to transfer funds to a second entity upon the occur-rence of specified events, under condi-tions whereby (a) the funds are legally available to creditors of the second entity and (b) those creditors may enforce the second entity's claims against the first entity under the agreement. Examples of indirect guarantees include agreements to advance funds if a second entity's in-come, coverage of fixed charges, or working capital falls below a specified minimum.

Financial Accounting Standards Board, Interpretation No. 34, *Disclosure of Indirect Guarantees of Indebtedness to Others: An Interpretation of FASB Statement No. 5,* paragraph 2 (1981).

Indorse: To sign on the back. Also spelled "endorse."

Indorsee: Party to whom or to whose order a special indorsement of an instrument is made.

Indorsement: Signature of the holder of an instrument made in connection with the negotiation of that instrument. An indorsement must be "written by or on behalf of the holder and on the instrument or on a paper so firmly affixed thereto as to become a part thereof." UCC Section 3-202. See special indorsement; blank indorsement; restrictive indorsement.

Indubitable equivalent: The equal in value; "equivalent" does not seem to need or benefit from a modifier, particularly one such as "indubitable," but the term is used in bankruptcy law and is enshrined in the Bankruptcy Code at 11 U.S.C. §361. Judge Hand origi-nated the phrase in *In re Murel Holding*

Company, 75 F. 2d 941, 942 (2d Cir. 1935), as "most indubitable equivalence."

Industrial bond: Bond issued by an industrial enterprise, other than a transportation company or public utility.

Industrial development bond: Bond issued by a state or subdivision of a state under the provisions of section 103(b) of the Internal Revenue Code, the proceeds of which are used for projects for private business, and the payment of which is made from payments made by that business for use of the project. If certain conditions are met, interest on industrial development bonds is not subject to federal income tax. *See* section 3(a)(2) of the Securities Act of 1933, 15 U.S.C. § 77c(a)(2); section 215(a) of the Tax Equity and Fiscal Responsibility Act of 1982. *See generally,* M. Rollinson, *Small Issue Industrial Development Bonds* (1976); Wade, *Industrial Development Bonds–The Capital Expenditure Rule for $10,000,000 Small Issues,* 34 Bus. Law. 1771 (1979).

Industrial Economics, Bureau of: Unit of the United States Department of Commerce responsible for collection of industrial economic data and preparation of forecasts and analyses of economic issues related to the industrial sector.

Industrial revenue bond: See industrial development bond.

Industry guide: 1. Statement issued by the Federal Trade Commission directed to a specific industry, providing guidance as to what practices the FTC considers lawful and unlawful. 16 C.F.R. § 1.5. 2. One of the guides issued by the Securities and Exchange Commission regarding preparation and filing of registration statements, 17 C.F.R. § 229.801, and disclosure under the Securities Exchange Act of 1934, 17 C.F.R. § 229.802. *See* SEC Release No. 33-6384 (1982).

Inflation: Rise in prices or decline in purchasing power of the monetary unit. *See* Financial Accounting Standards Board, Statement of Financial Accounting Standards No. 33, *Financial Reporting and Changing Prices* (1979).

Infringe: With respect to patents, "whoever without authority makes, uses or sells any patented invention, within the United States during the term of the patent therefor, infringes the patent." 35 U.S.C. § 271. With respect to copyrights, *see* 17 U.S.C. §§ 501–10; with respect to trademarks, *see* 15 U.S.C. §§ 1111–18, 1124.

Inherent coercion: Use of dominant economic power to foreclose competition without overt acts of coercion. *See FTC v. Texaco, Inc.,* 393 U.S. 223 (1968). *See generally* American Bar Association, Section of Antitrust Law, *Antitrust Law Developments* 171 (1975).

Injunction: Decree of a court of equity prohibiting or enjoining a party from doing some act that that party might be disposed to do that might injure the party obtaining the injunction in a way that could not be adequately redressed by an action at law. *See* Fed. R. Civ. Proc. 65; *Restatement, Second, Contracts* §§ 357–69 (1981). See also **preliminary**

injunction; temporary restraining order.

In pari delicto: At equal fault. Defense against suit, based on the assertion that the plaintiff is equally at fault with the defendant, and thus is not entitled to relief. As to private antitrust suits, *see Premier Elec. Constr. Co. v. Miller-Davis Co.*, 422 F.2d 1132 (7th Cir.), *cert. denied*, 400 U.S. 828 (1970); *see generally* American Bar Association, Section of Antitrust Law, *Antitrust Law Developments* 297 (1975).

In personam: Against the person. Most legal proceedings are in personam, against the person, rather than against property. Compare in rem.

In rem: Against the thing. A proceeding in rem is against property, rather than against a person. Actions in admiralty are usually in rem, against the vessel, instead of against the vessel owners. *See* Fed. R. Civ. Proc., Supplemental Rules for Certain Admiralty and Maritime Claims, Rule C, Rule E. Compare in personam.

Insecurity clause: Clause in a debt instrument or lease to the effect that the lender or lessor may accelerate the debt or terminate the lease at its option if it feels "insecure."

Insider: 1. Person subject to the reporting requirements of section 16(a) of the Securities Exchange Act of 1934, and the short-swing profit recapture provisions of section 16(b). This class includes "[e]very person who is directly or indirectly the beneficial owner of more than 10 per centum of any class of equity security ..." and officers and directors. 15 U.S.C. § 78p. 2. Person with access to material information about a public corporation before such information has been publicly announced. 3. In connection with the provisions of the Bankruptcy Code relating to insider preferences, the term "insider" includes, in the case of a corporation, directors, officers, persons in control, partnerships and partners of the debtor, and relatives of the foregoing. 11 U.S.C. § 101(25); *see* H.R. Rep. No. 95-595, 95th Cong., 1st Sess. 312 (1977).

Insider preference: Transfer to an "insider" within one year before bankruptcy that can be recovered by the trustee. *See* 11 U.S.C. § 547(b)(4)(B); *see* H.R. Rep. No. 95-595, 95th Cong., 1st Sess. 372 (1977). See insider.

Insolvency proceedings: Traditionally, voluntary proceedings by an insolvent entity to liquidate assets and make distribution to creditors, as opposed to bankruptcy proceedings, which were involuntary. Insolvency and bankruptcy are treated without distinction under the Bankruptcy Code. Under the Uniform Commercial Code, insolvency proceedings include "any assignment for the benefit of creditors or other proceedings intended to liquidate or rehabilitate the estate of the person involved." UCC Section 1-201(22).

Insolvent: 1. Unable to pay debts as they become due in the ordinary course of business. UCC Section 1-201(23); Model Business Corporation Act § 2(n); N.Y. Bus. Corp. Law. § 102(a)(8). *See Restatement, Second, Contracts* § 252 (1981). 2. Having liabilities in excess of assets. Under the federal Bankruptcy Code, "insolvent" means:

(A) with reference to an entity other than a partnership, financial condition such that the sum of such entity's debts is greater than all of such entity's property, at fair valuation, exclusive of—

(i) property transferred, concealed, or removed with intent to hinder, delay, or defraud such entity's creditors; and

(ii) property that may be exempted from property of the estate under section 522 of this title; and

(B) with reference to a partnership, financial condition such that the sum of such partnership's debts is greater than the aggregate of, at fair valuation—

(i) all such partnership's property, exclusive of property of the kind specified in subparagraph (A)(i) of this paragraph; and

(ii) the sum of the excess of the value of each general partner's separate property, exclusive of property of the kind specified in subparagraph (A)(ii) of this paragraph, over such partner's separate debts;

11 U.S.C. § 101(26). See H.R. Rep. No. 95-595, 95th Cong., 1st Sess. 312 (1977).

Installment contract: Under Article 2 of the Uniform Commercial Code–Sales, an installment contract is "one which requires or authorizes the delivery of goods in separate lots to be separately accepted, even though the contract contains a clause 'each delivery is a separate contract' or its equivalent." UCC Section 2-612. The buyer in an installment contract may reject any installment that is nonconforming, and under certain circumstances a default with respect to any installment may be regarded as a breach of the entire contract. UCC Section 2-612. The term "installment contract" may be used to mean a sale in which the purchase price is payable in installments, but such usage is inconsistent with the Uniform Commercial Code, and another term, such as "installment sale," should be used to describe such a transaction.

Installment sale: Sale in which the purchase price is paid in installments. See installment contract.

Institutional investor: Purchaser of securities that is a bank, insurance company, pension plan, or other financial institution. Institutional investors deal regularly in securities, and are presumed to be sophisticated in such matters; thus securities are often "privately" placed with these institutions without registration under the Securities Act of 1933, because the protection afforded by the registration process is unnecessary. See Securities and Exchange Commission, *Institutional Investor Study Report*, H.R. Doc. No. 62, 92d Cong., 1st Sess. (1971).

Instrument: For the purpose of Article 3 of the Uniform Commercial Code–Commercial Paper, "instrument" means a negotiable instrument. UCC Section 3-102. A broader definition is used in Article 9, Secured Transactions:

"Instrument" means a negotiable instrument (defined in Section 3-104), or a security (defined in Section 8-102) or any other writing which evidences a right to the payment of money and is not itself a security agreement or lease and is of a type which is in the ordinary course of business transferred by delivery with any necessary indorsement or assignment.

UCC Section 9-105(1)(i).

Insurable interest: Interest in property such that the person with the interest would suffer financially if a loss occurs. In a transaction for the sale of goods, a buyer acquires an insurable interest in the goods by identification of the goods as goods to which the contract refers, and a seller retains an insurable interest in goods "so long as title to or any security interest in the goods remains in him ... ." UCC Section 2-501.

Insurance: Method of transferring risk or pooling risk, involving a contract by which the insuror agrees to compensate the insured for losses due to specified risks, in consideration of payment of a premium.

Insurance company: For the purpose of the Securities Act of 1933, the term "insurance company" means;

a company which is organized as an insurance company, whose primary and predominant business activity is the writing of insurance or the reinsuring of risks underwritten by insurance companies, and which is subject to supervision by the insurance commissioner, or a similar official or agency, of a State or territory or the District of Columbia; or any receiver or similar official or any liquidating agent for such company, in his capacity as such.

Section 2(13); 15 U.S.C. § 77b(13). *See* Securities Act of 1934, section 3(a)(19), 15 U.S.C. § 78c(a)(19); Investment Company Act of 1940, section 2(a)(17), 15 U.S.C. § 80a-2(a)(17).

Insured bank: Bank in which the deposits are insured by the Federal Deposit Insurance Corporation.

Insured deposits: Bank deposits insured by the Federal Deposit Insurance Corporation.

Intangible assets: Goodwill, patents and patent rights, deferred charges, and unamortized bond premiums. *See* American Institute of Certified Public Accountants, Accounting Principles Board Opinion No. 17, *Accounting for Intangible Assets* (1970).

Intangible expenses: Development expenses of an oil or gas well, or a mine. Such expenses are deductible in the year incurred for federal income tax purposes.

Integrated agreement: "Writing or writings constituting a final expression of one or more terms of an agreement." *Restatement, Second, Contracts* § 209 (1981). An integrated agreement supersedes prior statements, and a "completely integrated agreement" supersedes consistent additional terms. *See Restatement, Second, Contracts* § 210 (1981).

Integrated disclosure: Method of compliance with the disclosure requirements of both the Securities Act of 1933 and the Securities Exchange Act of 1934 by filing periodic reports under the '34 act and incorporating those reports by reference in '33 act registrations. *See* SEC Release No. 33-6235, 45 Fed. Reg. 63693 (1980); SEC Release No. 33-6231, 45 Fed. Reg. 63630 (1980); SEC Releases Nos. 33-6383, 34-18524, 35-22407, 39-700, IC-12264, AS-306; 47 Fed. Reg. 11380 (1982).

Integration: Treatment of a number of offerings or sales of securities at different times or in different states as a single plan of financing. Individual offerings of securities may not be subject to the registration requirements of the Securities Act of 1933 because of the exemptions available for private placements (section 4(2)) or intrastate transactions (section 3(11)), but if integrated with other offerings and viewed as a single plan of financing, the exemptions may not be available. *See* SEC Release No. 33-4434 (1961); *Livens v. William D. Witter, Inc.*, 374 F. Supp. 1104 (D. Mass. 1974).

Intellectual property: Patents, copyrights, trademarks, and trade secrets.

Intended beneficiary: The beneficiary of a contractual promise is an "intended beneficiary" if

recognition of a right to performance in the beneficiary is appropriate to effectuate the intention of the parties and either

(a) the performance of the promise will satisfy an obligation of the promisee to pay money to the beneficiary; or

(b) the circumstances indicate that the promisee intends to give the beneficiary the benefit of the promised performance.

Restatement, Second, Contracts, § 302 (1981). An intended beneficiary may enforce the promised performance. § 304.

Inter alia: Among other things.

Inter-American Development Bank: Institution formed by the governments of the United States and several Latin American countries, which also has as members Israel and a number of countries of Europe. The bank is founded to further the economic and social development of its member countries by making loans. The funds for such loans come from loans and bonds issued in the United States, Europe, Israel, and Latin America. *See* Inter-American Development Bank Act, Pub. L. No. 86-147, 73 Stat. 299(1959), 22 U.S.C. § 283; Weiss, *Inter-American Development Bank,* in II W. Surrey & D. Wallace, Jr., ed., *A Lawyer's Guide to International Business Transactions* 117(1979).

Interchange rules: Rules promulgated by the Association of American Railroads regarding the maintenance of and settlement of hire charges for railroad equipment while on the lines of other railroads. Railroad companies interchange rolling stock among themselves, so that a shipment can be moved over the lines of several railroads in the same car. *See* Association of American Railroads, *Code of Car Service Rules, Freight.*

Interest: Compensation at a stated rate for the use of money borrowed. As to the scope of the term "interest" for the purpose of filing income tax returns, see I.R.C. § 6049(b).

Interest arbitrage: Trading in the money market to take advantage of differences in the interest rate of various types of money market instruments.

Interest coverage: Ratio of total income to bond interest.

Interest in land: For the purpose of the Statute of Frauds, an "interest in land" is "any right, privilege, power or immunity, or combination thereof, which is an interest in land under the law of property and is not 'goods' within the Uniform Commercial Code." *Restatement, Second, Contracts* §

127 (1981). *See Restatement, Property* §§ 1–9 (1936).

Interest rate futures contract: Contract for future delivery of a financial instrument. As defined by the Financial Accounting Standards Board, "Interest rate futures contracts are standardized contracts or agreements to make or take delivery of a standardized amount of a financial instrument of deliverable grade at a specified price during a specific month under conditions established by the commodity exchange on which the contracts are traded." Financial Accounting Standards Board, Technical Bulletin re APB Opinion No. 22, *Disclosure of Interest Rate Futures Contracts and Forward and Standby Contracts*, paragraph 3 (1981).

Interest rate implicit in the lease: As defined in Financial Accounting Standards Board, Statement of Financial Accounting Standards No. 13, *Accounting for Leases* (1976):

The discount rate that, when applied to (i) the minimum lease payments (as defined in paragraph 5(j)), excluding that portion of the payments representing executory costs to be paid by the lessor, together with any profit thereon, and (ii) the unguaranteed residual value (as defined in paragraph 5(i)) accruing to the benefit of the lessor, causes the aggregate present value at the beginning of the lease term to be equal to the fair value of the leased property (as defined in paragraph 5(c)) to the lessor at the inception of the lease, minus any investment tax credit retained by the lessor and expected to be realized by him.

Paragraph 5(k). See also **implicit rate.**

Intergovernmental Maritime Consultive Organization: An agency of the United Nations that establishes conventions for maritime matters, particularly regarding safety at sea and pollution of the oceans. IMCO conventions become adopted as the law of the sea by ratification of member nations. *See* Convention on the Intergovernmental Maritime Consultive Organization, March 6, 1948, 9 U.S.T. 621, T.I.A.S. 4044.

Interim dividend: Dividend declared during the fiscal year, before the income for the year has been finally established.

Interior, United States Department of: Cabinet-level department of the executive branch of the United States government responsible for the management of public lands and natural resources. Units of the Department of the Interior include the United States Fish and Wildlife Service, the National Park Service, the Bureau of Mines, the Geological Survey, the Bureau of Land Management, the Office of Surface Mining Reclamation and Enforcement, and the Bureau of Reclamation.

Interlock: Common directors or officers of two corporations. Interlocking directorates between banks and between competing corporations are prohibited by section 8 of the Clayton Act. *See United States v. Sears, Roebuck & Co.,* 111 F. Supp. 614 (S.D.N.Y. 1953); Federal Trade Commission, *Report on Interlocking Directorates* (1951); *see generally* American Bar Association, Section of Antitrust Law, *Antitrust Law Developments* 102 (1975). Dealings between common carriers and other corporations with common officers or directors are prohibited by section 10 of the Clayton Act unless competitive bidding is used. 15 U.S.C. § 20; *see* Walton, *Interlocks between Common Carriers and Companies Dealing with the Carrier,* 45 ICC Prac. J. 422 (1978); American Bar Association, Section of Antitrust Law, *Antitrust Law Developments* 436 (1975). *See* Cal. Corp. Code § 310. As to banks, see Regulation L, 12 C.F.R. § 212.

Intermediary: Entity that acts between parties in connection with a transaction or transactions. A financial institution may be so called because it acts as intermediary between borrowers and lenders.

Intermediary bank: Under the Uniform Commercial Code, "intermediary bank" means "any bank to which an item is transferred in course of collection except the depositary or payor bank." UCC Section 4-105.

Intermediate term: Used to describe fixed-income securities or loans with maturities of greater than one year and less than ten years.

Internal bond: Bond issued by a country payable in its own currency. Compare **external bond.**

Internal rate of return: Rate of return on an investment found by determining the discount rate that, when applied to the future cash flows, causes the present value of those cash flows to equal the investment. The formula is as follows:

$$A_0 = \frac{A_1}{(1+r)} + \frac{A_2}{(1+r)^2} + \ldots + \frac{A_n}{(1+r)^n}$$

in which A_0 is the initial investment, A_1 through A_n are the cash flows occurring at the end of the periods *1* through *n*, and *r* is the internal rate of return. The equation cannot be solved for *r*, so internal-rate-of-return problems must be solved by iteration; various values of *r* must be tested until the right one is found. Some hand-held calculators will solve simple internal-rate-of-return problems, but more complex problems require the use of a computer. *See* J. Van Horne, *Financial Management and Policy* 85 (4th ed. 1977).

Internal Revenue Bulletin: Weekly publication of the Internal Revenue Service containing Internal Revenue Service rulings and revenue procedures, and Treasury decisions, executive orders, legislation, and court decisions relating to federal tax matters. Twice a year the contents of the Internal Revenue Bulletins are consolidated in the Cumulative Bulletin.

Internal Revenue Code of 1954: Comprehensive legislation relating to federal income, estate, and gift taxes, passed in 1954 to replace the Internal Revenue Code of 1939. The tax code is still referred to as the Internal Revenue Code of 1954, even though it has been amended extensively since the year of its passage. Pub. L. No. 591, ch. 736, 68A Stat. 3 (1954).

Internal Revenue Service: Unit of the United States Department of the Treasury responsible for the administration and enforcement of the internal revenue (tax) laws, except those relating to alcohol, tobacco, firearms, and explosives. *See* I.R.C. § 7802.

International Accounting Standards Committee: Organization formed by the leading professional accounting bodies of Australia, Canada, France, Germany, Japan, Mexico, the Netherlands, the United Kingdom and Ireland, and the United States of America, to "formulate and publish in the public interest, standards to be observed in the presentation of audited financial statements and to promote their worldwide acceptance and observance." International Accounting Standards Committee, *Preface to Statements of International Accounting Standards* (1978).

International Bank for Reconstruction and Development: International organization, known as the World Bank, formed to assist in the development of poor member countries by promoting private foreign investment by guaranteeing loans and by making loans to supplement private investment. Loans must be for productive purposes related to reconstruction or development. The capital of the bank is subscribed by the member countries, mostly from a group of ten North American and European countries. The World Bank raises debt funds throughout the world, and has issued bonds and notes denominated in dollars. *See* Nurick, *The International Bank for Reconstruction and Development and the International Development Association,* in II W. Surrey & D. Wallace, Jr., ed., *A Lawyer's Guide to International Business Transactions* 49 (1979).

International Civil Aviation Organization: Agency of the United Nations, originally established at the International Civil Aviation Conference in Chicago in 1944. Its purposes are to develop principles and techniques of international air navigation and otherwise to foster the orderly growth of international civil aviation.

International Court of Justice: Principal judicial organ of the United Nations.

International Development Association: Affiliate of the World Bank that provides financing to developing countries on terms more favorable than those of conventional loans. *See* Nurick, *The International Bank for Reconstruction and Development and the International Development Association,* in II W. Surrey & D. Wallace, Jr., ed., *A Lawyer's Guide to International Business Transactions* 49 (1979).

International Development Cooperation Agency, United States: Independent agency of the United States government established as the central agency for economic aid to developing countries. Components of the IDCA are the Agency for International Development (AID), the Trade and Development Program, and the Overseas Private Investment Corporation (OPIC).

International Finance Corporation: Affiliate of the World Bank, created to promote productive private enterprise in developing countries, that does so by investing in such enterprises. *See* Richards, *International Finance Corporation,* in II W. Surrey & D. Wallace, Jr., ed., *A Lawyer's Guide to International Business Transactions* 97 (1979).

International Labor Affairs, Bureau of: Unit of the United States Department of Labor responsible for administering the trade adjustment assistance program under the Trade Act of 1974, which provides special benefits for workers adversely affected import competition.

International Monetary Fund: Organization established on July 22, 1944, by the United Nations Monetary and Financial Conference at Bretton Woods to promote stability in international currency exchange. The IMF lends funds to member nations to finance temporary balance of payments problems, to finance the expansion and balance growth of international trade, and to promote international monetary cooperation. Special drawing rights on the IMF provide member nations with a source of additional reserves. *See* The Articles of Agreement for the International Monetary Fund entered into force for the United States on December 27, 1945, 60 Stat. 1401; Bretton Woods Agreements Act, Pub. L. No. 171, ch. 339, 59 Stat. 512 (1945), 22 U.S.C. § 286. *See also* Special Drawing Rights Act, Pub. L. No. 90-349, 82 Stat. 188 (1968), 22 U.S.C. § 286n–r; Bretton Woods Agreements Act Amendments, Pub. L. No. 94-564, 90 Stat. 2660 (1976). *See generally* Gold, *The International Monetary Fund,* in II W. Surrey & D. Wallace, Jr., ed., *A Lawyer's Guide to International Business Transactions* 3 (1979).

International organization: For the purpose of the Internal Revenue Code, an international organization is a "public international organization entitled to enjoy privileges, exemptions, and immunities as an international organization under the International Or-

ganization Immunities Act (22 U.S.C. §§ 288—288f)." I.R.C. § 7701(a)(18).

International Telecommunication Union: Agency of the United Nations formed to establish and maintain standards and regulations for the international use of telegraph, telephone, and radio services.

International Trade Administration: Branch of the United States Department of Commerce responsible for programs relating to international trade, including the antidumping and countervailing duty laws within the meaning of Title VII of the Tariff Act of 1930.

International Trade Commission, United States: Independent agency of the United States government (formerly the United States Tariff Commission) that furnishes analyses and recommendations concerning international tariffs and trade to Congress and agencies of the federal government. *See* Pub. L. No. 271, ch. 463, 39 Stat. 756, 795 (1916); section 171 of the Trade Act of 1974, Pub. L. No. 93-618, 88 Stat. 1978, 2009 (1975); 19 U.S.C. § 2231; Tariff Act of 1930.

Interperiod tax allocation: Accounting apportionment of income taxes among periods. *See* American Institute of Certified Public Accountants, Accounting Principles Board Opinion No. 11, *Accounting for Income Taxes,* paragraph 12 (1967).

Interpleader: Action by the holder of money or property against which a number of parties may have claims to settle such claims in a consolidated proceeding, in a situation where such claims may be adverse to one another, or the money or property is insufficient to discharge all claims. *See* Fed. R. Civ. Proc. 22 (rule interpleader); 18 U.S.C. § 1335 (statutory interpleader). *See also State Farm Fire & Casualty Co. v. Tashire,* 386 U.S. 523 (1967).

Interpretation: Ascertainment of meaning. *Restatement, Second, Contracts* § 200 (1981). "Interpretation" is not the determination of legal effect; that is reserved to the word "construction." *See* Patterson, *The Interpretation and Construction of Contracts,* 64 Colum. L. Rev. 833 (1964). Compare **construction.**

Interpretative rule: Sections 553 (b)(A) and (d)(2) of the Administrative Procedure Act provide an exemption from the notice and hearing requirements of rule-making for "interpretative rules." The Attorney General's Manual on the Administrative Procedure Act defines such rules as "rules or statements issued by an agency to advise the public of the agency's construction of the statutes and rules which it administers." The distinction between interpretative rules and "legislative rules" (which are subject to the notice and hearing requirements) is sometimes difficult to draw. *See, e.g., Energy Reserves Group v. DOE,* 589 F. 2d 1082 (Temporary Emergency Court of Appeals, 1978); *see generally* 2 K. Davis, *Administrative Law Treatise* §§ 7:8-7:18 (2d ed. 1979).

Interrogatory: Written question by one party to a court action to another party, in the course of the process of discovery. *See* Fed. R. Civ. Proc. 33. See **discovery.**

Inter se: Among themselves.

Interstate commerce: See commerce; affecting commerce; commerce clause. *See also* section 2(7) of the Securities Act of 1933, 15 U.S.C. § 77b(7); section 3(a)(17) of the Securities Exchange Act of 1934, 15 U.S.C. § 78c(a)(17).

Interstate Commerce Act: Federal statute regulating railroads, certain trucking operations, and domestic water carriers. Act of Feb. 4, 1887, ch. 104, 24 Stat. 379; superseded in 1978 by Pub. L. No. 95-473, 92 Stat. 1337 (1978), 49 U.S.C. §§ 10101-11916.

Interstate Commerce Commission: Independent agency of the United States government that regulates the rates and service of interstate surface transportation companies, including railroads, motor carriers, and certain domestic water carriers. See **Interstate Commerce Act;** I. Sharfman, *The Interstate Commerce Commission* (1931).

Intervention: Action by a party, not originally named in a court action, to join in that action, when that party claims an interest in the subject of the main action, or has a claim with a question of law or fact in common with the main action. *See* Fed. R. Civ. Proc. 24; *Jones v. United Gas Improvement Corp.,* 69 F.R.D. 398 (E.D. Pa. 1975).

Intra-enterprise conspiracy: Conspiracy in restraint of trade in violation of the Sherman Act between a parent and subsidiary corporations or between corporations under common control. *See, e.g., United States v. Yellow Cab Co.,* 332 U.S. 218 (1947). *See generally*

American Bar Association, Section of Antitrust Law, *Antitrust Law Developments* 32 (1975).

Intrastate offering or intrastate sale: Offering or sale of securities within a state or territory utilizing the exemption from registration under the Securities Act of 1933 available under section 3(a)(11) thereof, 15 U.S.C. § 77c(a)(11). *See* SEC Rule 147, 17 C.F.R. § 230.147; *Chapman v. Dunn,* 414 F. 2d 153 (6th Cir. 1969). *See generally* Kant, *SEC Rule 147—A Further Narrowing of the Intrastate Offering Exemption,* 30 Bus. Law. 73 (1974).

Inventory: For the purpose of Article 9 of the Uniform Commercial Code—Secured Transactions, goods are "inventory" if they "are held by a person who holds them for sale or lease or to be furnished under contracts of service or if he has so furnished them, or if they are raw materials, work in process or materials used or consumed in a business. Inventory of a person is not to be classified as his equipment." UCC Section 9-109(4). "Inventory" is one of the classes of goods established under Article 9 for the purpose of determining certain rights and priorities, which may be different for the different classes of goods. The other classes are equipment, consumer goods, and farm products. The American Institute of Certified Public Accountants defines "inventory" as "the aggregate of those items of tangible personal property which (1) are held for sale in the ordinary course of business, (2) are in the process of production for such sale, or (3) are to be currently consumed in the production of goods or services to be available for sale." American Institute of Certified

Public Accountants, Accounting Research Bulletin No. 43, Ch. 4, *Inventory Pricing,* paragraph 2 (1953).

Inventory turnover: Ratio of annual cost of goods sold to average inventory.

Investee: Enterprise in which an investor invests.

Investigatory records: The Freedom of Information Act provisions for disclosure of information in the hands of government agencies have an exception for "matters that are ... investigatory records compiled for law enforcement purposes... ." 5 U.S.C. § 552(b)(7). This exception is intended to limit the discovery available to respondents in administrative proceedings to that available to respondents in federal judicial proceedings. *See* H.R. Rep. No. 1497, 89th Cong., 2d Sess. 11 (1965). The exception is available only if the prospect of enforcement proceedings is concrete. *Bristol-Myers Co. v. FTC,* 424 F. 2d 935, 939 (D.C. Cir.), *cert. denied,* 400 U.S. 824 (1970).

Investment adviser: As defined in the Investment Advisers Act of 1940, the term means:

any person who, for compensation, engages in the business of advising others, either directly or through publications or writings, as to the value of securities or as to the advisability of investing in, purchasing, or selling securities, or who, for compensation and as part of a regular business, issues or promulgates analyses or reports concerning securities; but does not include (A) a bank, or any bank holding company as defined in the Bank Holding Company Act of 1956, which is not an investment company; (B) any lawyer, accountant, engineer, or teacher whose performance of such services is solely incidental to the practice of his profession; (C) any broker or dealer whose performance of such services is solely incidental to the conduct of his business as a broker or dealer and who receives no special compensation therefor; (D) the publisher of any bona fide newspaper, news magazine or business or financial publication of general and regular circulation; (E) any person whose advice, analyses, or reports relate to no securities other than securities which are direct obligations of or obligations guaranteed as to principal or interest by the United States, or securities issued or guaranteed by corporations in which the United States has a direct or indirect interest which shall have been designated by the Secretary of the Treasury, pursuant to section (3)(a)(12) of the Securities Exchange Act of 1934, as exempted securities for the purpose of that Act; or (F) such other persons not within the intent of this paragraph, as the Commission may designate by rules and regulations or order.

Section 202(a)(11), 15 U.S.C. § 80b-2 (a)(11). *See* Securities Exchange Act of 1934, section 3(a)(20), 15 U.S.C. § 78c(a)(20); Investment Company Act of 1940, section 2(a)(20), 15 U.S.C. § 80a-2(c)(20); Cal. Corp. Code § 25009.

Investment Advisers Act of 1940: Federal statute to regulate the activities of investment advisers. Pub. L. No. 768, ch. 686, 54 Stat. 789, 847 (1940); 15 U.S.C. § 80b.

Investment banker: Person or institution that underwrites offerings of securities and otherwise acts as intermediary between sources of capital and users of capital. For the purpose of the Investment Company Act of 1940, an "investment banker" is a "person engaged in the business of underwriting securities issued by other persons, but does not include an investment company, any person who acts as an underwriter in isolated transactions but not as a part of a regular business, or any person solely by reason of the fact that such person is an underwriter for one or more investment companies." Section 2(a)(21), 15 U.S.C. § 80a-2(a)(21).

Investment by owners: Capital contribution. As defined by the Financial Accounting Standards Board:

Investments by owners are increases in net assets of a particular enterprise resulting from transfers to it from other entities of something valuable to obtain or increase ownership interests (or equity) in it. Assets are most commonly received as investments by owners, but that which is received may also include services or satisfaction or conversion of liabilities of the enterprise.

Financial Accounting Standards Board, Statement of Financial Accounting Concepts No. 3, *Elements of Financial Statements of Business Enterprises,* paragraph 52 (1980). Compare **distribution to owners.**

Investment company: The Investment Company Act of 1940 defines an "investment company" as an issuer of securities that:

(1) is or holds itself out as being engaged primarily, or proposes to engage primarily, in the business of investing, reinvesting, or trading in securities;

(2) is engaged or proposes to engage in the business of issuing face-amount certificates of the installment type, or has been engaged in such business and has any certificate outstanding; or

(3) is engaged or proposes to engage in the business of investing, reinvesting, owning, holding, or trading in securities, and owns or proposes to acquire investment securities having a value exceeding 40 per centum of the value of such issuer's total assets (exclusive of government securities and cash items) on an unconsolidated basis.

Section 3(a), 15 U.S.C. § 80a-3(a); "face amount certificate" is defined in section 2(a)(15). Section 3(c) provides certain exceptions, including brokers and dealers, banks, insurance companies, finance companies, and pension funds; 15 U.S.C. § 80a-3(c). *See* Securities Exchange Act of 1934, section 3(a)(19); 15 U.S.C. § 78c(a)(19). *Prudential Insurance Co. v. SEC*, 326 F. 2d 383 (3d Cir.), *cert. denied*, 327 U.S. 953 (1964). *See generally* Krupsky, *The Role of Investment Company Directors*, 32 Bus. Law. 1733 (1977). See also **regulated investment company; small business investment company; inadvertent investment company.**

Investment Company Act of 1940:
Federal statute regulating the activities of investment companies. Pub. L. No. 768, ch. 686, 54 Stat. 789 (1940); 15 U.S.C. § 80a. *See generally* Mackillop, *On Interpreting the Investment Company Act*, 64 A.B.A.J. 286 (1978).

Investment contract:
The term "investment contract" occurs in the definition of "security" in the Securities Act of 1933; a contract coming under this definition would be subject to the provisions of that act and the remedies available thereunder. Investment contract was defined in *SEC v. W. J. Howey Co.:*

An investment contract for purposes of the Securities Act means a contract, transaction or scheme whereby a person invests his money in a common enterprise and is led to expect profits solely from the efforts of a promoter or a third party, it being immaterial whether the shares in the enterprise are evidenced by formal certificates or by a nominal interest in the physical assets employed in the enterprise.

328 U.S. 293, 298 (1946). *See also United Housing Foundation, Inc., v. Forman*, 421 U.S. 837 (1975); *International Brotherhood of Teamsters, Chauffeurs, Warehouseman & Helpers of Am. v. Daniel*, 439 U.S. 551 (1979).

Investment discretion:
Under the Securities Exchange Act of 1934:

A person exercises "investment discretion" with respect to an account if, directly or indirectly, such person (A) is authorized to determine what securities or other property shall be purchased or sold by or for the account, (B) makes decisions as to what securities or other property shall be purchased or sold by or for the account even though some other person may have responsibility for such investment decisions, or (C) otherwise exercises such influence with respect to the purchase and sale of securities or other property by or for the account as the Commission, by rule, determines, in the public interest or for the protection of investors, should be subject to the operation of the provisions of this title and the rules and regulations thereunder.

Section 3(a)(35), 15 U.S.C. § 78c (a)(35).

Investment letter:
Letter of investment intent furnished by the purchaser of securities to establish that the securities are being purchased for investment and not "with a view to the distribu-

tion" of the securities, in order to qualify for the exemption from registration available under section 4(2) of the Securities Act of 1933. See private placement.

Investment security: See security; Uniform Commercial Code, Article 8—Investment Securities.

Investment tax credit: Credit against federal income taxes of 10%, more or less, of the cost of certain kinds of property acquired for use in a trade or business. *See* I.R.C. §§ 38, 46–50.

Investment value: With respect to a convertible security, the estimated price at which that security would sell if it were not convertible, based on its dividend or interest rate and other characteristics.

Ipso facto: By the fact itself. An ipso facto default clause in a debt instrument or lease provides that a default may be declared by the fact that the debtor or lessee is insolvent or bankrupt without a showing that an obligation under the instrument had been breached. Ipso facto clauses are generally ineffective when the borrower or lessee is under the protection of the bankruptcy laws. *See* 11 U.S.C. § 541(c)(1); H.R. Rep. No. 95-595, 95th Cong., 1st Sess. 369 (1977).

IRA: Individual retirement account.

IRB: Internal Revenue Bulletin.

IRC: Internal Revenue Code of 1954, as amended.

Irredeemable bond: Bond that does not mature and has no provision for principle recovery. The bondholder receives interest only.

Irrevocable credit; irrevocable letter of credit: Letter of credit that once established "as regards the customer" can be modified or revoked only with the consent of the customer, and once established "as regards the beneficiary" can be modified or revoked only with the consent of the beneficiary. UCC Section 5-106(2).

IRS: Internal Revenue Service.

ISO: Incentive stock option.

Isolated transaction: Single transaction by a foreign corporation, not in the course of a number of repeated transactions of like nature. An isolated transaction of itself would not constitute "doing business" and require qualification to do business in that jurisdiction. *See* Model Business Corporation Act § 106(j) (1979); *Franklin Enterprises Corp. v. Moore*, 226 N.Y.S. 2d 527 (1962); *see generally,* CT Corporation System, *What Constitutes Doing Business* 53 (1976).

Issue: With respect to negotiable instruments, issue means "the first delivery of an instrument to a holder or remitter." UCC Section 3-102. *See Bankhaus Hermann Lampe KG v. Mercantile-Safe Deposit and Trust Co.*, 466 F. Supp. 1133 (S.D. N.Y. 1979).

Issue date: For the purpose of the Internal Revenue Code provisions on capital gains and losses for the sale or exchange of debt securities, the issue date, or "date of original issue," is the date the issue was first sold to the public, or in the case of a private placement, the date of the sale by the issuer. I.R.C. § 1232(b)(3).

Issue price: For the purpose of the Internal Revenue Code provisions on capital gains and losses for the sale or exchange of debt securities, the issue price means "the initial offering price to the public (excluding bond houses and brokers) at which price a substantial amount of such bonds or other evidences of indebtedness were sold." In the case of a private placement, the issue price is the price to the first buyer. I.R.C. § 1232(b)(2).

Issuer: 1. With respect to securities, under the Securities Act of 1933:

The term "issuer" means every person who issues or proposes to issue any security; except that with respect to certificates of deposit, voting-trust certificates, or collateral-trust certificates, or with respect to certificates of interest or shares in an unincorporated investment trust not having a board of directors (or persons performing similar functions) or of the fixed, restricted management, or unit type, the term "issuer" means the person or persons performing the acts and assuming the duties of depositor or manager pursuant to the provisions of the trust or other agreement or instrument under which such securities are issued; except that in the case of an unincorporated association which provides by its articles for limited liability of any or all of its members, or in the case of a trust, committee, or other legal entity, the trustees or members thereof shall not be individually liable as issuers of any security issued by the association, trust, committee, or other legal entity; except that with respect to equipment-trust certificates or like securities, the term "issuer" means the person by whom the equipment or property is to be used; and except that with respect to fractional undivided interests in oil, gas, or other mineral rights, the term "issuer" means the owner of any such right or of any interest in such right (whether whole or fractional) who creates fractional interests therein for the purpose of public offering.

Section 2(4); 15 U.S.C. § 77b(4). *See* Securities Exchange Act of 1934, section 3(a)(8); 15 U.S.C. § 78c(a)(8); H.R. Rep. No. 85, 73d Cong., 1st Sess. 5 (1933); Landis, *The Legislative History of the Securities Act of 1933*, 28 Geo. Wash. L. Rev. 29, 37 (1959). *See also* Cal. Corp. Code § 25010. In leveraged lease transactions, the SEC has expressed the view that the owner-lessor, the nominal obligor on nonrecourse debt obligations secured by the lease and the equipment under lease, would not be regarded as the issuer; the lessee, whose undertakings are the underlying obligations of the transaction, would be the issuer. Stiles & Walker, *Leveraged Lease Financing of Capital Equipment*, 28 Bus. Law. 161, 177 (1972). Under Article 8 of the Uniform Commercial Code–Investment Securities, the term "issuer" includes a person who:

(a) places or authorizes the placing of his name on a security (otherwise than as authenticating trustee, registrar, transfer agent or the like) to evidence that it represents a share, participation or other interest in his property or in an enterprise or to evidence his duty to perform an obligation evidenced by the security; or

(b) directly or indirectly creates fractional interests in his rights or property which fractional interests are evidenced by securities; or

(c) becomes responsible for or in place of any other person described as an issuer in this section.

UCC Section 8-201(1). A guarantor is regarded as an issuer to the extent of his guaranty, even if the guaranty is not noted on the security. UCC Section 8-201(2). 2. With respect to letters of credit, the issuer is the bank or other person issuing the credit. UCC Section 5-103(1)(c). 3. With respect to bills of lading, warehouse receipts, and other documents of title, "issuer" means:

a bailee who issues a document except that in relation to an unaccepted delivery order it means the person who orders the possessor of goods to deliver. Issuer includes any person for whom an agent or employee purports to act in issuing a document if the agent or employee has real or apparent authority to issue documents, notwithstanding that the issuer received no goods or that the goods were misdescribed or that in any other respect the agent or employee violated his instructions.

UCC Section 7-102.

Issuer's lien: Lien upon a security in favor of the issuer thereof. *See* UCC Section 8-103.

ITC: 1. International Trade Commission. 2. Investment tax credit.

Item: For the purpose of Article 3—Commercial Paper and Article 4—Bank Deposits and Collections of the Uniform Commercial Code, "item" means "any instrument for the payment of money even though it is not negotiable but does not include money." UCC Section 4-104(1)(g).

Item of tax preference: See tax preference.

Iteration: Process of solving a problem by postulating a solution, testing that solution, then using the results of that test to postulate a better solution, testing again, and repeating the process until a solution with the desired degree of precision is found. Internal rate of return problems are solved by iteration.

ITU: International Telecommunication Union.

J

Jencks' rule: Rule that a defendant in an action is entitled to examine the records and reports used by the prosecution as the basis for its testimony. *Jencks v. United States,* 353 U.S. 657 (1957). The rule is applicable to administrative proceedings. *Great Lakes Airlines, Inc., v. CAB,* 291 F. 2d 354 (9th Cir.), *cert. denied,* 368 U.S. 890 (1961). *See* 18 U.S.C. § 3500.

Jingle rule: Rule of bankruptcy that partnership creditors may not participate in the distribution of the assets of a general partner until the general partner's separate creditors have been paid in full, and that the separate creditors of a partner may not participate in the distribution of partnership assets until the partnership creditors have been paid in full. "Firm assets to firm creditors; separate assets to separate creditors; anything left over from either goes to the other." *See* Uniform Partnership Act § 40(h). The jingle rule has been modified by the Bankruptcy Code. 11 U.S.C. § 723; *see* H.R. Rep. No. 95-595, 95th Cong., 1st Sess. 196 (1977).

Jobs tax credit: Credit against federal income taxes allowed to employers who hire from certain "targeted" groups, including handicapped people, economically disadvantaged young people, Vietnam veterans, welfare recipients, and former CETA employees. I.R.C. §§ 44B, 51–53

Joinder: Joining of claims asserted by a party against another party in a common court proceeding; joining of a person in an action of other parties if:

(1) in his absence complete relief cannot be accorded among those already parties, or (2) he claims an interest related to the subject of the action and is so situated that the disposition of the action in his absence may (i) as a practical matter impair or impede his ability to protect that interest or (ii) leave any of the persons already parties subject to a substantial risk of incurring double, multiple, or otherwise inconsistent obligations by reason of his claimed interest.

Fed. R. Civ. Proc. 18, 19. Joinder may also be permissive, if parties assert relief jointly, or if the action arises out of the same circumstances. Fed. R. Civ. Proc.

20. *See Provident Tradesmens Bank & Trust Co. v. Patterson,* 390 U.S. 102 (1968).

Joint: A joint obligation by two or more parties is an obligation for the same performance. *Restatement, Contracts, Second* § 288; *see* § 289. Compare **joint and several.** Many state statutes authorize separate suits against joint promisors as if each had agreed to be bound jointly and severally. *See Welch v. Sherwin,* 300 F. 2d 716, 718n (D.C. Cir. 1962).

Joint and several: A joint and several obligation by two or more parties is an obligation for separate performances, and the obligee may look to any party (several) or all parties (joint) for satisfaction of the obligation.

Joint stock association: Unincorporated association whose members hold shares of stock or other evidence of interest therein. *See* Del. Code Ann. tit. 8 § 254. A joint stock association can have many of the attributes of a corporation, including continuity of life, transferability of shares, and centralized management, but unlike a corporation, the holders of shares in a joint stock association do not have limited liability.

Joint stock company: 1. Joint stock association. 2. Corporate form used in Europe for larger enterprises and enterprises with public stock holdings. European joint stock companies are similar to American corporations, and have limited liability for stockholders. Management is by a board of directors, sometimes with two tiers, a supervisory board with outside directors and a managing board of employee-directors. Compare limited liability company.

Joint venture: In the broadest sense, any combination of businesses or individuals formed to undertake a specific project, whether a corporation, partnership, or contractual relationship. In a narrower sense, a contractual relationship for the purpose of a specific project that is not a partnership. Liability of the parties is limited to the contractual undertaking and one party cannot bind the others. The tax consequences of the undertaking flow through to the joint venturers, and the joint venture is not an independent entity for tax purposes. As to the antitrust aspects of joint ventures, see *United States v. Penn-Olin Chemical Co.,* 378 U.S. 158 (1964); *see generally* American Bar Association, Section of Antitrust Law, *Antitrust Law Developments* 86 (1975). See the definition of a "corporate joint venture" in American Institute of Certified Public Accountants, Accounting Principles Board Opinion No. 18, *The Equity Method of Accounting for Investments in Common Stock,* paragraph 3d (1971).

Judgment creditor: Creditor who has obtained a court judgment in respect of a debt.

Judicial dissolution: Dissolution of a corporation by court action in case of deadlock among directors or shareholders, petition of directors or shareholders in certain circumstances, or petition by a creditor in case of insolvency. Model Business Corporation Act § 97 (1979); N. Y. Bus. Corp. Law §§ 1101–5; Cal. Corp. Code §§ 1800–9. See **dissolution.**

Judicial lien: Lien obtained by judgment, levy, sequestration, or other legal or equitable process or proceeding. 11 U.S.C. § 101(27).

Jumbo CD: Certificate of deposit in a denomination of $100,000 or more.

Junior mortgage: Mortgage that is lower in priority of claims to another mortgage.

Junk bond: Bond that has a high risk of default or is in default.

Justice, United States Department of: Cabinet-level department of the executive branch of the United States government charged with enforcing federal laws (except those specifically assigned to other agencies) and representing the United States in legal proceedings. Divisions of the Department of Justice include the Antitrust Division, the Civil Division, the Civil Rights Division, the Criminal Division, the Land and Natural Resources Division, and the Tax Division. The Federal Bureau of Investigation is part of the Department of Justice, and U.S. Attorneys, U.S. Marshalls, and the Solicitor General work in the Department.

K

Keep-well: Undertaking by the parent of a contracting corporation to keep the contracting corporation in a position to discharge its contractual obligations by injecting capital as needed. A keep-well is an indirect and somewhat reluctant form of guaranty. See indirect **guarantee of indebtedness.**

KGaA: *Kommanditgesellschaft auf Aktien,* a form of business association under German law in which one partner must be a general partner (but that partner may be a corporation) and the board of directors has limited powers.

Know-how license: License for the use of unpatentable processes and techniques. As to the antitrust aspects of know-how licensing, see American Bar Association, Section of Antitrust Law, *Antitrust Law Developments* 351 (1975).

Knowledge: Conscious belief in the truth of a fact. *See Restatement, Second, Contracts* § 19, Comment b (1981). *See also* UCC Section 1-201(25). Compare **reason to know.**

L

Labor, United States Department of: Cabinet-level department of the executive branch of the United States government that administers federal programs designed to promote the welfare of wage earners. See also **National Labor Relations Board.**

Labor dispute: As defined in the National Labor Relations Act, "any controversy concerning terms, tenure or conditions of employment, or concerning the association or representation of persons in negotiating, fixing, maintaining, changing, or seeking to arrange terms or conditions of employment, regardless of whether the disputants stand in the proximate relation of employer and employee." Section 2(9), 29 U.S.C. § 152(9).

Labor Management Relations Act, 1947: Taft-Hartley Act; statute substantially amending the National Labor Relations Act, providing procedures for conciliation of labor disputes in emergency situations, and addressing other labor-related problems.Pub. L. No. 101, ch. 120, 61 Stat. 136 (1947).

Labor-Management Reporting and Disclosure Act of 1959: Federal statute amending the National Labor Relations Act and imposing certain reporting requirements and organizational safeguards on labor organizations. Also known as the Landrum-Griffin Act. Pub. L. No. 86-257, 73 Stat. 519 (1959).

Labor-Management Services Administration: Branch of the United States Department of Labor assigned responsibility for administration of the labor provisions of the Employee Retirement Income Security Act of 1974 (ERISA), the program to ensure veterans reemployment rights provided at 43 U.S.C. § 38, the Labor Management Reporting and Disclosure Act, and section 13(c) of the Urban Mass Transportation Act. The LMSA also provides technical and advisory services to employers and unions in connection with collective bargaining.

LAFTA: Latin American Free Trade Association.

Landrum-Griffin Act: Labor-Management Reporting and Disclosure Act of 1959.

Lanham Act: Trade-Mark Act of 1946; federal statute covering trademarks and trademark registration. Pub. L. No. 489, ch. 540, 60 Stat. 427 (1946); 15 U.S.C. 1051–1127.

LASH: Lighter aboard ship; a system of cargo carriage by water in which cargo is loaded into small barges, called lighters, and the lighter, with cargo, is loaded onto a larger, ocean-going vessel.

Last in, first out: Method of accounting in which it is assumed that the last purchases for inventory are then first used for sales. Compare first in, first out.

LDC: Less-developed country.

Leading-object rule: See main purpose rule.

Leakage: Sale of small amounts of unregistered securities pursuant to SEC Rule 144. 17 C.F.R. § 230.144; also called dribble.

Lease: Agreement for the occupation or use of property for a fixed period. Real property leases are conveyances for a limited term; personal property leases are contracts for the hire of the property. Real property leases are governed by property law, but personal property leases are governed by contract law. The results of a given type of controversy under the two branches of the law may not be the same. As to leases of real property, see *Friedman on Leases* (1974); as to leases of personal property, see B. Fritch & A. Reisman, ed., *Equipment Leasing–Leveraged Leasing* (2d ed. 1980); R. Contino, *Legal and Financial Aspects of Equipment Leasing Transactions* (1979). *See* Financial Accounting Standards Board, Statement of Financial Accounting Standards No. 13, *Accounting for Leases* (1976). See also **finance lease; true lease; leveraged lease; lease for security.**

Leaseback: Transaction in which an owner of property sells it to a financing party, and then leases it back.

Lease for security: Transaction that, while in form a lease, is in substance a conditional sale or security interest. The distinction between a "true" lease and a lease for security is sometimes difficult to make. See **security interest;** *see also* Rev. Rul. 55-540, 1955-2 C.B. 39; Rev. Proc. 75-21, 1975-1 C.B. 715; Coogan, *Is There a Difference Between a Long-Term Lease and an Installment Sale of Personal Property?* 56 N.Y.U. L. Rev. 1036 (1981).

Left-hand side: Rate at which a bank offers to sell foreign currency. Compare **right-hand side.**

Legal description: Description of a parcel of real property used in documents of conveyance, usually defining the boundaries by metes and bounds.

Legal investment laws: State laws regulating the kinds of investments that may be made by various classes of investors with fiduciary duties, such as insurance companies and savings banks. *See, e.g.,* New York Banking Law § 235. Legal investment laws are collected in the CCH Blue Sky Reports.

Legal list: List, published by the banking or insurance regulatory body of a state, showing the securities in which a regulated bank or insurance company may invest.

Legal rate of interest: Maximum rate of interest that may be charged on a loan, as established by law.

Legend: Statement placed on securities providing notice of restrictions on transfer, either because the securities are being issued in a transaction exempt from registration under the Securities Act of 1933, or a shareholders' agreement with respect to such securities is in effect. *See* SEC Release No. 33-5121, 36 Fed. Reg. 1525 (1970); Del. Code Ann. tit. 8 § 347(c); Cal. Corp. Code § 418.

Legislative facts: Facts related to general characteristics of an industry, or general reasons for administrative action, as compared to particular facts in a controversy (adjudicative facts). *See* Davis, *An Approach to Problems of Evidence in the Administrative Process,* 55 Harv. L. Rev. 364, 402 (1942). Compare adjudicative facts.

Legislative rule: The Attorney General's Manual on the Administrative Procedure Act defines "substantive rules" (which have since become more commonly referred to as "legislative rules") as "rules ... issued by an agency pursuant to statutory authority and which implement the statute ... Such rules have the force and effect of law." The distinction between legislative rules and interpretative rules (which are not subject to the notice and hearing requirements of the Administrative Procedure Act) has been very difficult to draw. *See, e.g., Energy Reserves Group v. DOE,* 589 F. 2d 1082 (Temporary Emergency Court of Appeals 1978); *see generally* 2 K. Davis, *Administrative Law Treatise* §§ 7:8-7:18 (2d ed. 1979). Compare interpretative rule.

Lemon provision: Provision of the Magnuson-Moss Warranty–Federal Trade Commission Improvement Act that requires the warrantor of consumer products under a full warranty to replace or provide a refund for products with defects that cannot be remedied after a reasonable number of efforts. 15 U.S.C. § 2304(a)(4).

Lender of last resort: Entity that undertakes to provide credit when it is otherwise unavailable. The Federal Reserve is the lender of last resort for member or nonmember banks or other entities in unusual circumstances involving a national or regional emergency where failure to obtain credit would have a severely adverse effect on the economy.

Lessee: Party to whom a lease is made; the party that has a right under a lease to possess certain property.

Lessee group: Term used in the Internal Revenue Service guidelines for advance rulings in leveraged lease transactions to include the lessee, any shareholder of the lessee, and any party related to the lessee under the rules for constructive ownership of stock set forth in section 318 of the Internal Revenue Code. *See* Rev. Proc. 75-21, 1975-1 C.B. 715.

Lessor: Party that grants a lease; the owner of property that gives a lessee a right of possession under a lease.

Letter for underwriters: See comfort letter.

Letter of advice: Communication from the drawer of a sight draft to the drawee that the described draft has been drawn. UCC Section 3-701.

Letter of credit: In Article 2 of the Uniform Commercial Code–Sales, "letter of credit" in a contract of sale means "an irrevocable credit issued by a financing agency of good repute and, where the shipment is overseas, of good international repute." UCC Section 2-325. See **financing agency**. Article 5 of the Uniform Commercial Code is specifically addressed to letters of credit, and uses this definition:

"Credit" or "letter of credit" means an engagement by a bank or other person made at the request of a customer and of a kind within the scope of this Article (Section 5-102) that the issuer will honor drafts or other demands for payment upon compliance with the conditions specified in the credit. A credit may be either revocable or irrevocable. The engagement may be either an agreement to honor or a statement that the bank or other person is authorized to honor.

UCC Section 5-103(1)(a). Not all engagements to honor drafts are treated as letters of credit under Article 5 of the Uniform Commercial Code. UCC Section 5-102. International practice with respect to letters of credit is covered by the Uniform Customs and Practice for Documentary Credits of the International Chamber of Commerce. *See gener-*

ally H. Harfield, *Letters of Credit* (1979).

Letter stock: Stock that has not been registered under the Securities Act of 1933, and that has been sold only to investors who have furnished an investment letter stating that the stock is being purchased for investment and not for resale.

Level accrual: Method of periodic accounting for interest income by dividing the amount of interest by the number of periods until payment thereof.

Level debt service: System of debt amortization whereby the combined payments of principal and interest on all payment dates are approximately equal; sometimes called mortgage amortization, because the principal amortization on home mortgages is usually calculated that way. The early payments will have a high proportion of interest, then as the principal balance is reduced the payments have less interest and a greater proportion of principal.

Leverage: Use of debt capital in an enterprise or particular financing to increase the effectiveness (and risk) of the equity capital invested therein.

Leverage contract: Contract for the delivery of a commodity incorporating credit or margin provisions. Usually successive purchases and sales can be made under a master contract, an initial down payment is required, and delivery is made upon payment in full. Leverage contracts for agricultural commodities are prohibited, and the Commodity Futures Trading Commission has the authority to regulate or prohibit leverage contracts for gold and silver bullion and coins. 7 U.S.C. § 23. *See* 17 C.F.R. § 31; 11 U.S.C. 761(13).

Leveraged buy-out: Purchase of all of the stock and assets of a company for cash, with operating management and an investor group putting up a small portion of the equity, and institutional investors providing additional equity and the remainder of the cash in the form of debt. The debt-equity ratio is usually very high. *See* Lederman, *Leveraged Buy-Outs,* 11 Inst. Sec. Reg. 165 (1980).

Leveraged lease: Lease transaction in which the owner or equity participant borrows a portion of the purchase price of the property being leased. The Financial Accounting Standards Board has promulgated a definition of leveraged lease for the purpose of accounting therefor that includes some additional elements—the debt is nonrecourse to the equity participant, and the investment of the equity participant declines in the early years of the lease and rises later. *See* Financial Accounting Standards Board, Statement of Accounting Standards No. 13, *Accounting for Leases,* paragraph 42 (1976). *See also* Rev. Proc. 75-21, 1975-1 C.B. 715. *See generally* B. Fritch & A. Reisman, ed., *Equipment Leasing—Leveraged Leasing* (2d ed. 1980); R. Contino, *Legal and Financial Aspects of Equipment Leasing Transactions* (1979).

Lex situs: Law of the place where the property is situated. The lex situs will always govern a matter involving real property, and it will sometimes govern a matter involving personal property.

Liability: As defined by the Financial Accounting Standards Board, "Liabilities are probable future sacrifices of economic benefits arising from present obligations of a particular entity to transfer assets or provide services to other entities in the future as a result of past transactions or events." Financial Accounting Standards Board, Statement of Financial Accounting Concepts No. 3, *Elements of Financial Statements of Business Enterprises,* paragraph 28 (1980). *See also* Financial Accounting Standards Board, Statement of Financial Accounting Standards No. 5, *Accounting for Contingencies,* paragraphs 69–73 (1975).

LIBOR: London interbank offered rate.

License: Grant of permission. Under the Administrative Procedure Act, the term "license" includes "the whole or a part of an agency permit, certificate, approval, registration, charter, membership, statutory exemption or other form of permission." 5 U.S.C. § 551(8).

Licensee: Party who acquires rights under license.

Licensing: Under the Administrative Procedure Act, the term "licensing" includes "agency process respecting the grant, renewal, denial, revocation, suspension, annulment, withdrawal, limitation, amendment, modification, or conditioning of a license." 5 U.S.C. § 551(9).

Licensor: Party who grants a license.

Lien: As defined in the Bankruptcy Code, a lien is a "charge against or interest in property to secure payment of a debt or performance of an obligation." 11 U.S.C. § 101(28); *see* H.R. Rep. No. 95-595, 95th Cong., 1st Sess. 312 (1977). See **security interest; tax lien.**

Lien creditor: For the purpose of Article 9 of the Uniform Commercial Code—Secured Transactions, a lien creditor is "a creditor who has acquired a lien on the property involved by attachment, levy or the like and includes an assignee for the benefit of creditors from the time of assignment, and a trustee in bankruptcy from the date of the filing of the petition or a receiver in equity from the time of appointment." UCC Section 9-301(3). A lien creditor has priority over an unperfected security interest. *See* UCC Section 9-301.

LIFO: Last in, first out.

Like grade and quality: The Robinson-Patman Act prohibition against price discrimination relates to goods of "like grade and quality." 15 U.S.C. § 13(a). "Grade and quality" are to be determined by the characteristics of the product itself, without reference to brand identification. *FTC v. Borden Co.,* 383 U.S. 637 (1966). *See* American Bar Association, Section of Antitrust Law, *Antitrust Law Developments* 113 (1975).

Like kind exchange: Exchange of property of "like kind" held for productive use or investment, which is not regarded as a taxable event. I.R.C. § 1031; *see also* I.R.C. §§ 1245(b)(4), 1250(d)(4).

Limited liability company. Corporate form used in Europe for smaller enterprises and enterprises that are owned by a limited number of shareholders. Boards of directors are not required, transfer of shares is restricted, and shares are usually evidenced only by notation on a register instead of by certificates. The American counterpart is a close corporation or closely held corporation. Compare **joint stock company.**

Limited partner: Partner in a partnership whose liability is limited by the terms of the partnership agreement. All partners in a partnership cannot be limited partners; at least one partner must be a general partner.

Limited partnership: Partnership with one or more general partners and one or more limited partners; the limited partners are not liable for the obligations of the partnership. *See* Uniform Limited Partnership Act, *e.g.,* Cal. Corp. Code §§ 15501–32. *See generally* Aslanides, Cardinalli, Haynsworth, Lane & Niesar, *Limited Partnerships—What's Next and What's Left?* 34 Bus. Law. 257 (1978).

Limited recourse: Transaction for the sale or assignment of accounts or chattel paper in which recourse to the seller or assignor is limited as to amount or time.

Limited reduction plan: Loan amortization plan that provides for reduction of only a portion of the principal amount prior to the maturity date.

Limited tax bond: Municipal bond payable only out of revenues from certain taxes, groups of taxes, or portions of taxes.

Limited use property: Property under lease that can only practically be used by the lessee at the expiration of the lease term. *See* Rev. Proc. 76-30, 1976-2 C.B. 647.

Limited warranty: Under the Magnuson-Moss Warranty–Federal Trade Commission Improvement Act, any warranty that is not a "full warranty" is a "limited warranty." 15 U.S.C. § 2303.

Line of commerce: Section 7 of the Clayton Act relates to the lessening of competition "in any line of commerce in any section of the country." 15 U.S.C. § 18. The relevant "line of commerce" is determined by reference to product markets and geographic markets. *See Brown Shoe Co. v. United States,* 370 U.S. 294 (1962); *see generally* American Bar Association, Section of Antitrust Law, *Antitrust Law Developments* 65 (1975).

Line of credit: Undertaking on the part of a financial institution to lend in the future, usually with a set limit of loans outstanding at any given time.

Liquid assets: Cash or other assets, such as marketable securities, that can be sold and converted to cash quickly.

Liquidated damages: Amounts stipulated by the parties to a contract as damages for the breach of that contract. Liquidated damages, to be enforceable, must represent a reasonable effort to estimate actual damages. A greater amount would be regarded as a penalty and be unenforceable. *Restatement, Second, Contracts* § 356. In contracts for the sale of goods, damages may be liquidated at "an amount which is reasonable in light of the anticipated or actual harm caused by the breach, the difficulties of proof of loss, and the inconvenience or nonfeasibility of otherwise obtaining an adequate remedy." UCC Section 2-718.

Liquidating dividend: Dividend paid out of liquidation or disposition of assets, rather than earnings.

Liquidation: Sale or conversion to cash; sale of assets of a corporation or business and distribution of proceeds to creditors and shareholders. *See* Model Business Corporation Act §§ 97–105 (1979); Del. Code Ann. tit. 8 §§ 291–303. See also **dissolution.**

Lis pendens: Pending suit. Usually used in the phrase "notice of lis pendens," indicating that a suit is pending with respect to certain property.

Listed: With respect to securities and options, listed for trading on a recognized exchange.

Little FTC act: State statute providing for private remedies for unfair or deceptive trade practices.

LNG: Liquefied natural gas.

Load: Fee charged by an open-end investment company in connection with the purchase of new shares. The load covers sales commissions and related costs.

Load line: See Plimsoll line.

Local business: Business over which the NLRB declines to assert jurisdiction, as authorized by section 14(c) of the National Labor Relations Act, 29 U.S.C. § 164(c).

Lockout: Employer action in terminating the employment of a group of employees by shutting down the plant or closing the employment location. A lockout is an unfair labor practice when used to discourage union activities, but not when dictated by business needs. *See American Ship Building Co. v. NLRB,* 380 U.S. 300 (1965).

Lockup: Agreement whereby the target of an unfriendly takeover attempt grants to a friendly potential acquiring company ("white knight") an option to purchase a large block of shares or a valuable property, thus keeping such shares or property out of reach of the unfriendly potential acquiring company.

London Interbank Offered Rate (LIBOR): Interest rate offered for short-term deposits of dollars in the most creditworthy international banks in London for a specified period (demand, three months, six months, nine months, or one year).

Long: Having a larger quantity of a commodity or security than one has agreed to sell.

Long term: In respect of debt obligations, when compared with short term, having a maturity of more than one year. Financial Accounting Standards Board, Statement of Financial Accounting Standards No. 6, *Classification of Short-term Obligations Expected to be Refinanced,* paragraph 2 (1975). When

compared with intermediate term, having a maturity of more than ten years.

Long-term capital gain: Under the Internal Revenue Code, a long-term capital gain is a "gain from the sale or exchange of a capital asset held for more than 1 year if and to the extent that such gain is taken into account in computing gross income." I.R.C. § 1222(3). Long-term capital gains are taxed at a lower rate than ordinary income. See **capital asset.**

Long-term capital loss: Under the Internal Revenue Code, a long-term capital loss is a "loss from the sale or exchange of a capital asset held for more than 1 year if and to the extent that such loss is taken into account in computing taxable income." I.R.C. § 1222(4). See **capital asset.**

Long-term contract: For federal income tax purposes, a building, construction, installation, or manufacturing contract that is not completed in the same taxable year in which it is entered into. *See* section 229 of the Tax Equity and Fiscal Responsibility Act of 1982.

Loss: As defined by the Financial Accounting Standards Board, "Losses are decreases in equity (net assets) from peripheral or incidental transactions of an entity and from all other transactions and other events and circumstances affecting the entity during a period except those that result from expenses or distributions to owners." Financial Accounting Standards Board, Statement of Financial Accounting Concepts No. 3, *Elements of Financial Statements* *of Business Enterprises,* paragraph 68 (1980). Compare **gain.**

Lot: In Article 2 of the Uniform Commercial Code–Sales, lot means "a parcel or a single article which is the subject matter of a separate sale or delivery, whether or not it is sufficient to perform the contract." UCC Section 2-105(5). If a contract for the sale of goods gives the seller the right to tender delivery in lots, payment can be demanded for each lot. UCC Section 2-307.

Lower of cost or market: In this phrase, used in connection with inventory evaluation, the word "market" means:

current replacement cost (by purchase or reproduction, as the case may be) except that:
(1) Market should not exceed the net realizable value (i.e., estimated selling price in the ordinary course of business less reasonably predictable costs of completion and disposal); and
(2) Market should not be less than net realizable value reduced by an allowance for an approximately normal profit margin.

American Institute of Certified Public Accountants, Accounting Research Bulletin No. 43, Ch. 4, *Inventory Pricing,* Statement 6 (1953).

Ltd.: Limited, referring to limited liability company; British corporation whose stock is not publicly traded. Compare **PLC.**

Luxibor: Luxembourg inter-bank offered rate for Deutschemark deposits, similar to LIBOR, the London inter-bank offered rate for dollar deposits in London.

M

Magnuson-Moss: The Magnuson-Moss Warranty–Federal Trade Commission Improvement Act, Pub. L. No. 93-637, 88 Stat. 2183 (1975); 15 U.S.C. §§ 44–46, 49–50, 52, 56–58, 2301–12. *See generally* Popper, *The New Federal Warranty Law: Guide to Compliance,* 32 Bus. Law. 399 (1977).

MAI: Member, Appraisal Institute.

Main purpose rule: Under the statute of frauds, a contract to answer for the duty of another (as guarantor or surety) must be in writing to be enforceable, with this exception, called the "main purpose" or "leading purpose" rule:

A contract that all or part of a duty of a third person to the promisee shall be satisfied is not within the Statute of Frauds as a promise to answer for the duty of another if the consideration for the promise is in fact or apparently desired by the promisor mainly for his own economic advantage, rather than in order to benefit the third person. If, however, the consideration is merely a premium for insurance, the contract is within the Statute.

Restatement, Second, Contracts § 116 (1981); *see* §§ 110, 112. *See generally* Morris, *The Leading Purpose Doctrine as Applied to the Statute of Frauds,* 62 W. Va. L. Rev. 339 (1960).

Maker: Party who executes an instrument, thus undertaking to be liable thereon.

Mallinkrodt rule: Six factors to be considered by the NLRB in determining whether a group of craftsmen should be treated as a separate bargaining unit, set out in *Mallinkrodt Chemical Works,* 162 N.L.R.B. 387, 397 (1966).

Management and Budget, Office of: Unit of the Executive Office of the President responsible for preparation of the federal budget and formulation of fiscal policy, and for coordinating the activities of the various federal agencies.

Managerial employee: Employee who formulates, determines, and carries out management policies. A managerial employee is not regarded as an "employee" under the National Labor Relations Act. *See NLRB v. Bell Aerospace Co.*, 416 U.S. 267 (1974).

Managing underwriter: In connection with an offering of securities:

The term "managing underwriter" includes an underwriter (or underwriters) who, by contract or otherwise, deals with the registrant; organizes the selling effort; receives some benefit directly or indirectly in which all other underwriters similarly situated do not share in proportion to their respective interests in the underwriting; or represents any other underwriters in such matters as maintaining the records of the distribution, arranging the allotments of securities offered or arranging for appropriate stabilization activities, if any.

17 C.F.R. § 230.405; 47 Fed. Reg. 11380, 11436 (1982).

Mandamus: Action to compel performance by a public official or a corporate officer of his prescribed duty.

Manufacturer's statement of origin: Document furnished by a manufacturer of a vehicle subject to vehicle registration laws, identifying the vehicle and its serial number, for use in registering the vehicle and obtaining a certificate of title.

MarAd: Maritime Administration.

Margin: Difference between the price of a security and the amount of cash paid by the purchaser; the amount borrowed for the purchase of securities.

Margin requirements: Regulations G, T, U, and X of the Federal Reserve System, limiting the amount that can be borrowed to purchase and hold securities. 12 C.F.R. §§ 207, 220, 221, 224. *See* section 7 of the Securities Exchange Act of 1934, 15 U.S.C. § 78g.

Maritime Administration: Branch of the United States Department of Transportation responsible for programs for the development, promotion, and operation of the United States merchant marine. MarAd administers the construction-differential and operating differential subsidy programs, the Title XI ship financing program, and the War Risk Insurance program, and maintains the National Defense Reserve Fleet of government-owned ships. *See* 46 C.F.R. § 201–391.

Maritime Commission: See Federal Maritime Commission.

Maritime lien: Claim against a vessel or right in a vessel provided by admiralty law as security for a debt with respect to the vessel. Maritime liens are enforced against the vessel *in rem,* and are not regarded as claims against the owner *in personam.* As to maritime liens for necessaries, see Merchant Marine Act, 1920, sections P–S, 46 U.S.C. §§ 971–75. *See* Ray, *Maritime Contract Liens,* 47 Tul. L. Rev. 587 (1973); Kriz, *Ship Mortgages, Maritime Liens, and their Enforcement: the Brussels Conventions of 1926 and 1962,* 1963 Duke L. J. 671.

Maritime Subsidy Board: Unit of the Maritime Administration that administers the programs of subsidy for the difference in operating cost between United States flag and foreign-flag vessels, and for the difference between construction costs in United States and foreign shipyards.

Market: Group of products and an associated geographic area. The definition of the products and the geographic area to be included in a market is an important and complex issue in an antitrust case. *See* United States Department of Justice, *Merger Guidelines* (1982). See also **lower of cost or market.**

Marketable: As defined for equity securities by the Financial Accounting Standards Board:

Marketable, as applied to an equity security, means an equity security as to which sales prices or bid and ask prices are currently available on a national securities exchange (i.e., those registered with the Securities and Exchange Commission) or in the over-the-counter market. In the over-the-counter market, an equity security shall be considered marketable when a quotation is publicly reported by the National Association of Securities Dealers Automatic Quotations System or by the National Quotations Bureau Inc. (provided, in the latter case, that quotations are available from at least three dealers). Equity securities traded in foreign markets shall be considered marketable when such markets are of a breadth and scope comparable to those referred to above. Restricted stock does not meet this definition.

Financial Accounting Standards Board, Statement of Financial Accounting Standards No. 12, *Accounting for Certain Marketable Securities,* paragraph 7b (1975); *see* Financial Accounting Standards Board, Interpretation No. 16, *Clarification of Definitions and Accounting for Marketable Equity Securities That Become Nonmarketable: An Interpretation of FASB Statement No. 12* (1977). See **restricted stock.**

Market extension merger: Merger between companies selling the same products but in different geographical markets. *See United States v. Atlantic Richfield Co.,* 297 F. Supp. 1061 (S.D.N.Y. 1969), *aff'd mem. sub nom. Bartlett v. United States,* 401 U.S. 986 (1971). *See generally* American Bar Association, Section of Antitrust Law, *Antitrust Law Developments* 79 (1975).

Market maker: Dealer willing to purchase or sell securities of a given type or of a given issuer at the market price for its own account, in order to maintain an orderly market, and so that every seller of that security will have a buyer, and every buyer a seller. As defined in the Securities Exchange Act of 1934:

The term "market maker" means any specialist permitted to act as a dealer, any dealer acting in the capacity of block positioner, and any dealer who, with respect to a security, holds himself out (by entering quotations in an inter-dealer communications system or otherwise) as being willing to buy and sell such security for his own account on a regular or continuous basis.

Section 3(a)(38), 15 U.S.C. § 78c(a)(38).

Market order: Order to buy or sell securities at the best price obtainable.

Market-out clause: Clause in a securities underwriting agreement providing for termination of the obligations of the underwriters if there should be a material adverse change in the market for the securities.

Market parity: In respect of convertible securities, equality of the market price and the conversion value.

Market power: The ability of one or more firms profitably to maintain prices above competitive levels. *See* United States Department of Justice, *Merger Guidelines* (1982).

Market price: Under the Uniform Commercial Code, when damages are to be determined by reference to market price in a case involving the sale of goods, such price is to be determined as of the place for tender, in the case of the seller's repudiation, or at the place of arrival, in the case of the buyer's rejection or revocation of acceptance. In either case, the market price is to be determined as of the time the buyer learns of the breach. UCC Section 2-713. In an action based on anticipatory repudiation, market price is to be determined as of the time the aggrieved party learns of the repudiation. UCC Section 2-723. Published quotations may be used to establish the market price. UCC Section 2-724.

Marshalling: Arranging or ranking in order. "Marshalling" is often used in the context of bankruptcy as "marshalling" assets–arranging the assets to secure the proper application of the assets toward claims.

Martin Act: Article 23-A of the New York General Business Law regarding fraudulent practices in respect of securities; New York's blue-sky law. N.Y. Gen. Bus. Law §§ 352–59-h.

Massachusetts trust: See business trust.

Matched sale-purchase agreement: Sale by the Federal Reserve of a security for immediate delivery to a dealer or foreign central bank, with an agreement to buy the security back within a specified period, usually seven days, at the same price. A matched sale-purchase agreement is the reverse of a repurchase agreement, and is sometimes called a reverse repurchase agreement.

Matching: Used in accounting to describe the recognition of expenses by associating costs with revenue on a cause and effect basis, or in a broader sense the process of expense recognition, or even the entire process of income determination. *See* American Institute of Certified Public Accountants, Accounting Principles Board Statement No. 4, Ch. 6, *Generally Accepted Accounting Principles–Pervasive Principles,* paragraph 11, n. 6 (1970).

Material: In connection with "material" misrepresentations in the context of contracts, "A misrepresentation is material if it would be likely to induce a reasonable person to manifest his assent, or if the maker knows that it would be likely to induce the recipient to do so." *Restatement, Second, Contracts* § 162(2) (1981); *see Nader v. Allegheny Airlines,* 445 F. Supp. 168, 174 (D.D.C. 1978). With respect to the requirement for furnishing information in registration statements and proxy statements, the term "material" limits the information required to "those matters to which there is a substantial likelihood that a reasonable investor would attach importance in determining whether to purchase the security registered."17 C.F.R. 230.405, SEC Release No. 33-6383, 47 Fed. Reg. 11380, 11436 (1982); 17 C.F.R. § 240.14a-9; *see TSC Industries, Inc. v. Northway, Inc.*, 426 U.S. 438 (1976); SEC Release No. 33-6333, 46 Fed. Reg. 41971, 41977 (1981). In connection with disclosure under rule 10b-5, "material" information has been held to encompass all information that is likely to affect the price of the stock (*SEC v. Texas Gulf Sulphur Co.*, 401 F. 2d 833, 848 (2d Cir. 1968), *cert. denied sub nom. Coates v. SEC*, 394 U.S. 976 (1969)), and has been held to depend on whether a reasonable man would attach importance to the information in question in determining his course of action (*List v. Fashion Park, Inc.*, 340 F.2d 457, 462 (2d Cir. 1965)). *See* Wiesen, *Disclosure of Inside Information–Materiality and Texas Gulf Sulphur*, 28 Md. L. Rev. 189 (1968). *See generally* Financial Accounting Standards Board, Statement of Financial Accounting Concepts No. 2, *Qualitative Characteristics of Accounting Information*, Appendix C (1980); Hewitt, *Developing Concepts of Materiality and Disclosure*, 32 Bus. Law. 887 (1977).

Materialman's lien: Lien on property arising by law to secure the payment of the price of materials used to construct or repair the property. A materialman's lien is usually treated in the same manner as a mechanic's lien. *See* UCC Section 9-310.

Materials Transportation Bureau: Unit of the United States Department of Transportation responsible for the administration and enforcement of laws relating to the transportion of hazardous materials and pipeline safety.

Mathematical or clerical error: The provisions of the Internal Revenue Code covering assessment and deficiency procedures treat mathematical or clerical errors somewhat differently from other circumstances giving rise to a deficiency proceeding, such as fraud. I.R.C. §§ 6211–16. The term "mathematical or clerical error" means an error in computation shown on the return, incorrect use of tables, inconsistent entries, omission of supporting information, and entry of a deduction or credit that exceeds a statutory limit. I.R.C. § 6213(g). Errors of this type would be apparent from examination of the return and are based on incorrect manipulation of accurately stated facts, thus fraud is not implied. See **footing error.**

Maturity: Date on which a debt security matures, and is to be completely paid off. In the case of securities with a sinking fund or principal amortization arrangement, the maturity is the date for the final payment of principal.

MBE: Minority Business Enterprise.

McCarran-Ferguson Act: Federal statute exempting the "business of insurance" from the Sherman, Clayton, and Federal Trade Commission Acts to the extent that it is "regulated by state law." Pub. L. No. 15, ch. 20, 59 Stat. 33 (1945); 11 U.S.C. §§ 1011–15. *See* Kimball & Boyce, *The Adequacy of State Insurance Rate Regulation: The McCarran-Ferguson Act in Historical Perspective*, 56 Mich. Law Rev. 545 (1958).

McFadden Act: Section 36 of the National Bank Act providing that national banks are subject to state laws in certain respects, particularly with respect to branching. Pub. L. No. 639, ch. 191, 44 Stat. 1224 (1927); 12 U.S.C. § 36.

Mechanic's lien: Lien on property arising by law, securing the payment of the price or value of work performed on the property. *See* UCC Section 9-310; II G. Gilmore, *Security Interests in Personal Property* 873 (1965). As to mechanics' liens on aircraft, see Sigman, *The Wild Blue Yonder: Interests in Aircraft under our Federal System*, 46 So. Calif. L. Rev. 316, 357 (1973).

Medium-term: Used to describe a fixed-income security or loan with a maturity of greater than one year and less than ten years.

Memorandum of agreement: Written memorandum of terms of agreement, resembling a contract, but intended as a record only, not to be enforceable by courts. Memoranda of agreement are often used to define relations between government agencies where a contract would be inappropriate.

Menge formula: Formula used to compute adjusted life insurance reserves for the purpose of allocating investment yield to policyholders. I.R.C. 805(c); see sections 261 and 263 of the Tax Equity and Fiscal Responsibility Act of 1982.

Merchant: In Article 2 of the Uniform Commercial Code–Sales, merchant means "a person who deals in goods of the kind or otherwise by his occupation holds himself out as having knowledge or skill peculiar to the practices or goods involved in the transaction or to whom such knowledge or skill may be attributed by his employment of an agent or broker or other intermediary who by his occupation holds himself out as having such knowledge or skill." UCC Section 2-104(1).

Merchantable: Under Article 2 of the Uniform Commercial Code–Sales, the sale of goods by a merchant with respect to goods of that kind carries with it an implied warranty as to merchantability of the goods sold. To be merchantable, goods must at least be such that:

(a) pass without objection in the trade under the contract description; and

(b) in the case of fungible goods, are of fair average quality within the description; and

(c) are fit for the ordinary purposes for which such goods are used; and

(d) run, within the variations permitted by the agreement, of even kind, quality and quantity within each unit and among all units involved; and

(e) are adequately contained, packaged, and labeled as the agreement may require; and

(f) conform to the promises or affirmations of fact made on the container or label if any.

UCC Section 2-314. See **implied warranty.**

Merchant bank: British financial institution performing the functions of an American investment banking house and certain other banking functions that would be prohibited to American investment bankers.

Merchant Marine Act, 1936: Statute creating the United States Maritime Commission, a federal regulatory and promotional body (whose duties have since been assigned to the Federal Maritime Commission and the Department of Commerce), and establishing programs for subsidy and assistance for the United States merchant marine. Title XI, providing for federal guaranties for vessel financing, was added in 1938. Pub. L. No. 835, ch. 858, 49 Stat. 1985 (1936), 46 U.S.C. §§ 1101–1295.

Merger: Absorption of one entity into another; combination of corporations. In the narrowest, technical sense, the term "merger" means a combination of two or more corporations into one of such corporations, but the term is also used in a broader sense to include consolidations and corporate combinations and acquisitions in which the original corporate entities are preserved. *See* United States Department of Justice, *Merger Guidelines* (1982). See also **consolidation; reorganization; statutory merger.**

Merger guidelines: Outline of the enforcement policy of the United States Department of Justice concerning acquisitions and mergers subject to section 7 of the Clayton Act or section 1 of the Sherman Act. United States Department of Justice, *Merger Guidelines* (1982).

MESBIC: Minority Enterprise Small Business Investment Corporation.

Midnight deadline: For the purpose of Article 3–Commercial Paper and Article 4–Bank Deposits and Collections of the Uniform Commercial Code, the "midnight deadline" with respect to a bank is "midnight on its next banking day following the banking day on which it receives the relevant item or notice or from which the time for taking action commences to run, whichever is later." UCC Section 4-104(1)(h).

Mil; mill: A thousandth part.

Mineral interests in properties: As defined by the Financial Accounting Standards Board:

Mineral interests in properties (hereinafter referred to as properties), which include fee ownership or a lease, concession, or other interest representing the right to extract oil or gas subject to such terms as may be imposed by the conveyance of that interest. Properties also include royalty interests, production payments payable in oil and gas, and other nonoperating interests in properties operated by others. Properties include those agreements with foreign governments or authorities under which an enterprise participates in the operation of the related properties or otherwise serves as the "producer" of the underlying reserves (see paragraph 53); but properties do not include other supply agreements or contracts that represent the right to purchase (as opposed to extract) oil and gas. Properties shall be classified as proved or unproved as follows:

    i. *Unproved properties*–properties with no proved reserves.

    ii. *Proved properties*–properties with proved reserves.

Financial Accounting Standards Board, Statement of Financial Accounting Standards No. 19, *Financial Accounting and Reporting by Oil and Gas Producing Companies,* paragraph 11a (1977).

Mineral production payment: See production payment.

Mineral resource asset: As defined by the Financial Accounting Standards Board:

Mineral resource assets are assets that are directly associated with and derive value from all minerals that are extracted from the earth. Such minerals include oil and gas, ores containing ferrous and non-ferrous metals, coal, shale, geothermal steam, sulphur, salt, stone, phosphate, sand, and gravel. Mineral resource assets include mineral interests in properties, completed and uncompleted wells, and related equipment and facilities, and other facilities required for purposes of extraction (FASB Statement No. 19, Financial Accounting and Reporting by Oil and Gas Producing Companies, paragraph 11). The definition does not cover support equipment because that equipment is included in the property, plant, and equipment for which current cost measurements are required by Statement 33.

Financial Accounting Standards Board, Statement of Financial Accounting Standards No. 39, *Financial Reporting and Changing Prices: Specialized Assets—Mining and Oil and Gas,* paragraph 5a (1980). See **mineral interests in properties.**

Minority Business Development Agency: Unit of the United States Department of Commerce that provides assistance for minority-owned businesses through local offices and the Interagency Council for Minority Business Enterprises and its network of local Minority Business Opportunity Committees.

Minority business enterprise set-aside: Provision of the Public Works Employment Act of 1977 that requires that, absent an administrative waiver, 10% of federal funds for public works projects must be used to procure services and supplies from businesses owned by members of minority groups. Pub. L. No. 95-28, 91 Stat. 116 (1977), 42 U.S.C. §§ 6701–10; *Fullilove v. Klutznick,* 448 U.S. 448 (1980).

Minority Enterprise Small Business Investment Corporation: Small Business Investment Corporation subject to section 301(d) of the Small Business Investment Act of 1958, 15 U.S.C. § 681(d). The term (and its acronym, MESBIC) is no longer used because the language of section 301(d) is not limited to minority groups, but speaks of "persons whose participation in the free enterprise system is hampered because of social or economic disadvantage." *See* S. Rep. No. 95-1070, 95th Cong., 2d Sess. (1978); Miller, *Small Business Investment Companies: Licensing, Tax and Securities Considerations,* 36 Bus. Law. 1679 (1981).

Minute book: Corporate record of the minutes of the meetings of the board of directors and special committees thereof.

Minutes: Record of the proceedings of a meeting.

Mirror-image rule: Rule of contract law that a counteroffer, if it is to operate to terminate an offeree's power to accept an offer, must relate to the same matter as the original offer and propose a substitute bargain. *Restatement, Second, Contracts* § 39 (1981). *See Uniroyal Inc. v. Chambers Gasket & Mfg. Co.,* 380 N.E. 2d 571 (Ind. App. 1978).

Misrepresentation: Assertion that is not in accord with the facts. *Restatement, Second, Contracts* § 159 (1981). *See* James, Jr., & Gray, *Misrepresentation,* 37 Md. L. Rev. 286 (1977), 488 (1978). Compare **mistake.**

Mistake: In connection with contracts, a belief that is not in accord with the facts. *Restatement, Second, Contracts* § 151 (1981). *See* Bronaugh, *Agreement, Mistake, and Objectivity in the Bargain Theory of Contract,* 18 Wm. & Mary L. Rev. 213 (1976).

Mitigate damages: Minimize the amount of damages due to breach of contractual duty. A party to a contract that has been breached by another has a duty to mitigate damages, and thus "damages are not recoverable for loss that the injured party could have avoided without undue risk, burden, or humiliation." *Restatement, Second, Contracts* § 350 (1981).

Mixed mortgage: Mortgage that covers a vessel and property other than a vessel. A mixed mortgage can have the status of a preferred mortgage under the Ship Mortgage Act, 1920, if it provides for separate discharge of the property that is not a vessel by payment of a specified portion of the mortgage indebtedness. *See* Ship Mortgage Act, 1920, section D, subdivision (e); 46 U.S.C. § 922(e); *see also The Emma Giles,* 15 F. Supp. 502 (D. Md. 1936).

MNC: Multi-national corporation.

Mobile goods: Under Article 9 of the Uniform Commercial Code–Secured Transactions, security interests in mobile goods are perfected under the law of the jurisdiction where the debtor is located, rather than where the goods are found. The term "mobile goods" is not specifically defined, but includes "goods which are mobile and which are of a type normally used in more than one jurisdiction, such as motor vehicles, trailers, rolling stock, airplanes, shipping containers, road building and construction machinery and commercial harvesting machinery and the like." UCC Section 9-103(3).

Modco: Modified coinsurance.

Model Business Corporation Act: Model law, drafted by the Committee on Corporate Laws of the Section of Corporation, Banking, and Business Law of the American Bar Association, which is the basis of the business corporation laws of 35 states (but not Delaware).

Model Debenture Indenture Provisions: Set of provisions for use in preparing indentures for corporate debenture issues, prepared by a committee of lawyers active in corporate financing and institutional investment. The model provisions are in a pre-printed booklet, and are incorporated by reference in the indenture that is specific for the debenture issue. American Bar Foundation, Corporate Debt Financing Committee, *Commentaries on Model Debenture Indenture Provisions, 1965; Model Debenture Indenture Provi-*

sions, *All Registered Issues, 1967; and Certain Negotiable Provisions Which May Be Included in a Particular Incorporating Indenture (1971).* See **Mortgage Bond Indenture Form.**

Modified coinsurance: Reinsurance agreement whereby the insurance company transferring risks retains ownership of the assets connected with the risks that are reinsured and retains the reserve liabilities connected with those risks. *See* section 255 of the Tax Equity and Fiscal Responsibility Act of 1982; I.R.C. § 811(c).

Modified half-year convention: See half-year convention.

Mohawk Valley formula: Program of strikebreaking involving public discredit of a union and unionization found to be a violation of the National Labor Relations Act in *Remington Rand, Inc.,* 2 N.L.R.B. 626 (1937).

M-1: Measure of the money supply. See money supply.

Monetary asset: Money or a claim to receive money the amount of which is fixed or determinable without reference to future prices of specific goods or services. Financial Accounting Standards Board, Statement of Financial Accounting Standards No. 33, *Financial Reporting and Changing Prices,* paragraph 47 (1979). *See* Financial Accounting Standards Board, Technical Bulletin re FASB Statement No. 33, *Classification as Monetary or Nonmonetary Items* (1981). See also **nonmonetary items.**

Monetary item: Monetary asset or liability.

Monetary liability: Obligation to pay a sum of money the amount of which is fixed or determinable without reference to future prices of specific goods or services. Financial Accounting Standards Board, Statement of Financial Accounting Standards No. 33, *Financial Reporting and Changing Prices,* paragraph 47 (1979). *See* Financial Accounting Standards Board, Technical Bulletin re FASB Statement No. 33, *Classification as Monetary or Nonmonetary Items* (1981). See also **nonmonetary items.**

Monetary-nonmonetary method: Method of translating assets and liabilities measured in foreign currency that translates monetary assets and liabilities at the current rate and nonmonetary assets and liabilities at the applicable historical rates. Financial Accounting Standards Board, Statement of Financial Accounting Standards No. 8, *Accounting for the Translation of Foreign Currency Transactions and Foreign Currency Financial Statements,* paragraphs 121, 126—128 (1975). Compare **current-noncurrent method; current rate method; temporal method.**

Monetary policy: Course of action by the Federal Reserve to influence the domestic and international economy with adjustments in the cost and availability of money and credit, by engaging in open market purchases and sales of government securities and tinkering with the discount rate and the reserve requirements. Compare **fiscal policy.**

Money: Medium of exchange, standard of value, and means to save or store purchasing power. The Uniform Commercial Code defines money as "a medium of exchange authorized or adopted by a domestic or foreign government as part of its currency." UCC Section 1-201(24). See money supply.

Money broker: Broker who specializes in finding short-term funds for money market borrowers and placing such funds for money market lenders.

Money market: Market for short-term, high quality credit instruments such as Treasury bills, commercial paper, bankers' acceptances, negotiable certificates of deposit, loans to and repurchase agreements with securities dealers, and federal funds. The market has no geographic location or formal structure, but functions on the telephone among banks, dealers in securities and commercial paper, and money brokers. *See* Parthemos, *The Money Market*, in T. Cook, ed., *Instruments of the Money Market* 5 (4th ed., 1977)

Money-market fund: Mutual fund that invests its assets, the capital contributed by its shareholders, in instruments of the money market.

Money-multiplier bond or money-multiplier note: Zero coupon bond or note; bond or note bearing no interest, issued at a deep discount, so the yield is the movement toward par value at maturity. The term "money-multiplier" is used because the return can be expressed as a multiple of the issue price; the original investment yields that return because with no interest payments, there is no requirement for reinvestment and thus the yield is not affected by a reinvestment rate.

Money-purchase pension plan: Type of defined-contribution pension plan in which the employer's contributions are allocated to specific individuals, usually as a percentage of compensation; the benefits to that individual are determined by the amounts so contributed. American Institute of Certified Public Accountants, Accounting Principles Board Opinion No. 8, *Accounting for the Cost of Pension Plans*, Appendix B, paragraph 19 (1966).

Money supply: The Federal Reserve defines monetary aggregates as follows:

M-1A: coin and currency, plus demand deposits, regardless of the financial institution where they are held, except foreign commercial banks and official institutions;

M-1B: M-1A plus other checkable deposits, including NOW accounts, ATS accounts, credit union share balances, and demand deposits at thrift institutions;

M-2: M-1B plus overnight repurchase agreements issued by commercial banks, overnight Eurodollar deposits held by U.S. nonbank residents at Caribbean branches of U.S. banks, money market mutual fund shares, and savings deposits and small time deposits at all depositary institutions;

M-3: M-2 plus large time deposits at all depositary institutions, and term repurchase agreements issued by commercial banks and savings and loan associations;

L: M-3 plus other Eurodollar holdings of U.S. residents other than banks, bankers acceptances, commercial paper, savings bonds, and liquid Treasury obligations.

Since January, 1982, the Federal Reserve has published only a single M-1 figure with the same coverage as M-1B. *See generally* Simpson, Williams, et al,

Recent Revisions in the Money Stock, 67 Fed. Res. Bull. 539 (1981); Simpson, *The Redefined Monetary Aggregates,* 66 Fed. Res. Bull. 97 (1980).

Monopolize: Section 2 of the Sherman Act prohibits monopolization, attempts to monopolize, and conspiracies to monopolize. 15 U.S.C. § 2. The offense of unlawful monopolization consists of "(1) the possession of monopoly power in the relevant market and (2) the willful acquisition or maintenance of that power as distinguished from growth or development as a consequence of a superior product, business acumen, or historic accident." *United States v. Grinnell Corp.,* 384 U.S. 563, 570 (1966). *See* American Bar Association, Section of Antitrust Law, *Antitrust Law Developments* 47 (1975).

Monopoly: In the context of section 2 of the Sherman Act, "the power to control market prices or exclude competition." *United States v. Grinnell Corp.,* 384 U.S. 563, 571 (1966). *See also American Tobacco Co. v. United States,* 328 U.S. 781, 811 (1946); *see generally* American Bar Association, Section of Antitrust Law, *Antitrust Law Developments* 48 (1975).

Moral obligation bond: Revenue bond with insufficient credit support from the project and its revenues, for which the state legislature undertakes a "moral obligation" to establish and replenish a fund to pay the interest and principal, if necessary.

Morning call: Daily telephone conversation between members of the staff of the board of governors of the Federal Reserve System in Washington and members of the staff of the New York Federal Reserve Bank to discuss and determine the adjustments to be made in monetary policy.

Mortgage: Conveyance of an interest in property, intended to secure performance of an obligation, that will become dead, or "mort," upon satisfaction of the obligation. The term usually refers to an interest in real property, but is also used for personal property (chattel mortgage), particularly for vessels. For the purpose of Article 9 of the Uniform Commercial Code–Secured Transactions, a mortgage means "a consensual interest created by a real estate mortgage, a trust deed on real estate, or the like." UCC Section 9-105(1)(j).

Mortgage Bond Indenture Form: Model form of trust indenture for use in corporate mortgage bond financings prepared by the Corporate Debt Financing Project of the American Bar Foundation. See also **Model Debenture Indenture Provisions.**

Mortgagee: Party to whom property is mortgaged (the lender or creditor). In the case of a preferred mortgage under the Ship Mortgage Act, 1920, mortgagee, "in the case of a mortgage involving a trust deed and a bond issue thereunder, means the trustee designated in such deed." 46 U.S.C. § 911. *See Chemical Bank New York Trust Co. v. S.S. Westhampton,* 358 F.2d 574 (4th Cir. 1965), *cert. denied,* 385 U.S. 921 (1966); Pub. L. No. 89-346, 79 Stat. 1305 (1965); H.R. Rep. No. 1116, 89th Cong., 1st Sess. (1965).

Mortgage participation certificate: Debt instrument representing an undivided interest in a group of conventional residential mortgages issued by the Federal Home Loan Mortgage Corporation. Principal and interest payments are made monthly, and the Federal Home Loan Mortgage Corporation guarantees the timely payment of the certificates regardless of the status of the underlying mortgages.

Mortgage subsidy bond: Under the Internal Revenue Code, a mortgage subsidy bond is an "obligation which is issued as part of an issue a significant portion of the proceeds of which are to be used directly or indirectly for mortgages on owner-occupied residences." I.R.C. § 103A(b). The interest on mortgage subsidy bonds is exempt from federal income taxes if certain requirements are met. I.R.C. § 103A. *See* section 220 of the Tax Equity and Fiscal Responsibility Act of 1982; Rev. Proc. 81-36.

Mortgagor: Party who subjects property to a mortgage; the debtor.

Most-favored-nation clause: Clause in a treaty giving to a nation or its citizens all of the privileges that a nation may give to any other nation or citizens; *e.g.*, Article I of the General Agreement on Tariffs and Trade. The term, although originating in the international treaty context, is sometimes used to describe similar clauses in labor contracts (in which a union agrees to give the contracting employer the most favorable terms it gives any employer) and in commercial agreements.

Motion picture films: As defined by the Financial Accounting Standards Board for the purpose of a supplement to its Statement of Financial Accounting Standards No. 33, *Financial Reporting and Changing Prices:*

the term motion picture films includes all types of films and videotapes and disks, including features, television specials, series, and cartoons that are (a) exhibited in theaters; (b) licensed for exhibition by individual television stations, groups of stations, networks, cable television systems, or other means; or (c) licensed for commercial reproduction (e.g., for the home viewing market).

Financial Accounting Standards Board, Statement of Financial Accounting Standards No. 46, *Financial Reporting and Changing Prices: Motion Picture Films,* paragraph 7 (1981).

MSO: Manufacturer's statement of origin.

MSRB: Municipal Securities Rulemaking Board.

MTB: Materials Transportation Bureau.

Multiple investment sinking fund method: Variation of the internal rate of return method of determining the yield on an investment in a leveraged lease transaction whereby the cash outflows towards the end of the transaction are regarded as additional investments and are assigned a different discount rate than the discount rate applied to the cash inflows. *See* Teichrow, Robichek & Montalbano, *An Analysis of Criteria for Investment and Financing Decisions Under Certainty,* 12 Management Science 151 (1965).

Municipal bond: Bond issued by a state or political subdivision of a state (not necessarily a municipality). The term is usually used in referring to an obligation of "a State, a Territory, or a possession of the United States, or any political subdivision of any of the foregoing, or of the District of Columbia," the interest on which would not be included in gross income for federal income taxes. *See* I.R.C. § 103. The Internal Revenue Code provision on computation of gross income for dealers in tax exempt securities have a special definition of the term "municipal bond." I.R.C. § 75(b). *See generally* Securities Industry Association, *Fundamentals of Municipal Bonds* (9th ed. 1973). See also **municipal securities.**

Municipality: Political subdivision or public agency or instrumentality of a state. 11 U.S.C. § 101(29); *see* H.R. Rep. No. 95-595, 95th Cong., 1st Sess. 312 (1977).

Municipal multiplier: Municipal bond with the characteristics of a money-multiplier bond.

Municipal securities: As defined in section 3(a)(29) of the Securities Exchange Act of 1934, securities that are "direct obligations of, or obligations guaranteed as to principal or interest by, a State or any political subdivision thereof, or any agency or instrumentality of a State or any political subdivision thereof, or any municipal corporate instrumentality of one or more States, or any security which is an industrial revenue bond ... " as defined in section 103(c)(2) of the Internal Revenue Code,

with certain qualifications. 15 U.S.C. § 78c(a)(29). *See generally* Peacock, *A Review of Municipal Securities and Their Status Under the Federal Securities Laws as Amended by the Securities Act Amendments of 1975,* 31 Bus. Law. 2037 (1976).

Municipal Securities Rulemaking Board: Federal agency established pursuant to section 15B of the Securities Exchange Act of 1934 (and the Securities Acts Amendments of 1975) to "adopt rules with respect to transactions in municipal securities effected by brokers, dealers, and municipal securities dealers." 15 U.S.C. § 78o-4(b).

Mutual fund: Investment company that sells shares to the public and uses the proceeds to buy securities. See **closed-end investment company; open-end investment company; regulated investment company.**

Mutual savings bank: State-chartered bank that can accept savings deposits and make loans, usually home mortgage loans. Mutual savings banks often have more diverse authority to accept deposits and make loans and investments than savings and loan associations, and in most states can offer checking accounts. Title XII of the Financial Institutions Regulatory and Interest Rate Control Act of 1978 gave the Federal Home Loan Bank Board authority to grant federal charters to mutual savings banks. *See* 12 C.F.R. §§ 575–78; I.R.C. § 591(b).

N

NAM: National Association of Manufacturers.

NASA: National Aeronautics and Space Administration.

NASAA: North American Securities Administrators Association.

NASD: National Association of Securities Dealers.

NASDAQ: National Association of Securities Dealers Automated Quotations.

National Aeronautics and Space Administration: Independent agency of the United States government that engages in aeronautical research and space exploration. *See* National Aeronautics and Space Act of 1958, Pub. L.No. 85-568, 72 Stat. 426 (1958); 42 U.S.C. §§ 2451–76; 14 C.F.R. §§ 1201–61.

National bank: National banking association; bank organized under the federal laws of the United States.

National Bureau of Standards: Unit of the United States Department of Commerce that provides a basis for physical measurements and provides scientific and technological services for government and industry, particularly in the fields of measurement and testing.

National Consumer Cooperative Bank: Independent financial institution sponsored by the United States government that provides financial and technical assistance to consumer cooperative organizations. *See* National Consumer Cooperative Bank Act, Pub. L. No. 95-351, 92 Stat. 499 (1978), 12 U.S.C. §§ 3001–50.

National Credit Union Administration: Independent agency of the United States government that charters, supervises, and insures federal credit unions and state-chartered credit unions that apply and qualify. The insurance program is called the National Credit Union Share Insurance Fund. The NCUA operates the Central Liquidity Facility, an emergency credit facility for member credit unions. *See* 12 U.S.C. § 1752a; 12 C.F.R. §§ 700–61.

National Environmental Policy Act: Federal statute establishing the Environmental Protection Agency and providing for a variety of measures for environmental protection to be employed by federal agencies, including preparation of an environmental impact statement for each major federal action. Pub. L. No. 91-190, 83 Stat. 852 (1970), 42 U.S.C. §§ 4321– 47. *See generally* Heyman, *et al, Complying with NEPA: Practice, Problems and Potential,* 29 Bus. Law. 1315 (1974).

National Highway Traffic Safety Administration: Branch of the United States Department of Transportation responsible for highway safety programs, including the promulgation of motor vehicle safety standards under the Motor Vehicle Safety Act of 1966 (Pub. L. No. 89-563, 80 Stat. 718 (1966)) and the Highway Safety Act of 1966 (Pub. L. No. 89-564, 80 Stat. 731 (1966), 23 U.S.C. §§ 401–3). NHTSA also promulgates standards for automotive fuel economy. *See* Highway Safety Act of 1970, Pub. L. No. 91-605, 84 Stat. 1739 (1970); 49 C.F.R. §§ 501–90.

National Labor Relations Act of 1935: Federal legislation, first passed as the Wagner Act in 1935 and subsequently amended by the Taft-Hartley Act and later legislation, providing a program of federal regulation of employer-union relations and collective bargaining. Pub. L. No. 2, ch. 372, 49 Stat. 449 (1935), 29 U.S.C. §§ 151–67.

National Labor Relations Board: Independent agency of the United States government responsible for the prevention of unfair labor practices by management and unions and for conducting elections among employees to decide on representation by labor organizations. The authority of the NLRB is established by the National Labor Relations Act. For railroad and air carriers, see **National Mediation Board.**

Nationally recognized statistical rating organization: This term, used by the Securities and Exchange Commission, is not defined, but Standard & Poor's Corporation, Moody's Investors Services, Inc., Fitch Investors Services, Inc., and Duff & Phelps, Inc. were regarded as such as of March 16, 1982. SEC Release No. 33-6383, 47 Fed. Reg. 11380, 11392 n. 54 (1982). *See* SEC Release No. 33-6336, 46 Fed. Reg. 42029 (1981); 17 C.F.R. § 240.15c3-1(c)(2)(vi)(F), 17 C.F.R. § 230.134; 17 C.F.R. § 230.436.

National Mediation Board: Independent agency of the United States government responsible for mediation of disputes over wages, hours, and working conditions among rail and air carriers and organizations representing their employees, and resolution of representation disputes and certification of employee organizations in the air and rail carrier industries. *See* Railway Labor Act; B. Aaron, B. Burgoon, *et al., The Railway Labor Act at Fifty* (1976).

National Oceanic and Atmospheric Administration: Branch of the United States Department of Commerce responsible for reporting and forecasting the weather, exploring and charting the oceans, and various programs relating to oceanography, meteorology, and marines fisheries. NOAA is responsible for licensing ocean thermal energy conversion facilities and for issuing licenses and permits for deep seabed mining of hard minerals. Units of NOAA include the National Weather Service (*see* 15 U.S.C. §§ 311–28), the National Ocean Survey (*see* 33 U.S.C. §§ 851–84), and the National Marine Fisheries Service (*see* 16 U.S.C. §§ 741—54).

National On-the-Job Training Program: Federal program administered by the Department of Labor of grants to labor organizations and trade management associations to operate special training programs for unemployed and disadvantaged persons.

National Pollutant Discharge Elimination System: Pollutant discharge system approved pursuant to a permit issued under section 402 of the Federal Water Pollution Control Act, as amended by the Clean Water Act of 1977, Pub. L. No. 95-217, 91 Stat. 1566 (1977); 33 U.S.C. § 1342.

National Railroad Adjustment Board: Unit of the National Mediation Board composed of an equal number of representatives of rail carriers and employee organizations which decides disputes on interpretation of agreements concerning rates of pay, rules, and working conditions in the railroad industry.

National Railroad Passenger Corporation: Government-sponsored corporation that provides rail passenger service. Amtrak, as it is called, owns trackage in the Northeast Corridor between Boston and Washington, but in other areas it operates by contracting with private railroad companies. *See* Rail Passenger Service Act, Pub. L. No. 91-518, 84 Stat. 1327 (1970), 45 U.S.C. §§ 541–645. *See generally* Adams, *The National Railroad Passenger Corporation—A Modern Hybrid Corporation Neither Private nor Public,* 31 Bus. Law. 601 (1976).

National Student Marketing: *SEC v. National Student Marketing Corp.,* 538 F. 2d 404 (D.C. Cir. 1976), *cert. denied sub nom. White & Case v. SEC,* 429 U.S. 1073 (1977), a significant case on the duty of counsel to disclose a client's possible wrongdoing.

National Technical Information Service: Unit of the United States Department of Commerce that provides public access to reports prepared by and for government agencies. The NTIS maintains a computer search service and sells reports in paper or microfiche form. *See* Pub. L. No. 776, ch. 936, 64 Stat. 823 (1950), 15 U.S.C. §§ 1151–57.

National Transportation Safety Board: Independent agency of the United States government that investigates and determines the cause of all civil aviation accidents, major rail, pipeline, and marine accidents, and selected highway accidents. *See* Independent Safety Board Act of 1974, Pub. L. No. 93-633, 88 Stat. 2166 (1974), 49 U.S.C. §§ 1901–7; 49 C.F.R. §§ 800–50.

NBS: National Bureau of Standards.

NCGA: National Council on Governmental Accounting.

NCITD: National Committee on International Trade Documentation.

NCUA: National Credit Union Administration.

Necessaries: Supplies and services essential to the operation of a vessel. Claims for debts for the furnishing of "necessaries" have a preferred status in admiralty. See **maritime lien;** Merchant Marine Act, 1920, subsections P–S, 46 U.S.C.§§ 971–75; *The Muskegon*, 275 F. 348 (2d Cir. 1921); G. Gilmore & C. Black, Jr., *The Law of Admiralty* 654 (1975).

Negative assurance: Form of comfort given with apparent reluctance by accountants:

Negative assurance consists of a statement by accountants to the effect that, as a result of specified procedures, nothing came to their attention that caused them to believe that specified matters do not meet a specified standard (e.g., that unaudited financial statements or condensed financial statements were not prepared in conformity with generally accepted accounting principles consistently applied).

American Institute of Certified Public Accountants, Statement on Auditing Standards No. 38, *Letters for Underwriters*, paragraph 2, n.2 (1981). Statements of negative assurance in accountants' letters to underwriters are the reason such letters are called "cold comfort" letters.

Negative carry: Excess of interest cost of money borrowed to make an investment over the earnings on that investment.

Negative goodwill: Excess of net asset value over the cost of an acquired company. *See* American Institute of Certified Public Accountants, Accounting Principles Board Opinion No. 16, *Accounting for Business Combinations*, paragraph 91 (1970).

Negative pledge: Covenant not to encumber corporate property with liens or security interests. *See* Coogan, Kripke & Weiss, *The Outer Fringes of Article 9: Subordination Agreements, Security Interests in Money and Deposits, Negative Pledge Clauses, and Participation Agreements*, 79 Harvard L. Rev. 229 (1965).

Negotiable: Capable of being transferred by endorsement or delivery so that the transferee acquires all rights. A warehouse receipt, bill of lading, or other document of title is negotiable:

(a) if by its terms the goods are to be delivered to bearer or to the order of a named person; or

(b) where recognized in overseas trade, if it runs to a named person or assigns.

Any other document is nonnegotiable. UCC Section 7-104. See **negotiable instrument.**

Negotiable instrument: Under Article 3 of the Uniform Commercial Code—Commercial Paper, to be negotiable an instrument must be in writing and must:

(a) be signed by the maker or drawer; and

(b) contain an unconditional promise or order to pay a sum certain in money and no other promise, order, obligation or power given by the maker or drawer except as authorized by this Article; and

(c) be payable on demand at a definite time; and

(d) be payable to order or to bearer.

UCC Section 3-104.

Negotiable order of withdrawal (NOW) account: Interest-earning account on which checks may be drawn.

Negotiated sale; negotiated offering: The issue of securities in a case where the price (and interest rate, in the case of debt securities) is determined by negotiation between the issuer and the underwriter (or purchaser, in a direct offering), rather than by competitive bidding.

Negotiating bank: Bank that purchases a draft that can be drawn against a letter of credit as a convenience to its customer, the beneficiary of the credit. The negotiating bank then presents the draft to the issuer or confirming bank for payment. *See* H. Harfield, *Letters of Credit* 11 (1979).

Negotiation: For the purpose of Article 3—Commercial Paper of the Uniform Commercial Code, negotiation of an instrument is the "transfer of an instrument in such form that the transferee becomes a holder. If the instrument is payable to order it is negotiated by delivery with any necessary indorsement; if payable to bearer it is negotiated by delivery." UCC Section 3-202.

Negotiation credit: Letter of credit that can be drawn upon by a party who purchases the beneficiary's draft on the credit. *See* H. Harfield, *Letters of Credit* 19 (1979).

NEPA: National Environmental Policy Act.

Net: Excluding all expenses and charges; after all deductions.

Net assets: Amount by which the total assets of a corporation exceed the total debts or liabilities of a corporation. Model Business Corporation Act § 2(i) (1979); Del. Code Ann. tit. 8, § 154; N.Y. Bus. Corp. Law § 102(a)(9).

Net capital gain: Excess of the net long-term capital gain for the taxable year over the net short-term capital loss for such year. I.R.C. § 1222(11).

Net capital loss: Excess of the losses from sales or exchanges of capital assets over the sum allowed under section 1211 of the Internal Revenue Code. Section 1211 limits the allowance for losses from sales or exchanges of capital assets to the extent of gains therefrom, in general. I.R.C. § 1222(10).

Net capital rule: Regulation of the Securities and Exchange Commission regarding minimum net worth of brokers and dealers. 17 C.F.R. § 240.15c3-1(c)(2).

Net current assets: The excess of current assets over current liabilities.

Net debt: Total indebtedness of an entity, less sinking fund accumulations and debt that is self-liquidating (such as industrial revenue bonds, in the case of a municipality).

Net income: The excess of revenue over expenses and the net increase in owner's equity of an enterprise for an accounting period from profit-directed activities. American Institute of Certified Public Accountants, Accounting Principles Board Statement No. 4, Ch. 5, *Basic Features and Basic Elements of Financial Accounting,* paragraph 21 (1970).

Net landed weight: Term in a contract for the sale of goods C.I.F. or C. & F. that means that the seller will reasonably estimate the weight, and that the payment due on tender of the documents called for by the contract will be based on such estimate, but the buyer and seller will adjust the final price based on the actual weight. UCC Section 2-321.

Net lease: Lease providing to the lessor a fixed stream of payments, net of all expenses and charges relating to the property, such as maintenance, insurance, and taxes. All such expenses and charges would be paid by the lessee, in addition to the fixed rentals. The term "net-net lease" is sometimes used in connection with real estate leases to mean a lease net of all costs to the landlord, and "net lease," in comparison, would mean a lease net of all costs except taxes. *See* 12 C.F.R. § 7.3400; *see generally* Howard & Howard, *Suggestions for Negotiating a Net Lease,* The Prac. Law., July 15, 1982, at 39.

Net long-term capital gain: Excess of long-term capital gains for the taxable year over the long-term capital losses for such year. I.R.C. § 1222(7).

Net long-term capital loss: Excess of long-term capital losses for the taxable year over the long-term capital gains for such year. I.R.C. § 1222(8).

Net operating loss: Excess of the deductions allowed by Chapter 1 of Subtitle A of the Internal Revenue Code (covering normal income taxes and surtaxes) over the gross income. I.R.C. § 172(c).

Net present value: Method of analyzing investment opportunities whereby the present values of future cash flows, discounted at an appropriate rate, are algebraically added, and the cost of the investment is subtracted from the total. The net present value of a stream of future cash flows is represented by the expression

$$\frac{A_1}{(1 + r)} + \frac{A_2}{(1 + r)^2} + \ldots +$$
$$\frac{A_n}{(1 + r)^n} - A_0$$

in which A_0 is the initial investment, A_1 through A_n are the cash flows occurring at the end of periods *1* through *n,* and *r* is the discount rate.

Net profit ratio: Excess of revenues over operating costs. "Net profit" is sometimes used interchangeably with net income, but is also used to mean net income before income deductions.

Net profit ratio: Ratio of net profit to sales for a given period.

Net quick assets: Excess of quick assets over current liabilities.

Net realizable value: Selling price less costs to sell.

Net short-term capital gain: Excess of short-term capital gains for the taxable year over the short-term capital losses for such year. I.R.C. § 1222(5).

Net short-term capital loss: Excess of short-term capital losses for the taxable year over the short-term capital gains for such year. I.R.C. § 1222(6).

Net weight: Weight not including the weight of the container.

Net working capital: The excess of current assets over current liabilities.

Net worth: Difference between assets and liabilities; in the case of a corporation, shareholders' equity.

New communities debenture: Obligation issued by the United States Department of Housing and Urban Development to provide assistance for new communities, pursuant to Title IV of the Housing and Urban Development Act of 1968 and Title VII of the Housing and Urban Development Act of 1970.

New York Convention: The United Nations Convention of 1958 on the Recognition and Enforcement of Foreign Arbitral Awards.

New York plan: Plan for the financing of railroad equipment based on a conditional sale agreement. The New York plan was developed in the last century as a companion to the Philadelphia plan, and was used in those states that gave effect to the reservation of title in a conditional vendor. Under the plan, the railroad purchases the equipment from the vendor or a group of vendors under a conditional sale agreement providing for installments of principal (usually payable annually for fifteen years) with interest (usually payable semiannually). The vendor or vendors immediately assign the indebtedness and the security interest in the equipment to a financial institution or a group acting through an agent, leaving the vendor or vendors with the equivalent of a cash sale and the financial institutions with an obligation of the railroad company, secured by an interest in the equipment. *See* D. Street, *Railroad Equipment Financing* (1959); K. Duncan, *Equipment Obligations* (1924). See also **Philadelphia plan.**

NG: No good (sometimes marked on a check to indicate insufficient funds).

NHTSA: National Highway Traffic Safety Administration.

NIFO: Next in, first out.

Nimble dividends: Most states permit corporate dividends to be paid only out of surplus, but Delaware and certain other states permit "nimble dividends," dividends that can be paid out of current net profits or profits from the preceding year, even if there is not any surplus. Del. Code Ann. tit. 8, § 170. *See* McCormick, *Nimble Dividends: Some States Do Permit Dividends Despite Deficit in Accumulated Earnings,* 88 J. of Accountancy 196 (1949).

NLRA: National Labor Relations Act of 1935.

NLRB: National Labor Relations Board.

NOAA: National Oceanic and Atmospheric Administration.

No action letter: Letter from the Securities and Exchange Commission or other government agency with enforcement powers, in response to a query about a contemplated course of action, to the effect that no enforcement action would be recommended by the agency staff if such course of action were followed; such a letter does not express an opinion on or approve the course of action contemplated.

No arrival, no sale: Delivery term in a contract for the sale of goods imposing on the seller the duty to ship conforming goods and leaving with the seller the risk of loss, but the seller assumes no obligation that the goods will arrive. If the goods fail to arrive, arrive late, or are damaged, the buyer may avoid the contract or may accept the goods with due allowance from the contract price. UCC Section 2-324, 2-613.

Noerr-Pennington doctrine: Doctrine that "the Sherman Act does not prohibit two or more persons from associating together in an attempt to persuade the legislature or the executive to take particular action with respect to a law that would produce a restraint or monopoly." *Eastern R.R. Presidents Conf. v. Noerr Motor Freight, Inc.*, 365 U.S. 127, 136 (1961); *United Mineworkers v. Pennington*, 381 U.S. 657 (1965). *See generally* Fischel, *Antitrust Liability for Attempts to Influence Government Action: The Basis and Limits of the Noerr-Pennington Doctrine*, 45 U. Chi. L. Rev. 80 (1977).

NOL: Net operating loss.

No-litigation certificate: Certificate, provided by an issuer of securities or its counsel, to the effect that there is no litigation pending or threatened that would impair the validity of the issue or the ability of the issuer to discharge its obligations on the securities.

No-load fund: Investment company that does not impose a "load," or charge, for the purchase of new shares.

Nolo contendere: I shall not contest it. Plea in a criminal matter, tantamount to guilty, but not an admission of guilt that can be used in a related civil case.

Nominal dollar accounting: Method of accounting that does not restate dollars into units of the same general purchasing power. Compare **constant dollar accounting;** see **current cost/nominal dollar accounting;** **historical cost nominal dollar accounting.**

Nominee: Partnership formed to act as record holder of securities held by institutional investors and financial intermediaries for their own account or for the account of their customers. See **street name.** *See generally* Securities and Exchange Commission, *Final Report on the Practice of Recording the Ownership of Securities in the Records of the Issuer in other than the Name of the Beneficial Owner of Such Securities* (1976).

Nonassessable: With respect to stock in a corporation, nonassessable means that the holders thereof have no obligation to the corporation other than the obligation to pay any unpaid portion of their subscription. *See* N.Y. Bus. Corp. Law §§ 628, 504(i).

Nonconsensual lien: Lien arising by action of law, rather than by contract.

Noncontributory pension plan: Pension plan in which the participants do not make contributions.

Noncumulative: When referring to preferred stock, meaning that dividends, once passed (by failure to be declared or paid on the scheduled date), do not accrue. See **cumulative preferred stock.**

Nonlegal: When referring to securities, meaning not conforming to the requirements of state law for investment by entities whose investments are restricted by legal investment laws, such as savings banks and insurance companies.

Nonmonetary items: Assets and liabilities that are not monetary. Financial Accounting Standards Board, Statement of Financial Accounting Standards No. 33, *Financial Reporting and Changing Prices,* paragraph 48 (1979). Nonmonetary assets include goods held for resale, assets used in the business, claims in amounts dependent on future prices, and residual rights such as good will and equity interests. Nonmonetary liabilities include obligations to furnish goods in specified quantities, not dependent on prices, and obligations to pay cash in amounts

dependent on future prices. *See* Financial Accounting Standards Board, Technical Bulletin re FASB Statement No. 33, *Classification as Monetary or Nonmonetary Items* (1981). See also **monetary asset; monetary liability.**

Nonnegotiable: Lacking one of more of the characteristics required for negotiability. See **negotiable; negotiable instrument.**

Nonnotification plan: Plan of assignment of accounts receivable or chattel paper to a lending institution without notifying the obligors on the accounts or chattel paper.

Nonrecourse: Form of secured debt in which the creditor agrees to limit its recourse to the borrower and to look only to the security. Accounts receivable and chattel paper may be assigned in a nonrecourse transaction, the lending institution agreeing to look only to such accounts or chattel paper for payment. The debt in a leveraged lease is usually nonrecourse, the creditor agreeing to look only to the lease and to the equipment under lease for satisfaction of the debt.

Nontaxable exchange: Exchange of property for which gain or loss is not recognized for federal income tax purpose. *See* I.R.C. §§1031–40.

No-sale doctrine: Doctrine that a transaction in securities is exempt from registration because no sale or offer to sell is involved, such as the case of a stock dividend or stock split. *See* SEC Release No. 33-4982 (1969).

Notation credit: Letter of credit that "specifies that any person purchasing or paying drafts drawn or demands for payment made under it must note the amount of the draft or demand on the letter or advice of credit ... ." UCC Section 5-108.

Note: Promissory note. For the purpose of Article 3 of the Uniform Commercial Code—Commercial Paper, a note is a written promise to pay money, other than a certificate of deposit. *See* UCC Sections 3-104, 3-105. As to treatment of notes as securities, see Sonnenschein, Jr., *Federal Securities Law Coverage of Note Transactions: The Antifraud Provisions,* 35 Bus. Law. 1567 (1980).

Note purchase agreement: Agreement among an issuer of promissory notes and the purchasers thereof providing for the commitment of the purchasers to purchase the notes and setting forth the conditions of such purchase.

Notice: Under the Uniform Commercial Code, a person has notice of a fact when:

(a) he has actual knowledge of it; or

(b) he has received a notice or notification of it; or

(c) from all the facts and circumstances known to him at the time in question he has reason to know that it exists.

UCC Section 1-201(25). The Uniform Commercial Code also sets forth the requirements for giving and receiving notice:

A person "notifies" or "gives" a notice or notification to another by taking such steps as may be reasonably required to inform the other in ordinary course whether or not such other actually comes to know of it. A person "receives" a notice or notification when

(a) it comes to his attention: or

(b) it is duly delivered at the place of business through which the contract was made or at any other place held out by him as the place for receipt of such communications.

UCC Section 1-201(26). The problem of effectiveness of receipt of notice at large corporations and other organizations is addressed in Section 1-201(27), generally placing a burden on organizations to exercise due diligence to communicate notices received to the correct individual in that organization. For notice of claim or defense with respect to negotiable instruments, see UCC Section 3-304. As to the notice requirements for copyrights, see 17 U.S.C. § 401. See also after notice and a hearing.

Notice of deficiency: Notice of deficiency in payment of federal income tax, issued pursuant to section 6212 of the Internal Revenue Code.

Notice of dishonor: Notice that payment or acceptance of an instrument has been refused or cannot be obtained. Under Article 3 of the Uniform Commercial Code—Commercial Paper, notice of dishonor may be oral or written and be in any terms that identify the instrument and state that it has been dishonored. UCC Section 3-508.

Notice of proposed rule making: Section 553 of the Administrative Procedure Act requires, as part of the administrative rule-making process, that a notice of proposed rule making be published in the Federal Register. Such a notice must include:

(1) a statement of the time, place, and nature of public rule-making proceedings;

(2) reference to the legal authority under which the rule is proposed; and

(3) either the terms of substance of the proposed rule or a description of the subjects and issues involved.

5 U.S.C. § 553(b).

Novation: "Substituted contract that includes as a party one who was neither the obligor nor the obligee of the original duty." *Restatement, Second, Contracts* § 280. Novation discharges the original duty. See **substituted contract.**

NOW account: Negotiable order of withdrawal account.

NPDES: National Pollutant Discharge Elimination System.

NRC: Nuclear Regulatory Commission.

NRSRO: Nationally recognized statistical rating organization.

NTIS: National Technical Information Service.

NTSB: National Transportation Safety Board.

Nuclear Regulatory Commission: Independent agency of the United States government responsible for licensing and regulating the construction and operation of nuclear reactors and the use of nuclear materials. The NRC was first organized as the Atomic Energy Commission in 1946 (Atomic Energy Act, Pub. L. No. 585, ch. 724, 60 Stat. 755, 919 (1946)); in 1974, the research and promotional aspects of atomic energy were transferred to the Department of Energy and the AEC was reconstituted as the NRC for licensing and regulatory functions. *See* Energy Reorganization Act of 1974, Pub. L. No. 93-438, 88 Stat. 1233, 1242 (1974), 42 U.S.C. §§ 5801–91; 10 C.F.R. ch. I.

Nunc pro tunc: Now for then; with retroactive effect.

NV: *Naamloze Vennootschap,* joint stock company organized under the laws of The Netherlands.

NYSE: New York Stock Exchange.

OAS: Organization of American States.

Obligor: One who is obliged; the debtor under a debt instrument or the lessee under a lease. For the purpose of the Trust Indenture Act of 1939:

The term "obligor", when used with respect to any such indenture security, means every person who is liable thereon, and, if such security is a certificate of interest or participation, such term means also every person who is liable upon the security or securities in which such certificate evidences an interest or participation; but such term shall not include the trustee under an indenture under which certificates of interest or participation, equipment trust certificates, or like securities are outstanding.

Section 303(12), 15 U.S.C. § 77ccc(12).

OBO: Vessel designed to carry ore, bulk freight, or oil.

Occupational Safety and Health Act of 1970: Federal statute providing for standards of safety in places of employment. Pub. L. No. 91-596, 84 Stat. 1590 (1970), 29 U.S.C. § 651–78.

Occupational Safety and Health Administration: Branch of the United States Department of Labor responsible for promulgating and enforcing standards and regulations under the Occupational Safety and Health Act of 1970.

Occupational Safety and Health Review Commission: Independent agency of the United States government that rules on disagreements arising out of safety and health inspections by the Occupational Safety and Health Administration.

Ocean thermal energy conversion facility: Facility that is "standing or moored in or beyond the territorial sea of the United States and which is designed to use temperature differences in ocean water to produce electricity or another form of energy capable of being used to perform work, ..." Section 3(11) of the Ocean Thermal Energy Conversion Act of 1980, Pub. L. No. 96-320, 94 Stat. 974, 42 U.S.C. § 9101–67. Ocean thermal energy conversion facilities are subject to federal licensing. *See* S. Rep. No. 96-721,

96th Cong., 2d Sess. (1980); H.R. Rep. No. 96-994, 96th Cong., 2d Sess. (1980).

OCED: Office of Comprehensive Employment Development of the United States Department of Labor.

Odd lot: Lot other than a round lot; in the case of stock, a lot of less than 100 shares.

OECD: Organization for Economic Cooperation and Development.

OFCCP: Office of Federal Contract Compliance Programs.

Offer: "Manifestation of willingness to enter into a bargain, so made as to justify another person in understanding that his assent to that bargain is invited and will conclude it." *Restatement, Second, Contracts* § 24 (1981). Offer and acceptance are essential elements of a contract. See **acceptance;** *Restatement, Second, Contracts* §§ 17–70 (1981); UCC Sections 2-205, 2-206. The Securities Act of 1933 uses a broad and somewhat complex definition:

The term "offer to sell", "offer for sale", or "offer" shall include every attempt or offer to dispose of, or solicitation of an offer to buy, a security or interest in a security, for value. The terms defined in this paragraph and the term "offer to buy" as used in subsection (c) of section 5 shall not include preliminary negotiations or agreements between an issuer (or any person directly or indirectly controlling or controlled by an issuer, or under direct or indirect common control with an issuer) and any underwriter or among underwriters who are or are to be in privity of contract with an issuer (or any person directly or indirectly controlling or controlled by an issuer, or under direct or indirect common control with an issuer). Any security given or delivered with, or as a bonus on account of, any purchase of securities or any other thing, shall be conclusively presumed to constitute a part of the subject of such purchase and to have been offered and sold for value. The issue or transfer of a right or privilege, when originally issued or transferred with a security, giving the holder of such security the right to convert such security into another security of the same issuer or of another person, or giving a right to subscribe to another security of the same issuer or of another person, which right cannot be exercised until some future date, shall not be deemed to be an offer or sale of such other security; but the issue or transfer of such other security upon the exercise of such right of conversion or subscription shall be deemed to be a sale of such other security.

Section 2(3); 15 U.S.C. § 77b(3); *see* SEC Release No. 33-6337, 46 Fed. Reg. 42029 (1981); 17 C.F.R. §§ 230.137, 230.138, 230.139. See also **issuer; sale.**

Offering circular: Document describing an issue of securities, similar to a prospectus, but used in circumstances in which registration of the securities under the Securities Act of 1933 is not required, such as an issue of municipal bonds. *See* 17 C.F.R. §§ 256, 259.

Offering statement: Statement required to be filed with the Securities and Exchange Commission in lieu of a registration statement in connection with an issue of securities exempt from registration pursuant to Regulation A. 17 C.F.R. § 230.255.

Officer: The by-laws of a corporation usually specify the officers thereof and describe their duties. For the purpose of securities regulation, the term "officer" means "a president, vice president, secretary, treasurer or principal financial officer, comptroller or principal accounting officer, and any person routinely performing corresponding functions with respect to any organization whether incorporated or unincorporated." 17 C.F.R. § 230.405, 47 Fed. Reg. 11380, 11436 (1982); 17 C.F.R. § 240.12b-2. See also **executive officer**.

Offset: Right of a bank to apply amounts on deposit in a debtor's account to a debt in default. *See* D. Melinkoff, *The Language of the Law* 244 (1963). See also **setoff**.

Oil payment: See production payment.

OMB: Office of Management and Budget.

On demand: For the purpose of Article 3 of the Uniform Commercial Code—Commercial Paper, instruments payable on demand include "those payable at sight or on presentation and those in which no time for payment is stated." UCC Section 3-108.

One-month liquidation: Liquidation of a corporation within one calendar month, which limits the recognition of gain under section 333 of the Internal Revenue Code.

OPEC: Organization of Petroleum Exporting Countries.

Open-end credit: Line of credit that may be used repeatedly up to a certain limit; also called revolving credit.

Open-end fund: Open-end investment company.

Open-end investment company: Investment company (also called open-end fund) that sells additional shares to new participants and redeems shares from participants upon request. The value of each share is the value of investments and other assets of the fund divided by the number of shares outstanding. The Investment Company Act of 1940 defines an "open-end company" as "a management company which is offering for sale or has outstanding any redeemable security of which it is the issuer." Section 5(a)(1), 15 U.S.C. § 80a-5(a)(1). Compare closed-end investment company.

Open-end lease: Lease, used as a financing device, that requires the lessee to pay to the lessor at the end of the lease term the difference, if any, between a specified amount and the value of the leased property when it is returned to the lessor. Thus the risk of value decrease of the leased property is placed on the lessee. Compare closed-end lease.

Open market operations: Purchases and sales of government and certain other securities by the New York Federal Reserve Bank as an instrument of monetary policy.

Open order: Order to buy or sell securities at a designated price.

Open price term: Term in a contract for the sale of goods that leaves open or for later determination the price of the goods. Under Article 2 of the Uniform Commercial Code–Sales, a contract with the price not settled can be binding. UCC Section 2-305.

Operating agreement: Agreement among joint venturers in a mining project, providing for management of the project.

Operating-differential subsidy: Program of federal subsidy to operators of United States flag liners and bulk cargo vessels in United States-foreign commerce, with the objective of equalizing operating cost differences between United States flag and foreign vessels. *See* Title VI of the Merchant Marine Act, 1936, 46 U.S.C. §§ 1171–83.

Operating expense: Expense incurred in operations of an enterprise, excluding income deductions such as interest and income taxes.

Operating lease: Equipment lease in which the lessee provides maintenance services and that usually has a short term relative to the life of the equipment, or is cancellable by the lessee. The Financial Accounting Standards Board defines an operating lease as any lease other than a capital lease, a somewhat broader definition. Financial Accounting Standards Board, Statement of Financial Accounting Standards No. 13, *Accounting for Leases,* paragraph 6 (1976). Compare **finance lease.**

Operating loss: Excess of deductions over revenues in a taxable year.

Operating ratio: For a transportation company, operating expenses divided by revenues.

OPIC: Overseas Private Investment Corporation.

Opinion: In connection with contracts, "An assertion is one of opinion if it expresses only a belief, without certainty, as to the existence of a fact or expresses only a judgment as to quality, value, authenticity, or similar matters." *Restatement, Second, Contracts* § 168 (1981). See **misrepresentation.**

Opinion of counsel: Expression of belief by a lawyer as to a legal conclusion or legal question. *See Legal Opinions to Third Parties: An Easier Path, A Report by the Special Committee on Legal Opinions in Commercial Transactions, New York County Lawyers' Association,* 34 Bus. Law. 1891 (1979); American Bar Association, Section of Corporate, Banking and Business Law, Committee on Developments in Business Financing, *Legal Opinions Given in Corporate Transactions,* 33 Bus. Law. 2389 (1978); Fuld, *Lawyers' Standards and Responsibilities in Rendering Opinions,* 33 Bus. Law. 1295 (1978); Babb, Barnes, Gordon & Kjellenberg, *Legal Opinions to Third Parties in Corporate Transactions,* 32 Bus. Law. 553 (1977); Fuld, *Legal Opinions in Business Transactions–An Attempt to Bring Some Order out of Some Chaos,* 28 Bus. Law. 915 (1973).

Opportunity cost: The anticipated return from alternative use of assets (such as selling them). American Institute of Certified Public Accountants, Accounting Principles Board Statement No. 4, Ch. 6, *Generally Accepted Ac-*

counting Principles—Pervasive Principles, paragraph 28 (1970).

Option: Right, exercisable at the option of the holder (and thus not an obligation), to buy or sell a security or commodity at a given price within, or at, a given time. *See* 7 U.S.C. § 6c(a)(B); 17 C.F.R. § 32.1(a).

Optional payment bond: Bond that gives the holder the right to receive payment in two or more currencies.

Option contract: Contract to keep an offer open; "promise which meets the requirements for formation of a contract and limits the promisor's power to revoke an offer." *Restatement, Second, Contracts* § 25 (1981). *See Humble Oil & Refining Co. v. Cox,* 207 Va. 197, 148 S.E. 2d 756 (1966).

Option tender bond: Put bond; bond, usually issued by a municipality, with a feature that permits the holder to put the bond to the indenture trustee for redemption at face value prior to maturity. The issuer usually arranges for a letter of credit from a financial institution, whereby that institution agrees to buy bonds from the indenture trustee at face value so that the trustee can pay the holder exercising the put. An option tender bond provides protection against erosion of the value of the bond due to increases in interest rates.

Or: As used in legislation and legal documents, the word "or" usually denotes both the conjunctive and the disjunctive, so that one of a series connected by "or" would not necessarily exclude the others, unless the context clearly indicates exclusive alternatives,

such as "yes or no." *See, e.g.,* 11 U.S.C. § 102(5); Treas. Reg. § 1.368-2(h).

Order: 1. For the purpose of Article 3 of the Uniform Commercial Code—Commercial Paper:

An "order" is a direction to pay and must be more than an authorization or request. It must identify the person to pay with reasonable certainty. It may be addressed to one or more persons jointly or in the alternative but not in succession.

UCC Section 3-102. See **payable to order;** UCC Section 3-110. 2. Under the Administrative Procedure Act, the term "order" means "the whole or a part of a final disposition, whether affirmative, negative, injunctive, or declaratory in form, of an agency in a matter other than rule making but including licensing." 5 U.S.C. § 551(6). Compare **rule making; rule; licensing.**

Order bill; order bill of lading: Negotiable bill of lading. Compare straight bill; see bill of lading; negotiable.

Ordinary course: See buyer in ordinary course of business.

Ordinary income: Income, including income from the sale or exchange of property, that is neither a "capital asset" (I.R.C. § 1221) nor "property used in the trade or business" (I.R.C. § 1231(b)). I.R.C. § 64.

Ordinary loss: Loss, including a loss from the sale or exchange of property, that is not a "capital asset" (I.R.C. § 1221). I.R.C. § 65.

Organization: For the purpose of the Uniform Commercial Code, the term "organization" includes "a corporation, government or governmental subdivision or agency, business trust, estate, trust, partnership or association, two or more persons having a joint or common interest, or any other legal or commercial entity." UCC Section 1-201(28).

Organizational expenditure: For the purpose of the Internal Revenue Code, an "organizational expenditure" is an expenditure incidental to the creation of a corporation, chargeable to capital account and of a character which, if expended in connection with the creation of a corporation having a limited life, would be amortizable over such life. I.R.C. § 248(b). Organizational expenditures can be amortized over 60 months. I.R.C. § 248.

Original issue discount: For the purpose of determining capital gains on debt securities, the "original issue discount" is "the difference between the issue price and the stated redemption price at maturity." If the original issue discount is less than 0.25% of the redemption price multiplied by the number of years to maturity, it is treated as being zero. I.R.C. § 1232(b). *See* I.R.C. § 1232A; section 231 of the Tax Equity and Fiscal Responsibility Act of 1982.

OSHA: 1. Occupational Safety and Health Administration. 2. Occupational Safety and Health Act of 1970.

OSM: Office of Surface Mining Reclamation and Enforcement of the United States Department of the Interior.

OTEC: Ocean thermal energy conversion. See **ocean thermal energy conversion facility.**

Output contract: Contract for sale of goods or services in which the quantity is determined by the output of the seller. Under Article 2 of the Uniform Commercial Code–Sales, the output under such a contract must occur in good faith and not be unreasonably disproportionate to a stated estimate or normal output. UCC Section 2-306. See **requirements contract.**

Outside director: Member of corporate board of directors who is not a member of management.

Out turn: Term in a contract for the sale of goods C.I.F. or C. & F., that means that the seller will reasonably estimate the weight and the payment due on tender of the documents called for by the contract will be based on such estimate, but the buyer and seller will adjust the final price based on the actual weight. UCC Section 2-321.

Over-allocation; over-allotment: Allocation or allotment of the managers of an underwriting syndicate of more securities to the selling group than are actually planned for the issue.

Overdraft: Issuance of checks in amounts greater than the balance in the account.

Overdraft checking account: Line of credit in connection with a checking account that permits overdrafts, with a finance charge on the amount of the overdraft.

Overhead: Business costs not related to units of production, such as costs of maintenance of facilities.

Overissue: 1. With respect to securities, overissue means the "issue of securities in excess of the amount which the issuer has the corporate power to issue." UCC Section 8-104. 2. With respect to documents of title for fungible goods, overissue means the issue of documents of title representing quantities greater than that actually in the possession of the issuer. *See* UCC Section 7-402.

Overseas: For the purpose of Article 2 of the Uniform Commercial Code–Sales, a shipment by water or air is overseas "insofar as by usage of trade or agreement it is subject to the commercial, financing or shipping practices characteristic of international deep water commerce." UCC Section 2-323.

Overseas Private Investment Corporation: Independent agency of the executive branch of the United States government, operating within the International Development Cooperation Agency, established to facilitate investment in developing countries by United States investors. OPIC offers loan guarantees for private investment in eligible projects and also makes its own loans. *See* Pub. L. No. 91-175, 83 Stat. 805 (1969); 22 U.S.C. §§ 2191–2200a; 22 C.F.R. §§ 705–10. *See* Hunt, *The Overseas Private Investment Corporation,* in II W. Surrey & D. Wallace, Jr., ed., *A Lawyer's Guide to International Business Transactions* 275 (1979).

Over-the-counter: Transaction in securities that are not listed on a securities exchange, or a security that is not so listed.

Overview committee: Committee of corporate board of directors formed to provide objective review by directors free of personal interest in the matters under consideration, such as audit, nominations, and compensation. *See The Overview Committees of the Board of Directors,* 35 Bus. Law. 1335 (1980).

Owner-trustee: Trustee for the equity participants in a lease transaction, owning the equipment in its name (as trustee) and entering into the lease and debt agreement.

P

PAC: Political action committee.

Package licensing: Licensing of a patent together with the licensing of other patents or the sale of equipment or services. If the primary patent license is being used as leverage to sell other patents or other unpatented goods and services, an illegal "tying" arrangement is present. *See United States Plywood Corp. v. General Plywood Corp.*, 370 F. 2d 500 (6th Cir. 1966). *See generally* American Bar Association, Section of Antitrust Law, *Antitrust Law Developments* 341 (1975).

Panama Convention: The Inter-American Convention of 1975 on International Commercial Arbitration.

Par: Equal to the face value.

Parent corporation: Corporation owning a substantial proportion of the stock of a corporation or chain of corporations; *See* I.R.C. § 425(e); Cal. Corp. Code § 175. *See also* International Accounting Standards Committee, Statement of International Accounting Standards 3, *Consolidated Financial Statements*, paragraph 4 (1976).

Pari passu: Equally, without preference.

Parol evidence rule: Rule of contract law that evidence of prior agreements or contemporaneous oral agreements cannot be used to modify the terms of a written contract. *Restatement, Second, Contracts* § 213. Article 2 of the Uniform Commercial Code–Sales adopts the rule for contracts for the sale of goods:

Terms with respect to which the confirmatory memoranda of the parties agree or which are otherwise set forth in a writing intended by the parties as a final expression of their agreement with respect to such terms as are included therein may not be contradicted by evidence of any prior agreement or of a contemporaneous oral agreement but may be explained or supplemented

(a) by course of dealing or usage of trade (Section 1-205) or by course of performance (Section 2-208); and

(b) by evidence of consistent additional terms unless the court finds the writing to have been intended also as a complete and exclusive statement of the terms of the agreement.

UCC Section 2-202.

Partial liquidation: For the purpose of the Internal Revenue Code, a distribution of stock not essentially equivalent to a dividend, in redemption of part of the stock of the corporation pursuant to a plan and occurring within the taxable year in which the plan is adopted or the next taxable year. I.R.C. § 302(e). *See* section 222 of the Tax Equity and Fiscal Responsibility Act of 1982; *Fowler Hosiery Co. v. Commissioner,* 301 F. 2d 394 (7th Cir. 1962); Rev. Rul. 81-3, 1981-1 C.B. 125.

Participating preferred stock: Preferred stock that is entitled to dividends, in addition to the regular dividends, related to the dividends declared on common stock.

Participation agreement: 1. Agreement among the lead bank in a loan transaction and other banks participating in the loan. *See* Hutchins, *What Exactly is a Loan Participation?* 9 Rutgers Camden L. J. 447 (1978); Stahl, *Loan Participations: Lead Insolvency and Participants' Rights,* 94 Banking L. J. 882 (1977), 95 Banking L. J. 38 (1978); Coogan, Kripke & Weiss, *The Outer Fringes of Article 9: Subordination Agreements, Security Interests in Money and Deposits, Negative Pledge Clauses, and Participation Agreements,* 79 Harv. L. Rev. 229 (1965); Simpson, *Loan Participations: Pitfalls for Participants,* 31 Bus. Law. 1977 (1976). 2. Agreement among the borrower or lessee and the financing parties to a loan or lease transaction, providing the terms of the financing commitments (debt and equity, if any) and the conditions of closing.

Participation certificate: Evidence of interest in a fund or group of securities or other obligations, such as mortgages. See also **certificate of participation; mortgage participation certificate.**

Partner: Member of a partnership. *See* I.R.C. § 7701(a)(2).

Partnership: Association of two or more persons to carry on as co-owners a business for profit. Uniform Partnership Act § 6(1), Cal. Corp. Code § 15006. *See Cox v. Hickman,* 8 H.L. Cas. 268 (1860). Partners are each liable for the debts of the partnership, except limited partners, whose liability is limited to the amount contributed. In a limited partnership, there must be at least one general partner, who is liable for the partnership debts. For the purpose of the Internal Revenue Code, the term "partnership" includes "a syndicate, group, pool, joint venture, or other unincorporated organization, through or by means of which any business, financial operation, or venture is carried on, and which is not, within the meaning of this title, a trust or estate or a corporation." I.R.C. § 7701(a)(2); *see* I.R.C. § 761(a). For the use of the term in the Bankruptcy Code, see H.R. Rep. No. 95-595, 95th Cong., 1st Sess. 196 (1977). *See generally* Walthall, Rheuban, Rollinson, & Talley, *Partnership Law: A Selected Bibliography,* 35 Bus. Law. 659 (1980).

Partnership trust: Arrangement for participation by more than one equity participant in a lease financing transaction, whereby the equity participants are the grantors and beneficiaries of a trust that owns the equipment. If properly arranged, such a trust will permit the tax incidents of the transaction to pass through to the beneficiaries. *See* Treas. Reg. § 301.7701-2.

Party: 1. Person or group that forms one side in an action. Under the Administrative Procedure Act, the term "party" includes "a person or agency named or admitted as a party, or properly seeking and entitled as of right to be admitted as a party, in an agency proceeding, and a person or agency admitted by an agency as a party for limited purposes." 5 U.S.C. § 551(3). 2. For the purpose of the Uniform Commercial Code, a party is "a person who has engaged in a transaction or made an agreement within this Act." Third parties are expressly excluded. UCC Section 1-201(29). The Official Comment adds that the term "party" includes a person acting through an agent.

Party in interest: Under the Employee Retirement Income Security Act of 1974, the term "party in interest," with respect to an employee benefit plan, includes:

- administrators, counsel, and employees of the plan;
- a person providing service to the plan;
- the employer of any employees covered by the plan, or the owner of a 50% or more interest therein;
- an employee organization whose members are covered by the plan;
- a corporation or other organization of which 50% or more of the control is owned by the foregoing; and

- an employee, officer, director, or 10% shareholder or partner in the foregoing.

ERISA § 3(14); 29 U.S.C. § 1002(14). Most types of transactions between the plan and a "party in interest" are prohibited. See **prohibited transaction.**

Par value: The face value of a security. In the case of debt securities, the principal amount, payable at maturity.

Passing off: Sale, or "passing off," of products as those of a competitor. "Passing off" would lead to a cause of action for damages, and would be a violation of section 5 of the Federal Trade Commission Act, 15 U.S.C. § 45. *See, e.g., Waltham Watch Co. v. FTC,* 318 F.2d 28 (7th Cir.), *cert. denied,* 375 U.S. 944 (1963); *see generally* American Bar Association, Section of Antitrust Law, *Antitrust Law Developments* 184 (1975).

Passing-on doctrine: Defense to private action for damages for price discrimination or price fixing, based on the assertion that the plaintiff was able to "pass on" the higher cost to its customers, and thus did not suffer economic harm. *See, e.g., Hanover Shoe, Inc., v. United Shoe Machinery Corp.,* 392 U.S. 481 (1968). *See generally* American Bar Association, Section of Antitrust Law, *Antitrust Law Developments* 285 (1975); Schaefer, *Passing-On Theory in Antitrust Treble Damage Actions: An Economic and Legal Analysis,* 16 Wm. & Mary L. Rev. 883 (1975).

Pass-through: Security representing an undivided interest in a group of obligations, usually mortgages, issued by the institution that has taken the mortgages as mortgagee or purchased the mortgages. Pass-throughs are usually issued by government agencies that have purchased mortgages from private institutions, but may be issued by private institutions directly. See **mortgage participation certificate.**

Patent: Right "to exclude others from making, using, or selling" a particular invention in the United States for a period of seventeen years. 35 U.S.C. § 154.

Patent and Trademark Office: Branch of the United States Department of Commerce that administers the system for the issuance of patents and the registration of trademarks.

Patent misuse: Defense to patent infringement suits based on the principle that a court should not give relief to a party who is guilty of improper conduct in licensing the patent or marketing the patented product. A finding of misuse would render the patent unenforceable, not invalid. Patent misuse may involve a violation of the antitrust laws; *see Zenith Radio Corp. v. Hazeltine Research, Inc.,* 395 U.S. 100 (1969); *see generally* American Bar Association, Section of Antitrust Law, *Antitrust Law Developments* 328 (1975).

Patronage dividend: Dividend paid by a cooperative or corporation operating on a cooperative basis to a shareholder determined on the basis of quantity or units of output (or throughput, in the case of pipelines) of the cooperative or corporation taken or used by the shareholder, or determined on the basis of net earnings attributable to the business done with the shareholder. *See* I.R.C. § 1388(a). *See generally* I.R.C. §§ 1381–88.

Payable: Debt or liability; account payable.

Payable through: An instrument that is payable through a bank "designates that bank as a collecting bank to make presentment but does not of itself authorize the bank to pay the instrument." UCC Section 3-120.

Payable to bearer: Under Article 3–Commercial Paper of the Uniform Commercial Code, an instrument, to be treated as a negotiable instrument, must be "payable to order or to bearer." UCC Section 3-104(1)(d). An instrument is payable to bearer if by its terms it is payable to:

(a) bearer or the order of bearer; or

(b) a specified person or bearer; or

(c) "cash" or the order of "cash", or any other indication which does not purport to designate a specific payee.

UCC Section 3-111. See **bearer**; UCC Section 1-201(5).

Payable to order: Under Article 3–Commercial Paper of the Uniform Commercial Code, an instrument, to be treated as a negotiable instrument, must be "payable to order or to bearer." UCC Section 3-104(1)(d). An instrument is "payable to order" if by its terms it is payable "to the order or assigns of any person therein specified with reasonable certainty, or to him or his order, or when it is conspicuously designated on its face as 'exchange' or the like and and names a payee." UCC Section 3-110.

Pay any bank: When these words are endorsed on an item covered by Article 4 of the Uniform Commercial Code—Bank Deposits and Collections, only a bank may acquire the rights of a holder of that item, unless the item has been returned to the customer initiating collection or has been specially endorsed by a bank to a person who is not a bank. UCC Section 4-201(2).

Pay-as-you-go pension plan: Pension plan in which the employer makes payments to retired employees as the benefits become due; funds are not accumulated for future benefits.

Payee's indorsement required: A bank may supply the indorsement of its customer on a check or other item taken for collection, unless the words "payee's indorsement required" or similar words appear on the item. UCC Section 4-205.

Paying agent: Entity, usually a bank or trust company, that handles the payment of principal and interest, or dividends, on an issue of securities to the holders. The Trust Indenture Act of 1939 defines a paying agent as "any person authorized by an obligor" on securities issued under an indenture "(A) to pay the principal of or interest on such security on behalf of such obligor, or (B) if such security is a certificate of interest or participation, equipment trust certificate, or like security, to make such payment on behalf of the trustee." Section 303(13), 15 U.S.C. § 77ccc(13).

Paying bank: Bank designated by the issuer of a letter of credit to effect payment, usually in a location convenient to the beneficiary.

Payment guaranteed: Under Article 3 of the Uniform Commercial Code—Commercial Paper, such words or equivalent words added to a signature on an instrument mean that "the signer engages that if the instrument is not paid when due he will pay it according to its tenor without resort by the holder to any other party." UCC Section 3-416(1). See also collection guaranteed.

Payor bank: For the purpose of Article 3—Commercial Paper and Article 4—Bank Deposits and Collections of the Uniform Commercial Code, "payor bank" means "a bank by which an item is payable as drawn or accepted." UCC Section 4-105.

PAYSOP: Payroll tax credit employee stock ownership plan.

PBGC: Pension Benefit Guaranty Corporation.

PC: Participation certificate.

P/E: Price/earnings ratio.

PEFCO: Private Export Funding Corporation.

Pendente lite: Pending the suit. A court may order preservation of the status quo or other relief pending the disposition of a suit. *See, e.g, United States v. Cities Service Co.,* 289 F. Supp. 133 (D. Mass. 1968), *appeal dismissed,* 410 F.2d 662 (1st Cir. 1969).

Pension Benefit Guaranty Corporation: Corporation, wholly-owned by the United States government, established by Title IV of the Employee Retirement Income Security Act of 1974 (ERISA) to provide insurance for benefits under private pension plans.

Pension plan: Arrangement whereby a company undertakes to provide its retired employees with benefits that can be determined or estimated in advance. American Institute of Certified Public Accountants, Accounting Principles Board Opinion No. 8, *Accounting for the Cost of Pension Plans,* paragraph 8 (1966).

Peppercorn: Nominal amount, or token.

Peppercorn option: Option to purchase property under lease for a nominal or token amount at the expiration of the lease term. See double-dip lease.

Percentage depletion: Special method of computing the depletion allowance for extraction of minerals (a deduction from gross income for federal income tax) whereby a percentage of gross income can be taken as the depletion allowance. The depletion allowance reduces the basis of the property, but unlike cost depletion, percentage depletion is not limited to that basis, and may continue even after the basis of the depletable property has been reduced to zero. I.R.C. § 613. See cost depletion.

Percentage lease: Lease of commercial property in which the rents are calculated as a percentage of gross sales or sales over a specified amount.

Percentage-of-completion method: Method of accounting for long-term construction-type contracts that recognizes income from time to time as work on the contract proceeds. *See* American Institute of Certified Public Accountants, Accounting Research Bulletin No. 45, *Long-Term Construction-Type Contracts* (1955); International Accounting Standards Committee, Statement of International Accounting Standards 11, *Accounting for Construction Contracts* (1979). Compare completed-contract method.

Per diem: By the day.

Perfect: Used as a verb in connection with a security interest under the Uniform Commercial Code to mean to obtain priority over other conflicting claims in the same collateral. A security interest cannot be perfected until it has attached, and the additional steps of filing or taking possession of the collateral are taken. A perfected security interest is not perfect, however. *See* UCC Section 9-303.

Permanent differences: Differences between taxable income and pretax accounting income that will not be offset by corresponding differences in other periods. American Institute of Certified Public Accountants, Accounting Principles Board Opinion No. 11, *Accounting for Income Taxes,* paragraph 12f (1967); *see* American Institute of Certified Public Accountants, *Accounting for Income Taxes, Accounting Interpretations of APB Opinion No. 11,* paragraphs 48-55 (1969). Compare timing differences.

Permanent financing: In a transaction involving financing during the period of construction or an interim period, which is to be replaced by long-term financing, the long-term financing is sometimes called the "permanent" financing, even though the financing will eventually be retired.

Perpetual bond: Bond which does not mature, and for which there is no provision for principal recovery. The holder receives only interest.

Per se violation: Practice that is a violation of the antitrust laws "per se," or of itself, without further inquiry as to the anticompetitive effect. The Sherman Act and other antitrust laws are written in broad terms, prohibiting, for example, "combinations . . . in restraint of trade." Ordinarily it would be necessary to show the anticompetitive effect of the defendant's activities in any prosecution. Over the years, however, courts have determined "that there are certain practices which because of their pernicious effect on competition and lack of any redeeming virtue are conclusively presumed to be illegal without elaborate inquiry as to the precise harm they have caused or the business excuse for their use." *Northern Pacific Ry. v. United States,* 356 U.S. 1, 5 (1958). Thus engaging in such a practice is "per se" illegal, and proof of the defendant's having engaged in such a practice is sufficient for conviction under the antitrust laws without the need to show the anticompetitive effect. Examples of "per se" violations of the Sherman Act are horizontal price fixing, resale price maintenance, division of markets, and collective refusals to deal. *See generally* American Bar Association, Section of Antitrust Law, *Antitrust Law Developments* 2 (1975); Bork, *The Rule of Reason and the Per Se Concept: Price Fixing and Market Division,* 74 Yale L. J. 775 (1965), 75 Yale L. J. 373 (1966). See also **rule of reason.**

Person: In most business and business law situations, and in this dictionary, the meaning of the term "person" is not confined to natural persons, but includes organizations and artificial persons, such as corporations. *See, e.g.,* 1 U.S.C.§ 1; 5 U.S.C. § 551(2); section 8 of the Sherman Act, 15 U.S.C. § 7; section 1 of the Clayton Act, 15 U.S.C. § 12; section 2(1) of the National Labor Relations Act, 29 U.S.C. § 152(1). Section 2(2) of the Securities Act of 1933 defines person to mean "an individual, a corporation, a partnership, an association, a joint-stock company, a trust, any unincorporated association, or a government or political subdivision thereof." 15 U.S.C. § 77b(2). *See also* section 3(a)(9) of the Securities Exchange Act of 1934, 15 U.S.C. § 78c(a)(9). The Internal Revenue Code definition includes within the meaning of the term "person" an "individual, a trust, estate, partnership, association, company or corporation." I.R.C. § 7701(a)(1). *See also* I.R.C. §7343. The Bankruptcy Code does not include governmental units or estates and trusts, but uses the word "entity" to include such. 11 U.S.C. §§ 101(14), (30); *see* H.R. Rep. No. 95-595, 95th Cong., 1st Sess. 313 (1977). The Uniform Commercial Code definition of person includes "an individual or an organization." UCC Section 1-201(30). See **organization.** The term "individual" is usually used to denote a natural person.

Personal holding company: For the purpose of the Internal Revenue Code, a corporation that derives at least 60 percent of its "adjusted ordinary gross income" (defined in I.R.C. § 543(b)(2)) from "personal holding company income," and more than 50 percent in value of its outstanding stock is owned, directly or indirectly, by not more than five individuals. I.R.C. § 542(a). See I.R.C. § 542(c) for exceptions. *See generally* I.R.C. §§ 541–47.

Personal holding company income: Under the Internal Revenue Code, income that consists of dividends, certain rents, certain mineral, oil and gas royalties, copyright royalties, film rents, use of corporate property by a shareholder, personal service contracts, and estates and trusts. I.R.C. § 543(a). See personal holding company.

Personal property: Usually property of a movable nature, but also including any property not constituting a freehold interest in land.

Personal Property Security Act: Canadian counterpart of Article 9 of the Uniform Commercial Code–Secured Transactions. *E.g.*, Ont. Rev. Stat. c. 344 (1970); Man. Rev. Stat. c. 5/P35 (1973). *See generally* Canadian Commercial Law Guide (CCH), paragraph 1700.

Person associated with a broker or dealer: For the purpose of the Securities Exchange Act of 1934:

The term "person associated with a broker or dealer" or "associated person of a broker or dealer" means any partner, officer, director, or branch manager of such broker or dealer (or any person occupying a similar status or performing similar functions), any person directly or indirectly controlling, controlled by, or under common control with such broker or dealer, or any employee of such broker or dealer, except that any person associated with a broker or dealer whose functions are solely clerical or ministerial shall not be included in the meaning of such term for the purposes of section 15(b) of this title (other than paragraph (6) thereof).

Section 3(a)(18), 15 U.S.C. § 78c(a)(18). For "person associated with a municipal securities dealer," see section 3(a)(32) of the Securities Exchange Act of 1934, 15 U.S.C. § 78c(a)(32).

Person in the position of a seller: Under Article 2 of the Uniform Commercial Code–Sales, a "person in the position of seller" may exercise the rights of a seller to withhold or stop delivery, resell, and recover incidental damages, under certain circumstances. UCC Sections 2-707, 2-705, 2-706, 2-710. The term "person in the position of seller" includes "as against a principal an agent who has paid or become responsible for the price of goods on behalf of his principal or anyone who otherwise holds a security interest or other right in goods similar to that of a seller." UCC Section 2-707.

PERT: Program evaluation and review technique; a method of planning engineering and construction projects by constructing a network of tasks and their interaction. The method, similar to CPM (critical path method), uses estimates of the time needed to accomplish individual tasks and the relationship of the completion of tasks to the initiation of others to estimate the time required to complete the entire project. The method will show the effect of delays in a particular element of the project on the completion schedule for the entire project. PERT is more complex than CPM in that it provides estimates of the range of time required to complete a project (earliest, latest, most likely) and is designed for implementation by a computer. *See, e.g.,* B. Baker & R. Eris, *An Introduction to PERT-CPM.*

Phantom stock option, phantom stock plan: Method of supplemental compensation for employees to provide the benefit of a stock option plan without a requirement for purchase of stock by the employee. Supplemental compensation, in the form of cash or stock, is paid based on increases in the market price of the employer's stock over a specified period. *See* Note, *Phantom Stock Plans,* 76 Harv. L. Rev. 619 (1963). See also **stock appreciation right.**

Phase-by-phase method: Method of reporting the consolidated taxable income of an affiliated group in which individual income and expense items are aggregated for the entire group and then the taxable income of the group is determined. Compare **bottom-line method.**

Philadelphia plan: Method of financing railroad equipment developed in the nineteenth century to create a nonpossessory interest in the equipment in jurisdictions that did not give effect to the reservation of title in a vendor under a conditional sale. The Philadelphia plan is based on a bailment-lease, in which the equipment is nominally owned by a trustee for the financing parties, and is leased to the railroad with rentals being calculated to recover the principal of the investment with "dividends" thereon. At the end of the lease term, when all payments have been made, title to the equipment passes to the railroad without additional payment. *See* Adkins & Billyou, *Current Developments in Railroad Equipment Financing,* 12 Bus. Law. 207 (1957); K. Duncan, *Equipment Obligations* (1924).

Pierce the corporate veil: To disregard the corporate entity and hold the stockholders liable when necessary to achieve justice: "a corporation will be looked upon as a legal entity as a general rule, and until sufficient reason to the contrary appears; but when the notion of legal entity is used to defeat public convenience, justify wrong, protect fraud, or defend crime, the law will regard the corporation as an association of persons." *United States v. Milwaukee Refrigerator Transit Co.,* 142 F. 247, 255 (E.D. Wis. 1905). *See Northern Ill. Gas Co. v. Total Energy Leasing Corp.,* 502 F. Supp. 412 (N.D. Ill. 1980); Krendl & Krendl, *Piercing the Corporate Veil: Focusing the Inquiry,* 55 Denver L. J. 1 (1978). With respect to federal income taxes, *see, e.g., Gregory v. Helvering,* 293 U.S. 465 (1935).

Pilot sale: Sale intended to constitute the first use of a trademark in commerce, establishing a claim of ownership of the mark.

PLC: Public limited company; British corporation whose stock is publicly traded.

Pledge: The bailment of property to a creditor as security for an obligation. A pledge is different from mortgages and other types of security interests in that the creditor keeps pledged property in his possession until the obligation is discharged.

Plimsoll line: Load line; a line painted on the hull of a vessel indicating the depth to which the ship may safely be loaded. The load line was proposed by Samuel Plimsoll, adopted for British vessels by the Merchant Shipping Act in 1890, and established internationally by the International Safety at Sea and Load-Line Conventions in 1930. Some vessels have higher, "summer" marks, permitting loading to a greater depth during seasons when bad weather is not anticipated. *See* International Convention on Load Lines, April 5, 1966, 18 U.S.T. 1857, T.I.A.S. No. 6331.

Plus: In the case of securities quoted in fractions, an additional half increment. For example, if the quotation is in 1/32nds, "plus" is an additional 1/64th.

PN: Project note.

Point: In the case of stock, one dollar; in the case of bonds, one percentage point (usually ten dollars, because most bonds have a par value of $1000); in the case of indices or averages, such as the Dow Jones Industrial Average, a unit of one, the whole number, and not a fraction or decimal. See basis point.

Points: Fee charged by a lending institution for making a loan, each point equaling one percent of the amount of the loan.

Pooling agreement: Agreement among ocean carriers that "provides for the division of the cargo carryings or earnings and/or losses among the parties in accordance with a fixed formula." 46 C.F.R. § 522.2(a)(3).

Pooling of interests method: Method of accounting for business combinations in a situation where the combination is effected by an exchange of voting common stock; under this method, the assets and liabilities of the corporations that were combined are carried into the combined corporation without change, and the income of the combined corporation includes the income of the corporations that were combined back to the beginning of the current accounting period. *See* American Institute of Certified Public Accountants, Accounting Principles Board Opinion No. 16, *Accounting for Business Combinations,* paragraphs 12–14 (1970); SEC Accounting Series Release No. 130, 37 Fed. Reg. 20937 (1972); Fiflis, *Accounting for Mergers, Acquisitions and Investments, in a Nutshell: The Interrelationships of, and Criteria for, Purchase or Pooling, the Equity Method, and Parent-Company-Only and Consolidated Statements,* 37 Bus. Law. 89 (1981). Compare **purchase method.**

Pork barrel: Used to describe legislation designed to benefit a Congressman's home district by construction of public works or military facilities therein.

Portability: With respect to pension plans, the feature that permits participation in the plan to continue when the employee changes employers.

Portfolio: Securities held or owned by an investor.

Port of documentation: Home port; port where documents and records concerning a vessel are kept. *See* Home Port Act, Pub. L. No. 420, ch. 235, 43 Stat. 947 (1925); 46 U.S.C.§§ 18, 1011–14; 46 C.F.R. § 67.19.

Positive carry: Excess of earnings on an investment over the interest on money borrowed to purchase the investment.

Post-effective amendment: Amendment to a registration statement after it has become effective, in order to cure an inaccuracy in the original statement, or to reflect the price obtained in competitive bidding. *See* SEC Rules 470–79, 17 C.F.R.§ 230.470–79, 47 Fed. Reg. 11380, 11445 (1982).

Potential competition: Pro-competitive influence on the firms in a market by the presence of a potential competitor "in the wings." Potential competition is sometimes used as a basis for challenging mergers. *See FTC v. Proctor & Gamble Co.*, 386 U.S. 568 (1967); *United States v. Penn-Olin Chemical Co.*, 378 U.S. 158 (1964); *see generally* United States Department of Justice, *Merger Guidelines* 29 (1982); O'Brien, *The Legal Evolution of Potential Competition and Its Application to Banking,* 30 Bus. Law. 1181 (1975).

Praecipium: Part of the fee paid by a borrower in a Eurocredit transaction that is retained by the lead manager of the syndicate after payment of fees to other members of the syndicate.

Preemptive right: Right of a stockholder of a corporation to participate in new issues or offerings of stock in the same proportion that his holdings bear to the total outstanding stock of that corporation. Such rights are usually available only if the certificate of incorporation so provides. *See* Model Business Corporation Act §§ 26, 26A (1979); N. Y. Bus. Corp. Law § 622; Del. Code Ann. Tit. 8 § 102(b)(3); Cal. Corp. Code § 204(a)(2). *See generally* Drinker, Jr., *The Preemptive Right of Shareholders to Subscribe to New Shares,* 43 Harv. L. Rev. 586 (1930).

Preferred dividend coverage: Ratio of net income after taxes and debt service to preferred dividends payable for a given period, usually one year.

Preferred maritime lien: Lien having priority over a preferred mortgage under the Ship Mortgage Act, 1920. Preferred maritime liens include liens prior in time to the preferred mortgage and liens arising out of tort claims, claims for wages, general average, and salvage. 46 U.S.C. § 953.

Preferred mortgage: Type of mortgage used in vessel financing, sanctioned by the Ship Mortgage Act, 1920, and correlative legislation in other countries. *See* 46 U.S.C. §§ 911–83; Gyory, *Security at Sea: A Review of the Preferred Ship Mortgage,* 31 Fordham L. Rev. 231 (1962).

Preferred stock: Stock entitled to a preference in the distribution of dividends or assets over other classes of stock. Model Business Corporation Act §§ 15, 16 (1979); N.Y. Bus. Corp. Act

§ 501(b); *see* Del. Code Ann. tit. 8 § 151. Preferred stock usually bears dividends at a fixed rate. See **cumulative preferred stock; participating preferred stock.** As to the distinction between preferred stock and debt for tax purposes, see I.R.C. § 385; Treas. Reg. § 1-385, 47 Fed. Reg. 164 (1982).

Preliminary injunction: Injunction granted before trial, upon hearing, where prompt injunctive relief is necessary to prevent irreparable harm. In federal courts the trial on the action on the merits may be advanced and consolidated with the hearing on the application for preliminary injunction. *See* Fed. R. Civ. Proc. 65.

Preliminary prospectus: Prospectus prepared for submission to the Securities and Exchange Commission in connection with a registration statement. A prospectus does not become final until the registration statement has become "effective," and if used before the effective date, it must bear a legend, printed in red, that the prospectus is preliminary. *See* SEC Release No. 33-6383, 47 Fed. Reg. 11380 (1982); 17 C.F.R. § 230.430. See **red herring.**

Premarket notification: 1. Notification to the the Federal Trade Commission of a pending merger or acquisition. See **Hart-Scott-Rodino Antitrust Improvements Act of 1976.** 2. Notification to the Environmental Protection Agency prior to the manufacture of any "new chemical substance" or manufacture or processing of any existing chemical substance for a "significant new use." Section 5(a)(1) of the Toxic Substances Control Act, 15 U.S.C. § 2604(a)(1).

Premium: 1. Additional or extra amount; difference between the price at which a security is offered or sold and the face amount or par value, if the price exceeds such face amount or par value. 2. Consideration for a contract of insurance.

Prepayment: Payment of the principal of a loan prior to the time when due.

Prepayment penalty or prepayment premium: Premium or penalty charge imposed by a lending institution for prepaying a loan.

Present fairly in conformity with generally accepted accounting principles: In the Statement of Auditing Standards by the American Institute of Certified Public Accountants, *The Meaning of "Present Fairly in Conformity with Generally Accepted Accounting Principles" in the Independent Auditor's Report* (1975), the AICPA states that:

The auditor's opinion that financial statements present fairly an entity's financial position, results of operations, and changes in financial position in conformity with generally accepted accounting principles should be based in his judgment as to whether (a) the accounting principles selected and applied have general acceptance ... ; (b) the accounting principles are appropriate in the circumstances ... ; (c) the financial statements, including the related notes, are informative of matters that may affect their use, understanding, and interpretation ... ; (d) the information presented in the financial statements is classified and summarized in a reasonable manner, that is, neither too detailed nor too condensed ... ; and (e) the financial statements reflect the underlying events and transactions in a manner that presents the financial position, results of operations, and changes in financial position stated within a range of acceptable limits, that is, limits that are reasonable and practical to attain in financial statements.

Paragraph 4. See **generally accepted accounting principles.**

Presenting bank: Under Article 4–Bank Deposits and Collections of the Uniform Commercial Code, presenting bank means "any bank presenting an item except a payor bank." UCC Section 4-105.

Presentment: For the purpose of Article 3–Commercial Paper and Article 4–Bank Deposits and Collections of the Uniform Commercial Code, "Presentment is a demand for acceptance or payment made upon the maker, acceptor, drawee or other payor by or on behalf of the holder." UCC Section 3-504(1). Presentment may be made by mail, through a clearing house, or at the place specified for acceptance or payment (or if there be none, at the place of business of the party to accept or pay). UCC Section 3-504(2).

Present sale: For the purpose of Article 2 of the Uniform Commercial Code–Sales, present sale means "a sale which is accomplished by the making of the contract." UCC Section 2-106.

Present value: Value of a payment or item of property, to be paid, received, or realized in the future, determined as of the present time by reducing the future value by an appropriate discount rate, compounded, for the intervening period. See **discount.** In pension plan valuations, the present value may be determined by including computations of the probability of such factors as mortality and withdrawal.

Presumption: Under the Uniform Commercial Code, "'Presumption' or 'presumed' means that the trier of fact must find the existence of the fact presumed unless and until evidence is introduced which would support a finding of its non-existence." UCC section 1-201(31).

Pretax accounting income: Income or loss for a period, before deducting related tax expense or adding related tax income.

Price amendment: Amendment to a registration statement filed with the Securities and Exchange Commission under the Securities Act of 1933 reflecting the price established for the securities. The price amendment is usually filed on the day or the day before the registration statement is to become effective, and acceleration is usually asked for and received so that the interval between establishing the price and selling the securities is short.

Price discrimination: Sale of commodities of like kind or quality to different purchasers at different prices. Price discrimination resulting in competitive injury is a violation of section 2(a) of the Robinson-Patman Act, 15 U.S.C. § 13(a). *See generally* American Bar Association, Section of Antitrust Law, *Antitrust Law Developments* 106 (1975).

Price/earnings ratio: Ratio of the current market price of a stock to the annual earnings per share.

Primary earnings per share: Earnings attributable to each share of common stock outstanding, including common stock equivalents. Compare fully-diluted earnings per share; see earnings per share.

Primary jurisdiction: Doctrine that an administrative agency should hear a given controversy on a matter within its purview before resorting to the courts. Primary jurisdiction may be exclusive, preempting court jurisdiction over certain matters, or nonexclusive, requiring administrative agency review before resorting to court proceedings. *See Ricci v. Chicago Mercantile Exchange,* 409 U.S. 289 (1973); *see generally* American Bar Association, Section of Antitrust Law, *Antitrust Law Developments* 412 (1975).

Primary offering: Offering of securities by the issuer. Compare **secondary offering.**

Prime rate: Rate of interest publicly announced by a bank from time to time for short-term, unsecured loans to its business customers with the highest credit standing. The prime rate may not be the lowest rate of interest available, because banks may offer special types of loans at lower rates in certain circumstances. The prime rate is used by banks as the basis for determining the interest on many types of loans that have a "floating" rate to reflect market conditions from time to time. The prime rate may once have been based on actual loans made, but it has become an artificial thing, established by banks by announcement. *See An Analysis of Prime Rate Lending Practices at the Ten Largest United States Banks, Staff Report for the Committee on Banking, Finance and Urban Affairs, House of Representatives,* Committee Print 97-2, 97th Cong., 1st Sess. (1981).

Principal: 1. Employer of an agent. 2. Party whose obligation is guaranteed.

Principal underwriter: In connection with a securities offering registered under the Securities Act of 1933, a "principal underwriter" is an underwriter "in privity of contract with the issuer of the securities as to which he is underwriter, the term 'issuer' having the meaning given in sections 2(4) and 2(11) of the Act." 17 C.F.R. 230.405, 47 Fed. Reg. 11380, 11436 (1982). See also **managing underwriter.**

Prior redemption privilege: Privilege extended to holders of debt securities that have been called to present their securities for redemption prior to the call date or maturity date.

Privacy Act of 1974: Federal law providing safeguards to limit use of information about an individual by agencies of the federal government. Pub. L. No. 93-579, 88 Stat. 1896 (1974); 5 U.S.C. § 552a. *See A Citizens' Guide on How to Use the Freedom of Information Act and the Privacy Act in Requesting Government Documents,* H.R. Rep. No. 95-793, 95th Cong., 1st Sess. (1977); Feldman & Gordin, Jr., *Privacy and Personal Information Reporting: The Legislative Boom,* 35 Bus. Law. 1259 (1980).

Private activity bond: Industrial development bond or municipal bond used to finance educational expense or to benefit charitable, religious, or educational organizations. Interest on private activity bonds will not be exempt from federal income taxes pursuant to section 103 of the Internal Revenue Code unless certain reporting requirements are met. I.R.C. § 103(l); section 215(b) of the Tax Equity and Fiscal Responsibility Act of 1982.

Private car line: Company that owns railroad cars for lease and hire to railroad companies and shippers. The car line is not private; the cars are. Private cars are railroad cars not owned by a railroad.

Private Export Funding Corporation: Private corporation owned by banks and industrial corporations that provides financing for exports by United States enterprises.

Private offering: See private placement.

Private placement: Issuance of securities under circumstances "not involving any public offering," so that registration of the securities pursuant to the Securities Act of 1933 is not necessary because of the exemption available under section 4(2), 15 U.S.C. § 77d(2). *See* SEC Release No. 33-6389, 47 Fed. Reg. 11251 (1982); 17 C.F.R. §§ 230.501–5; *SEC v. Ralston Purina Co.*, 346 U.S. 119 (1953); Kinderman, *The Private Offering Exemption: An Examination of Its Availability under and outside Rule 146,* 30 Bus. Law. 921 (1975); Schneider, *The Statutory Law of Private Placements,* 14 Rev. Sec. Reg. 869 (1981).

Private ruling: Ruling by the Internal Revenue Service on a question presented by a taxpayer regarding the tax treatment of a particular transaction or situation. *See* Kasischke, *New Procedures to Obtain an IRS Ruling,* 11 Tax Advisor 580 (1980).

Private sale: Under the Uniform Commercial Code, a private sale is a sale that is not a public sale, but is effected by solicitation and negotiation conducted either directly or through a broker. *See* UCC Section 2-706, Official Comment, Point 4.

Private sector pass-through: Security backed by mortgages that is issued by a private financial institution, similar to mortgage pass-through securities issued by federal agencies.

Privilege: Interest that is not a right.

Privity: Direct relationship as parties to a contract.

Proceeds: Under Article 9 of the Uniform Commercial Code–Secured Transactions, proceeds include "whatever is received upon the sale, exchange, collection or other disposition of collateral or proceeds." Insurance payments may be proceeds, under certain circumstances. "Money, checks, deposit accounts, and the like" are "cash proceeds"; all other proceeds are "non-cash proceeds." UCC Section 9-306. In most circumstances, a security interest in collateral continues in identifiable proceeds upon the sale or other disposition of the collateral. UCC Section 9-306(2).

Process of posting: For the purpose of Article 4 of the Uniform Commercial Code—Bank Deposits and Collections, "process of posting" means the usual procedure followed by a bank in determining to pay an item and recording the payment. The process may include verification of signature, ascertaining that sufficient funds are available, stamping the item "paid," and entering a charge to the customer's account. UCC Section 4-109.

Processing agreement: Agreement to pay for processing or materials at a given plant, for a fixed period at a given minimum rate at an established price. Such an agreement, obtained from a creditworthy party, is intended to provide a basis for the financing of the processing plant.

Product extension merger: Merger of companies selling related or complementary products. Such mergers may be attacked on antitrust grounds because of the elimination of potential competition. *See, e.g., United States v. Standard Oil Co. (New Jersey)*, 253 F. Supp. 196 (D.N.J. 1966); *see generally* American Bar Association, Section of Antitrust Law, *Antitrust Law Developments* 79, 82 (1975).

Production credit association: Borrower-owned financial institution organized pursuant to Title II of the Farm Credit Act of 1971. Production credit associations make loans to farmers, ranchers, commercial fishermen, persons engaged in on-the-farm services, and rural residents.

Production payment: Right to a specified share in the proceeds of production from a mineral property. The right may be specified in monetary terms or in terms of a quantity of oil and gas. Liability for the payment is usually limited to the production from that property, and is secured by the minerals in place. *See* I.R.C. § 636; Financial Accounting Standards Board, Statement of Financial Accounting Standards No. 19, *Financial Accounting and Reporting by Oil and Gas Companies,* paragraphs 43b, 47a (1977).

Productive assets: Assets employed in production, rather than held for sale in the ordinary course of business.

Profitability index: Measure of the desirability of an investment opportunity, consisting of the ratio of the sum of the present value of future cash flows to the initial cash investment; also called benefit/cost ratio. *See* Schwab & Lustig, *A Comparative Analysis of the Net Present Value and the Benefit-Cost Ratio as Measures of the Economic Desirability of Investments,* 24 J. of Finance 507 (1969).

Profit and loss statement: Statement of income.

Profit center: Component of a business that sells primarily to outside markets and for which information about revenue and profitability is accumulated. Financial Accounting Standards Board, Statement of Financial Accounting Standards No. 14, *Financial Reporting for Segments of a Business Enterprise,* paragraph 13 (1976).

Profit-sharing plan: Form of pension or employee benefit plan in which contributions are made by an employer out of profits, with no requirement for such contributions, and the benefits are determined by the amount contributed.

Pro forma: As a matter of form. Pro forma financial statements reflect hypothetical or proposed situations, such as combined statements of planned merger partners and estimates of future financial results.

Progress payments: Payments on a construction, consulting, development, or other contract involving special work by the seller for the buyer, made by the buyer as work progresses instead of holding back the entire amount until the project is complete or the item delivered. As to the availability of investment tax credit for progress expenditures, see I.R.C. § 46(d).

Pro hac vice: For this particular occasion.

Prohibited transaction: 1. Transaction between a pension plan and a "party in interest," prohibited by the Employee Retirement Income Security Act of 1974. "Prohibited transactions" include:

(A) sale or exchange, or leasing, of any property between the plan and a party in interest;

(B) lending of money or other extension of credit between the plan and a party in interest;

(C) furnishing of goods, services, or facilities between the plan and a party in interest;

(D) transfer to, or use by or for the benefit of, a party in interest, of any assets of the plan; or

(E) acquisition, on behalf of the plan, of any employer security or employer real property in violation of section 407(a).

ERISA section 406(a)(1). The terms "employer security," "employer real property," and "party in interest" are specifically defined in ERISA. *See* I.R.C. § 4975. *See generally* Cummings, *Purposes and Scope of the Fiduciary Provisions under the Employee Retirement Income Security Act of 1974*, 31 Bus. Law. 15 (1975); *ERISA and the Investment Management and Brokerage Industries, Five Years Later*, 35 Bus. Law. 189 (1979). 2. Transaction that would result in the loss by an organization of its tax-exempt status under the Internal Revenue Code. Prohibited transactions include loans without adequate security and a reasonable rate of interest, excessive compensation, preferential service, sales with less than adequate consideration, and other diversion of property or income to the creator of or a substantial contributor to the organization, or a member of the family of or a corporation controlled by such a person. I.R.C. § 503(b).

Project agreement: Agreement among owners, contractors, and unions providing that there will be no strike or lockout during the period of a construction project. *See* Nolan & O'Brien, *Project Agreements—A Modern Dilemma*, 36 Bus. Law. 1751 (1981).

Project financing arrangement: As defined by the Financial Accounting Standards Board in connection with disclosure of long-term obligations:

The financing of a major capital project in which the lender looks principally to the cash flows and earnings of the project as the source of funds for repayment and to the assets of the project as collateral for the loan. The general credit of the project entity is usually not a significant factor, either because the entity is a corporation without other assets or because the financing is without direct recourse to the owner(s) of the entity.

Financial Accounting Standards Board, Statement of Financial Accounting Standards No. 47, *Disclosure of Long-Term Obligations*, Appendix B (1981). *See generally* P. Nevitt, *Project Financing* (2d ed. 1978).

Promise: In connection with contracts, "A promise is a manifestation of intention to act or refrain from acting in a specified way, so made as to justify a promisee in understanding that a commitment has been made." *Restatement, Second, Contracts* § 2(1) (1981). *See* 1 Corbin, *Contracts* § 13 (1963 & Supp. 1980). For the purpose of Article 3 of the Uniform Commercial Code—Commercial Paper, "a promise is an undertaking to pay and must be more than an acknowledgment of an obligation." UCC Section 3-102.

Promisee: Party to whom a promise is made. *See Restatement, Second, Contracts* § 2(3) (1981).

Promisor: Party making a promise. *See Restatement, Second, Contracts* § 2(2) (1981).

Promissory note: Written, unconditional promise to pay a sum certain, at a definite time or on demand, to the holder or to his order. If a promissory note meets the requirements of negotiability set forth in Article 3 of the Uniform Commercial Code, it can be transferred and enforced by a transferee against the maker without setoff for any claims of the maker against the transferor.

Promoter: For the purpose of registration statements and reports filed under the securities laws:

The term "promoter" includes—

(i) Any person who, acting alone or in conjunction with one or more other persons, directly or indirectly takes initiative in founding and organizing the business or enterprise of an issuer, or

(ii) Any person who, in connection with the founding and organizing of the business or enterprise of an issuer, directly or indirectly receives in consideration of services or property, or both services and property, 10 percent or more of any class of securities of the issuer or 10 percent or more of the proceeds from the sale of any class of such securities. However, a person who receives such securities or proceeds either solely as underwriting commissions or solely in consideration of property shall not be deemed a promoter within the meaning of this paragraph if such person does not otherwise take an active part in founding and organizing the enterprise.

17 C.F.R. § 230.405, 47 Fed. Reg. 11380, 11436 (1982); SEC Regulation S-X, 17 C.F.R. § 210.1-02(r); 17 C.F.R. § 240.12b-2. *See Old Dominion Copper Mining & Smelting Co. v. Bigelow*, 203 Mass. 159, 89 N.E. 193, 201 (1909).

Properly payable: Under Article 4—Bank Deposits and Collections of the Uniform Commercial Code, properly payable "includes the availability of funds for payment at the time of decision to pay or dishonor." UCC Section 4-104(1)(i).

Property from the estate: Property over which a bankrupt estate has control or possession. The phrase is used in the automatic stay provisions of the Bankruptcy Code, 11 U.S.C. § 362(a)(3). An official definition is not provided in the statute; the foregoing definition is found in the legislative history. H.R. Rep. No. 95-595, 95th Cong., 1st Sess. 341 (1977).

Property of the estate: All legal or equitable interests of a debtor in property, wherever located, when a case is commenced under the Bankruptcy Code. For a full listing of the property that would be included in the "estate" created by the commencement of a case under the Bankruptcy Code, see 11 U.S.C. § 541. *See also* H.R. Rep. No. 95-595, 95th Cong., 1st Sess. 367 (1977).

Property used in the trade or business: For the purpose of the Internal Revenue Code provisions on capital gains, "property used in the trade or business" means "property used in the trade or business, of a character which is subject to the allowance for depreciation provided in section 167, held for more than 1 year, . . ." that is inventory, property held for sale to customers, copyrights and similar property, publications of the United States (unless purchased at the price at which offered to the public), timber, coal, domestic iron ore, livestock, and unharvested crops. I.R.C. § 1231(b).

Pro rata: In proportion; according to interest.

Prospectus: Preliminary, or prospective, statement or description of business proposition or project; usually used in connection with an issue of securities. Under the Securities Act of 1933:

The term "prospectus" means any prospectus, notice, circular, advertisement, letter, or communication, written or by radio or television, which offers any security for sale or confirms the sale of any security; except that (a) a communication sent or given after the effective date of the registration statement (other than a prospectus permitted under subsection (b) of section 10) shall not be deemed a prospectus if it is proved that prior to or at the same time with such communication a written prospectus meeting the requirements of subsection (a) of section 10 at the time of such communication was sent or given to the person to whom the communication was made, and (b) a notice, circular, advertisement, letter, or communication in respect of a security shall not be deemed to be a prospectus if it states from whom a written prospectus meeting the requirements of section 10 may be obtained and, in addition, does no more than identify the security, state the price thereof, state by whom orders will be executed, and contain such other information as the Commission, by rules or regulations deemed necessary or appropriate in the public interest and for the protection of investors, and subject to such terms and condition as may be prescribed therein, may permit.

Section 2(10); 15 U.S.C. § 77b(10). *See* section 10, 15 U.S.C. § 77j; section 303(3) of the Trust Indenture Act of 1939, 15 U.S.C. § 77ccc(3); SEC Rule 134, 17 C.F.R. § 230.134.

Pro tanto: For so much, as far as it goes.

Protective filing: The filing of a financing statement in respect of personal property under lease under Section 9-408 of the Uniform Commercial Code. Such a filing is not required to protect the rights of the owner and lessor in leased property in most jurisdictions, but the filing is made in case a court were to construe the lease as "lease intended as security" rather than a true lease, and treat the owner and lessor as a secured party. See **security interest.**

Protective order: Order of a court limiting methods and scope of discovery to protect a person from "annoyance, embarrassment, oppression, or undue burden or expense... ." Fed. R. Civ. Proc. 26(c).

Protest: For the purpose of Article 3–Commercial Paper and Article 4–Bank Deposits and Collections of the Uniform Commercial Code, "A protest is a certificate of dishonor made under the hand and seal of a United States consul or vice consul or a notary public or other person authorized to certify dishonor by the law of the place where dishonor occurs." UCC Section 3-509(1). A protest must identify the instrument, certify that due presentment has been made (or the reason why it is excused), and must certify that the instrument has been dishonored by nonacceptance or nonpayment. UCC Section 3-509(2).

Proved area: The part of a property to which proved reserves have been specifically attributed. Financial Accounting Standards Board, Statement of Financial Accounting Standards No. 19, *Financial Accounting and Reporting by Oil and Gas Producing Companies,* paragraph 275 (1977).

Proved oil and gas reserves: The Securities and Exchange Commission defines "proved oil and gas reserves" as "the estimated quantities of crude oil, natural gas, and natural gas liquids which geological and engineering data demonstrate with reasonable certainty to be recoverable in future years from known reservoirs under existing economic and operating conditions, ..." Regulation S-X, 17 C.F.R. § 210.4-10(a)(2). The definition goes on in some detail about when reservoirs are considered "proved," when reserves that are recoverable by improved techniques can be included, and certain oil and gas that should not be included. Definitions of "proved developed oil and gas reserves" and "proved undeveloped reserves" are also included in Regulation S-X. 17 C.F.R. §§ 210.4-10(a)(3), 210.4-10(a)(4); *see* SEC Accounting Series Release No. 257, 43 Fed. Reg. 60404 (1978). The Financial Accounting Standards Board defers to Regulation S-X with respect to these definitions. Financial Accounting Standards Board, Statement of Financial Accounting Standards No. 25, *Suspension of Certain Accounting Requirements for Oil and Gas Producing Companies,* paragraph 7 (1979).

Proven properties; proved properties: Properties with proved reserves. 17 C.F.R. 210.4-10(a)(5); Financial Accounting Standards Board, Statement of Financial Accounting Standards No. 19, *Financial Accounting and Reporting by Oil and Gas Producing Companies,* paragraph 11 (1977). See **mineral interests in properties.**

Proviso: Condition set forth in a document, usually preceded by the words *"provided, however"* or the like.

Proximate cause: That which produces the damage or injury; if the injury is caused by a sequence of events, the last event in the causative chain. In the case of an action by a buyer for consequential damages for the seller's breach in a sale of goods, such damages include "injury to person or property proximately resulting from any breach of warranty." UCC Section 2-715(2). The question of "proximate" turns on "whether it was reasonable for the buyer to use the goods without such inspection as would have revealed the defects." UCC Section 2-715(2), Official Comment, Point 5.

Proxy: Authority to act for a shareholder in voting shares. Cal. Corp. Code § 178. *See* Model Business Corporation Act § 33 (1979); N.Y. Bus. Corp. Law § 609; Del. Code Ann. Tit. 8 § 212.

Proxy holder: Person to whom a proxy is given. Cal. Corp. Code § 179.

Proxy rules: Rules relating to solicitation of proxies and preparation of proxy statements promulgated by the Securities and Exchange Commission pursuant to section 14(a) of the Securities Exchange Act of 1934, 15 U.S.C. § 78n(a). SEC Regulation 14A, 17 C.F.R. § 240.14a. *See also* SEC Regulation 14C, 17 C.F.R. § 240.14c. *See* SEC Release No. 34-17424 (1981).

Proxy statement: Statement furnished to holders of voting securities in connection with a solicitation of proxies. Under most circumstances, proxy statements must comply with the requirements of the proxy rules promulgated by the Securities and Exchange Commission pursuant to section 14(a) of the Securities and Exchange Act of 1934, 15 U.S.C. § 78n(a). *See* SEC Regulation 14A, 17 C.F.R. § 240.14a.

Prudent man rule: Rule requiring a fiduciary to exercise the same care and diligence that a prudent man would use in the conduct of his own affairs. As originally expressed in *Harvard College v. Amory,* a trustee should "observe how men of prudence, discretion and intelligence manage their own affairs, not in regard to speculation, but in regard to the permanent disposition of their funds, considering the probable income, as well as the probable safety of the capital to be invested." 26 Mass. (9 Pickering) 446, 461 (1830). *See Matter of the Bank of New York, Bank of New York v. Spitzer,* 43 App. Div. 2d 105 (1st Dept.) *aff'd,* 35 N.Y. 2d 512 (1974). The prudent man rule is often incorporated in state statutes regarding the legality of investments by savings banks, insurance companies, and others in fiduciary situations, and has been included in ERISA, 29 U.S.C. § 1104(a)(1)(B), and section 11(c) of the Securities Act of 1933, 15 U.S.C. 77k(c).

Psuedo corporation: Subchapter S corporation.

PTE: Prohibited transaction exemption.

PTO: Patent and Trademark Office.

Publication: With respect to copyrights, "publication" is

the distribution of copies or phonorecords of a work to the public by sale or other transfer of ownership, or by rental, lease, or lending. The offering to distribute copies or phonorecords to a group of persons for purposes of further distribution, public performance, or public display, constitutes publication. A public performance or display of a work does not of itself constitute publication.

17 U.S.C. § 101.

Public corporation: 1. Corporation whose stock has been registered with the Securities and Exchange Commission pursuant to the Securities Act of 1933 and can be publicly traded, or is required to file reports with the Securities and Exchange Commission pursuant to the Securities Exchange Act of 1934. *See* Financial Accounting Standards Board, Statement of Financial Accounting Standards No. 33, *Financial Reporting and Changing Prices,* paragraph 22h (1979). 2. Corporation formed as an instrumentality of government or for public purposes, as a municipal corporation. *E.g.,* N. Y. Gen. Const. Law § 66(1).

Public housing bonds and notes: Obligations issued by local housing authorities and agencies, guaranteed by the United States government.

Public housing program-project notes: Obligations of local housing authorities secured by an agreement of the United States to make loans sufficient to pay the principal of and interest on the notes.

Public interest: An elusive term, difficult or impossible to define objectively, but useful for subjective application to reach the desired result in individual cases in which a court or administrative agency must determine whether some activity or situation is in the "public interest." As to the public interest requirement for a proceeding by the Federal Trade Commission under section 5 of the Federal Trade Commission Act (15 U.S.C. § 45), see American Bar Association, Section of Antitrust Law, *Antitrust Law Developments* 166 (1975). As to "public interest" justification for immunity to antitrust laws under section 15 of the Shipping Act, 1916 (46 U.S.C. § 814), see *Federal Maritime Commission v. Aktiebolaget Svenska Amerika Linien,* 390 U.S. 238, 243 (1968).

Publicly: Under the copyright law, to perform or display a work "publicly" means·

(1) to perform or display it at a place open to the public or at any place where a substantial number of persons outside of a normal circle of a family and its social acquaintances is gathered; or

(2) to transmit or otherwise communicate a performance or display of the work to a place specified by clause (1) or to the public, by means of any device or process, whether the members of the public capable of receiving the performance or display receive it in the same place or in separate places and at the same time or at different times.

17 U.S.C. § 101.

Public offering: Offering of securities registered under the Securities Act of 1933. Certain securities exempt from the registration requirements of the Securities Act by section 3 thereof may also be offered to the public, but such an offering is not usually styled as a "public offering."

Public policy: An elusive term, difficult to define objectively, but useful for subjective application in the furtherance of justice in particular cases. For example, a court may refuse to enforce a particular term of a contract because it is found to be inconsistent with "public policy." In connection with the unenforceability of contract terms on grounds of "public policy":

A public policy against enforcement of promises or other terms may be derived by the court from

(a) legislation relevant to such a policy, or

(b) the need to protect some aspect of the public welfare, as is the case for judicial policies against, for example,

(i) restraint of trade,

(ii) impairment of family relations, and

(iii) interference with other protected interests.

Restatement, Second, Contracts § 179 (1981); *see, e.g. Homestead Supplies, Inc., v. Executive Life Insurance Co.,* 81 Cal. App. 3d 978, 147 Cal. Rptr. 22 (1978).

Public policy committee: Committee of the board of directors of a corporation to address social issues and handle disclosure of socially significant information. McGrath, *Corporate Directorship Practices: The Public Policy Committee* (1980).

Public sale: References to "public sale" in the Uniform Commercial Code usually mean sale at auction. UCC Section 2-706, Official Comment, point 4.

Public Utility Holding Company Act of 1935: Federal legislation limiting the use of holding companies to own and acquire utility companies. Pub. L. No. 333, ch. 687, 49 Stat. 803 (1935), 15 U.S.C. § 79

Public utility property: For the purpose of the investment tax credit provisions of the Internal Revenue Code, "public utility property" is property used predominantly in the trade or business of the furnishing or sale of electrical energy, water, or sewage disposal services, gas through a local distribution system, or telephone, domestic telegraph, or other communication services, including microwave, if such furnishing or sale is subject to rate regulation. I.R.C. § 46(c)(3). As to "15-year public utility property," see accelerated cost recovery system, I.R.C. § 168.

Puffing: Expression of opinion by a seller as to the favorable qualities of the object being sold, not constituting a representation as to fact. The term is often preceded by the word "mere."

Purchase: Under the Uniform Commercial Code, the term "purchase" includes "taking by sale, discount, negotiation, mortgage, pledge, lien, issue or reissue, gift or any other voluntary transaction creating an interest in property." UCC Section 1-201(32).

Purchase agreement: Agreement between an issuer of securities and the purchaser or underwriter of those securities, providing the terms of such purchase. This term is usually used in connection with a private placement, the term "underwriting agreement" being used in public offerings.

Purchase fund: Fund established in connection with an issue of debt securities to be used by the issuer to prepay or redeem the securities prior to maturity. A purchase fund is similar to a sinking fund, but a purchase fund is not required to be used for prepayment or redemption, as is a sinking fund.

Purchase method: Method of accounting for business combinations in situations where the acquisition involves consideration other than voting common stock, or other requirements of the "pooling of interests" method are not met. The purchase method treats the acquisition as an acquisition of the assets and an assumption of the liabilities of the acquired corporation; any excess of purchase price must be treated as goodwill and amortized by the acquiring corporation in succeeding years. *See* American Institute of Certified Public Accountants, Accounting Principles Board Opinion No. 16, *Accounting for Business Combinations*, paragraph 11 (1970); Fiflis, *Accounting for Mergers, Acquisitions and Investments, in a Nutshell: The Interrelationships of, and Criteria for, Purchase or Pooling, the Equity Method, and Parent-Company-Only and Consolidated Statements*, 37 Bus. Law. 89 (1981). Compare pooling of interests method.

Purchase money mortgage: Mortgage given by a purchaser of real property to the seller to secure an unpaid portion of the purchase price.

Purchase money security interest: Security interest that is taken by a seller of goods to secure part of the price, or taken by a financer who gives value to enable a purchaser to acquire rights in goods. *See* UCC Section 9-107. A purchase money security interest has priority over certain other types of security interests. *See* UCC Section 9-312, 9-301(2). *See generally* Gilmore, *The Purchase Money Priority*, 76 Harv. L. Yev. 1333 (1963).

Purchaser: Under the Uniform Commercial Code, "a person who takes by purchase." UCC Section 1-201(33). The Bankruptcy Code definition is broader, including a "transferee of a voluntary transfer, and the immediate or mediate transferee of such a transferee." 11 U.S.C. § 101(32); *see* H.R. Rep. No. 95-595, 95th Cong., 1st Sess. 313 (1977).

Purpose statement: Statement by a borrower, required by Federal Reserve Regulation U, as to the use to which the proceeds of a loan secured by stock are to be put. 12 C.F.R. § 221.

Pursuant to commitment: Under Article 9 of the Uniform Commercial Code—Secured Transactions, an advance is made "pursuant to commitment" if "the secured party has bound himself to make it, whether or not a subsequent event of default or otherevent not within his control has relieved or may relieve him from his obligation." UCC Section 9-105(1)(k). This phrase is used in the rules relating to priority of future advances in UCC Sections 9-301(4), 9-307(3), and 9-312(7).

Put: Right or option to sell, or "put," a given security or piece of property at a specified price at a specified time, to the party who has given the "put." The opposite of a call.

Put bond: Option tender bond.

Quad R Act: Railroad Revitalization and Regulatory Reform Act of 1976.

Qualified mortgage bond: Mortgage bond qualified under section 103A of the Internal Revenue Code, the interest on which is exempt from federal income taxes. I.R.C. § 103A(c)(1).

Quantity discount: Discount on the price of commodities for purchase in certain quantities. An exception to the price discrimination prohibition of the Robinson-Patman Act is provided for "differentials which make only due allowance for differences in the cost of manufacture, sale, or delivery resulting from the differing methods or quantities in which such commodities are to such purchasers sold or delivered: ... ." 15 U.S.C. § 13(a). See cost justification.

Quantity limit proviso: The Robinson-Patman Act prohibition against price discrimination has an exception for cost-justified quantity discounts. See **quantity discount.** That exception is further qualified by the "quantity limit proviso":

Provided, however, that the Federal Trade Commission may, after due investigation and hearing to all interested parties, fix and establish quantity limits, and revise the same as it finds necessary, as to particular commodities or classes of commodities, where it finds that available purchasers in greater quantities are so few as to render differentials on account thereof unjustly discriminatory or promotive of monopoly in any line of commerce; and the foregoing shall then not be construed to permit differentials based on differences in quantities greater than those so fixed and established.

15 U.S.C. § 13(a). *See FTC v. B. F. Goodrich Co.*, 242 F.2d 31 (D.C. Cir. 1957); *see generally* American Bar Association, Section of Antitrust Law, *Antitrust Law Developments* 140 (1975).

Quasi-contract: Obligation of a contractual nature not arising from an express contract, but imputed from circumstances or relationships between parties, in order to achieve justice. *See*

Restatement of Restitution; Bloomgarden v. Coyer, 479 F. 2d 201 (D.C. Cir. 1973).

Quasi-reorganization: Restatement of assets, capital stock, and surplus of a corporation; also called corporate readjustment. *See* American Institute of Certified Public Accountants, Accounting Research Bulletin No. 43, Ch. 7A, *Quasi-Reorganization or Corporate Readjustment* (1953); SEC Accounting Series Release No. 25, 11 Fed. Reg. 10923 (1941).

Quick assets: Cash and other assets that can be converted to cash within a short time, perhaps a month, such as government securities and other marketable securities and accounts receivable.

Quick assets ratio, quick ratio: Ratio of quick assets to current liabilities.

Quiet enjoyment clause: Clause in a lease of real or personal property confirming the right of the lessee to the quiet enjoyment of the premises or property so long as the lessee fulfills its obligations under the lease. A quiet enjoyment clause would be used in a lease of property that would be, or become subject to, a mortgage or security interest, in order to protect the lessee from efforts of the secured party to oust the lessee from possession in the event of default by the owner under the mortgage or security agreement. A quiet enjoyment clause is also useful in a sublease.

Quitclaim deed: Deed releasing any claim or interest, but without any representation or undertaking that there exists any such claim or interest.

Quorum: The number of shareholders or directors required to be in attendance at a meeting for action taken to be valid. In the case of directors, a majority usually constitutes a quorum, unless the certificate of incorporation or by-laws specifies a higher proportion. *See* Model Business Corporation Act §§ 32, 40 (1979); N.Y. Bus. Corp. Law § 707, 709; Del. Code Ann. tit. 8 § 141(b), 211(c); Cal. Corp. Code §§ 307(a)(7), 602.

Quo warranto: By what authority. Proceeding to challenge authority. *See* Cal. Corp. Code § 1801.

R

Racketeer Influenced and Corrupt Organizations Act: Statute providing federal remedies for racketeering activities; Title IX of the Organized Crime Control Act of 1970. Pub. L. No. 91-452, 84 Stat. 922, 941 (1970), 18 U.S.C. §§ 1961–68.

Rail carrier: For the purpose of regulation by the Interstate Commerce Commission, the term "rail carrier" means "a person providing railroad transportation for compensation." 49 U.S.C. § 10102(17). See **railroad**.

Railroad: The Bankruptcy Code provides special rules for railroad reorganizations, and defines "railroad" as a "common carrier by railroad engaged in the transportation of individuals or property or owner of trackage facilities leased by such a common carrier." 11 U.S.C. § 101(33); *see* H.R. Rep. No. 95-595, 95th Cong., 1st Sess. 313 (1977). For the purpose of regulation by the Interstate Commerce Commission, the term "railroad" includes:

(A) a bridge, car float, lighter, and ferry used by or in connection with a railroad;

(B) the road used by a rail carrier and owned by it or operated under an agreement; and

(C) a switch, spur, track, terminal, terminal facility, and a freight depot, yard, and ground, used or necessary for transportation.

49 U.S.C. § 10102(18). See also **rail carrier.**

Railroad Retirement Board: Independent agency of the United States government responsible for the administration of the federal retirement, survivor, unemployment, and sickness benefit programs for railroad workers. *See* Railroad Retirement Act of 1935, Pub. L. No. 399, ch. 812, 49 Stat. 967 (1935); Railroad Retirement Act of 1974, Pub. L. No. 93-445, 88 Stat. 1305 (1974); 45 U.S.C. §§ 231–31t; Railroad Unemployment Insurance Act, Pub. L. No. 722, ch. 680, 52 Stat. 1094 (1938); 45 U.S.C. §§ 351–67.

Railroad Revitalization and Regulatory Reform Act of 1976: Federal legislation implementing reorganization of certain railroads in bankruptcy, providing assistance to railroads, and reforming certain procedures of the Interstate Commerce Commission. Pub. L. No. 94-210, 90 Stat. 31 (1976).

Railway Association, United States: Agency of the United States government formed by the Regional Rail Reorganization Act of 1973 to plan and supervise the reorganization and rehabilitation of railroads in the northeast United States after the bankruptcy of the Penn Central and other railroads in the region.

Railway Labor Act: Federal legislation regulating employer-union relations and collective bargaining in the railroad and airline industries. Pub. L. No. 257, ch. 347, 44 Stat. 577 (1926); 45 U.S.C. §§ 151–88. *See generally* B. Aaron, B. Burgoon, et al, *The Railway Labor Act at Fifty* (1976).

Ralston Purina: *SEC v. Ralston Purina Co.,* 346 U.S. 119 (1953), an important case on the availability of the private placement exemption from registration under section 4(2) of the Securities Act of 1933.

RAN: Revenue anticipation note.

Rapid amortization: Method of accelerated depreciation available for railroad equipment and pollution control equipment under the Internal Revenue Code, whereby the owner of the asset may elect to depreciate (or amortize) the cost of the asset over 60 months, on a straight-line basis. I.R.C. §§ 169, 184.

Rate agreement: Agreement among ocean carriers regarding rates, similar to a conference agreement, but permitting individual member carriers to vary from an agreed rate upon notice to the other carriers. 46 C.F.R. § 522.2(a)(2).

Rating: Classification of an issue of securities into categories of investment safety by a private rating agency, such as Moody's Investors Service, Inc., or Standard & Poor's Corporation. *See* SEC Release No. 33-6336, 46 Fed. Reg. 42024 (1981).

RCRA: Resource Conservation and Recovery Act.

REA: Rural Electrification Administration.

Readjustment: Restatement of assets, capital stock, and surplus of a corporation; also called quasi-reorganization. *See* American Institute of Certified Public Accountants, Accounting Research Bulletin No. 43, Ch. 7A, *Quasi-Reorganization or Corporate Readjustment* (1953).

Real estate investment trust: Corporation, trust, or other business association engaged in real estate transactions, whose income, if the requirements of sections 856 and 857 of the Internal Revenue Code are met, is taxed only to the beneficiaries. I.R.C. § 856(a), (c). *See also* Cal. Corp. Code § 23000, limiting the term to unincorporated associations operated by a trustee for holders of transferable shares in the trust estate.

Realization: Process of converting noncash resources and rights into money; sale of assets for cash or claims to cash. Financial Accounting Standards Board, Statement of Financial Accounting Concepts No. 3, *Elements of Financial Statements of Business Enterprises,* paragraph 83 (1980). Compare recognition.

Reallowance: Discount allowed to favored investors by members of an underwriting syndicate, by passing on part of the underwriters discount.

Real property: Land and whatever is erected or growing upon the land. The distinction between real and personal property is difficult to make on occasion, and a given piece of property can change its nature, by being affixed to or severed from land.

Reasonable: This term resists formulation of an objective method and is normally used subjectively to reach a desired result, by judging whether the action or interpretation in question is "reasonable." *See* D. Melinkoff, *The Language of the Law* 301 (1963). As to "reasonable time," see UCC Section 1-204, but it may not be helpful. As to the "reasonable needs of the business" in connection with the Federal income tax on corporations improperly accumulating surplus, see I.R.C. § 537. As to "reasonable investigation" and "reasonable ground for belief" for the purpose of section 11(c) of the Securities Act of 1933, see due diligence; 17 C.F.R. 230.176, 47 Fed. Reg. 11380, 11433 (1982).

Reason to know: A number of questions in the law of contracts turn on whether a person has "reason to know" certain facts. For example, a contract may be formed by a manifestation of assent by conduct if the person engaging in the conduct knows or has "reason to know" that the other party may infer from his conduct that he assents. The draftsmen of the *Restatement, Second, Contracts* explain what constitutes "reason to know" as follows:

A person has reason to know a fact, present or future, if he has information from which a person of ordinary intelligence would infer that the fact in question does or will exist. A person of superior intelligence has reason to know a fact if he has information from which a person of his intelligence would draw the inference. There is also reason to know if the inference would be that there is such a substantial chance of the existence of the fact that, if exercising reasonable care with reference to the matter in question, the person would predicate his action upon the assumption of its possible existence.

Restatement, Second, Contracts § 19, comment b (1981).

Recapitalization: "[R]eshuffling of a capital structure within the framework of an existing corporation." *Helvering v. Southwest Consolidated Corp.,* 315 U.S. 194 (1942). *See* I.R.C. § 368; Treas. Reg. § 1.368-2(e); CCH Federal Tax Reporter paragraph 2551.459. See also reorganization.

Recapture: Liability for federal income taxes due to a change in the circumstances that justified a deduction or credit. Investment credit is subject to recapture if the property for which the credit has been taken is disposed of or ceases to be "section 38 property" before the expiration of the "recovery" period determining the amount of the credit (three or five years, in most cases). I.R.C. § 47. Depreciation deductions and accelerated cost recovery deductions are subject to recapture if the property is sold for an amount in excess of its depreciated basis. I.R.C. § 1245. *See* section 205(a) of the Tax Equity and Fiscal Responsibility Act of 1982.

Receipt: 1. Instrument given by a party receiving goods, securities, or money acknowledging such receipt. 2. Under Article 2 of the Uniform Commercial Code–Sales, "receipt" of goods means "taking physical possession of them." UCC Section 2-103(1)(c).

Receivable: Amount owing to an entity; account receivable.

Receivables rule: "Notes or accounts receivable due from officers, employees, or affiliated companies must be shown separately and not included under a general heading such as notes receivable or accounts receivable." American Institute of Certified Public Accountants, Accounting Research Bulletin No. 43, Ch. 1A, paragraph 5 (1934).

Receiver: Person appointed by a state court to supervise the affairs of an insolvent corporation, or the dissolution and distribution of assets of a corporation because of insolvency or deadlock. Del. Code Ann. tit. 8 §§ 291–303. See custodian; judicial dissolution; receivership.

Receivership: 1. Control by a receiver appointed pursuant to state law. Under certain state statutes, receivers may be appointed to operate a corporation and dispose of its property in certain circumstances, such as judicial dissolution, an action brought by a judgment creditor to sequester assets, or an action to preserve the assets of a corporation. *E.g.,* N.Y. Bus. Corp. Law §§ 1201–18; Del. Code Ann. tit. 8 §§ 291–303. Most bankruptcy and insolvency proceedings are conducted under federal law, however. 2. Loose term for bankruptcy. Before 1933, equity receiverships were often used to effect corporate reorganizations in federal courts, but that method was replaced by the reorganization provisions of Chapter X of the Bankruptcy Act, which evolved in the period 1933–1938. The Bankruptcy Act has since been replaced by the Bankruptcy Code. Receiverships had no statutory basis, but were developed using the equity powers of the courts. Creditors would petition the court to appoint a receiver to administer the assets of an insolvent corporation for the benefit of creditors; this action protected the assets of the corporation from seizure by creditors, thus permitting an orderly plan of liquidation or reorganization to be developed and implemented. If reorganization was contemplated, a new corporation would be organized by the creditors and other claimants, and the new corporation would purchase the assets of the old at a judicial sale which would strip the assets of claims. Most of the purchase price was paid with value established for the claims against the insolvent company. *See I Report of the Commission on the Bankruptcy Laws of the United States,* H.R. Doc. No. 93-137, 93d Cong., 1st Sess. 238 (1973).

Reciprocal dealing: Use of purchasing power to obtain an advantage in the sale of products. Certain types of reciprocal arrangements have been held to be violations of section 1 of the Sherman Act and section 7 of the Clayton Act. *See, e.g., United States v. General Dynamics Corp.,* 258 F. Supp. 36 (S.D.N.Y. 1966). *See generally* American Bar Association, Section of Antitrust Law, *Antitrust Law Developments* 28, 84 (1975).

Reclamation, Bureau of: Unit of the United States Department of the Interior that is responsible for the "reclamation" of arid and semiarid land in the western part of the United States by the construction of dams and waterways. *See* Reclamation Act of 1902, Pub. L. No. 161, ch. 1093, 32 Stat. 388 (1902); 43 U.S.C. § 391.

Recognition: Process of formally recording or incorporating an item in the financial statements of an entity. Financial Accounting Standards Board, Statement of Financial Accounting Concepts No. 3, *Elements of Financial Statements of Business Enterprises,* paragraph 83 (1980). Compare **realization.**

Recomputed basis: Basis of depreciable property with certain adjustments used in the determination of recapture from the disposition thereof. I.R.C. § 1245(a)(2).

Recordation: Filing of interests in real property under state law, evidence of security interests in or leases of aircraft under section 503 of the Federal Aviation Act of 1958, or railroad rolling stock under section 11303 of Title 49 of the United States Code.

Record date: Date on which the books for the transfer of corporate shares are closed, and the identity of shareholders determined, for the purpose of distribution of dividends or voting at meetings of shareholders. *See* Model Business Corporation Act § 30 (1979); Del. Code Ann. tit. 8 § 213.

Recording act: State statute providing for recordation of interests in real property and sometimes other types of property, such as railroad rolling stock.

Records: Under the Securities Exchange Act of 1934, the term "records" means "accounts, correspondence, memorandums, tapes, discs, papers, books, and other documents or transcribed information of any type, whether expressed in ordinary or machine language." Section 3(a)(37), 15 U.S.C. § 78c(a)(37). See also **agency records.**

Recoverable amount: Current worth of the net amount of cash expected to be recoverable from the use or sale of an asset. Financial Accounting Standards Board, Statement of Financial Accounting Standards No. 33, *Financial Reporting and Changing Prices,* paragraphs 62, 63 (1979).

Recovery period: Period over which accelerated cost recovery deductions with respect to a particular piece of property may be taken against federal income tax. The recovery period is established by statute for various types of property, and replaces the concept of "useful life" under the old depreciation provisions. *See* I.R.C. §§ 168(b), 168(f)(2)(C); accelerated cost recovery system; recovery property.

Recovery property: Under section 168 of the Internal Revenue Code (the provision covering the accelerated cost recovery system introduced by the Economic Recovery Tax Act of 1981), recovery property means

tangible property of a character subject to the allowance for depreciation—

(A) used in a trade or business, or

(B) held for the production of income.

Recovery property need not be new, but the term does not include property placed in service by the taxpayer before January 1, 1981; such property is subject to depreciation under prior provisions of the Internal Revenue Code (section 167). Recovery property may be "3-year property," "5-year property," "10-year property," "15-year real property," or "15 year public utility property," depending on the period for accelerated cost recovery assigned by the statute. I.R.C. § 168(c). *See* I.R.C. § 168(e) for exceptions. *See also* section 206 of the Tax Equity and Fiscal Responsibility Act of 1982.

Redeemable preferred stock: Preferred stock subject to mandatory redemption requirements or whose redemption is outside of the control of the issuer. *See* SEC Accounting Series Release No. 268, 44 Fed. Reg. 45610 (1979).

Redemption: Buying back; purchase by the issuer of securities of all or a portion of the issue. For redemption of shares of a corporation, see Model Business Corporation Act § 67 (1979). Redemption in the case of debt securities may be mandatory, by a sinking fund provision, or optional, perhaps with a premium paid over par.

Redemption, right of: Under Article 9 of the Uniform Commercial Code—Secured Transactions, a debtor has the right to redeem collateral after default on a security agreement before the secured party has disposed of it by tendering fulfillment of all obligations secured by the collateral and the expenses reasonably incurred by the secured party in exercising his remedies. UCC Section 9-506.

Red herring: Preliminary prospectus; prospectus prepared for submittal to the Securities and Exchange Commission in connection with a registration statement. A red herring prospectus would not have been approved by the SEC, and thus bears a legend, printed in red, that the prospectus is preliminary. When the registration process is complete, the prospectus is revised to reflect the comments of the SEC, and is issued in final form without the red legend. *See* SEC Release No. 33-6383, 47 Fed. Reg. 11380 (1982); 17 C.F.R. § 230.430.

Reed-Bullwinkle Act: Federal statute amending the Interstate Commerce Act to authorize the Interstate Commerce Commission to grant antitrust immunity for rate-fixing agreements among motor carriers in "furtherance of the national transportation policy." Pub. L. No. 662, ch. 491, 62 Stat. 472 (1948); *see* 49 U.S.C. § 10706(b).

Refunding: Replacement of corporate debt with new debt.

Refusal, right of: Right to purchase property at the same price as that offered by another.

Refusal to deal: See collective refusal to deal.

Regional Rail Reorganization Act Cases: Supreme court cases deciding the constitutionality of the Regional Rail Reorganization Act of 1973. 419 U.S. 102 (1974).

Regional Rail Reorganization Act of 1973: Law creating the United States Railway Association and implementing certain other measures to solve the crisis following the bankruptcy of the Penn Central and other railroads in the Northeast. Pub. L. No. 93-236, 87 Stat. 985 (1974).

Registered: When used to describe securities, meaning that the holder is registered with the issuer, trustee, or transfer agent. Under Article 8 of the Uniform Commercial Code—Investment Securities, a security is in "registered" form "when it specifies a person entitled to the security or to rights it evidences and when its transfer may be registered upon books maintained for that purpose by or on behalf of an issuer or the security so states." UCC Section 8-102(1)(c).

Registered agent: Agent of corporation, registered with the appropriate state agency, upon whom process, notice, and demand to be served on the corporation may be served. *See* Model

Business Corporation Act §§ 12, 14 (1979); N.Y. Bus. Corp. Law § 305; Del. Code Ann. tit. 8 §§ 102(a)(2), 132.

Registered holding company: Public utility holding company registered under section 5 of the Public Utility Holding Company Act of 1935. *See* section 2(a)(12) of said act, 15 U.S.C. § 79b(a)(12); *see also* I.R.C. § 1083(b).

Registered investment adviser: Investment adviser registered with the Securities and Exchange Commission under the Investment Advisers Act of 1940. *See* section 203 of said act, 15 U.S.C. § 80b-3; investment adviser.

Registered investment company: Investment company registered with the Securities and Exchange Commission under the Investment Company Act of 1940. *See* section 8 of said act, 15 U.S.C. § 80a-8; investment company.

Registered office: Office of a corporation, registered with the appropriate state agency, where lists of shareholders and certain records are required to be kept. Model Business Corporation Act § 12 (1979); Del. Code Ann. tit. 8 § 102(a)(2).

Registrar: Agent for an issuer of securities, usually a bank or trust company, that maintains records of ownership of the securities and issues and exchanges certificates.

Registration statement: Statement filed with the Securities and Exchange Commission pursuant to section 6 of the Securities Act of 1933 in respect of an issue of securities, and "any amendment thereto and any report, document, or memorandum filed as part of such statement or incorporated therein by reference." Securities Act of 1933, section 2(8); 15 U.S.C. § 77b(8). *See* 17 C.F.R. § 229.500–802; SEC Release No. 33-6383, 47 Fed. Reg. 11380 (1982).

Regular way: In connection with the transfer of a security, regular way delivery means delivery of and payment for the security the next day for government securities, and within five business days for corporate and municipal securities. *See* New York Stock Exchange, *Directory and Guide,* Rule 64-66.

Regulated investment company: For the purpose of the Internal Revenue Code, a regulated investment company is an investment company that is registered under the Investment Company Act of 1940 as a management company or as a unit investment trust, or that is a common trust fund or similar fund excluded by section 3(c)(3) of said act from the definition of "investment company" and is not included in the definition of "common trust fund" of the Internal Revenue Code. I.R.C. § 851(a). If a regulated investment company so elects, and meets the requirements of sections 851–5 of the Internal Revenue Code, it is not taxed on the amount of its income that is distributed to shareholders.

Regulated public utility: For the purpose of the Internal Revenue Code, a regulated public utility is a corporation engaged in the furnishing or sale of electric energy, gas, water, or sewerage disposal service, or transportation, if the rates for such furnishing or sale are regulated; a common carrier gas pipeline subject to the jurisdiction of the Federal Power Commission (that is what the code says, but the duties of the FPC have been taken over by the Federal Energy Regulatory Commission); a railroad; a petroleum pipeline subject to federal or state rate regulation; a telephone or telegraph company subject to rate regulation; an air carrier subject to regulation by the Civil Aeronautics Board; a water carrier subject to regulation by the Interstate Commerce Commission or the Federal Maritime Board; unless, in each case, less than 80% of its income is derived from such activities. I.R.C. § 7701(a)(33).

Regulation 8B: Regulation of the Securities and Exchange Commission regarding the filing of registration statements pursuant to section 8 of the Investment Company Act of 1940. 17 C.F.R. § 270.8b.

Regulation 9: Regulation of the Comptroller of the Currency regarding the conduct of fiduciary business by national banks. *See* Pub. L. No. 87-722, 76 Stat. 668 (1962). 12 U.S.C. § 92a.

Regulation 12B: Regulation of the Securities and Exchange Commission regarding procedures for filing reports with the SEC pursuant to the Securities Exchange Act of 1934. 17 C.F.R. § 240.12b; SEC Release No. 33-6383, 47 Fed. Reg. 11380 (1982).

Regulation 14A: Regulation of the Securities and Exchange Commission regarding proxy statements and solicitation of proxies. 17 C.F.R. § 240.14a.

Regulation 14C: Regulation of the Securities and Exchange Commission regarding distribution of proxy statements and other information. 17 C.F.R. §§ 240.14c.

Regulation 14D: Regulation of the Securities and Exchange Commission regarding tender offers. 17 C.F.R. § 240.14d.

Regulation 14E: Regulation of the Securities and Exchange Commission regarding unlawful tender offer practices. 17 C.F.R. § 240.14e.

Regulation A: 1. Regulation of the Securities and Exchange Commission covering the exemption from registration of certain classes of securities issued in amounts not in excess of $1,500,000 in any one year. 17 C.F.R. §§ 230, 251–64. 2. Regulation of the Federal Reserve System covering extension of credit by Federal Reserve Banks. 12 C.F.R. § 201.

Regulation AA: Regulation of the Federal Reserve System covering unfair or deceptive acts and practices. 12 C.F.R. § 227.

Regulation B: Regulation of the Federal Reserve System regarding equal credit opportunity, prohibiting discrimination by lenders. 12 C.F.R. § 202. *See generally* Geary, *Equal Credit Opportunity–An Analysis of Regulation B,* 31 Bus. Law. 1641 (1976).

Regulation BB: Regulation of the Federal Reserve System regarding com-

munity reinvestment requirements. 12 C.F.R. § 228.

Regulation C: 1. Regulation of the Securities and Exchange Commission regarding the form and content of registration statements. 17 C.F.R. §§ 230.400–94. *See* SEC Release No. 33-6383, 47 Fed. Reg. 11380 (1982). 2. Regulation of the Federal Reserve System regarding disclosure of data on home mortgages, pursuant to the Home Mortgage Disclosure Act of 1975, Title III of Pub. L. No. 94-200, 89 Stat. 1125, 12 U.S.C. §§ 2801–9. 12 C.F.R. § 203.

Regulation D: 1. Regulation of the Securities and Exchange Commission covering the private placement exemption from registration under the Securities Act of 1933. Regulation D supersedes Rules 146, 240, and 242. 17 C.F.R. §§ 230.501–6. *See* SEC Release 33-6339 (1980), SEC Release No. 33-6389, 47 Fed. Reg. 11251 (1982). 2. Regulation of the Federal Reserve specifying reserves to be maintained by member banks. 12 C.F.R. § 204.

Regulation E: Regulation of the Federal Reserve System covering electronic fund transfers. 12 C.F.R. § 205.

Regulation F: Regulation of the Federal Reserve System regarding securities of member state banks. 12 C.F.R. § 206.

Regulation G: Regulation of the Federal Reserve System covering extension of credit secured by margin securities by persons other than banks, brokers, or dealers. 12 C.F.R. § 207. See also

Regulation T; Regulation U; Regulation X.

Regulation H: Regulation of the Federal Reserve System covering membership by state banks. 12 C.F.R. § 208.

Regulation I: Regulation of the Federal Reserve System covering ownership of stock in the Federal Reserve by member banks. 12 C.F.R. § 209.

Regulation J: Regulation of the Federal Reserve System covering collection of checks and transfer of funds. 12 C.F.R. § 210.

Regulation K: Regulation of the Federal Reserve System covering international banking operations, including Edge Act corporations and agreement corporations. 12 C.F.R. § 211.

Regulation L: Regulation of the Federal Reserve System covering the prohibition of interlocks among directors, officers and employees of member banks and other banks under section 8 of the Clayton Act, 15 U.S.C. § 19. 12 C.F.R. § 212.

Regulation N: Regulation of the Federal Reserve System covering relations with foreign banks and bankers. 12 C.F.R. § 214.

Regulation O: Regulation of the Federal Reserve System regarding loans to officers, directors, and shareholders. 12 C.F.R. § 215.

Regulation P: Regulation of the Federal Reserve System regarding security devices and procedures. 12 C.F.R. § 216.

Regulation Q: Regulation of the Federal Reserve System setting ceilings on rates of interest payable on deposits. 12 C.F.R. § 217.

Regulation R: Regulation of the Federal Reserve System regarding relationships with securities dealers. 12 C.F.R. § 218.

Regulation S: Regulation of the Federal Reserve System regarding reimbursement for providing financial records. 12 C.F.R. § 219.

Regulation S-K: "Standard Instructions for Filing Forms under Securities Act of 1933 and Securities Exchange Act of 1934"; the regulation of the Securities and Exchange Commission covering the nonfinancial statement portions of registration statements and reports and proxy statements. 17 C.F.R. § 229. This regulation is intended as "the repository for the uniform disclosure requirements" of documents filed with the Securities and Exchange Commission under the Securities Act of 1933 and the Securities Exchange Act of 1934. SEC Release No. 33-6383, 47 Fed. Reg. 11380 (1982). Regulation S-K was initially adopted by SEC Release No. 33-5893, 42 Fed. Reg. 65554, 65561 (1977). *See* SEC Release No. 33-6332, 46 Fed. Reg. 41925 (1981); SEC Release No. 33-6338, 46 Fed. Reg. 42042 (1981); SEC Release No. 34-17517, 46 Fed. Reg. 11954 (1981).

Regulation S-X: Regulation of the Securities and Exchange Commission covering the form and content of financial statements required to be filed as a part of registration statements and in connection with reports furnished pursuant to the Securities Exchange Act of 1934, the Public Utility Holding Company Act of 1935, and the Investment Company Act of 1940. 17 C.F.R. § 210. *See* SEC Accounting Series Releases No. 280, 281 45 Fed. Reg. 63660, 63682 (1980); SEC Release No. 33-6357 (1981).

Regulation T: Regulation of the Federal Reserve System covering extension of credit by brokers and dealers for securities transactions. 12 C.F.R. § 220.

Regulation U: Regulation of the Federal Reserve System covering extension of credit by banks for securities transactions. 12 C.F.R. § 221.

Regulation V: Regulation of the Federal Reserve System covering loan guaranties for defense production. 32A C.F.R. § 1505.

Regulation X: Regulation of the Federal Reserve System covering borrowers who obtain credit for securities transactions. 12 C.F.R. § 224.

Regulation Y: Regulation of the Federal Reserve System covering bank holding companies. 12 C.F.R. § 225.

Regulation Z: Regulation of the Federal Reserve System covering truth in lending practices. 12 C.F.R. § 226.

Rehabilitation credit: Credit against federal income taxes available for expenditures for the rehabilitation of buildings 30 years old or older, and certified historic structures. I.R.C. §§ 48(o)(8), 46(a)(2)(F).

Reinsurance: Insurance for an insurer; contract of insurance entered into by original insurer with another insurer (the reinsurer) to pass on the risk.

Reinvestment rate: In calculating the return on an investment, the rate of return assumed on the reinvestment of interest and principal payments (or in the case of a lease, rents) received on the investment prior to maturity. *See* M. Stigum, *Money Market Calculations: Yields, Break-Evens, and Arbitrage* 67, 113 (1981).

Reissue patent: Patent reissued after discovery of a defect in the original patent or claim, covering the invention disclosed in the original patent, but in accordance with a new and amended application. 35 U.S.C. §§ 251–52.

REIT: Real estate investment trust.

Release: "Writing providing that a duty owed to the maker of the release is discharged immediately or on the occurrence of a condition." *Restatement, Second, Contracts* § 284(1) (1981).

Relevant market: The "area of effective competition" within which defendants to an antitrust action operate. *Standard Oil Co. of Calif. v. United States,* 337 U.S. 293, 299 n.5 (1949). The determination of the relevant market, the foundation of many antitrust cases, is often very difficult, and must include consideration of the product market and the geographic market. *See generally* American Bar Association, Section of Antitrust Law, *Antitrust Law Developments* 48 (1975).

Reliance interest: In connection with a contract, the "reliance interest" is the interest of a promisee "in being reimbursed for loss caused by reliance on the contract by being put in as good a position as he would have been in had the contract not been made." *Restatement, Second, Contracts* § 344 (1981). The purpose of judicial remedies for breach of contract is the protection of the expectation interest, the reliance interest, and the restitution interest. *See* Hudec, *Restating the "Reliance Interest,"* 67 Cornell L. Rev. 704 (1982); Fuller & Perdue, Jr., *The Reliance Interest in Contract Damages*, 46 Yale L.J. 52 (1936).

Relief: Under the Administrative Procedure Act, "relief" includes:

the whole or part of an agency—

(A) grant of money, assistance, license, authority, exemption, exception, privilege, or remedy;

(B) recognition of a claim, right, immunity, privilege, exemption, or exception; or

(C) taking of other action on the application or petition of, and beneficial to, a person;

5 U.S.C. § 551(11).

Remarketing agreement: Undertaking to secure a replacement lessee or buyer for leased equipment, in the event of default or early termination of the lease. *See* Financial Accounting Standards Board, Statement of Financial Accounting Standards No. 13, *Accounting for Leases*, paragraph 21 (1976).

Remedy: Under the Uniform Commercial Code, "any remedial right to which an aggrieved party is entitled with or without resort to a tribunal."

UCC Section 1-201(34). Self-help remedies, an important body of rights under the Uniform Commercial Code, are expressly contemplated by this definition. For remedies in the sale of goods, see UCC Sections 2-701–25. For remedies in secured transactions, see UCC Sections 9-501–7. For remedies for breach of contract generally, see *Restatement, Second, Contracts* §§ 344–85 (1981).

Remitting bank: For the purpose of Article 4 of the Uniform Commercial Code–Bank Deposits and Collections, remitting bank means "any payor or intermediary bank remitting for an item." UCC Section 4-105.

Renegotiable rate mortgage: Mortgage whose interest rate can be revised, at specified intervals and within certain limits, by the mortgagee. "Renegotiable" is rarely the correct term, because the mortgagee usually sets the new rate unilaterally.

Renegotiation: Process of determination by a government contracting agency of excessive profits under a government contract. Renegotiation Act of 1951, 65 Stat. 7 (1951); 50 U.S.C. App. §§ 1211–33; *see* I.R.C. § 1481(a)(1)(A).

Reorganization: 1. Proceeding for the reorganization of the business and capital structure of an enterprise under chapter 11 of the Bankruptcy Code, 11 U.S.C. §§ 1101–74; *see generally* H.R. Rep. No. 95-595, 95th Cong., 1st Sess. 220 (1977); Trost, *Business Reorganizations Under Chapter 11 of the New Bankruptcy Code*, 34 Bus. Law. 1309 (1979). *See also* I.R.C. §§ 371, 372, and 374. 2. Merger, recapitalization, or other reorganization of corporate structure. For the purpose of the Internal Revenue Code, reorganization means:

(A) a statutory merger or consolidation;

(B) the acquisition by one corporation, in exchange solely for all or a part of its voting stock (or in exchange solely for all or a part of the voting stock of a corporation which is in control of the acquiring corporation), of stock of another corporation if, immediately after the acquisition, the acquiring corporation has control of such other corporation (whether or not such acquiring corporation had control immediately before the acquisition);

(C) the acquisition by one corporation, in exchange solely for all or a part of its voting stock (or in exchange solely for all or a part of the voting stock of a corporation which is in control of the acquiring corporation), of substantially all of the properties of another corporation, but in determining whether the exchange is solely for stock the assumption by the acquiring corporation of a liability of the other, or the fact that property acquired is subject to a liability, shall be disregarded;

(D) a transfer by a corporation of all or a part of its assets to another corporation if immediately after the transfer the transferor, or one or more of its shareholders (including persons who were shareholders immediately before the transfer), or any combination thereof, is in control of the corporation to which the assets are transferred; but only if, in pursuance of the plan, stock or securities of the corporation to which the assets are transferred are distributed in a transaction which qualifies under section 354, 355, or 356 (of the Internal Revenue Code).

(E) a recapitalization;

(F) a mere change in identity, form, or place of organization of one corporation, however effected; or

(G) a transfer by a corporation of all or part of its assets to another corporation in a title 11 or similar case; but only if, in pursuance of the plan, stock or securities of the corporation to which the assets are transferred are distributed in a transaction which qualifies under section 354, 355, or 356 (of the Internal Revenue Code).

I.R.C. § 368(a). *See* Treas. Reg. § 1.368-2. The various types of reorganizations are often referred to by the letters identifying each clause; thus an exchange reorganization is known as a "B" reorganization or merger, and an acquisition of assets is known as a "C" reorganization or merger. This classification is adopted in other statutes; *e.g.* Cal. Corp. Code § 181. See **merger; consolidation; statutory merger; statutory consolidation.**

Replevin: Action brought to recover goods unlawfully taken. As to a buyer's right to replevin for goods identified to the contract, see UCC Section 2-716.

Repo: Repurchase agreement.

Reporting person: Person subject to the reporting requirements of section 16(a) of the Securities Exchange Act of 1934, and the short-swing profit recapture provisions of section 16(b). This class includes "Every person who is directly or indirectly the beneficial owner of more than 10 per centum of any class of equity security. . ." and officers and directors. 15 U.S.C. § 78p.

Representative: One who represents another, in any particular or general capacity. The term "representative" does not have a special legal meaning, as do "agent" and "trustee," but should include those terms. Under the Uniform Commercial Code, the term "representative" includes "an agent, an officer of a corporation or association, and a trustee, executor or administrator of an estate, or any other person empowered to act for another." UCC Section 1-201(35).

Repudiation: In connection with contracts,

A repudiation is

(a) a statement by the obligor to the obligee indicating that the obligor will commit a breach that would of itself give the obligee a claim for damages for total breach under § 243, or

(b) a voluntary affirmative act which renders the obligor unable or apparently unable to perform without such a breach.

Restatement, Second, Contracts § 250 (1981). *See* UCC Section 2-610.

Repurchase agreement: Form of short-term loan, usually by banks to securities dealers, in which the lender buys a security for immediate delivery and agrees to sell the security back at the same price by a specific date (usually within 15 days and sometimes overnight), and receives interest at a specified rate. *See* Monhollon, *Dealer Loans and Repurchase Agreements,* in T. Cook, ed., *Instruments of the Money Market* 49 (4th ed. 1977).

Requirements contract: Agreement by a user of materials or goods to purchase its requirements, perhaps for a given plant or operation, from a supplier. A requirements contract usually does not provide for minimum purchases. Under Article 2 of theUniform Commercial Code–Sales, the measure of requirements under such a contract must be made in good faith, and must not be "unreasonably disproportionate" to a stated estimate or normal requirements. UCC Section 2-306. The converse of a requirements contract is an output contract.

Resale price maintenance: Agreement between a supplier and its customers to fix prices at which the commodities supplied are resold; also called vertical price fixing. *See California Retail Liquor Dealers Assn. v. Midcal Aluminum, Inc.,* 445 U.S. 97 (1980); *United States v. Colgate & Co.,* 250 U.S. 300 (1919). *See generally* American Bar Association, Section of Antitrust Law, *Antitrust Law Developments* 7 (1975).

Rescission: An agreement of rescission is "an agreement under which each party agrees to discharge all of the other party's remaining duties of performance under an existing contract." *Restatement, Second, Contracts* § 283 (1981).

Research: As defined by the Financial Accounting Standards Board:

Research is planned search or critical investigation aimed at discovery of new knowledge with the hope that such knowledge will be useful in developing a new product or service . . . or a new process or technique . . . or in bringing about a significant improvement to an existing product or process.

Financial Accounting Standards Board, Statement of Financial Accounting Standards No. 2, *Accounting for Research and Development Costs,* paragraphs 8, 24–30 (1974); *see* Financial Accounting

Standards Board, Interpretation No. 6, *Applicability of FASB Statement No. 2 to Computer Software: An Interpretation of FASB Statement No. 2* (1975); International Accounting Standards Committee, Statement of International Accounting Standards 9, *Accounting for Research and Development Activities* (1978). Compare development.

Research and experimental expenditures: In connection with the deduction permitted under section 174 of the Internal Revenue Code for "research and experimental expenditures," such expenditures mean "expenditures incurred in connection with the taxpayer's trade or business which represent research and development costs in the experimental or laboratory sense." The term includes expenditures for pilot models and plants, but not for surveys or promotions. Treas. Reg. § 1-174-2(a)(1). *See also* I.R.C. § 44F.

Reserve recognition accounting: Method of accounting proposed for use by oil and gas producing companies that reflects:

(1) Proved oil and gas reserves as assets on the balance sheet;

(2) Additions to proved reserves and changes in valuations of proved reserves in the income statement; and

(3) All costs associated with finding and developing additions to proved oil and gas reserves, together with all costs determined to be nonproductive during the accounting period, in the income statement.

SEC Accounting Series Release No. 253, 43 Fed. Reg. 40688 (1978); *see* SEC Accounting Series Release No. 289, 46 Fed. Reg. 15496 (1981).

Reserve requirements: Percentage of customer deposits that banks must set aside in the form of reserves. The reserve requirement ratio determines the expansion of deposits (and loans made therefrom) that can be supported by a given dollar amount of reserves. The Federal Reserve can raise or lower reserve requirements for member banks within limits, and uses this authority as an instrument of monetary policy. 12 C.F.R. § 204. See bank reserves.

Reserves: Amounts held by financial institutions in the form of liquid or marketable assets as reserves against liabilities. For example, balances maintained with the Federal Reserve by member banks as reserves against deposit liabilities, and amounts held in certain qualified investments by insurance companies as reserves against liabilities to policy holders. *See, e.g.,* N.Y. Ins. Law. §§ 80, 81.

Reservoir: As defined by the Financial Accounting Standards Board, "A porous and permeable underground formation containing a natural accumulation of producible oil or gas that is confined by impermeable rock or water barriers and is individual and separate from other reservoirs." Financial Accounting Standards Board, Statement of Financial Accounting Standards No. 19, *Financial Accounting and Reporting by Oil and Gas Producing Companies,* Appendix C (1977).

Residual value: The value of leased property at the end of the lease term.

Residuum rule: Principle that a reviewing court must set aside an administrative finding unless the finding is supported by "a residuum" of evidence that would be admissible in a jury trial. *Carroll v. Knickerbocker Ice Co.*, 218 N.Y. 435, 113 N.E. 507 (1916); *see Richardson v. Perales*, 402 U.S. 389 (1971); K. Davis, *Administrative Law Text* 277 (1972).

Res judicata: The matter decided; principle that a final judgment on a given controversy is conclusive and binding as to the matter decided. *See Cromwell v. County of Sac*, 94 U.S. 351 (1876). Compare collateral estoppel.

Resource Conservation and Recovery Act: Federal statute regulating the handling of waste materials. Pub. L. No. 94-580, 90 Stat. 2795 (1976); 42 U.S.C. § 6901–86. *See generally* Rosbe, *RCRA and Regulation of Hazardous and Nonhazardous Solid Wastes–Closing the Circle of Environmental Control*, 35 Bus. Law. 1519 (1980); *Resource Conservation and Recovery Act of 1976–The Newest Environmental "Sleeper,"* 33 Bus. Law. 2555 (1977).

Respondent: Party named in an action; defendant. The term has its roots in actions in equity, but is currently commonly used to identify the party who is the subject of a government enforcement action or prosecution.

Restitution interest: In connection with a contract, the "restitution interest" is the interest of a promisee "in having restored to him any benefit that he has conferred on the other party." *Restatement, Second, Contracts* § 344 (1981) *see* §§ 371–77. The purpose of judicial remedies for breach of contract is the protection of the expectation interest, the reliance interest, and the res-

titution interest. *See* Perillo, *Restitution in a Contractual Context,* 73 Colum. L. Rev. 1208 (1973). As to a buyer's right to restitution from a defaulting seller, see UCC Section 2-718.

Restraint of trade: Section 1 of the Sherman Act prohibits contracts, combinations, and conspiracies "in restraint of trade or commerce ... ." 15 U.S.C. § 1. The Sherman Act is "designed to be a comprehensive charter of economic liberty aimed at preserving free and unfettered competition as the rule of trade," and thus the term "restraint of trade" takes in a broad range of practices in restraint of competition. *Northern Pac. Ry. v. United States,* 356 U.S. 1, 4 (1958). Practices held to be "in restraint of trade" include horizontal and vertical price-fixing, divisions of territory or customers, refusals to deal, certain mergers, reciprocal dealing arrangements, tying arrangements, and exclusive dealing arrangements. *See generally* American Bar Association, Section of Antitrust Law, *Antitrust Law Developments* 1 (1975). In connection with the common law prohibition against contracts "in restraint of trade," "A promise is in restraint of trade if its performance would limit competition in any business or restrict the promisor in the exercise of a gainful occupation." *Restatement, Second, Contracts* § 186 (1981).

Restricted stock: 1. Stock transferred by an employer to employees, and subject to restrictions on transfer or substantial risk of forfeiture. The transaction becomes taxable to the employee when the restrictions are lifted or the risk of forfeiture ceases. I.R.C. § 83. 2. Stock obtained in a transaction exempt from registration under the Securities Act of 1933, such as a private placement under section 4(2), and thus subject to restrictions on resale. 3. For the purposes of the Financial Accounting Standards Board distinction from marketable securities, restricted stock means:

securities for which sale is restricted by a governmental or contractual requirement except where such requirement terminates within one year or where the holder has the power by contract or otherwise to cause the requirement to be met within one year. Any portion of the stock which can reasonably be expected to qualify for sale within one year, such as may be the case under Rule 144 or similar rules of the Securities and Exchange Commission, is not considered restricted.

Financial Accounting Standards Board, Statement of Financial Accounting Standards No. 12, *Accounting for Certain Marketable Securities,* paragraph 7, n. 3 (1975).

Restricted subsidiary: Subsidiary of a corporation that is bound by the restrictive covenants that the parent corporation has given in debt agreements.

Restrictive endorsement: Endorsement of an instrument that restricts the actions of the next holder. Under Article 3—Commercial Paper of the Uniform Commercial Code, an endorsement is restrictive if it:

(a) is conditional; or

(b) purports to prohibit further transfer of the instrument; or

(c) includes the words "for collection", "for deposit", "pay any bank", or like terms signifying a purpose of deposit or collection; or

(d) otherwise states that it is for the benefit or use of the indorser or of another person.

UCC Section 3-205. For the effect of a restrictive endorsement, see UCC Section 3-206.

Results of operations: Information presented in the statement of income and statement of retained earnings; revenue, expenses, and net income. *See* American Institute of Certified Public Accountants, Accounting Principles Board Opinion No. 9, *Reporting the Results of Operations* (1966).

Retained earnings: Earned surplus. *See* Cal. Corp. Code § 500.

Retrofit: Modification of equipment to comply with standards or requirements with retroactive effect, that is, affecting equipment already in service as well as equipment subsequently manufactured. The term usually is encountered in connection with aircraft that must be modified by FAA regulation or order.

Revenue: As defined by the Financial Accounting Standards Board:

Revenues are inflows or other enhancements of assets of an entity or settlements of its liabilities (or a combination of both) during a period from delivering or producing goods, rendering services, or other activities that constitute the entity's ongoing major or central operations.

Financial Accounting Standards Board, Statement of Financial Accounting Concepts No. 3, *Elements of Financial Statements of Business Enterprises,* paragraphs 63, 64 (1980).

Revenue Act of 1978: Amendment to the Internal Revenue Code. Pub. L. No. 95-600, 92 Stat. 2763 (1978); *see* U.S. Congress, Joint Committee on Taxation, *General Explanation of the Revenue Act of 1978* (1979).

Revenue anticipation note: Short-term note issued by a state, municipality, or local public authority or agency to cover cash needs pending receipt of revenues.

Revenue bond: Bond, usually a municipal bond, that is to be serviced solely out of the revenues from a particular project, such as a toll bridge. Compare **general obligation bond**.

Reverse exoneration: Defense to suit against a surety that requires a creditor to bring suit against the debtor on demand of the surety. *See* Harrington, *Reverse Exoneration: The Accommodation Party's Forgotten Defense,* 4 Lending L. F. 3 (1980).

Reverse FOIA suit: Suit by a party that has furnished information to the government to prevent disclosure of that information under the Freedom of Information Act. *See Chrysler Corp. v. Brown,* 441 U.S. 281 (1979); Note, *The Reverse-FOIA Lawsuit: Routes to Nondisclosure After Chrysler,* 46 Brooklyn L. Rev. 269 (1980).

Reverse merger: Merger in which the acquiring corporation is merged into the acquired corporation.

Reverse repurchase agreement: The opposite of a repurchase agreement; see **matched sale-purchase agreement**.

Reverse stock split: Pro rata combination of all the outstanding shares of a class of corporate stock into a smaller number of shares of the same class. *See* Cal. Corp. Code § 182.

Review Commission: Occupational Safety and Health Review Commission.

Revocable credit: Letter of credit that may be modified or revoked by the issuer without notice to or consent from the account party or beneficiary. UCC Section 5-106(3).

Revolving credit agreement: Commitment on the part of a bank or group of banks to make short-term loans from time to time, up to a certain maximum amount outstanding at any given time.

Rev. Proc.: Revenue procedure.

Rev. Rul.: Revenue ruling.

RICO: Racketeer Influenced and Corrupt Organizations Act.

Right-hand side: Rate at which a bank offers to buy foreign currencies. Compare **left-hand side**.

Right of redemption: See redemption, right of.

Right of refusal: See refusal, right of.

Right of setoff: See setoff.

Rights: Under the Uniform Commercial Code, the term "rights" includes "remedies." UCC Section 1-201(36).

Rights offering: Distribution to shareholders of rights to purchase securities prior to the public offering thereof. *See* SEC Rule 10b-8, 17 C.F.R. 240.10b-8.

Right-to-work law: State law providing that the right of persons to work may not be denied on account of membership or nonmembership in any labor union or labor organization. *See* section 14(b) of the National Labor Relations Act, 29 U.S.C. § 164(b).

Risk arbitrage: Trading in securities that are the subject of a tender offer. Tender offers are ordinarily made at a price in excess of the current market price, and a risk arbitrageur will take a position in the securities in the hope that the offer will be consummated.

Robinson-Patman Act: Robinson-Patman Anti-Discrimination Act; federal statute amending section 2 of the Clayton Act to prohibit price discrimination. Pub. L. No. 692, ch. 592, 49 Stat. 1526 (1936); 15 U.S.C. §§ 13, 13a–c, 21a. *See generally* American Bar Association, Section of Antitrust Law, *Antitrust Law Developments* 106 (1975).

Roll-over: To renew at maturity. When a debt security reaches maturity, it may be renewed or "rolled over" with the original holder, or be rolled over by sale of other securities, using the proceeds to pay the principal of the original securities. An instrument with a specific roll-over provision usually specifies that the renewal be at the rate of interest prevailing at the time of roll-over.

Roly-poly CD: Series of consecutive certificates of deposit under which the buyer of the certificates agrees to purchase an equivalent dollar amount of new certificates upon maturity for as long a period as the contract calls for. The buyer may sell his current CDs, but remains liable for the purchase of the new issues under the contract. Roly-poly CDs may be fixed-rate, in which the new issues carry the same rate of interest as the original certificates, or floating rate, in which the new issues carry the then-current market rate.

ROM: Roll-over mortgage.

Round lot: Normal trading unit of securities: 100 shares of stock, or $100,000 par value of bonds.

Royalty: Compensation for use of property, usually of an intellectual nature, such as patented and copyrighted works.

Rozelle rule: Rule, named after Alvin Ray "Pete" Rozelle, commissioner of the National Football League, that a football team hiring a player whose contract with another team has expired must compensate that other team. *Mackey v. Nat'l Football League*, 543 F. 2d 606, 609 n. 1. (8th Cir. 1976). That case held that the Rozelle rule was an unreasonable restraint of trade under the Sherman Act, and also held that the nonstatutory exemptions to the antitrust laws available to labor groups are also available to nonlabor parties where such parties are parties to a collective bargaining agreement relating to mandatory subjects of bargaining. The latter holding is called the rule in the

Rozelle case, and in the labor law context, may be called simply the Rozelle rule.

RRA: Reserve recognition accounting.

RRB replacement property: Replacement track material installed by a railroad company and subject to special recovery periods under the accelerated cost recovery system. I.R.C. 168(f)(3).

RRM: Renegotiable rate mortgage.

Rule: Under the Administrative Procedure Act:

"rule" means the whole or a part of an agency statement of general or particular applicability and future effect designed to implement, interpret, or prescribe law or policy or describing the organization, procedure, or practice requirements of an agency and includes the approval or prescription for the future of rates, wages, corporate or financial structures or reorganizations thereof, prices, facilities, appliances, services or allowances therefor or of valuations, costs, or accounting, or practices bearing on any of the foregoing.

5 U.S.C. § 551(4).

Rule making: Under the Administrative Procedure Act, rule making means "agency process for formulating, amending, or repealing a rule." 5 U.S.C. § 551(5). *See also* 5 U.S.C. § 553. See rule.

Rule of law: Principle of the supremacy of law, controlling the decisions of government administrators and courts.

Rule of reason: Doctrine that the Sherman Act prohibition against com-

binations in restraint of trade was meant to apply only to those combinations that unreasonably restrain competition. *Standard Oil Co. v. United States,* 221 U.S. 1, 59 (1911); *see also Board of Trade of the City of Chicago v. United States,* 246 U.S. 231 (1918); *see generally* Bork, *The Rule of Reason and the Per Se Concept: Price Fixing and Market Division,* 74 Yale L. J. 775 (1965), 75 Yale L. J. 373 (1966). See also **per se violation.**

Rule of 72: Method for estimating compound interest based on the fact that 7.2% compounded annually will double the amount of the initial investment in ten years. The number of years required to double an investment can be estimated by dividing the interest rate into 72.

Rule of 78: Formula for allocation of interest to each payment of a loan payable in installments, used to determine the amount due if the loan is prepaid. To determine the amount of interest payable for any period, the total interest is multiplied by a fraction, the numerator of which is the number of periods remaining and the denominator of which is the sum of the digits that represent each period (similar to sum-of-the-digits depreciation). The denominator can also be determined by the formula $n(n + 1)/2$, where n is the number of periods. For a loan of twelve periods (a one-year loan payable in monthly installments), the denominator is 78—hence the name of the rule. *See generally* Hunt, *The Rule of 78: Hidden Penalty for Prepayment in Consumer Credit Transactions,* 55 B.U. L. Rev. 331 (1975); Neifeld, *The Rule of 78ths—The Sum of the Digits Method for Computing*

Refunds, 13 Personal Fin. L. Q. 8 (1978).

Rule 2(e): Regulation of the Securities and Exchange Commission providing for the discipline of attorneys and accountants practicing before the commission. 17 C.F.R. § 201.2(e). *See generally* Marsh, Jr., *Rule 2(e) Proceedings,* 35 Bus. Law. 987 (1980).

Rule 10b-5: Regulation of the Securities and Exchange Commission regarding fraud in connection with the purchase and sale of securities. 17 C.F.R. § 240.10b-5. *See Ernst & Ernst v. Hochfelder,* 425 U.S. 185 (1976); A. Jacobs, *The Impact of Rule 10b-5* (1976).

Rule 10b-6: Regulation of the Securities and Exchange Commission regarding manipulative practices in the distribution of securities, prohibiting an issuer from bidding for or purchasing a security of the same class until the distribution is completed. 17 C.F.R. § 240.10b-6.

Rule 13e-3: Regulation of the Securities and Exchange Commission regarding "going private" transactions. 17 C.F.R. § 240.13e-3. *See* Gannon, *An Evaluation of the SEC's New Going Private Rule, 7 J. Corp. L. 55 (1981).*

Rule 14a-8: Regulation of the Securities and Exchange Commission providing for inclusion of shareholder proposals in proxy materials. 17 C.F.R. § 240.14a-8. *See* Securities and Exchange Commission, *Staff Report on Corporate Accountability B1* (1980).

Rule 23: Rule of the Federal Rules of Civil Procedure regarding class actions.

Rule 144: Regulation of the Securities and Exchange Commission relating to resale of securities originally issued in a transaction exempt from registration. 17 C.F.R. § 230.144. *See generally* Fogelson, *Rule 144—A Summary Review,* 37 Bus. Law. 1519 (1982).

Rule 146: Regulation of the Securities and Exchange Commission relating to issuance of securities in a transaction "not involving a public offering." Rule 146 provided a "safe harbor," a set of conditions for which the private placement exemption of section 4(2) of the Securities Act of 1933 will be considered applicable, but the rule did not exclusively state the conditions for the exemption. *See* Kinderman, Jr., *The Private Offering Exemption: An Examination of Its Availability under and outside Rule 146,* 30 Bus. Law. 921 (1975). Rule 146 has been superseded by Rule 506 under Regulation D, 17 C.F.R. § 230.506. *See* SEC Release No. 33-6389, 47 Fed. Reg. 11251 (1982).

Rule 176: Regulation of the Securities and Exchange Commission identifying certain circumstances bearing on the reasonableness of the investigation conducted to discharge one's obligation under section 11(b) of the Securities Act of 1933. 17 C.F.R. § 230.176. *See* SEC Release No. 33-6383, 47 Fed. Reg. 11380 (1982). See **due diligence.**

Rule 240: Regulation of the Securities and Exchange Commission regarding the private placement exemption from registration for certain small issues. Rule 240 has been superseded by Rule 504 under Regulation D, 17 C.F.R. §

230.504; *see* SEC Release No. 33-6389 47 Fed. Reg. 11251 (1982).

Rule 242: Regulation of the Securities and Exchange Commission regarding the private placement exemption from registration for certain transactions. Rule 242 has been superseded by Rule 505 under Regulation D, 17 C.F.R. § 230.505; *see* SEC Release No. 33-6389, 47 Fed. Reg. 11251 (1982).

Rule 415: Regulation of the Securities and Exchange Commission establishing conditions for "shelf registration," registration covering securities of a given type to be offered in a two-year period. 17 C.F.R. 230.415. *See* SEC Release No. 33-6383, 47 Fed. Reg. 11380 (1982).

Ruling: Determination of law or policy by an administrative agency, usually without a formal proceeding (other than application), and often in an individual case.

Runaway shop: Place of employment that is transferred to another location. If done to evade collective bargaining responsibilities, such a transfer is regarded as an unfair labor practice. *See, e.g, Garwin Corp.,* 153 N.L.R.B. 664 (1965), *enforced in part sub nom. Local 57, International Ladies' Garment Workers' Union v. NLRB,* 374 F. 2d 295 (D.C. Cir. 1967).

Rural Electrification Administration: Agency of the United States Department of Agriculture that provides low-cost loans (at five or two percent interest) and loan guarantees to finance electric and telephone facilities in the rural areas of the United States. *See* Rural Electrification Act of 1936, Pub. L. No. 605, ch. 432, 49 Stat. 1363 (1936); 7 U.S.C. §§ 901–50.

Rural Telephone Bank: Agency of the United States government, affiliated with the Rural Electrification Administration, that makes loans to telephone systems.

S

S-1: See form S-1.

S-2: See form S-2.

S-3: See form S-3.

S-5: See form S-5.

S-6: See form S-6.

S-8: See form S-8.

S-11: See form S-11.

S-14: See form S-14.

S-15: See form S-15.

S-18: See form S-18.

SA: 1. *Société Anonyme,* joint stock company organized under the laws of France. 2. *Sociedad Anomina,* joint stock company organized under the laws of Spain.

SAB: Staff Accounting Bulletin.

Safe Drinking Water Act: Title XIV of the Public Health Service Act cover-ing the safety of public water supplies. Pub. L. No. 93-523, 88 Stat. 1660 (1974); 42 U.S.C. §§ 300f–j.

Safe harbor: Set of objective standards for the availability of specific legal treatment that may otherwise be subjective in application. For a "safe harbor" for treatment of a securities transaction as one "not involving a public offering," and thus having available the exemption from registration afforded by section 4(2) of the Securities Act of 1933, see SEC Regulation D, 17 C.F.R. §230.506. For a "safe harbor" for treatment of a given transaction as a lease for tax purposes, see **safe harbor lease.**

Safe harbor lease: Lease transaction with respect to which an election under section 168(f)(8) of the Internal Revenue Code has been made. This section, added by the Economic Recovery Tax Act of 1981, provides that a transaction shall be treated as a lease for federal income tax purposes even though certain characteristics, such a fixed-price purchase option, are present that might disqualify the transaction as a lease under previous Internal Revenue Service interpretations (Rev. Proc. 75-21, 1975-1 C.B. 715; Rev. Rule. 55-540, 1955-2 C.B. 39). Section 208(a) of the Tax Equity and Fiscal Responsibility Act of 1982 modified the benefits of safe harbor leasing, and repealed the safe harbor lease provisions effective for leases entered into after December 31, 1983.

Said to contain: Words of qualification of the description of goods in a bill of lading, relieving the issuer of the bill from liability for misdescription of the goods under certain circumstances. UCC Section 7-301.

Sale: For the purpose of Article 2 of the Uniform Commercial Code–Sales, a sale is "the passing of title from the seller to the buyer for a price." UCC Section 2-106(1). As to passage of title, see UCC Section 2-401. For the purpose of the Robinson-Patman Act prohibition on price discrimination, the term "sale" (in the form "sold") does not include leases, licensing arrangements, agency or consignment arrangements, loans, and contracts for services. *See* American Bar Association, Section of Antitrust Law, *Antitrust Law Developments* 110 (1975). Under the Securities Act of 1933, "The term 'sale' or 'sell' shall include every contract of sale or disposition of a security or interest in a security, for value." Section 2(3), 15 U.S.C. § 77b(3). *See* section 3(a)(14) of the Securities Act of 1934, 15 U.S.C. § 78c(a)(14); section 303(2) of the Trust Indenture Act of 1939, 15 U.S.C. § 77ccc(2). The term "sale" is to be broadly construed in application of the securities laws, *SEC v. National Securities, Inc.,* 393 U.S. 453 (1969).

Sale and leaseback, sale-leaseback: Financing transaction in which the owner of property sells that property to an investing party or group, and then that party or group leases it back to the seller. *See* Financial Accounting Standards Board, Statement of Financial Accounting Standards No. 28, *Accounting for Sales with Leasebacks* (1979).

Sale on approval: Under Article 2 of the Uniform Commercial Code–Sales, a sales transaction is a "sale on approval" if the goods may be returned by the buyer even though they conform to the contract and the goods are delivered primarily for use by the buyer. UCC Section 2-326(1). See **sale or return.** Goods held by the buyer under a "sale on approval" are not subject to claims of the buyer's creditors until acceptance; goods held under a "sale or return" are subject to such claims, unless certain precautions are taken. UCC Section 2-326(2). *See also* UCC Section 2-327.

Sale or return: Under Article 2 of the Uniform Commercial Code–Sales, a sales transaction is a "sale or return" if the goods may be returned by the buyer even though they conform to the contract and the goods are delivered primarily for resale by the buyer. UCC Section 2-326(1). See **sale on approval.** Unless certain precautions are taken, goods held by the buyer under a "sale or return" are subject to claims of the buyer's creditors; goods held under a "sale on approval" are not subject to such claims until acceptance. UCC Section 2-326(2). *See also* UCC Section 2-327.

Sallie Mae: Student Loan Marketing Association, or a security issued thereby.

Salvage value: Value of an asset when the owner retires it from service. The salvage value must be considered when calculating depreciation, but for purposes of federal income tax deductions under the accelerated cost recovery system, salvage value is ignored (or treated as zero). *See* I.R.C. §§ 167, 168.

Same-day funds: Funds that, when transferred, are available the same day for further transfer or withdrawal in cash, such as federal funds.

Samurai bond: Bond denominated in yen and issued in Japan for non-Japanese borrowers.

Sanction: Under the Administrative Procedure Act:

"sanction" includes the whole or part of an agency—

(A) prohibition, requirement, limitation, or other condition affecting the freedom of a person;

(B) withholding of relief;

(C) imposition of penalty or fine;

(D) destruction, taking, seizure, or withholding of property;

(E) assessment of damages, reimbursement, restitution, compensation, costs, charges, or fees;

(F) requirement, revocation, or suspension of a license; or

(G) taking other compulsory or restrictive action;

5 U.S.C. § 551(10).

SAR: Stock appreciation right.

Sarl: *Société à responsabilité limitée,* limited liability company organized under the laws of France.

SAS: Statement of Auditing Standards.

Savings and loan association: Financial institution that accepts interest-bearing time deposits and invests those deposits in high-quality securities (usually in accordance with legal investment laws) and mortgages on real property, usually residential property. Most savings and loan associations are technically owned by the depositors, who receive shares in the association for their deposits.

Savings bank: Financial institution that accepts interest-bearing time deposits and invests these deposits in high-quality securities (usually in accordance with legal investment laws) and mortgages on real property.

SBA: Small Business Administration.

SBIC: Small Business Investment Company.

Scienter: Mental state embracing intent to deceive, manipulate, or defraud. *Ernst & Ernst v. Hochfelder,* 425 U.S. 185, 193 n. 12 (1976). *See* Bucklo, *The Supreme Court Attempts to Define Scienter under Rule 10b-5: Ernst & Ernst v. Hochfelder,* 29 Stan. L. Rev. 213 (1977).

Scrip: Document issued by a corporation evidencing fractional shares. *See, e.g.,* N.Y. Bus. Corp. Law § 509; Del. Code Ann. tit. 8 § 155.

SDR: Special Drawing Right.

Seal: Piece of wax or wafer impressed with a stamp, or mark intended as a such, on a contract that once created a "contract under seal," which operated as an enforceable contract without the need for consideration. *Restatement, Second, Contracts* §§ 95–109 (1981). Most United States jurisdictions have abolished the distinction between sealed and unsealed contracts, making the use of a seal ineffective. Article 2 of the Uniform Commercial Code–Sales renders seals inoperative for contracts for the sale of goods. UCC Section 2-203. In some jurisdictions, the use of a corporate seal on an instrument purporting to be executed by authority of a corporation is prima facie evidence that the instrument was so executed. *E.g.,* N.Y. Bus. Corp. Law § 107. *See also* N.Y. Gen. Const. Law §§ 43, 45.

Seasonable: Timely; within a proper time. Under the Uniform Commercial Code, an action is taken seasonably when it is taken "at or within the time agreed or if no time is agreed at or within a reasonable time." UCC Section 1-204(3). With respect to checks and other items covered by Article 4 of the Uniform Commercial Code–Bank Deposits and Collections, a collecting bank taking proper action before its midnight deadline following receipt of the item acts seasonably, although a longer period may be seasonable. UCC Section 4-202(2).

SEC: Securities and Exchange Commission.

Secondary boycott: Action to induce a person to cease dealing or doing business with another person. A description of secondary boycott activity is set forth in the prohibition in respect thereof in section 8(b) of the National Labor Relations Act:

It shall be an unfair labor practice for a labor organization or its agents–...

(4) (i) to engage in, or to induce or encourage any individual employed by any person engaged in commerce or in an industry affecting commerce to engage in, a strike or refusal in the course of his employment to use, manufacture, process, transport, or otherwise handle or work on any goods, articles, materials, or commodities or to perform any services; or (ii) to threaten, coerce, or restrain any person engaged in commerce or in an industry affecting commerce, where in either case the object thereof is ...

(B) forcing or requiring any person to cease using, selling, handling, transporting, or otherwise dealing in the products of any other producer, processor, or manufacturer, or cease doing business with any other person.... .

29 U.S.C. § 158(b). *See, e.g., Local 761, International Union of Electrical, Radio & Machine Workers v. NLRB,* 366 U.S. 667 (1961).

Secondary market: Market for securities after the initial offering, and after the underwriting syndicate has disbanded. Compare **after-market.**

Secondary offering: Offering of securities by security holders, rather than the issuer. Compare **primary offering.**

Secondary party: For the purpose of Article 3–Commercial Paper, and Article 4–Bank Deposits and Collections, of the Uniform Commercial Code, secondary party means "a drawer or endorser." UCC Section 3-102(1)(e).

Second mortgage: Mortgage with a claim against property junior in priority to another, "first" mortgage.

Section: When referring to land, a parcel of one square mile.

Section 38 property: Property for which the investment tax credit is available under section 38 of the Internal Revenue Code. Section 38 property is not defined in section 38 of the Internal Revenue Code, but in section 48(a). In general, the term includes "tangible personal property." Buildings, structural components thereof, and air conditioning and heating units are not included, but the term does include certain property that might be regarded as real property under state law, such as storage facilities and tanks, escalators and elevators, and property "used as an integral part of manufacturing, production, or extraction or of furnishing transportation, communications, electrical energy, gas, water, or sewage disposal services ... ." I.R.C. § 48(a)(1). The term "section 38 property" does not, however, include property used "predominantly outside the United States," certain property used for lodging, property used by tax-exempt organizations and governmental units, livestock, certain property of foreign origin, and certain boilers fueled by oil or gas. I.R.C. § 48(a)(2)–(10).

Section 179 property: Depreciable business property, the cost of which can be treated as an expense, and a deduction taken against federal income taxes in the taxable year when first placed in service. I.R.C. § 179(a). In general, "section 179 property" means "recovery property" (I.R.C. § 168) that is "sec-

tion 38 property" (I.R.C. § 48(a)) and is acquired by purchase for use in a trade or business. I.R.C. § 179(d). The dollar amount of this deduction is very limited. I.R.C. § 179(b).

Section 341 assets: Property held for a period of less than three years that is stock in trade or inventory and certain other property. I.R.C. § 341(b)(3). If a corporation is formed or availed of principally for the purchase of "section 341 assets," it would be regarded as a "collapsible corporation," and gain from the sale of its stock would be treated as ordinary income instead of capital gains. I.R.C. § 341. See **collapsible corporation.**

Section 1244 stock: Stock in a small business corporation on which losses can be treated as ordinary losses instead of as capital losses for federal income taxes. In order to qualify as "section 1244 stock," the stock must be issued for money or other property, and the corporation must have derived more than 50 percent of its gross receipts from sources other than royalties, rents, dividends, interest, annuities, and sales or exchanges of stocks or securities. A small business corporation, for this purpose, is one with a capitalization of not more than $1,000,000. I.R.C. § 1244.

Section 1245 property: Depreciable property on which any gain from the disposition would be taxed as ordinary income to the extent of depreciation and amortization previously taken. In general, the term covers personal property. Buildings and structural components thereof are not included, but the term does include certain property that might be regarded as real property under state law, such as storage facilities and tanks, escalators and elevators, and property "used as an integral part of manufacturing, production, or extraction or of furnishing transportation, communications, electrical energy, gas, water, or sewage disposal services ... ." I.R.C. § 1245(a)(3).

Section 1245 recovery property: Depreciable property on which any gain from the disposition would be taxed as ordinary income, to the extent of accelerated cost recovery system deductions previously taken. Section 1245 recovery property is recovery property as defined in section 168 of the Internal Revenue Code, other than certain real property with a recovery period of 15 years. I.R.C. § 1245(a)(5).

Section 1250 property: Real property, other than section 1245 property, that is subject to the allowance for depreciation under section 167 of the Internal Revenue Code. I.R.C. § 1250(c).

Secured party: Party holding a security interest. Under Article 9 of the Uniform Commercial Code–Secured Transactions, a "secured party" is a "lender, seller or other person in whose favor there is a security interest, including a person to whom accounts or chattel paper have been sold. When the holders of obligations issued under an indenture of trust, equipment trust agreement or the like are represented by a trustee or other person, the representative is the secured party; ... ." UCC Section 9-105(1)(m). Article 9 substitutes the term "secured party" for traditional terms such as conditional sale vendor and mortgagee in transactions involving security interests in personal property.

Securities Act of 1933: Federal legislation requiring the disclosure of details concerning issues of securities by a process of registration with the SEC, except in certain circumstances, and providing remedies for fraud in the issuance of securities. Pub. L. No. 22, ch. 38, 48 Stat. 74 (1933); 15 U.S.C. § 77a–aa. *See* Landis, *The Legislative History of the Securities Act of 1933,* 28 Geo. Wash. L. Rev. 29 (1959).

Securities and Exchange Commission: Independent regulatory agency of the United States government formed to protect the interests of the public and investors against malpractices in the securities and financial markets. The SEC was established by the Securities Exchange Act of 1934, and it administers that act and the Securities Act of 1933, the Public Utility Holding Company Act of 1935, the Trust Indenture Act of 1939, the Investment Company Act of 1940, and the Investment Advisors Act of 1940. Pursuant to those laws, the SEC receives registration statements for securities offerings, and regulates securities markets, securities dealers, mutual funds and other investment companies, investment advisers and counselors, and companies controlling electric and gas utilities. Pursuant to the Bankruptcy Code, the SEC advises the parties to a reorganization and the court with respect to the fairness and feasibility of proposed plans of reorganization.

Securities Exchange Act of 1934: Federal statute creating the Securities and Exchange Commission and providing for registration of certain issuers of securities, the filing of periodic and special reports by certain issuers of securities, and certain securities exchange safeguards. Pub. L. No. 291, ch. 404, 48 Stat. 881 (1934); 15 U.S.C. § 78a–kk.

Securities Investor Protection Act of 1970: Statute creating the Securities Investor Protection Corporation. Pub. L. No. 91-598, 84 Stat. 1636 (1970), 15 U.S.C. §§ 78aaa–lll.

Securities Investor Protection Corporation: Government corporation created by the Securities Investor Protection Act of 1970 to provide insurance for losses of investors due to financial difficulties of brokers and dealers. *See* 17 C.F.R. § 300.

Securities laws: The Securities Act of 1933, Pub. L. No. 22, ch. 38, 48 Stat. 74 (1933), 15 U.S.C. §§ 77a–aa; the Securities Exchange Act of 1934, Pub. L. No. 291, ch. 404, 48 Stat. 881 (1934), 15 U.S.C. §§ 78a–kk; the Trust Indenture Act of 1939, Pub. L. No. 253, ch. 411, 53 Stat. 1149 (1939), 15 U.S.C. §§ 77aaa–bbbb; the Investment Company Act of 1940, Pub. L. No. 768, ch. 686, 54 Stat. 789 (1940), 15 U.S.C. §§ 80a; the Investment Advisors Act of 1940, Pub. L. No. 768, ch. 686, 54 Stat. 789, 847 (1940), 15 U.S.C. §§ 80b; and the Securities Investor Protection Act of 1970, Pub. L. No. 91-598, 84 Stat. 1636 (1970), 15 U.S.C. §§ 78aaa–lll. Depending on the circumstances, the Banking Act of 1933 (the Glass-Steagall Act), Pub. L. No. 66, ch. 89, 48 Stat. 162 (1933), and the Public Utility Holding Company Act of 1935,

Pub. L. No. 333, ch. 687, 49 Stat. 803 (1935), 15 U.S.C. §§ 79–79z, may be regarded as securities laws. See also **blue-sky laws.**

Security: 1. Collateral for a loan. See security interest. 2. Medium of investment, evidence of an obligation or right to participate in earnings or distribution of property. The primary source of a definition of the term "security" is section 2(1) of the Securities Act of 1933:

The term "security" means any note, stock, treasury stock, bond, debenture, evidence of indebtedness, certificate of interest or participation in any profit-sharing agreement, collateral trust certificate, preorganization certificate or subscription, transferable share, investment contract, voting-trust certificate, certificate of deposit for a security, fractional undivided interest in oil, gas, or other mineral rights, or, in general, any interest or instrument commonly known as a "security", or any certificate of interest or participation in, temporary or interim certificate for, receipt for, guarantee of, or warrant or right to subscribe to or purchase, any of the foregoing.

15 U.S.C. § 77b(1). As to employee benefit plans as securities, see SEC Release 33-6188 (1980). Related laws administered by the Securities and Exchange Commission use similar definitions; *see* section 3(a)(10) of the Securities Exchange Act of 1934 and section 2(a)(16) of the Public Utility Holding Company Act of 1935. *See also* ERISA § 3(20), 29 U.S.C. 1002(20). The securities law definition has been the subject of considerable litigation because a broad construction of the definition permits the use of securities law remedies by the SEC and by private liti-

gants; *e.g.*, *Marine Bank v. Weaver*, 455 U.S. ... (1982), 50 U.S.L.W. 4285. A troublesome aspect of the Securities Act definition is its exemplary, rather than analytical, nature; the term seems to defy analytical definition but like obscenity, a court may know it when it sees it. Court decisions have attempted to take a flexible approach, and the decisions have often turned on whether the court was in a mood to permit the securities laws to be used to provide a remedy for the particular swindle in question. Nevertheless, some standards such as "economic reality" have emerged from the decisions. *See, e.g.*, Hannan & Thomas, *The Importance of Economic Reality and Risk in Defining Federal Securities*, 25 Hastings L.J. 219 (1974); Faust, *What is a Security?* 33 Sec. Reg. L.J. 219 (1975). The Interstate Commerce Act (which predates the Securities Act of 1933) uses a somewhat less broad definition; as it appears in the successor statute, Title 49 of the United States Code, security means "a share of capital stock, a bond, or other evidence of interest in, or indebtedness of, a carrier." 49 U.S.C. § 11301(a)(2). Despite the remedial nature of the section in which this definition appears, the term has been narrowly construed in this context. *Association of Am. Railroads v. United States*, 603 F. 2d 953 (D.C. Cir. 1979). The Bankruptcy Code adopts a definition similar to the Securities Act definition, but modeled after the proposed Federal Securities Code; the Bankruptcy Code definition also is exemplary rather than analytical. The term includes:

(i) note;
(ii) stock;
(iii) treasury stock;
(iv) bond;

(v) debenture;
(vi) collateral trust certificate;
(vii) pre-organization certificate or subscription;
(viii) transferable share;
(ix) voting trust certificate;
(x) certificate of deposit;
(xi) certificate of deposit for security;
(xii) investment contract or certificate of interest or participation in a profit-sharing agreement or in an oil, gas, or mineral royalty or lease, if such contract or interest is the subject of a registration statement filed with the Securities and Exchange Commission under the provisions of the Securities Act of 1933 (15 U.S.C. § 77a et seq.), or is exempt under section 3(b) of such Act (15 U.S.C. § 77c(b)) from the requirement to file such a statement;
(xiii) interest of a limited partner in a limited partnership;
(xiv) other claim or interest commonly known as a "security"; and
(xv) certificate of interest or participation in, temporary or interim certificate for, receipt for, or warrant or right to subscribe to or purchase or sell, a security·....

11 U.S.C. § 101(35)(A). The Bankruptcy Code definition specifically excludes certain interests that might be regarded as "securities" under laws regulating the issue and sale of securities:

(i) currency, check, draft, bill of exchange, or bank letter of credit;
(ii) leverage transaction, as defined in section 761(13) of this title;
(iii) commodity futures contract or forward commodity contract;
(iv) option, warrant, or right to subscribe to or purchase or sell a commodity futures contract;
(v) option to purchase or sell a commodity;
(vi) contract or certificate specified in clause (xii) of subparagraph (A) of this paragraph that is not the subject of such a registration statement filed with the Se-

curities and Exchange Commission and is not exempt under section 3(b) of the Securities Act of 1933 (15 U.S.C. § 77c(b)) from the requirement to file such a statement; or

(vii) debt or other evidence of indebtedness for goods sold and delivered or services rendered; ... .

11 U.S.C. § 101(35)(B); *see* H.R. Rep. No. 95-595, 95th Cong., 1st Sess. 313 (1977). The term is not defined in the Internal Revenue Code (except for the purpose of section 1236; I.R.C. § 1236 (c)), but has been construed in *Camp Wolters Enterprises, Inc.*, 22 T.C. 737, *aff'd* 230 F. 2d 555 (5th Cir.), *cert. denied*, 352 U.S. 826 (1956); *United States v. Hertwig*, 398 F. 2d 452 (5th Cir. 1968). State blue-sky laws also cover securities, and sometimes provide a definition. Like the definition under the Securities Act of 1933, the state definitions are broadly stated (although usually less detailed), and require broad construction because of the remedial nature of securities regulation laws. A definition for a different purpose appears in Article 8 of the Uniform Commercial Code—Investment Securities:

A "security" is an instrument which

(i) is issued in bearer or registered form; and

(ii) is of a type commonly dealt in upon securities exchanges or markets or commonly recognized in any area in which it issued or dealt in as a medium for investment; and

(iii) is either one of a class or series or by its terms is divisible into a class or series of instruments; and

(iv) evidences a share, participation or other interest in property or in an enterprise or evidences an obligation of the issuer.

UCC Section 8-102. This definition, for the purpose of Article 8, is addressed to the documentary aspects of a security, because Article 8 is intended to be "a negotiable instruments law dealing with securities." UCC Section 8-101, Official Comment. See also **investment contract.**

Security agreement: Agreement that creates or provides for a security interest. *See* UCC Section 9-105(1)(l); 11 U.S.C. § 101(36); H.R. Rep. No. 95-595, 95th Cong., 1st Sess. 314 (1977).

Security interest: Term created by the Uniform Commercial Code to describe an interest in personal property or fixtures that secures payment or performance of an obligation, and that entitles the holder thereof to take the property or fixtures upon default. The term "security interest" replaces and merges the concepts of lien and of title retention for security under conditional sale agreements and some types of leases. The Uniform Commercial Code definition appears in Section 1-201(37):

"Security interest" means an interest in personal property or fixtures which secures payment or performance of an obligation. The retention or reservation of title by a seller of goods notwithstanding shipment or delivery to the buyer (Section 2-401) is limited in effect to a reservation of a "security interest". The term also includes any interest of a buyer of accounts or chattel paper which is subject to Article 9. The special property interest of a buyer of goods on identification of such goods to a contract for sale under section 2-401 is not a "security interest", but a buyer may also acquire a "security interest" by complying with Article 9. Unless a lease or consignment is intended as security, reservation of title thereunder is not a "security interest" but a consignment is in any event subject to the provisions on consignment sales (Section 2-326).

The term as used in the Bankruptcy Code is broader, and includes interests in real property. It is defined simply as a "lien created by agreement." 11 U.S.C. § 101(37); *see* H.R. Rep. No. 95-595, 95th Cong., 1st Sess. 314 (1977). The most difficult interpretive problems arise in attempting to distinguish between certain lease forms that are intended for security and are in substance security interests, and true leases. The code definition continues:

Whether a lease is intended as security is to be determined by the facts in each case; however, (a) the inclusion of an option to purchase does not of itself make the lease one intended for security, and (b) an agreement that upon compliance with the terms of the lease the lessee shall become or has the option to become the owner of the property for no additional consideration or for a nominal consideration does make the lease one intended for security.

For a fifteen-page lesson in how to read the seven sentences of the Uniform Commercial Code definition of "security interest," see Coogan, *Leases of Equipment and Some Other Unconventional Security Devices: An Analysis of UCC Section 1-201(37) and Article 9,* 1973 Duke L.J. 909. *See also* Rev. Proc. 55-540, 1955-2 C.B. 39.

Security title: Interest of a secured party in equipment used as collateral for a financing, nominally identified as title for the purposes of a title-retention type of security agreement but diminished by the adjective "security" to avoid some implications, such as strict liability, of ownership. The term has been used in aircraft financing; *see* section 504 of the Federal Aviation Act, 49 U.S.C. § 1404.

Segment of a business: In accounting terminology, a component of a business entity whose activities represent a major line of business or class of customer. A segment may be a division or department, or a subsidiary corporation; but its assets, operations, and activities must be clearly distinguishable. American Institute of Certified Public Accountants, Accounting Principles Board Opinion No. 30, *Reporting the Results of Operations—Reporting the Effects of Disposal of a Segment of a Business, and Extraordinary, Unusual and Infrequently Occurring Events and Transactions,* paragraph 13 (1973); *see also* Financial Accounting Standards Board, Statement of Financial Accounting Standards No. 14, *Financial Reporting for Segments of a Business Enterprise,* paragraph 10 (1976).

Self-regulatory organization: For the purpose of securities regulation and the Securities Exchange Act of 1934, a self-regulatory organization is a "national securities exchange, registered securities association, or registered clearing agency, or (solely for the purposes of sections 19(b), 19(c), and 23(b) of this title) the Municipal Securities Rulemaking Board established by section 15B of this title." Section 3(a)(26), 15 U.S.C. § 78c(a)(26). *See* Securities and Exchange Commission, *Staff Report on Corporate Accountability* H1 (1980). For the purpose of the Commodity Exchange Act and commodities futures regulation, see 17 C.F.R. § 1.3.

Self-underwriting rule: Rule 15b10-9 under the Securities Exchange Act of 1934, regarding participation by broker-dealers in the public distribution of their own securities. 17 C.F.R. § 240.15b10-9.

Sell: See sale.

Seller: Under Article 2 of the Uniform Commercial Code–Sales, "seller" means "a person who sells or contracts to sell goods." UCC Section 2-103(1)(d).

Send: For the purposes of the Uniform Commercial Code:

"Send" in connection with any writing or notice means to deposit in the mail or deliver for transmission by any other usual means of communication with postage or cost of transmission provided for and properly addressed and in the case of an instrument to an address specified thereon or otherwise agreed, or if there be none to any address reasonable under the circumstances. The receipt or any writing or notice within the time at which it would have arrived if properly sent has the effect of a proper sending.

UCC Section 1-201(38).

Senior debt: All debt that is not subordinated to other liabilities, and thus has first claim on the assets of an enterprise.

Senior equity: Equity interests that would have priority over common stock; preferred stock.

Senior security: Debt or equity security having priority over common stock as to distribution of earnings and assets.

Sensitivity analysis: Analytical technique whereby various independent variables are changed through a given range and the effect of the dependent variable, or solution, is observed. Sensitivity analysis will show how the yield on a leveraged lease investment responds to changes in assumptions such as residual value or debt-equity ratio.

Separability clause: Clause in a statute or contract reciting that the provisions thereof are separable, and the invalidity of one does not affect the others. *E.g.,* Cal. Corp. Code § 19. See severability.

Separate account: For the purpose of the Securities Act of 1933, a separate account is an "account established and maintained by an insurance company ... under which income, gains and losses, whether or not realized, from assets allocated to such account, are, in accordance with the applicable contract, credited to or charged against such account without regard to other income, gain, or losses of the insurance company." Section 2(14); 15 U.S.C. § 77b(14). *See* section 3(a)(19) of the Securities Exchange Act of 1934, 15 U.S.C. § 78c(a)(19); section 2(a)(37) of the Investment Company Act of 1940, 15 U.S.C. § 80a-2(a)(37); ERISA § 3(17, 29 U.S.C. § 1002(17).

Separate discharge: Discharge of the claim or lien against one of the vessels subject to a fleet mortgage by payment of a specified portion of the mortgage indebtedness. *See* Ship Mortgage Act, 1920, subsection D(f); 46 U.S.C. § 922(f); *The Emma Giles,* 15 F. Supp. 502 (D. Md. 1936).

Serial: When used to describe bonds or other debt securities, meaning issued in a series with maturities of differing duration. The principal amount of the entire issue is thus amortized over the life of the issue, as bonds mature serially from time to time, but the principal amount of an individual bond will remain outstanding in full until the maturity of that bond.

Service mark: "Mark used in the sale or advertising of services to identify the services of one person and distinguish them from the services of others." The term includes titles, character names, and distinctive features of radio or television programs. 15 U.S.C. § 1027. See **trademark.**

Service well: As defined by the Financial Accounting Standards Board:

A service well is a well drilled or completed for the purpose of supporting production in an existing field. Wells in this class are drilled for the following specific purposes: gas injection (natural gas, propane, butane, or flue gas), water injection, steam injection, air injection, salt-water disposal, water supply for injection, observation, or injection for in-situ combustion.

Financial Accounting Standards Board, Statement of Financial Accounting Standards No. 19, *Financial Accounting and Reporting by Oil and Gas Producing Companies,* Appendix C (1977). See also **development well; stratigraphic test well.**

Setoff: Right of a creditor in a bankruptcy proceeding to set off, or deduct, from the amount owed by the debtor an amount owed by the creditor to the debtor. *See* 11 U.S.C. § 553; H.R. Rep. No. 95-595, 95th Cong., 1st Sess. 183 (1977). *See generally* Freeman, *Setoff under the New Bankruptcy Code: The Effect on Bankers,* 97 Banking L. J. 484 (1980).

Settle: For the purpose of Article 4–Bank Deposits and Collections, of the Uniform Commercial Code, "settle" means "to pay in cash, by clearing house settlement, in a charge or credit or by remittance, or otherwise as instructed. A settlement may be either provisional or final." UCC Section 4-104(1)(j).

Settlement date: Date on which payment is made for a security, usually four business days after the date of the transaction or trade.

Severability: Concept that one part of an agreement can be enforced even though another part is unenforceable on grounds of public policy, under certain circumstances, by apportioning the parties' performances into corresponding pairs of part performances. *See Restatement, Second, Contracts* § 183 (1981).

Share: Unit of proprietary interest in a corporation or an unincorporated association. Model Business Corporation Act § 2(d) (1979); N. Y. Bus. Corp. Law § 501; Cal. Corp. Code § 184. *See* 17 C.F.R. § 230.405, 47 Fed. Reg. 11380, 11436 (1982). The terms "share" and "stock" are almost interchangeable; "share" and "shareholder" are used in the Model Business Corporation Act, the New York Business Corporation Law, and the California Corporations Code, whereas "stock" and "stockholder" are used in the Delaware Corporation Law. When modified by an adjective or used as an adjective, "share" often becomes "stock," as in "common stock" and "stock split."

Share certificate: Instrument evidencing shares in a corporation.

Share dividend: Dividend paid in shares of stock instead of cash. *See* Model Business Corporation Act § 45 (1979); N. Y. Bus. Corp. Law § 511; Del. Code Ann. Tit. 8 § 173.

Shareholder: Holder of a share of stock in a corporation or a unit of interest in an unincorporated association. The term is used in the Model Business Corporation Act and the New York Business Corporation Law, but the term "stockholder" is used in the Delaware Corporation Law. Under the Internal Revenue Code, the term "shareholder" includes "a member in an association, joint-stock company, or insurance company." I.R.C. § 7701(a)(8). In some situations the term is limited to holders of record; Cal. Corp. Code § 185.

Shareholder proposal rule: Rule 14a-8 of the Securities and Exchange Commission.

Shareholders' agreement: Agreement among shareholders in a closely held corporation, or among the shareholders and the corporation, regarding corporate management, voting of shares, disposition of shares, and other matters. *See* Model Business Corporation Act § 34 (1979); N. Y. Bus. Corp. Law § 620; Cal. Corp. Code §§ 186, 300(b); Del. Code Ann. tit. 8 § 218(c).

Shareholders' equity: Book value of assets minus liabilities; net worth.

Shareholders' equity is evidenced by common stock and preferred stock, and includes capital and surplus.

Shark repellent: Provision in corporate charter or other corporate instruments designed to impede hostile takeover attempts. *See generally* Black & Smith, *Antitakeover Charter Provisions: Defending Self-Help for Takeover Targets,* 36 Wash. & Lee L. Rev. 699 (1979); Hochman & Folger, *Deflecting Takeovers: Charter and By-Law Techniques,* 34 Bus. Law. 537 (1979).

Shelf registration: Registration statement filed with the Securities and Exchange Commission covering all securities of a given type planned to be issued in a two-year period. *See* SEC Release No. 33-6334, 46 Fed. Reg. 42001 (1981); SEC Release No. 33-6383, 47 Fed. Reg. 11380 (1982); 17 C.F.R. 230.415.

Shelter provision: Rule with respect to negotiable instruments and investment securities that, upon delivery of an instrument or security, the purchaser acquires the right therein which his transferor had or had actual authority to convey. UCC Section 8-301. *See Gruntal v. U.S. Fidelity & Guaranty Co.,* 254 N.Y. 468, 173 N.E. 682 (1930).

Sherman Act: Sherman Anti-Trust Act; federal statute prohibiting contracts, combinations, and conspiracies "in restraint of trade" and monopolies and attempts to monopolize trade or commerce. Act of July 2, 1890, ch. 647, 26 Stat. 209; 15 U.S.C. §§ 1–7. The Sherman Act has been characterized as "a comprehensive charter of economic liberty aimed at preserving free and unfettered competition as the rule of trade." *Northern Pac. Ry. v. United States,* 356 U.S. 1, 4 (1958). *See generally* American Bar Association, Section of Antitrust Law, *Antitrust Law Developments* 1 (1975).

Shields plan: Plan by underwriters, involved in the underwriting of an issue of securities preceded by a distribution of rights to purchase such securities, to purchase such rights in the market and to sell an equivalent number of the securities, in order to reduce the exposure to decline in the market price for the securities between the time the underwriter commits to do the underwriting (at a set price) and the actual issue of the securities. See **rights offering.**

Shingle rule: Rule that by holding himself out as a broker or dealer (hanging out a shingle), a person makes an implied representation to his customers that he will deal fairly and in accordance with high standards of conduct. *See* William Harrison Keller, Jr., 38 S.E.C. 900, 905 (1959); E. Weiss, *Registration and Regulation of Brokers and Dealers 104* (1965).

Shipment contract: Contract for the sale of goods under which the seller bears the expense of shipment to a given destination, but not the risk of loss. See **C.I.F.; C.& F.;** UCC Section 2-504. Compare **destination contract.**

Ship Mortgage Act, 1920: Section 30 of the Merchant Marine Act, 1920, creating the preferred mortgage as a maritime lien, enforceable in federal courts, and providing for priority of the preferred mortgage over certain other

types of maritime liens. Pub. L. No. 261, ch. 250, 41 Stat. 988, 1000, 46 U.S.C. § 911–83. *See generally* Smith, *Ship Mortgages,* 47 Tul. L. Rev. 608 (1973). The constitutionality of the Ship Mortgage Act was established in *Detroit Trust Co. v. The Thomas Barlum,* 293 U.S. 21 (1934).

Shipper's weight, load, and count: Words of qualification of the description of goods in a bill of lading, relieving the issuer of the bill from liability for misdescription of the goods, under certain circumstances. UCC Section 7-301.

Shipping Act, 1916: Federal statute providing for regulation of United States ocean shipping by the Federal Maritime Commission, and imposing certain restrictions on the ownership and transfer of vessels registered under United States law. Pub. L. No. 260, ch. 451, 39 Stat. 728 (1916); 46 U.S.C. §§ 801–42.

Ship's husband: Person appointed by the owners of a vessel to manage the affairs of that vessel.

Shop right: Right of an employer to an employee's invention.

Short: Owning fewer shares of a security or units of a commodity than one has agreed to sell.

Short-dated bills: Treasury bills of very short maturities, usually less than a month. See **cash management bills.**

Short-form merger: Merger pursuant to statute in a situation where the parent owns 90 percent or more of the stock of the subsidiary that is to be merged into the parent. Cal. Corp. Code § 1110; Del. Code Ann. Tit. 8 § 253.

Short-form registration: Registration of securities under the Securities Act of 1933 using an abbreviated or condensed form, such as form S-3.

Short sale: Sale of security or commodity not owned by the seller, with the intention of meeting the delivery requirements by a subsequent purchase of the same security or commodity. If the price drops, the seller can cover the short sale by purchasing at the market and make a profit. If the price rises, the seller incurs a loss in covering the short sale.

Short-swing profits: Profits on securities transactions within a six-month period by a "person who is directly or indirectly the beneficial owner of more than 10 per centum of any class of equity security" and officers and directors of the issuer of the securities. Short-swing profits by such persons "shall inure to and be recoverable by the issuer" pursuant to section 16(b) of the Securities Exchange Act of 1934, 15 U.S.C. § 78p(b).

Short term: Used to describe loans and fixed-income securities having a maturity of one year or less. *See* Financial Accounting Standards Board, Statement of Financial Accounting Standards No. 6, *Classification of Short-term Obligations Expected to be Refinanced,* paragraph 2 (1975). Compare long term; intermediate term.

Short-term capital gain: Under the Internal Revenue Code, the term "short-term capital gain" means "gain from the sale or exchange of a capital asset held for not more than 1 year, if and to the extent such gain is taken into account in computing gross income." I.R.C. § 1222(1). See capital asset; long-term capital gain.

Short-term capital loss: Under the Internal Revenue Code, the term "short-term capital loss" means "loss from the sale or exchange of a capital asset held for not more than 1 year if and to the extent that such loss is taken into account in computing taxable income." I.R.C. § 1222(2). See capital asset; long-term capital loss.

SIBOR: Singapore interbank offered rate. See London interbank offered rate.

Signature: For the purpose of Article 3—Commercial Paper, of the Uniform Commercial Code, "A signature is made by use of any name, including any trade or assumed name, upon any instrument, or by any word or mark used in lieu of a written signature." UCC Section 3-401. See also signed.

Signature guaranty: See guarantee of the signature.

Signed: For the purposes of the Uniform Commercial Code, the term "signed" includes "any symbol executed or adopted by a party with present intention to authenticate a writing." UCC Section 1-201(39). The Official Comment to this section elaborates on the term "authentication," suggesting that almost anything will do: "Authentication may be printed, stamped, or written; it may be by initials or by thumbprint. ... The question always is whether the symbol was executed or adopted by the party with present intention to authenticate the writing."

Simple interest: Interest calculated by applying the interest rate to the principal amount for the full period in question, without compounding, or adding interest to the principal.

Sinking fund: Fund fed by regular payments designed to retire indebtedness or to meet future obligations. A sinking fund may be held in the form of cash or securities, pending application against the obligation, but more common is the situation whereby sinking fund payments are used to immediately retire a part of the outstanding securities in an issue, providing the equivalent of a regular amortization. In the latter case, a sinking fund is a complicated way to express the simple concept of installment payments. In an analysis of yield on an investment in a leveraged lease transaction, the term "sinking fund" is an analytic device to earmark certain cash flows for later reinvestment, without actually creating a fund.

SIP: State implementation plan.

SIPA: Securities Investor Protection Act of 1970.

SIPC: Securities Investor Protection Corporation.

Skimming: Removal of cash before counting as income in order to evade taxes thereon.

SL: *Sociedad de responsabilidad limitada,* limited liability company organized under the laws of Spain.

SLMA: Student Loan Marketing Association.

SLOB: Substantial lender on own book.

Small Business Administration: Independent agency of the United States government whose purpose is to assist small business enterprises by making loans, providing management assistance, and advocating the interests of small businesses before other federal agencies. The SBA regulates Small Business Investment Companies and provides financing by direct loans and guarantees of debenture offerings. *See* Small Business Act, Pub. L. No. 85-536, 72 Stat. 384 (1958), 15 U.S.C. §§ 631–47; Small Business Investment Act of 1958, Pub. L. No. 85-699, 72 Stat. 689 (1958), 15 U.S.C. §§ 661–96; 13 C.F.R. §§ 101–31.

Small business corporation: For the purposes of Subchapter S of the Internal Revenue Code, the term "small business corporation" means a domestic corporation that does not have more than 25 shareholders, does not have a shareholder who is not an individual, does not have a nonresident alien as a shareholder, and does not have more than one class of stock. I.R.C. § 1371(a). A "small business corporation" may elect not to be subject to federal income tax, pursuant to Subchapter S, I.R.C. §§ 1371–79.

Small Business Investment Company: Privately owned company that supplies venture capital and loans to small business. SBICs are regulated by the Small Business Administration, and the SBA makes loans to and guarantees the debentures of SBIC's. *See* I.R.C. §§ 1242, 1243. *See generally* Miller, *Small Business Investment Companies: Licensing, Tax and Securities Considerations,* 36 Bus. Law. 1679 (1981).

Small issue exemption: The interest on industrial development bonds issued by a municipality is not exempt from federal income taxes, with certain exceptions, one of which is for "small issues" of $10,000,000 and less. I.R.C. § 103(b)(6). *See also* section 214(a) of the Tax Equity and Fiscal Responsibility Act of 1982; Rev. Rul. 81-216, 1981-2 C.B. 21. *See generally* M. Rollinson, *Small Issue Industrial Development Bonds* (1976); Wade, *Industrial Development Bonds—The Capital Expenditure Rule for $10,000,000 Small Issues,* 34 Bus. Law. 1771 (1979).

SMSA: Standard Metropolitan Statistical Area.

SNG: Synthetic natural gas.

Sovereign immunity: Doctrine that a government entity is immune from suit without its consent. The doctrine extends to foreign sovereigns in United States courts (*L'Invincible,* 14 U.S. (1 Wheat) 238 (1816)), but acts of a commercial nature are excluded from the immunity (*Bank of the United States v. Planters' Bank of Ga.,* 22 U.S. (9 Wheat) 904 (1824)). *See Dunhill v. Republic of Cuba,* 425 U.S. 682 (1976); *United States v. Deutsches Kalisyndikat Gesellschaft,* 31 F. 2d 199 (S.D.N.Y. 1929). The doctrine is codified by the Foreign Sovereign Immunities Act of 1976, Pub. L. No. 94-583, 90 Stat. 2891 (1976); 28 U.S.C. §§ 1602–11.

Special bill: Treasury bill maturing shortly after a tax due date, instead of the usual three-month, six-month, and 52-week bills.

Special Drawing Rights: Type of international money created by the International Monetary Fund and allocated to its member nations. SDRs are only accounting entries, and are not backed by currency or precious metal. Subject to certain conditions, a nation that has a balance of payments deficit can use SDRs to settle debts to another nation or to the International Monetary Fund. *See* Gold, *The International Monetary Fund,* in II W. Surrey & D. Wallace, Jr., ed., *A Lawyer's Guide to International Business Transactions* 3, 10 (1979).

Special indorsement: Under Article 3–Commercial Paper of the Uniform Commercial Code, a special indorsement "specifies the person to whom or to whose order it makes the instrument payable. Any instrument specially indorsed becomes payable to theorder of the special indorsee and may be further negotiated only by his indorsement." UCC Section 3-204(1).

Special interest account: Interest-bearing account in a commercial bank in states where use of the term "savings account" by commercial banks is prohibited.

Specialist: Broker and member of the New York Stock Exchange responsible for executing trades and making a market in a given stock or group of stocks.

Specially advised: When referring to letters of credit, "specially advised" means that information as to the establishment of the credit is conveyed to the beneficiary by an intermediary party, rather than directly by the issuer. See **advising bank.**

Specific performance: Equitable remedy requiring a party to perform a contractual obligation according to its specific terms, where money damages would be an inadequate remedy. Specific performance is an unusual remedy, difficult to enforce. *See Restatement, Second, Contracts* § 357, 359–69 (1981). *See generally* Schwartz, *The Case for Specific Performance,* 89 Yale L. J. 271 (1979); Kronman, *Specific Performance,* 45 U. Chi. L. Rev. 351 (1978). A buyer of goods may have the right to specific performance by the seller under certain circumstances. *See* UCC Section 2-716.

Spin-off: Reorganization of a corporation or corporate assets into two or more corporations by transferring part of the assets of the corporation to a corporation controlled by the transferor, and distributing stock or securities of the transferee corporation to the shareholders of the transferor corporation, without a surrender by the shareholders of stock. *See* I.R.C. § 355. Compare split-off; split-up.

Split-off: Reorganization of a corporation or corporate assets into two or more corporations by transferring part of the assets of the corporation to a corporation controlled by the transferor,

and by distributing stock or securities of the transferee corporation to the shareholders of the transferor corporation, in exchange for part of their stock. *See* I.R.C. § 355. Compare **spin-off; split-up.**

Split-up: Corporate reorganization into two or more corporations by transferring all of the assets of the corporation to two or more new corporations in exchange for their stock, and then liquidating and distributing shares of the new corporations to the shareholders of the original corporation. Compare **spin-off; split-off.**

Spot market: Market for a commodity for immediate delivery, "on the spot," rather than for future delivery or under long-term supply contract.

Spot payment: Single payment.

Spot rate: Cost per unit of a commodity, currency, or service for immediate delivery, "on the spot." *See* Financial Accounting Standards Board, Statement of Financial Accounting Standards No. 8, *Accounting for the Translation of Foreign Currency Transactions and Foreign Currency Financial Statements,* Appendix E (1975). A spot charter rate is the rate for a single voyage, rather than for a longer-term charter.

Spot rate curve: Plot, similar to a yield curve, showing the relationship of the discount rate for future spot payments to the time (of maturity) of those payments. The spot rate curve is useful in examining the price of the various components of stripper bonds.

Spread: 1.Difference between prices or rates of the same commodity, security, or transaction in different circumstances, as the difference between ask and bid prices of securities, or the difference between the price paid by an underwriter of a security in an offering and the price for which the security is sold. 2. Straddle.

Squeeze-out merger: Merger pursuant to statute in which the parent owns 90 percent or more of the stock of the subsidiary that is to be merged into the parent. *See* Del. Code Ann. Tit. 8 § 253, Cal. Corp. Code § 1110. Holders of interests of less than 10 percent cannot block the merger, and can be "squeezed out" (with appraisal rights). Del. Code Ann. Tit. 8 § 253(d). *See* freeze-out.

SREA: Society of Real Estate Appraisers, or Senior Real Estate Analyst, the highest designation of that society.

SRO: Self-regulatory organization.

Stabilization: The placing of a bid for securities for the purpose of stabilizing the price of that security. Stabilization may be practiced by underwriters of an issue of securities in order to prevent a decline in price. *See* SEC Rule 10b-7, 17 C.F.R. § 240.10b-7.

Staff Accounting Bulletin: Publication of the Division of Corporate Finance or the Office of Chief Accountant of the Securities and Exchange Commission representing interpretations and practices of SEC staff in administering the disclosure requirements of the securities laws. SABs are not statements of the Securities and Exchange Commission, and do not bear official commission approval.

Staggers Rail Act of 1980: Federal legislation providing for reduction in the level of economic regulation of railroad companies, and covering certain aspects of railroad bankruptcies. Pub. L. No. 96-448, 94 Stat. 1895 (1980). *See generally* Note, *The Staggers Rail Act of 1980: Authority to Compete with Ability to Compete*, 12 Trans. L. J. 301 (1982). As to constitutionality of the bankruptcy provisions, see *Railway Labor Executives Association v. Gibbons*, 455 U.S. . . . (1982), 50 U.S.L.W. 4258.

Stale: 1. A stale check is one presented more than six months after its date. A bank is not required to honor a stale check. UCC Section 4-404. 2. A stale security is one in which presentation and surrender of the security for payment of money or delivery of securities was set for a date more than one year prior, or which has been in default for more than two years. Article 8 of the Uniform Commercial Code–Investment Securities, provides that a purchaser of a security is charged with notice of any defect in a stale security. UCC Section 8-203. Section 8-305 provides shorter periods for staleness in respect of redemption or exchange (one year) and surrender for payment (six months), after which time a purchaser would be regarded as having notice of adverse claims.

Standby contract: Optional delivery forward "put" contract for financial instruments. The buyer of a standby pays a fee for the right to sell to the writer a specified financial instrument at a specified future date at a specified price or yield; the seller, or writer, stands ready to buy the instrument at the other party's option. Financial Accounting Standards Board, Technical Bulletin re APB Opinion No. 22, *Disclosure of Interest Rate Futures Contracts and Forward and Standby Contracts,* paragraph 5 (1981).

Standby letter of credit: Letter of credit that can be drawn upon only if another transaction is not consummated or another obligation is not met. *See Republic Nat'l Bank of Dallas v. Northwest Nat'l Bank of Fort Worth,* 578 S.W. 2d 109 (Sup. Ct. Tex. 1978).

Standstill agreement: Agreement by one party not to engage in a tender offer for the other party's securities.

Stare decisis: Principle that courts should abide by or follow precedent cases.

Start-up expenditure: For the purpose of the Internal Revenue Code, the term "start-up expenditure" means any amount paid or incurred in connection with investigating the creation or acquisition of an active trade or business or the creation of an active trade or business which, if paid or incurred in connection with the expansion of an existing trade or business, would be allowable as a deduction in the taxable year paid or incurred. Start-up expenditures may, at the election of the taxpayer, be treated as deferred expenses and allowed as a deduction ratably over a period of not less than six months. I.R.C. § 195.

State: As used in federal statutes, the term "State" usually includes the District of Columbia and territories and possessions of the United States. *E.g.,* section 3(a)(16) of the Securities Act of 1934, 15 U.S.C. § 78c(a)(16).

State, United States Department of: Cabinet-level department of the executive branch of the United States government that has the responsibility for the foreign affairs of the United States.

Stated capital: Sum of (1) the par value of all shares of a corporation having a par value that have been issued, (2) the amount of consideration received by a corporation for all shares of the corporation without par value that have been issued, except such part of such consideration as shall have been allocated to capital surplus, and (3) such other amounts as have been transferred to stated capital of the corporation, whether upon distribution of share or otherwise, minus all reductions from such sum permitted by law. Model Business Corporation Act § 2(j) (1979); N.Y. Bus. Corp. Law §§ 102(a)(12), 506. The Delaware corporation law does not use the term, but "capital" has substantially the same meaning thereunder. Del. Code Ann. tit. 8 § 154.

Statement of changes in financial position: Statement that summarizes for the period the resources made available to finance the activities of an enterprise and the uses to which such resources have been put. International Accounting Standards Committee, Statement of International Accounting Standards, Statement 7, *Statements of Changes in Financial Position,* paragraph 1 (1977). *See* American Institute of Certified Public Accountants, Accounting

Principles Board Opinion No. 19, *Reporting Changes in Financial Position* (1971). A statement of changes in financial position will include a statement of income, a statement of retained earnings, and perhaps other statements. American Institute of Certified Public Accountants, Accounting Principles Board Statement No. 4, *Basic Concepts and Accounting Principles Underlying Financial Statements of Business Enterprises*, Ch. 2, paragraph 4–7 (1970).

Statement of condition: Balance sheet for a bank, prepared daily.

Statement of financial position: Balance sheet; accounting statement presenting assets, liabilities, and owners' equity. American Institute of Certified Public Accountants, Accounting Principles Board Statement No. 4, *Basic Concepts and Accounting Principles Underlying Financial Statements of Business Enterprises,* Ch. 2, paragraph 3 (1970).

Statement of income: Accounting statement presenting the revenues, expenses, gains, losses, and net income for the accounting period. American Institute of Certified Public Accountants, Accounting Principles Board Statement No. 4, *Basic Concepts and Accounting Principles Underlying Financial Statements of Business Enterprises,* Ch. 2, paragraph 4 (1970). Also called profit and loss statement.

Statement of retained earnings: Accounting statement presenting net income and items such as dividends and adjustments of the net income of prior periods. American Institute of Certified Public Accountants, Accounting Principles Board Statement No. 4, *Basic*

Concepts and Accounting Principles Underlying Financial Statements of Business Enterprises, Ch. 2, paragraph 5 (1970).

Statement of source and application of funds: Statement of changes in financial position.

Statute of Frauds: Requirement of law, based on the Statute of 29 Charles II, c. 3, that contracts be in writing to be enforceable, if the contract cannot be performed within a year or involves a decedent's estate, a guarantee, a sale of an interest in land, or a sale of personal property for a price greater than a specified amount. *Restatement, Second, Contracts,* §§ 110–50; N.Y. Gen. Oblig. Law §§ 5-701, 5-703. Section 1-206 of the Uniform Commercial Code adopts $5000 as the maximum amount for enforcement of contracts of sale of personal property without a writing identifying the subject matter and signed by the party against whom enforcement is sought. The limit for a sale of goods is $500, but a writing is not necessary if the goods are to be specially manufactured (and such manufacture has commenced or commitments have been made for their procurement) or if the party against whom enforcement is sought admits to the contract in court proceedings. UCC Section 2-201. The sale of securities and establishment of security interests are governed by separate rules (Sections 8-319 and 9-203). *See generally* Duesenberg, *The Statute of Frauds in its 300th Year: The Challenge of Admissions in Court and Estoppel,* 33 Bus. Law. 1859 (1978).

Statute of Limitations: Statute that prohibits legal action after the lapse of a certain period of time after the cause of action arose. Under the Uniform Commercial Code, the Statute of Limitations for contracts for the sale of goods is four years. UCC Section 2-725. For the Statute of Limitations with respect to federal income tax, see I.R.C. §§ 6501–2.

Statutory consolidation: Consolidation of two or more corporations into a new corporation pursuant to state statute. Model Business Corporation Law § 72 (1979); N. Y. Bus. Corp. Law §§ 901–9; Del. Code Ann. Tit. 8 §§ 251–62. See I.R.C. § 368(a); Treas. Reg. § 1.368-2. See also merger; statutory merger; reorganization.

Statutory disqualification: Disqualification of a member of a stock exchange or other "self-regulatory organization" by operation of the provisions of the Securities Exchange Act of 1934. Section 3(a)(39), 15 U.S.C. § 78c(a)(39).

Statutory law: Law as enacted in statutes, as opposed to law developed by courts, and sometimes as opposed to regulations of administrative agencies that interpret laws enacted in statutes.

Statutory lien: Lien arising by statute. As used in the Bankruptcy Code:

"statutory lien" means lien arising solely by force of a statute on specified circumstances or conditions, or lien of distress for rent, whether or not statutory, but does not include security interest or judicial lien, whether or not such interest or lien is provided by or is dependent on a statute and whether or not such interest or lien is made fully effective by statute.

11 U.S.C. § 101(38); see H.R. Rep. No. 95-595, 95th Cong., 1st Sess. 314

(1977). Tax liens and mechanics' liens are statutory liens. See security interest; judicial lien.

Statutory merger: Merger of two or more corporations into one of such corporations pursuant to state statute. Model Business Corporation Law § 71 (1979); N. Y. Bus. Corp. Law §§ 901–9; Del. Code Ann. Tit. 8. §§ 251–62; Cal. Corp. Code §§ 1100–12. See I.R.C. § 368(a); Treas. Reg. § 1.368-2. See also merger; statutory consolidation; reorganization.

Statutory underwriter: Purchaser of securities that comes under the definition of "underwriter" in section 2(11) of the Securities Act of 1933, even though that purchaser is not an underwriter in the business sense. See underwriter.

Stock: 1. Share or unit of interest in a corporation or an unincorporated association; see 17 C.F.R. § 230.405, 47 Fed. Reg. 11380, 11436 (1982). The terms "share" and "stock" are almost interchangeable; "share" and "shareholder" are used in the Model Business Corporation Act and the New York Business Corporation Law, whereas "stock" and "stockholder" are used in the Delaware Corporation Law, with an occasional reference to "shares of stock." The Internal Revenue Code uses "stock," but the holders thereof are termed "shareholders." Under that code, the term "stock" includes "shares in an association, joint-stock company, or insurance company." I.R.C. § 7701(a)(7). See also I.R.C. § 1083(f). 2. Inventory.

Stock appreciation right: Right entitling an employee to receive cash, stock, or a combination of cash and stock in an amount equivalent to the excess, if any, of the market value of a stated number of shares of the employer's stock over a stated price. Financial Accounting Standards Board, Interpretation No. 28, *Accounting for Stock Appreciation Rights and Other Variable Stock Option or Award Plans: An Interpretation of APB Opinions No. 15 and 25,* Appendix A (1978). *See generally* Herzel & Perlman, *Stock Appreciation Rights,* 33 Bus. Law. 749 (1978).

Stock certificate: Instrument evidencing stock or shares in a corporation.

Stock dividend: Dividend paid in stock instead of cash; distribution of stock accompanied by a transfer of retained or undistributed profit to capital. *See* Model Business Corporation Act § 45 (1979); N. Y. Bus. Corp. Law § 511; Del. Code Ann. Tit. 8 § 173. A stock dividend is prompted by a desire to give shareholders "some ostensible separate evidence of a part of their respective interests in accumulated corporate earnings without distribution of cash or other property . . . ." American Institute of Certified Public Accountants, Accounting Research Bulletin No. 43, Ch. 7B, *Stock Dividends and Stock Split-Ups,* paragraph 1 (1953). See also **stock split.**

Stockholder: Holder of a share of stock in a corporation or a unit of interest in an unincorporated association. The term is used in the Delaware corporation law, but the term "shareholder" is used in the Model Business Corporation Act, the New York Business Corporation Law,

and the Internal Revenue Code. See stock; share.

Stock option: Option granted an employee to purchase shares of the employer's stock at a stated price.

Stock power: Power of attorney for the transfer of stock.

Stock relief: In the United Kingdom, a deduction from income taxes for increases in the carrying amount of inventory (inventory is called "stock" in the United Kingdom). *See* Financial Accounting Standards Board, Statement of Financial Accounting Standards No. 31, *Accounting for Tax Benefits Related to U.K. Tax Legislation Concerning Stock Relief,* paragraph 1 (1979).

Stock split: Pro rata division, other than by a stock dividend, of all of the outstanding shares of stock of a class into a greater number (usually a multiple) of shares of stock of the same class. *See* Cal. Corp. Code § 188. A stock split is prompted by "a desire to increase the number of outstanding shares for the purpose of effecting a reduction in their unit market price and, thereby, of obtaining wider distribution and improved marketability of the shares." American Institute of Certified Public Accountants, Accounting Research Bulletin No. 43, Ch. 7B, *Stock Dividends and Stock Split-Ups,* paragraph 2 (1953). See also **stock dividend.**

Stop limit order: Order to buy or sell a security at the limit price, or a better price if obtainable, when a transaction occurs at the specified "stop" price (or above the stop price, in the case of buy order, and below, in the case of a sell order).

Stop order: Order to buy or sell a security when a transaction occurs at the specified "stop" price (or below the stop price, in the case of buy order, and above, in the case of a sell order).

Stop-transfer: Instruction to the transfer agent of an issue of securities to stop transfer of the securities unless certain conditions are complied with. *See* SEC Release No. 33-5121 (1970).

Straddle: Combination of offsetting positions in futures contracts for commodities or securities. "Straddles," or "spreads," usually involve simultaneous purchase and sale of contracts for delivery of the same commodity at different times in anticipation of profits from price movement during the intervening period; but an "intermarket straddle" involves contracts for different commodities in anticipation of profits from relative price movement. For the purpose of the Internal Revenue Code, the term "straddle" means "offsetting positions with respect to personal property." The code further says that "A taxpayer holds offsetting positions with respect to personal property if there is a substantial diminution of the taxpayer's risk of loss from holding any position with respect to personal property by reason of his holding 1 or more other positions with respect to personal property (whether or not of the same kind)." I.R.C. § 1092(c). *See* I.R.C. § 1256; S. Rep. No. 97-144, 97th Cong., 1st Sess. 143 (1981). *See generally* Lee, *The Taxation of Commodity Straddles under the Economic Recovery Tax Act of 1981*, Prac. Law., Jan. 15, 1982, at 11.

Straight bankruptcy: Bankruptcy proceedings intended to liquidate the assets of the debtor, rather than reorganization.

Straight bill; straight bill of lading: Nonnegotiable bill of lading. Compare order bill; see bill of lading; negotiable.

Straight credit; straight letter of credit: Letter of credit with no commitment or obligation to any party except the beneficiary. Compare negotiation credit.

Straight-line depreciation: Method of depreciation whereby the amount of depreciation is taken in equal parts over the useful life of the property, so that a plot of the asset balance over time will produce a straight line from the original cost to the salvage value.

Straight reduction plan; straight term plan: Plan of amortization of a debt involving equal payments of principal at specified intervals, with interest on the then unpaid balance.

Stratigraphic test well: As defined by the Financial Accounting Standards Board:

A stratigraphic test is a drilling effort, geologically directed, to obtain information pertaining to a specific geologic condition. Such wells customarily are drilled without the intention of being completed for hydrocarbon production. This classification also includes tests identified as core tests and all types of expendable holes related to hydrocarbon exploration. For purposes of this Statement, stratigraphic test wells (sometimes called "expendable wells") are classified as follows:

1. Exploratory-type stratigraphic test well. A stratigraphic test well not drilled in a proved area.

2. Development-type stratigraphic test well. A stratigraphic test well drilled in proved area.

Financial Accounting Standards Board, Statement of Financial Accounting Standards No. 19, *Financial Accounting and Reporting by Oil and Gas Producing Companies,* Appendix C (1977). *See* 17 C.F.R. § 210.4-10(a)(13).

Straw man: Individual, not having an actual interest in a transaction, who enters into a contract as a convenience to the actual parties in interest, or to avoid disclosure of an actual party in interest. Traditionally, an individual willing to act as a witness in court proceedings, who made known his occupation by displaying a straw in his shoe.

Street name: Nominee name used by brokers to register securities held for their own account or the account of customers. See **nominee.** *See generally* Securities and Exchange Commission, *Final Report on the Practice of Recording the Ownership of Securities in the Records of the Issuer in Other than the Name of the Beneficial Owner of Such Securities* (1976).

Strict liability: Liability arising not out of a proven act or omission, or fault on the part of the party held liable, but strictly from the circumstance of ownership or possession. Strict liability is usually pursuant to a specific statute, and applies to owners of property with special potential for causing harm, such as automobiles and aircraft.

Strike suit: Derivative action by stockholders.

Stripped bond; stripper bond: Debt security that has had the coupons representing interest payments stripped away. Each of the coupons and the corpus of the security then represents a claim on a single payment at its respective maturity, and each can be treated as a zero-coupon bond and traded at a discount. For federal income tax treatment, see I.R.C. § 1232B; section 232(a) of the Tax Equity and Fiscal Responsibility Act of 1982.

Student Loan Marketing Association: Government-sponsored private corporation formed to promote the secondary market in student loans made under the Guaranteed Student Loan Program. The SLMA (Sallie Mae) makes advances secured by and purchases student loans from financial institutions, and finances its operations by issuing debt securities, guaranteed by the Secretary of Education.

Subchapter S: Sections 1371–79 of the Internal Revenue Code, permitting certain "small business corporations" to elect not to be subject to federal income taxes; in such a case, the gains and losses of the corporation pass through to the shareholders.

Subchapter S corporation: Corporation electing not to be subject to federal income taxes pursuant to subchapter S of the Internal Revenue Code. I.R.C. §§ 1371–79. Also called pseudo-corporation; tax-option corporation. See small business corporation.

Submission agreement: Agreement to submit a given controversy to arbitration. *See generally* G. Goldberg, *A*

Lawyer's Guide to Commercial Arbitration 6 (1977).

Subordinate: Lower or inferior in rank or priority.

Subordinated debt: Debt that is subordinate to senior debt, and can be satisfied out of the assets of the enterprise only after the debt to which it is subordinate has been satisfied.

Subordination agreement: Agreement to assert a claim only after another claim has been discharged. A subordination agreement may include a provision for the subordinated party to turn over subordinated payments to the superior creditor upon failure of the common debtor to pay the superior creditor, but such an agreement does not of itself create a security interest in the subordinated payments. UCC Section 1-209. *See* Coogan, Kripke & Weiss, *The Outer Fringes of Article 9: Subordination Agreements, Security Interests in Money and Deposits, Negative Pledge Clauses, and Participation Agreements*, 79 Harv. L. Rev. 229 (1965). As to subordination agreements in bankruptcy, see 11 U.S.C. 510(a), H.R. Rep. No. 95-595, 95th Cong., 1st Sess. 359 (1977).

Subpart F income: Foreign income earned by a foreign corporation but taxable to a United States taxpayer owning more than 50% of such corporation, even if not distributed to that taxpayer. I.R.C. § 952(a). *See generally* Liebman, *Note on the Tax Treatment of Joint Venture Income Under Subpart F: An Addendum*, 32 Bus. Law. 1819 (1977); Liebman, *The Tax Treatment of Joint Venture Income*

Under Subpart F: Some Issues and Alternatives, 32 Bus. Law. 341 (1977).

Subpoena: Order to appear and give testimony. *See* Fed. R. Civ. Proc. 45.

Subpoena duces tecum: Order to appear and give testimony, and to produce specified documents. *See* Fed. R. Civ. Proc. 45(b).

Subrogation: Substitution of one party for another with respect to a claim or right; acquisition of the rights of another against a third party by payment of a claim or guaranty owed by that third party. An insurance carrier will acquire by subrogation the rights of its insured against the party causing the damage, and a guarantor will acquire the rights of the recipient of the guaranty against the obligor whose obligation was guaranteed.

Subscription: Agreement to purchase shares in a corporation. *See* N. Y. Bus. Corp. Law § 503.

Subscription adviser: Publisher of investment advisory letters by subscription for a fee. *See generally* Comment, *The Regulation of Investment Advice: Subscription Advisers and Fiduciary Duties*, 63 Mich. L. Rev. 1220 (1965).

Subsequent purchaser: Under Article 8–Investment Securities of the Uniform Commercial Code, a subsequent purchaser is a person "who takes other than by original issue." UCC Section 8-102(2).

Subsidiary: Corporation owned or controlled by another corporation. *See*

Cal. Corp. Code § 189; International Accounting Standards Committee, Statement of International Accounting Standards 3, *Consolidated Financial Statements,* paragraph 4 (1976); American Institute of Certified Public Accountants, Accounting Principles Board Opinion No. 18, *The Equity Method of Accounting for Investments in Common Stock,* paragraph 3c (1971). See also control.

Substantial evidence test: Principle of court review of administrative agency action in which the court confines itself to the question of whether the agency acted within its power and whether there was substantial evidence to support the agency action. *ICC v. Louisville & N. R.R.,* 227 U.S. 88 (1913). *See Consolidated Edison Co. v. NLRB,* 305 U.S. 197, 229 (1938); *NLRB v. Columbian Enameling & Stamping Co.* 306 U.S. 292, 300 (1939). Compare de novo review.

Substituted contract: "Contract that is itself accepted by the obligee in satisfaction of the obligor's existing duty." *Restatement, Second, Contracts* § 279 (1981). A substituted contract discharges the original duty. See novation.

Successful efforts method: Method of accounting for oil and gas activities in which costs that cannot be directly related to the discovery of specific oil and gas reserves are charged to expense. Financial Accounting Standards Board, Statement of Financial Accounting Standards No. 19, *Financial Accounting and Reporting by Oil and Gas Producing Companies,* paragraphs 102, 111–19 (1977). *See* SEC Regulation S-X, 17 C.F.R. § 210.4-10(b); SEC Accounting Release No. 253, 43 Fed. Reg. 40688 (1978). Compare full cost method.

Sui generis: The only one of its kind.

Sum certain: Under Article 3–Commercial Paper of the Uniform Commercial Code, for a promise or order to pay in writing to be a negotiable instrument it must, among other things, be for a "sum certain." UCC Section 3-104. A specified sum is a "sum certain" even though it is to be paid:

(a) with stated interest or by stated installments; or

(b) with stated different rates of interest before and after default or a specified date; or

(c) with a stated discount or addition if paid before or after the date fixed for payment; or

(d) with exchange or less exchange, whether at a fixed rate or at the current rate; or

(e) with costs of collection or an attorney's fee or both upon default.

UCC Section 3-106.

Summary prospectus: Condensed form of prospectus prepared for an issue of securities pursuant to SEC Rule 431, 17 C.F.R. 230.431, 47 Fed. Reg. 11380, 11440 (1982).

Summary review: Review by the Securities and Exchange Commission staff of a registration statement that is apparently well prepared or is based on an earlier registration statement, in which only a few written or oral comments are provided and the review process is handled expeditiously. SEC Release No. 33-5231 (1972). Compare **cursory review.**

Sum-of-the-years' digits: Method of depreciation whereby the original cost of the property, less salvage value, is multiplied by a fraction, the numerator of which is the number of years of remaining useful life, and the denominator of which is the sum of the digits for each of such years. For property having a useful life of five years, the fraction for the first year would be $5/(5+4+3+2+1)$, or $5/15$; for the second year, the fraction is $4/15$. *See* Treas. Reg. § 1.167(b)-3. Compare **declining balance.** See also **rule of 78.**

Sunshine Act: Government in the Sunshine Act, Pub. L. No. 94-409, 90 Stat. 1241 (1976); 5 U.S.C. § 552b. The Sunshine Act provides for public conduct of the business of federal agencies, with certain exceptions. Many states also have sunshine laws.

Superfund: Fund created by the Comprehensive Environmental Response, Compensation and Liability Act of 1980 to provide compensation for damage from spillage of oil and other substances. 42 U.S.C. §§ 9601–7.

Superpriority: Special priority for the claim of a secured creditor in the distribution of the property of a bankrupt estate, to the extent that "adequate protection" has not been provided by the trustee of the estate. 11 U.S.C. § 507(b).

Supertanker: Very large crude carrier, a tank vessel of 200,000 deadweight tons or more.

Supplementary earnings per share: Computation of earnings per share, other than primary or fully diluted earnings per share, that gives effect to conversions that took place during the period or shortly thereafter as though they had occurred at the beginning of the period (or date of issuance, if later). American Institute of Certified Public Accountants, Accounting Principles Board Opinion No. 15, *Earnings per Share,* Appendix D (1968).

Surety: One who undertakes to fulfill an obligation for another if that person fails to do so. Surety and guarantor are nearly synonymous; if there is a distinction, it is that a surety joins in the obligation of the principal from the outset and in the same instrument, while a guarantor provides its undertakings in a separate instrument. Under the Uniform Commercial Code, the term "surety" includes "guarantor." UCC Section 1-201(40).

Surety bond: Bond or guaranty given by a surety.

Surface Mining Reclamation and Enforcement, Office of: Unit of the United States Department of the Interior established by the Surface Mining Control and Reclamation Act of 1977, Pub. L. No. 95-87, 91 Stat. 445 (1977), 30 U.S.C. §§ 1201–1328. The OSM develops standards for regulating the surface effects of coal mining, assists the states in developing regulatory programs, and administers the Abandoned Mine Fund, a fund created by a tax on coal mining used to reclaim and restore land and water resources damaged by past coal mining.

Surplus: Excess of net assets of a corporation over its stated capital. Model Business Corporation Act § 2(k) (1979); N. Y. Bus. Corp. Law §§ 102(a)(13), 517; Del. Code Ann. Tit. 8 § 154. See **earned surplus**.

Suspends payments: Under Article 4–Bank Deposits and Collections of the Uniform Commercial Code, "suspends payments" with respect to a bank means that the bank "has been closed by order of the supervisory authorities, that a public officer has been appointed to take it over or that it ceases or refuses to make payments in the ordinary course of business." UCC Section 4-104(1)(k).

Swap: 1. Trade of bankers' acceptances acquired by a drawee bank for acceptances drawn on other banks. 2. Tax-free exchange of property under section 1031 of the Internal Revenue Code. 3. Simultaneous purchase and sale of foreign currency for different delivery periods, usually one transaction for immediate delivery and the other for future delivery, in order to eliminate foreign exchange risk.

Swap arrangements: Arrangement among the Federal Reserve and certain foreign central banks and the Bank of International Settlements for short-term reciprocal lines of credit. Through swap arrangements, the Federal Reserve can borrow foreign currency to buy dollars in the foreign exchange market, and can provide dollars to foreign central banks.

Swing loan: Bridge loan; loan to provide funds for the purchase of property, to be repaid out of the sale of other property shortly thereafter.

SWU: Separative work unit, a measure of energy that takes into account the energy needed to produce that energy.

Sympathy strike: Strike in sympathy with employees of another employer. *See* section 7 of the National Labor Relations Act, 29 U.S.C. § 57.

Syndicate: Group of investment bankers formed to underwrite a given issue of securities, or group of banks involved in a Eurobond issue.

Synthetic Fuels Corporation: Corporation established pursuant to Title I of the Energy Security Act to provide financial assistance to bring about commercial production of synthetic fuel. Pub. L. No. 96-294, 94 Stat. 611, 633 (1980); 42 U.S.C. §§8701—8795. *See generally* Pozen, *Synthetic Fuels Corporation, Investment Bank or Government Agency?* 36 Bus. Law. 953 (1981).

T

TAB: Tax-anticipation bill.

Taft-Hartley Act: Labor-Management Relations Act, 1947.

Tail: Difference between the average price at an auction for United States Treasury securities and the lowest price (the stop-out price) accepted by the Treasury on a given issue.

Take-and-pay contract: Agreement to purchase a specified minimum quantity of a product or service over a specified period of time. The obligation under a take-and-pay contract is conditioned upon the provision of the product or service, unlike a take-or-pay contract.

Take-or-pay contract: Agreement to make periodic payments of a certain amount over specified period of time; such payments are designated as the price for delivery of a service or product over the period of the obligation, but the payments must be made whether or not the service is provided or the product furnished. This unconditional obligation can be used as the basis for financing the project used to provide the service or furnish the product. See Financial Accounting Standards Board, Statement of Financial Accounting Standards No. 47, *Disclosure of Long-Term Obligations,* Appendix B (1981).

Take-out commitment: Commitment by a lending institution to furnish long-term financing, and "take out" of the financing an interim lender or a construction lender.

TAN: Tax anticipation note.

Tandem stock option: Two stock options, issued together, in which the exercise of one affects the right to exercise the other. See incentive stock option.

Tangible expenses: Expenses incurred in the development of a mineral project that are capitalized and subject to depreciation and depletion. Compare intangible expenses.

Targeted jobs credit: Credit against federal income tax for a portion of wages paid to certain economically disadvantaged employees. I.R.C. § 51; *see* section 233 of the Tax Equity and Fiscal Responsibility Act of 1982.

Targeted Outreach Program: Federal program, administered by the Department of Labor, to assist young persons, mainly members of minority groups, to qualify for and obtain jobs in skilled trades.

Tariff: 1. Schedule of taxes levied upon goods moving across international borders, usually by the importing nation, or one of such taxes. 2. Schedule of rates and charges for transportation, usually filed by the transportation company with a regulatory agency.

Taxable income: For a corporation, gross income minus the deductions allowed by the Internal Revenue Code. I.R.C. § 63(a). *See* American Institute of Certified Public Accountants, Accounting Principles Board Opinion No. 11, *Accounting for Income Taxes,* paragraph 12d (1967).

Taxable year: The calendar year, or the fiscal year ended during such calendar year, upon the basis of which taxable income is calculated for federal income taxes. I.R.C. § 7701(a)(23). *See* Treas. Reg. 1.441-1(b).

Tax-anticipation bill: Form of Treasury bill designed to smooth out the uneven flow of tax receipts while providing corporations with an attractive investment for funds accumulated for tax payments. Tax anticipation bills usually mature a week after tax due dates, but are accepted at par for payment of tax liability. *See* Nelson, *Tax Anticipation Bills,* in T. Cook, ed., *Instruments of the Money Market* 21 (4th ed., 1977).

Tax-anticipation note: Short-term security issued by a municipality to cover cash needs pending receipt of tax revenues.

Tax benefit transfer: Form of sale and leaseback transaction, sanctioned by I.R.C. § 168(f)(8) (added by the Economic Recovery Tax Act of 1981), in which the lessee transfers the tax attributes of equipment to a lessor in consideration of cash and a purchase money note. The lessor then leases the equipment back to the lessee under a lease in which the rentals exactly equal the obligations under the note. Thus no money changes hands after the initial cash payment to the lessee by the lessor, and the transaction, although styled a lease, is tantamount of a sale of the investment credit and accelerated cost recovery deductions with respect to the equipment by the lessee to the lessor. These transactions are used in situations where the lessee has insufficient tax liability to fully utilize the tax benefits of equipment ownership. The economic benefits of tax benefit transfers were significantly reduced by the Tax Equity and Fiscal Reponsibility Act of 1982, and such transactions will not be sanctioned after December 31, 1983. See **safe harbor lease.**

Tax Court, United States: Federal court, located in Washington, D.C., with jurisdiction to decide controversies involving income, estate, gift, and personal holding company taxes, to redetermine excise taxes and penalties imposed on private foundations, to render declaratory judgments relating to the qualification of pension plans, and to make certain other determinations relating to tax matters.

Tax Division: Division of the United States Department of Justice that represents the United States and its officers in all civil and criminal cases arising under the internal revenue laws, except cases in the United States Tax Court.

Tax Equity and Fiscal Responsibility Act of 1982: Federal legislation intended to produce additional revenue through tax increases and reform measures and reductions in federal spending. Pub. L. No. 97-248, 96 Stat. 324 (1982). *See* S. Rep. No. 97-494, 97th Cong., 2d Sess. (1982); H.R. Rep. No. 97-404, 97th Cong., 2d Sess. (1981); H.R. Rep. No. 97-760, 97th Cong., 2d Sess. (1982).

Tax-exempt debt: Obligation of a government entity on which the interest income is not subject to federal income taxes. *See* I.R.C. § 103.

Tax lien: Lien imposed on a taxpayer's property to secure the payment of taxes. Liens may be imposed by action of tax authorities, as in the case of federal income taxes, or may be automatic after a certain period, as in the case of local real estate taxes. See **federal tax lien.**

Tax-option corporation: Subchapter S corporation.

Taxpayer: For the purpose of the Internal Revenue Code, "any person subject to any internal revenue tax." I.R.C. § 7701(a)(14). *See also* I.R.C. § 1313(b).

Tax preference: For the purpose of the add-on minimum tax provided by section 56 of the Internal Revenue Code, "items of tax preference" for corporations include the excess of accelerated depreciation over straight-line depreciation on depreciable real property (I.R.C. § 57(a)(2)), the excess of accelerated depreciation over straight-line depreciation on leased personal property that is not recovery property (I.R.C. § 57(a)(3)), the excess of percentage depletion over the property's adjusted basis (I.R.C. § 57(a)(8)), the excess of rapid amortization over ordinary methods of depreciation (I.R.C. § 57(a)(4), (5), and (10)), the excess of the fair market value of stock received under a qualified or restricted stock option plan over the option price (I.R.C. § 57(a)(6)), excess intangible drilling costs (I.R.C. § 57(a)(11)), and the excess of accelerated cost recovery deductions over straight-line depreciation (I.R.C. § 57(a)(12)). *See* I.R.C. § 57 (b); section 204(b) of the Tax Equity and Fiscal Responsibility Act of 1982.

Tax Reform Act of 1976: Amendment to the Internal Revenue Code. Pub. L. No. 94-455, 90 Stat. 1520 (1976).

Tax shelter: Investment, a significant part of the yield of which is due to savings on taxes on other income, or a delay in the payment of taxes.

T-bill: Treasury bill.

TBT: Tax benefit transfer.

T.D.: Treasury Decisions.

Technical Corrections Act of 1979: Legislation, ostensibly to correct technical problems with the Revenue Act of 1978, but with some new changes in tax law. Pub. L. No. 96-222, 94 Stat. 194 (1980). *See* S. Rep. No. 96-498, 96th Cong., 2d Sess.(1979).

Technology Assessment, Office of: Agency of the United States Congress that provides congressional committees with assessments and studies that identify the social and physical consequences expected to accompany various policy choices affecting the use of technologies. *See* Technology Assessment Act of 1972, Pub. L. No. 92-484, 86 Stat. 797 (1972), 2 U.S.C. §§ 471–81.

TEFRA: Tax Equity and Fiscal Responsibility Act of 1982.

Telegram: Strictly, a communication by telegraph. The Uniform Commercial Code uses a broader definition, however, and includes "a message transmitted by radio, teletype, cable, any mechanical method of transmission, or the like." UCC Section 1-201(41).

Temporal method: Method of translating assets and liabilities measured in foreign currency that translates cash, receivables and payables, and assets and liabilities carried at present or future prices at the current rate and assets and liabilities carried at past prices at the applicable historical rates. Financial Accounting Standards Board, Statement of Financial Accounting Standards No. 8, *Accounting for the Translation of Foreign Currency Transactions and Foreign Currency Financial Statements,* paragraphs 121, 123-125 (1975).

Temporary restraining order: Injunctive relief granted without notice to an opposing party in circumstances in which "immediate and irreparable injury, loss, or damage will result to the applicant before the adverse party or his attorney can be heard in opposition... ." Fed. R. Civ. Proc. 65(b).

Ten-day rule: Rule of the New York Stock Exchange that a broker may vote the proxies of customers's stock held in the broker's street name if the broker requests voting instructions and does not receive them by a specified time before the meeting. New York Stock Exchange Rule 451, 452. The American Stock Exchange has similar rules.

Tender of delivery: Performance of a contract of sale by the seller; under Article 2 of the Uniform Commercial Code–Sales, "tender of delivery" requires that the seller "put and hold conforming goods at the buyer's disposition and give the buyer any notification reasonably necessary to enable him to take delivery." UCC Section 2-503. *See also* UCC Sections 2-504, 2-507.

Tender offer: Invitation to holders of certain securities to tender the same at a certain price for cash. The term is not defined in the securities laws, and the Securities and Exchange Commission has declined to offer a definition as to what extent of stock acquisition constitutes a "tender offer" that requires disclosure by filing a Schedule 13D under the Securities Exchange Act of 1934. *See* section 13(d) of the Securities Exchange Act of 1934, 15 U.S.C. 78m(d); 17 C.F.R. 240.13d. *See generally* M. Lipton & E. Steinberger,

Takeovers and Freezouts (1978); E. Aranow, H. Einhorn & G. Berlstein, *Developments in Tender Offers for Corporate Control* (1977); Einhorn & Blackburn, *The Developing Concept of "Tender Offer": An Analysis of the Judicial and Administrative Interpretations of the Term,* 23 N.Y.L.S. L. Rev. 379 (1978); Lipton, *Open Market Purchases,* 32 Bus. Law. 1321 (1977); Note, *The Developing Meaning of "Tender Offer" under the Securities Exchange Act of 1934,* 86 Harv. L. Rev. 1250 (1973). See also **creeping tender offer;** compare **exchange offer.**

Term: As a portion of a promise, agreement, or contract:

(1) A term of a promise or agreement is that portion of the intention or assent manifested which relates to a particular matter.

(2) A term of a contract is that portion of the legal relations resulting from the promise or set of promises which relates to a particular matter, whether or not the parties manifest an intention to create those relations.

Restatement, Second, Contracts § 5 (1981). The second clause refers to contract terms supplied by law as well as terms agreed to by the parties. For the purposes of the Uniform Commercial Code, term means "that portion of an agreement which relates to a particular matter." UCC Section 1-201(42).

Term CD: Certificate of deposit with a term of greater than one year.

Termination: Under Article 2 of the Uniform Commercial Code–Sales, "termination" of a contract for the sale of goods "occurs when either party pursuant to a power created by agreement or law puts an end to the contract otherwise than for its breach. On 'termination' all obligations which are still executory on both sides are discharged but any rights based on prior breach or performance survives." UCC Section 2-106(3). See **cancellation.**

Termination statement: Statement filed by a secured party, in the same public office as a financing statement, to the effect that the secured party no longer claims a security interest under the financing statement referred to in the termination statement. UCC Section 9-404. Like a financing statement, a termination statement is usually in a special form approved by the secretary of state of the state in question.

Term loan: Loan made by a bank for a term of more than 90 days.

Term RP: Repurchase agreement for a period longer than overnight.

Territorial restriction: Restriction imposed by a supplier and its dealers on the geographic area in which goods may be sold by individual dealers. *See Continental TV, Inc. v. GTE Sylvania, Inc.,* 433 U.S. 36 (1977); *United States v. Arnold, Schwinn & Co.,* 388 U.S. 365 (1967). *See generally* Weisberg, *Continental TV v. GTE Sylvania: Implications for Horizontal, as Well as Vertical Restraints on Distributors,* 33 Bus. Law. 1757 (1978). As to territorial restrictions in international licensing, see Adelman & Brooks, *Territorial Restraints in International Technology Agree-*

ments after Topco, 17 Antitrust Bull. 763 (1968). See also **vertical restraint.**

TEU: Twenty-foot equivalent unit, a measure of the capacity of container ships and container handling equipment. Containers are approximately eight feet high and wide, and twenty, thirty, forty, or forty-five feet long. A TEU is the equivalent of twenty-foot long container.

Texas Gulf Sulphur: *SEC v. Texas Gulf Sulphur Co.,* 401 F. 2d 833 (2d Cir. 1968), *cert. denied sub nom. Coates v. SEC,* 394 U.S. 976 (1969); significant case regarding disclosure of information affecting securities and rule 10b-5 under the Securities Exchange Act of 1934. See **material.**

Thin capitalization: Capitalization of a corporation with relatively low equity capital, buttressed by loans from the stockholders. If the equity capitalization is "thin"—insufficient for the needs of the business—the stockholder loans will be treated as additional equity, and interest will be taxed as dividends. *See, e.g., Kelley v. Commissioner,* 326 U.S. 521 (1946). See also **Deep Rock doctrine.**

Third party: Party not joining in the contract in question as signatory party

Third party beneficiary: Third party with rights under a contract, even though it has not joined in as a signatory party. See **intended beneficiary.**

Three-name paper: Market instrument with three obligors. A banker's acceptance can become three-name paper if sold by a bank that is not the original drawer or the drawee, because such an acceptance represents the obligation of the drawee bank which has accepted it, the drawer who has endorsed it upon negotiation, and the selling bank which also has endorsed it.

Three R act: Regional Rail Reorganization Act of 1973.

Thrift institution: Financial institution organized primarily to accept and reinvest deposits of personal savings. Mutual savings banks, savings and loan associations, and credit unions are lumped in the general term "thrift institutions."

Through bill; through bill of lading: Bill of lading embodying undertakings to be performed in part by persons as a agents of the issuer or by connecting carriers. *See* UCC Section 7-302, 49 U.S.C. § 11707.

Throughput and deficiency agreement: Agreement entered into between a pipeline company and a group of shippers of the commodity (usually oil) whereby the shippers agree to make certain minimum periodic shipments through the pipeline and pay the set tariff. If at the end of a given period the pipeline company has insufficient cash to meet its expenses and debt obligations, each shipper must make up the deficiency pro rata in accordance with its shipping commitments. Each shipper making such payment receives a credit therefor on the books of the pipeline company for advance payment for shipments, and the tariffs are then adjusted to consume this advance in future shipments. Throughput and deficiency obligations entered into by creditworthy shippers are often used as the basis for financing a pipeline project; the unconditional nature of these obligations satisfies lending institutions, but these obligations have not been regarded as balance sheet items for the shipper. *See generally* Financial Accounting Standards Board, Statement of Financial Accounting Standards No. 47, *Disclosure of Long-Term Obligations* (1981).

Throughput contract: As defined by the Financial Accounting Standards Board:

An agreement between a shipper (processor) and the owner of a transportation facility (such as an oil or natural gas pipeline or a ship) or a manufacturing facility that provides for the shipper (processor) to pay specified amounts periodically in return for the transportation (processing) of a product. The shipper (processor) is obligated to provide specified minimum quantities to be transported (processed) in each period and is required to make cash payments even if it does not provide the contracted quantities.

Financial Accounting Standards Board, Statement of Financial Accounting Standards No. 47, *Disclosure of Long-Term Obligations,* Appendix B (1981). See also **throughput and deficiency agreement.**

TIA: Trust Indenture Act of 1939.

T.I.A.S.: Treaties and Other International Acts Series, pamphlets published by the United States Department of State.

Tie-in: See **tying arrangement.**

TIGR: Treasury investment growth receipt; an interest in a fund of zero-coupon Treasury bonds of a certain maturity (the zero-coupon bonds are stripped regular bonds or their coupons–see **stripper bonds**). Also called CATS, Certificates of Accrual on Treasury Securities, depending on the investment banking house that arranges the issue.

Time charter: Charter for the services of a vessel for a fixed period of time. The vessel owner provides the crew and operates the vessel for voyages specified by the charterer. See also **voyage charter; bare-boat charter.**

Time deposit: Deposit with a bank for specified minimum period, or for which a notice period is provided for withdrawal.

Time of issuance: In accounting for the effect of convertible securities on earnings per share, the "time of issuance generally is the date when agreement as to terms has been reached and announced, even though such agreement is subject to certain further actions, such as directors' or shareholders' approval." American Institute of Certified Public Accountants, Accounting Principles Board Opinion No. 15, *Earnings per Share,* Appendix D (1968).

Time order: Order for the purchase or sale of securities for execution at a specified time. A time order may be a market order, for execution at the market, or may be limited as to price.

Time-price doctrine: Doctrine that an installment sale with a higher price for deferred payments than for immediate payment in full does not violate usury laws, however great the difference between the two prices. *Verbeck v. Clymer,* 202 Cal. 557, 261 P. 1017 (1927).

Timing differences: Differences between taxable income and pretax accounting income for a period that arise because the period in which some items of revenue and expense are included in taxable income does not coincide with the period in which they are included in accounting income. Timing differences are offset by corresponding and opposite differences in other periods. International Accounting Standards Committee, Statement of International Accounting Standards 12, *Accounting for Taxes on Income,* paragraph 5 (1979); *see* American Institute of Certified Public Accountants, Accounting Principles Board Opinion No. 11, *Accounting for Income Taxes,* paragraph 12e (1967); American Institute of Certified Public Accountants, Accounting for Income Taxes, *Accounting Interpretation of APB Opinion No. 11,* paragraphs 35—47 (1969). Compare **permanent differences.**

TIN: Taxpayer identification number.

Tippee: Person who receives a tip; usually used in connection with the receipt of information affecting corporate securities that is not available to the public. *See SEC v. Texas Gulf Sulphur Co.,* 401 F. 2d 833 (2d Cir. 1968), *cert. denied sub nom. Coates v. SEC,* 394 U.S. 976 (1969).

Title: 1. Name by which anything is known. 2. Evidence of ownership of property. The concept of title has only limited meaning for personal property since the near-universal adoption of the Uniform Commercial Code, because the rights of parties in personal property will be determined from circumstances other than the recited location of title. Motor vehicles, however, have documents of title under most state laws, providing evidence of ownership. *See* UCC Section 2-401.

Title insurance: Insurance against loss due to defects in the title to property.

Title XI: Title XI of the Merchant Marine Act, 1936, added in 1938 to provide a system of federal guaranties for the financing of vessel construction. *See* Pub. L. No. 705, ch. 600, 52 Stat. 953, 969 (1938); 46 U.S.C. § 1271–79. *See generally* Cook, Jr., *Government Assistance in Financing, Title XI Federal Guarantees,* 47 Tul. L. Rev. 653 (1973).

T.M.: Technical Memorandum, a publication of the Internal Revenue Service.

To arrive: Delivery term in a contract for the sale of goods that means the same as "no arrival, no sale" in a contract calling for delivery to the buyer, but in a C.I.F. or C.& F. contract, the term "to arrive" operates to relieve the seller of the duty to deliver goods only to the extent that any loss is not covered by the insurance required by the contract. UCC Section 2-324, Official Comment, Point 4.

TOFC: Trailer on flat car.

Tolling contract: Take or pay contract.

Tombstone: Newspaper advertisement announcing an offer of securities. Such advertisements must be carefully constructed so as not to constitute a prospectus or an offer, and thus contain only certain basic information, arranged in a conservative fashion that resembles the text on a tombstone. *See* section 2(10) of the Securities Act of 1933, 15 U.S.C. § 77B(10). See also prospectus.

Tom next: Tomorrow next; two days hence. Used in connection with transactions in Eurodollar deposits and foreign exchange transactions in which the value date is two days after the transaction has been agreed upon.

TOP: Targeted Outreach Program.

Toxic Substances Control Act: Federal legislation regulating the environmental aspects of the manufacture and use of chemical substances. Pub. L. No. 94-469, 90 Stat. 2003 (1976); 15 U.S.C. §§ 2601–29. *See* S. Rep. No. 94-698, 94th Cong., 2d Sess. (1976); H.R. Rep. No. 94-1341, 94th Cong. 2d Sess. (1976). *See generally* Zener, *The Toxic Substances Control Act, Federal Regulation of Commercial Chemicals,* 32 Bus. Law. 1685 (1977).

Trade acceptance: Draft drawn by an exporter on an importer which has been accepted by that importer.

Trade discount: Discount offered for prompt payment of bills.

Trademark: In the narrow, technical sense, a trademark is a "word, name, symbol, or device or any combination thereof adopted and used by a manufacturer or merchant to identify his goods and distinguish them from those manufactured or sold by others." 15 U.S.C. § 1127. In a broader sense, the term includes service marks, certification marks, and collective marks, as well as "true" trademarks. *See generally,* 1 McCarthy, *Trademarks and Unfair Competition* § 3.2 (1973); Diamond, *Untangling the Confusion in Trademark Terminology,* 78 Pat. & T.M. Rev. 197 (1980).

Trade name: The terms "trade name" and "commercial name" include:

individual names and surnames, firm names and trade names used by manufacturers, industrialists, merchants, agriculturists, and others to identify their businesses, vocations, or occupations; the names or titles lawfully adopted and used by persons, firms, associations, corporations, companies, unions, and any manufacturing, industrial, commercial, agricultural, or other organizations engaged in trade or commerce and capable of suing and being sued in a court of law.

15 U.S.C. § 1127.

Trade Regulation Rule: Rule promulgated by the Federal Trade Commission defining "with specificity acts or practices which are unfair or deceptive acts or practices in or affecting commerce." 16 C.F.R. § 1.8. *See* Section 18 of the Federal Trade Commission Act, 15 U.S.C. § 57a. *See also National Petroleum Refiners Association v. FTC,* 482 F. 2d 672 (D.C. Cir. 1973), *cert. denied,* 415 U.S. 951 (1974).

Trade secret: As defined in the comments to the Restatement of Torts:

A trade secret may consist of any formula, pattern, device or compilation of information which is used in one's business, and which gives him an opportunity to obtain an advantage over competitors who do not know or use it. It may be a formula for a chemical compound, a process of manufacturing, treating or preserving materials, a pattern for a machine or other device, or a list of customers. It differs from other secret information in a business in that it is not simply information as to single or ephemeral events in the conduct of business, as, for example, the amount or other terms of a secret bid for a contract. . . . A trade secret is a process or device for the continuous use in the operation of the business. Generally it relates to the production of goods, as, for example, a machine or formula for the production of an article. It may, however, relate to the sale of goods or to other operations in the business, such as a code for determining discounts, rebates or other concessions in a price list or catalogue, or a list of specialized customers, or a method of bookkeeping or other office management.

Restatement, Torts § 757, comment (b) (1939). *See Aronson v. Quick Point Pencil Co.*, 440 U.S. 257, 266 (1979); 1 Milgrim, *Trade Secrets* § 2.09 (1980). A more succinct, and perhaps narrower, definition was used in the context of the Freedom of Information Act exemption for trade secrets in *Consumers Union of United States, Inc., v. Veterans Administration*, 301 F. Supp. 796, 801 (S.D.N.Y. 1969): "an unpatented, secret, commercially valuable plan, appliance, formula, or process, which is used for the making, preparing, compounding, treating, or processing of articles or materials which are trade commodities."

Trade Secrets Act: Provision of federal law prohibiting United States government employees from disclosing trade secrets of private persons and corporations obtained in investigations or from reports. 18 U.S.C. § 1905. *See* H.R. Rep. No. 880, Pt. I, 94th Cong., 2d Sess. 23 (1976).

Transacting business: See doing business.

Transaction: As defined by the Financial Accounting Standards Board:

A transaction is a particular kind of external event, namely, an external event involving transfer of something of value (future economic benefit) between two (or more) entities. The transaction may be an exchange in which each participant both receives and sacrifices value, such as purchases or sales of goods or services; or the transaction may be a nonreciprocal transfer in which an entity incurs a liability or transfers an asset to another entity (or receives an asset or cancellation of a liability) without directly receiving (or giving) value in exchange. Nonreciprocal transfers contrast with exchanges, which are reciprocal transfers, and include, for example, investments by owners, distributions to owners, impositions of taxes, gifts, charitable contributions, and thefts.

Financial Accounting Standards Board, Statement of Financial Accounting Concepts No. 3, *Elements of Financial Statements of Business Enterprises*, paragraph 77 (1980).

Transfer: For the purpose of the Bankruptcy Code, "transfer" is defined broadly as "every mode, direct or indirect, absolute or conditional, voluntary or involuntary, of disposing of or parting with property or with an interest in property, including retention of title as a security interest." 11 U.S.C. § 101(40); *see* H.R. Rep. No. 95-595, 95th Cong., 1st Sess. 314 (1977).

Transferable credit; transferable letter of credit: Letter of credit under which the beneficiary can transfer its rights to draw on the credit to a party who can substitute its own performance for that of the beneficiary. *See* UCC Section 5-116.

Transfer agent: Agent of a corporation empowered to handle transfers of securities of a given issue; registrar. The term is defined in section 3(a)(25) of the Securities Act of 1934:

The term "transfer agent" means any person who engages on behalf of an issuer of securities or on behalf of itself as issuer of securities in (A) countersigning such securities upon issuance; (B) monitoring the issuance of such securities with a view to preventing unauthorized issuance, a function commonly performed by a person called a registrar; (C) registering the transfer of such securities; (D) exchanging or converting such securities; or (E) transferring record ownership of securities by bookkeeping entry without physical issuance of securities certificates. The term "transfer agent" does not include any insurance company or separate account which performs such functions solely with respect to variable annuity contracts or variable life policies which it issues or any registered clearing agency which performs such functions solely with respect to options contracts which it issues.

15 U.S.C. § 78c(a)(25).

Transfer statutes: Sections 9 and 37 of the Shipping Act, 1916, which prohibit transfer of an interest in a vessel documented under the laws of the United States to a person not a citizen without the approval of the Maritime Commission. 46 U.S.C.§§ 808, 835. *See* McDonald, *Documentation and Transfer of Vessels; Transfer of United States Vessels to Aliens,* 47 Tul. L. Rev. 511 (1973).

Translation: With respect to foreign currency, the process of expressing amounts denominated or measured in one currency in terms of another currency by use of the exchange rate. Financial Accounting Standards Board, Statement of Financial Accounting Standards No. 8, *Accounting for the Translation of Foreign Currency Transactions and Foreign Currency Financial Statements,* Appendix E (1975). *See* Brooks, *Currency Translations in the Registration Statements of Foreign Issuers,* 35 Bus. Law. 435 (1980).

Transmitting utility: Under Article 9 of the Uniform Commercial Code–Secured Transactions, a transmitting utility is "any person primarily engaged in the railroad, street railway or trolley bus business, the electric or electronics communication transmission business, the transmission of goods by pipeline, or the transmission or the production and transmission of electricity, steam, gas or water, or the provision of sewer service." UCC Section 9-105(1)(n). The Uniform Commercial Code has special rules for the filing of financing statements and continuation statements against transmitting utilities. *See* UCC Sections 9-401, 9-403.

Transportation: Under the United States Transportation Code, the successor to the Interstate Commerce Act, the term "transportation" includes:

(A) a locomotive, car, vehicle, motor vehicle, vessel, warehouse, wharf, pier, dock, yard, property, facility, instrumentality, or equipment of any kind related to the movement of passengers or property, or both, regardless of ownership or an agreement concerning use; and

(B) services related to that movement, including receipt, delivery, elevation, transfer in transit, refrigeration, icing, ventilation, storage, handling, and interchange of passengers and property.

49 U.S.C. 10103(23).

Transportation, United States Department of: Cabinet-level department of the executive branch established to coordinate the activities of the various executive branch programs for the separate transportation modes, and to develop national transportation policies. Units of DOT include the United States Coast Guard, the Federal Aviation Administration, the Federal Highway Administration, the Federal Railroad Administration, the National Highway Traffic Safety Administration, the Urban Mass Transportation Administration, and the Materials Transportation Bureau. *See* Department of Transportation Act, Pub. L. No. 89-670, 80 Stat. 931 (1966), 49 U.S.C. §§ 1651–59.

Transportation Code: Title 49 of the United States Code, covering ground transportation. The Interstate Commerce Act has been revised and has become part of the Transportation Code, but other federal statutes relating to ground transportation await codification.

Transportation contract: Long-term contract for transportation by vessel, having certain characteristics of take-or-pay contracts and throughput and deficiency agreements. Because such contracts are unconditional, they can be used to support the financing of the vessel.

TRASOP: Tax Reduction Act Stock Ownership Plan.

Treas. Reg.: Treasury Regulations; regulations of the United States Department of the Treasury, for the most part regarding taxes. Treasury regulations in respect of the Internal Revenue Code are numbered the same as the code sections, preceded by "1."; thus Treas. Reg. § 1.167 relates to I.R.C. § 167.

Treasurer's check: Check issued by a bank.

Treasury, United States Department of the: Cabinet-level department of the executive branch of the United States government responsible for the fiscal operations of the government and certain law enforcement functions. *See* 31 U.S.C. §§ 1001–37.

Treasury bill: Short-term obligation of the United States issued by the Treasury. Treasury bills are issued in minimum denominations of $10,000, and usually have initial maturities of three, six, or twelve months. Treasury bills are issued and sold at prices lower than the face value, so that the yield to the investor is the difference between the amount received when the bills mature or are sold and the price paid. Treasury bills are evidenced by a book entry and receipt, not an actual certificate. *See* Monhollon, *Treasury Bills,* in T. Cook, ed., *Instruments of the Money Market* 13 (4th ed., 1977).

Treasury bond: Obligation of the United States issued by the Treasury, with a maturity of more than ten years. Bonds pay interest semi-annually, with the principal payable at maturity. Treasury bonds are issued in registered or bearer form.

Treasury note: Obligation of the United States issued by the Treasury, with medium-term maturity (between one and ten years). Notes pay interest semi-annually, with the principal payable at maturity. Treasury notes are issued in registered or bearer form.

Treasury securities: Obligations of the United States issued by the Treasury as a means of borrowing money to meet government expenditures not covered by tax revenues. Treasury securities are categorized as bills, notes, or bonds, depending on the date of maturity.

Treasury share; treasury stock: Shares of a corporation that have been issued, subsequently acquired by the corporation, and have not been cancelled. Treasury shares are deemed to be "issued" shares, but not "outstanding" shares. Model Business Corporation Act § 2(h) (1979); N.Y. Bus. Corp. Law. § 102(a)(14). *See* Del. Code Ann. Tit. 8 §§ 160, 243.

Treasury stock method: In accounting for earnings per share, the "treasury stock method" is "A method of recognizing the use of proceeds that would be obtained upon exercise of options and warrants in computing earnings per share. It assumes that any proceeds would be used to purchase common stock at current market prices." American Institute of Certified Public Accountants, Accounting Principles Board Opinion No. 15, *Earnings per Share,* Appendix D (1968).

Triangular reorganization: Reorganization in which a corporation creates a wholly-owned subsidiary which is used to acquire shares in a third corporation by exchanging its own shares or the shares of the parent. The acquired corporation can then be liquidated with its assets going to the subsidiary, or the acquired corporation can survive as a second-tier subsidiary. *See* Stutsman, Jr., *Triangular Mergers,* 50 Taxes 820 (1972).

TRO: Temporary restraining order.

True lease: Instrument styled as a lease that really is a lease; lease in which the nominal lessor is regarded as the actual owner of the leased property for the purpose of establishing the right to tax benefits or possession. Many instruments, styled as leases, are not regarded as true leases because the lessee has rights under the instrument more consistent with ownership than with a leasehold interest, and the interest of the lessor is more consistent with that of a secured party. See **security interest; lease for security.**

Trust: Right in property held by one for the benefit of another.

Trust deed: Instrument creating an interest in property to secure a loan or other obligation, similar to a mortgage.

Trustee: Party appointed to administer a trust, or who owns property, not for its own account, but for the benefit of another.

Trust indenture: Instrument, entered into by an issuer of debt securities and a corporate trustee, under which the trustee acts for the holders of the securities. A trust indenture will contain provisions relating to the duties of the trustee, the issuance and reissuance of the securities, and the handling of payments made by the issuer of the securities. Often the trust indenture will be combined with a security agreement or mortgage (mortgage indenture), the trustee holding the rights in the collateral for the benefit of the holders of the securities. A trust indenture used in an issue of securities registered under the Securities Act of 1933 must comply with the requirements of the Trust Indenture Act of 1939. *See* American Bar Foundation, Corporate Debt Financing Committee, *Commentaries on Model Debenture Indenture Provisions, 1965; Model Debenture Indenture Provisions, All Registered Issues, 1967; and Certain Negotiable Provisions Which May Be Included in a Particular Incorporating Indenture* (1971); Rodgers, *The Corporate Trust Indenture Project,* 20 Bus. Law. 551 (1965). For a mortgage indenture, see American Bar Foundation, *Mortgage Bond Indenture Form* (1981). Trust indentures are typically lengthy and cumbersome documents; for a proposed simplified form that has the blessing of the SEC staff, see McDaniel, *A Simplified Indenture,* 13 Rev. of Securities Reg. 871 (1980);

SEC Release 33-6279 (1981). See also indenture.

Trust Indenture Act of 1939. Federal legislation requiring trust indentures used in connection with an offering of securities registered under the Securities Act of 1933 to have certain provisions. Pub. L. No. 253, ch. 411, 53 Stat. 1149 (1939); 15 U.S.C. § 77aaa–bbbb.

Trust plate: Plate attached to a railroad locomotive indicating the existence of an interest in that locomotive to secure a financial obligation. Trust plates are sometimes used on other types of railroad rolling stock, but a painted stencil is more common. The term came about because railroad equipment is often financed by means of an equipment trust, and under old state recording statutes that were relied upon before the advent of federal recording provisions for interests in railroad equipment (49 U.S.C. § 11303), marking of each unit by the use of plate or other means showing the name of the trustee was necessary. *E.g.,* Cal. Pub. Util. Code § 7578.

TSCA: Toxic Substances Control Act.

Tunney Act: Antitrust Procedures and Penalties Act.

Turnkey contract: Contract for the construction of a complete plant or facility, with all equipment, ready for operation. In the United States a "turnkey" contract usually includes the construction of the building, but in Europe the purchaser may supply the building to the contractor's specifications, with the contractor supplying and installing the remaining facilities and equipment needed to make the plant operational.

Two-class method: Method of calculating earnings per share that treats common stock equivalents as though they were common stocks with different dividend rates. American Institute of Certified Public Accountants, Accounting Principles Board Opinion No. 15, *Earnings per Share*, Appendix D (1968).

Two-name paper: Market instrument with two obligors. An example is a bankers' acceptance, representing the obligation of the drawee bank which has accepted it, and the drawer, who endorses the acceptance when he sells it.

Twyne's case: Old English case holding that a transfer of ownership without transfer of possession was void as against creditors of the transferor. *Twyne's case* is the basis of the common law prejudice against nonpossessory interests in personal property. 3 Co. Rep. 80b, 76 Eng. Rep. 809 (Star Chamber, 1601).

Tying arrangement: Arrangement whereby a seller conditions the sale of a product or service on the buyer's purchase of another product or service. Tying arrangements usually violate section 1 of the Sherman Act (15 U.S.C. § 1). *See, e.g., Times-Picayune Publishing Co. v. United States*, 345 U.S. 594 (1953). *See generally* American Bar Association, Section of Antitrust Law, *Antitrust Law Developments* 38 (1975); Bauer, *A Simplified Approach to Tying Arrangements: A Legal and Economic Analysis*, 33 V and. L. Rev. 283 (1980).

U

UCC: Uniform Commercial Code.

UCC-1: Designation used in many states for the form of financing statement for filing under the Uniform Commercial Code. UCC Section 9-402. See financing statement.

UCC-3: Designation used in many states for the form for filing of continuation statement, termination statement, assignment of security interest, amendment of financing statement, and release under the Uniform Commercial Code. UCC Sections 9-402, 9-403, 9-404, 9-405. See financing statement.

UCP: Uniform Customs and Practice for Documentary Credits, a publication of the International Chamber of Commerce regarding letters of credit.

ULCC: Ultra large crude carrier; tank vessel of 400,000 deadweight tons or more.

Ultimate facts; ultimate finding: Finding of a court in a given case expressed as a conclusion of law or a mixed conclusion of fact and law. The ultimate finding is the objective of the proceeding. Compare basic facts.

Ultra vires: Beyond the scope of corporate powers; defense to an action against a corporation based on the lack of power or capacity of the corporation to perform an act or make a conveyance. *See* Model Business Corporation Act § 7 (1979); N. Y. Bus. Corp. Law § 203; Del. Code Ann. Tit. 8 § 124; Cal. Corp. Code § 208.

UMTA: Urban Mass Transportation Administration.

Unauthorized: Under the Uniform Commercial Code, an unauthorized signature or endorsement is one "made without actual, implied or apparent authority and includes a forgery." UCC Section 1-201(43).

UNCITRAL: United Nations Commission on International Trade Law.

Unclean hands: Defense to an action for damages or equitable relief based on the assertion that the plaintiff is guilty of inequitable behavior and is thus not entitled to the relief sought. *See, e.g., Heldman v. United States Lawn Tennis Association*, 354 F. Supp. 1241 (S.D.N.Y. 1973).

Unconditional: Under Article 3–Commercial Paper of the Uniform Commercial Code, for a promise or order to pay in writing to be a negotiable instrument it must, among other things, be "unconditional." UCC Section 3-104. A promise or order otherwise unconditional is not made conditional if the instrument:

(a) is subject to implied or constructive conditions; or

(b) states its consideration, whether performed or promised, or the transaction which gave rise to the instrument, or that the promise or order is made or the instrument matures in accordance with or "as per" such transaction; or

(c) refers to or states that it arises out of a separate agreement or refers to a separate agreement for rights as to payment or acceleration; or

(d) states that it is drawn under a letter of credit; or

(e) states that it is secured, whether by mortgage, reservation of title or otherwise; or

(f) indicates a particular account to be debited or any other fund or source from which reimbursement is expected; or

(g) is limited to payment out of a particular fund or the proceeds of a particular source, if the instrument is issued by a government or governmental agency or unit; or

(h) is limited to payment out of the entire assets of a partnership, unincorporated association, trust or estate by or on behalf of which the instrument is issued.

However, a promise or order is not unconditional if the instrument:

(a) states that it is subject to or governed by any other agreement; or

(b) states that it is to be paid only out of a particular fund or source except as provided in this section.

UCC Section 3-105.

Unconditional purchase obligation: Obligation to transfer funds in the future for fixed or minimum quantities of goods or services at fixed or minimum prices (for example, as in take-or-pay contracts or throughput contracts). Unconditional purchase obligations having certain characteristics must be disclosed in financial statements. Financial Accounting Standards Board, Statement of Financial Accounting Standards No. 47, *Disclosure of Long-Term Obligations*, paragraph 6 (1981).

Unconscionable: Under Article 2 of the Uniform Commercial Code–Sales, a court may refuse to enforce a contract for the sale of goods, or a clause thereof, if it finds that such contract or clause is "unconscionable." The term resists precise definition beyond its dictionary meaning of contrary to the dictates of conscience, but can be used by a court for subjective evaluation of specific actions or circumstances to achieve a just result. UCC Section 2-302. Certain provisions limiting consequential damages may be considered unconscionable. UCC Section 2-719. *See* Fort, *Understanding Unconscionability: Defining the Principle*, 9 Loy. Chi. L. J. 765 (1978); Leff, *Unconscionability and the Code–The Emperor's New Clause*, 115 Univ. of Pa. L. Rev. 485 (1967).

UNCTAD: United Nations Conference on Trade and Development, a code of conduct in business practices and licensing for the benefit of developing nations.

Under protest: Words indicating the reservation of rights while performing under a contract that is subject to a dispute, so that such performance does not prejudice the rights reserved. *See* UCC Section 1-207.

Under reservation: A shipment of goods by a seller "under reservation" means that the seller has reserved a security interest in the goods. Procurement of a negotiable bill of lading to himself or his own order reserves in the seller a security interest in the goods. UCC Section 2-505.

Underwriter: 1. Person who agrees to purchase securities from the issuer, usually with a view toward resale. Under the Securities Act of 1933, the term "underwriter" includes "any person who has purchased from an issuer with a view to, or offers or sells for the issuer in connection with, the distribution of any security, or participates or has a direct or indirect participation in any such undertaking, or participates or has a participation in the direct or indirect underwriting of any such undertaking; . . . ." In this definition, the term "issuer" has some added gloss, including, in addition to parties covered by the definition of issuer in section 2(4) of the Securities Act, "any person under direct or indirect common control with the issuer." Thus parties that may not be underwriters in the business sense may come under this definition, and be regarded as "statutory" underwriters.

Securities Act of 1933, section 2(11), 15 U.S.C. § 77b(11). *See* section 202a(2) of the Investment Advisors Act of 1940, 15 U.S.C. § 80b-2(a)(20); section 3(a)(20) of the Securities Exchange Act of 1934, 15 U.S.C. § 78c(a)(20); section 303(4) of the Trust Indenture Act of 1939, 15 U.S.C. § 77ccc(4). 2. Person who insures another; insurer.

Underwriting agreement: Agreement between an issuer of securities and the underwriter (or managing underwriter of a group), setting forth the terms and conditions of the commitment of the underwriter. See **best-efforts underwriting; firm commitment underwriting.**

Undoable: Not doable; a transaction that is undoable is one that cannot be placed or done, not one that can be undone.

Unenforceable contract: Contract "for the breach of which neither the remedy of damages nor the remedy of specific performance is available, but which is recognized in some other way as creating a duty of performance, though there has been no ratification." *Restatement, Second, Contracts* § 8 (1981). *See Daugherty v. Kessler,* 264 Md. 281, 286 A. 2d 95 (1972). Compare **voidable contract.**

Uneven rent: Rent in a lease that is not the same amount for each period. The Internal Revenue Service may regard rents that are uneven to an extent greater than ten percent as prepaid or deferred rent. Rev. Proc. 75-21, section 5.01, 1975-1 C.B. 715.

Unfair labor practice: Practice prohibited by section 8 of the National Labor Relations Act, 29 U.S.C. §§ 152(8), 158.

Unfair method of competition: Section 5 of the Federal Trade Commission Act declares unlawful "unfair methods of competition in or affecting commerce, and unfair or deceptive acts or practices in commerce... ." 15 U.S.C. § 45(a). The unfair practices prohibited by this statute may extend beyond the "letter or the spirit of the antitrust laws... ." *FTC v. Sperry & Hutchinson Co.*, 405 U.S. 233, 239 (1972). *See generally* American Bar Association, Section of Antitrust Law, *Antitrust Law Developments* 168, 174 (1975).

UNIDROIT: International Institute for the Unification of Private Law.

Uniform Commercial Code: Proposed uniform law relating to commercial transactions, including sales, commercial paper, bank deposits and collections, documents of title, investment securities, and secured transactions, prepared by The American Law Institute and the National Conference of Commissioners on Uniform State Laws. The Uniform Commercial Code is only the law to the extent that it has been adopted by the legislature of the state in question. Almost all states adopted the 1962 Official Text, with local variations. The 1972 Official Text has supplanted the 1962 version in most states, and is expected to become universal, except perhaps in Louisiana. The references to the Uniform Commercial Code herein, unless otherwise stated, mean the 1972 Official Text.

Uniform Securities Act: Proposed uniform or model law for the state regulation of securities promulgated by the National Conference of Commissioners on Uniform State Laws. The Uniform Securities Act has been adopted, with some variations, by thirty-four states; the remaining states have their own distinct securities, or "blue-sky," laws. *See generally*, L. Loss & E. Cowett, *Blue Sky Laws* (1958).

Union shop: Place of employment where employees are required to join and continue membership in the union whose contract covers such employees. Membership is not required as a condition of initial employment, only of continued employment.

United States Code: Statutes of the United States, arranged in a code incorporating all amendments. Some more recent statutes, such as the Bankruptcy Code and the Transportation Code, have been specifically enacted as titles of the United States Code, while others, such as the various securities laws, are published as part of the code for convenience although the "official" version is the statute itself.

United States person: For the purpose of the Internal Revenue Code, the term "United States person" means a citizen or resident of the United States, a domestic partnership, a domestic corporation, and any estate or trust, other than a foreign estate or trust. I.R.C. § 7701(a)(30). *See also* I.R.C. § 957(d).

United States Railway Association: Government corporation created by the Regional Rail Reorganization Act of 1973 to plan and finance the reorganization and rehabilitation of the bankrupt railroads in the Northeast.

Unit investment trust: As defined in the Investment Company Act of 1940, an "investment company which (A) is organized under a trust indenture, contract of custodianship or agency, or similar instrument, (B) does not have a board of directors, and (C) issues only redeemable securities, each of which represents an undivided interest in a unit of specified securities; but does not include a voting trust." Section 4(2), 15 U.S.C. § 80a-4(2). *See* I.R.C. § 851(f). See also **investment company.**

Unit of account: Multicurrency unit, a composite of the currencies of a group of countries. Examples are the ECU, European Currency Unit, the EUA, European Unit of Account, the EURCO, European Composite Unit, and SDR units based on International Monetary Fund Special Drawing Rights.

Unit train: Train-length group of railroad cars assigned to specific service, and not broken up in classification yards. Coal is often moved in unit trains.

Unprocessed natural resources: Mineral resource assets, timberlands, and growing timber. Financial Accounting Standards Board, Statement of Financial Accounting Standards No. 39, *Financial Reporting and Changing Prices: Specialized Assets—Mining and Oil and Gas,* paragraph 5d (1980).

Unproved properties: Properties with no proved reserves. See **mineral interests in properties.**

Unrealized profit rule:

Unrealized profit should not be credited to income account of the corporation either directly or indirectly, through the medium of charging against such unrealized profits amounts which would ordinarily fall to be charged against income accounts. Profit is deemed to be realized when a sale in the ordinary course of business is effected, unless the circumstances are such that the collection of the sale price is not reasonably assured. An exception to the general rule may be made in respect of inventories in industries (such as packing-house industry) in which owing to the impossibility of determining costs it is a trade custom to take inventories at net selling prices, which may exceed cost.

American Institute of Certified Public Accountants, Accounting Research Bulletin No. 43, Ch. 1A, paragraph 1 (1934).

Unregistered securities: Securities that have been issued without registration under the Securities Act of 1933, usually in a transaction exempt from registration under section 4 thereof.

Unrelated business income: Business income of tax-exempt entities that is taxable because it is unrelated to the exercise or performance of the charitable, educational, or other purpose constituting the basis of the exemption of the entity from federal income taxes. I.R.C. §513.

Unrestricted subsidiary: Subsidiary of a corporation that is not subject to the restrictive covenants entered into by the parent corporation.

Unsecured debt: Debt not secured by an interest in specifically identified property, but representing a claim on the general assets of the debtor.

U.N.T.S.: United Nations Treaty Series.

Unusual items: Gains or losses that derive from events or transactions that are distinct from the ordinary activities of an enterprise and therefore are not expected to recur frequently or regularly. International Accounting Standards Committee, Statement of International Accounting Standards 8, *Unusual and Prior Period Items and Changes in Accounting Policies,* paragraph 3 (1978).

Unwind: To reverse a transaction in an effort to restore the parties to their respective positions as if the transaction had not been done.

Upjohn: *Upjohn Co. v. United States,* 449 U.S. 383 (1981), a significant case on the attorney-client privilege where a corporation is the client. *See* Gergacz, *Attorney-Corporate Client Privilege,* 37 Bus. Law. 461 (1982).

Upset price: Price below which an object shall not be sold.

Upstream merger: Merger of a subsidiary into its parent. *See* Del. Code Ann. Tit. 8 § 253.

Urban Mass Transportation Administration: Unit of the United States Department of Transportation responsible for the urban mass transportation assistance programs under the Urban Mass Transportation Act of 1964, Pub. L. No. 88-365, 78 Stat. 302 (1964), 49 U.S.C. § 1601-11.

Urban renewal program—project notes: Obligations of local public agencies, secured by an agreement of the United States to pay the principal and interest of such obligations. This agreement is endorsed on each note, and is regarded as incontestable in the hands of the bearer. These notes are similar to public housing program—project notes.

Usage: Habitual or customary practice. *Restatement, Second, Contracts* § 219 (1981); *see* §§ 220–22.

Usage of trade: Under the Uniform Commercial Code, agreements are to be interpreted by reference to the course of dealing between the parties and usage of trade, not by a layman's interpretation or a strict legal construction. A usage of trade is

any practice or method of dealing having such regularity of observance in a place, vocation or trade as to justify an expectation that it will be observed with respect to the transaction in question. The existence and scope of such a usage are to be proved as facts. If it is established that such a usage is embodied in a written trade code or similar writing the interpretation of the writing is for the court.

UCC Section 1-205. *See Restatement, Second, Contracts* § 222 (1981); *Lipschutz v. Gordon Jewelry Corp.,* 373 F. Supp. 375 (S.D. Tex. 1974). See also **course of dealing.**

U.S.C.: United States Code.

Useful life: Life of a depreciable asset used in calculating depreciation. For the purpose of accelerated cost recovery deductions (the equivalent of depreciation) from federal income tax, the useful life is called the "recovery period" and is established by statute for specific types of property. I.R.C. § 168. The useful life employed for property not eligible for the accelerated cost recovery system may be determined by "facts and circumstances," or according to the asset depreciation range and class life system. *See* Rev. Proc. 72-10, 1972-1 C.B. 721; Rev. Proc. 77-10, 1977-1 C.B. 548. The useful life for the purpose of calculating depreciation for tax purposes is somewhat artificial and arbitrary, and may not be the same as the useful life for accounting purposes, which is closer to the normal meaning of the words. As defined by the International Accounting Standards Committee in Statement of International Accounting Standards 4, *Depreciation Accounting* (1976), "Useful life is either (a) the period over which a depreciable asset is expected to be used by the enterprise; or (b) the number of production or similar units expected to be obtained from the asset by the enterprise."

Use-or-pay contract: Take-or-pay contract.

USRA: United States Railway Association.

U.S.T.: United States Treaties and Other International Agreements.

Usury: The charging of interest at a rate greater than that permitted by law. *See* N. Y. Gen. Oblig. Law. § 5-501.

V

Validly issued: When used with respect to stock in an opinion of counsel, validly issued means that the issuance of the stock was duly authorized, proper consideration was given, and appropriate stock certificates were properly executed. *Legal Opinions to Third Parties: An Easier Path,* 34 Bus. Law. 1891, 1910 (1979).

Valuation allowance: Net unrealized loss (the amount by which aggregate cost exceeds market value) for a portfolio of securities. Financial Accounting Standards Board, Statement of Financial Accounting Standards No. 12, *Accounting for Certain Marketable Securities,* paragraph 7f (1975).

Value: Under the Uniform Commercial Code, value means more than money or tangible property, and includes contractual obligations and binding commitments:

Except as otherwise provided with respect to negotiable instruments and bank collections (Sections 3-303, 4-208 and 4-209) a person gives "value" for rights if he acquires them
    (a) in return for a binding commitment to extend credit or for the extension of immediately available credit whether or not drawn upon and whether or not a chargeback is provided for in the event of difficulties in collection; or

(b) as security for or in total or partial satisfaction of a pre-existing claim; or

(c) by accepting delivery pursuant to a pre-existing contract for purchase; or

(d) generally, in return for any consideration sufficient to support a simple contract.

UCC Section 1-201(44). *See generally* Davenport, *The Value of "Value" in a Purchase Money Security Interest,* 28 Baylor L. Rev. 667 (1976). In the case of negotiable instruments, a holder takes the instrument for "value":

(a) to the extent that the agreed condition has been performed or that he acquires a security interest in or a lien on the instrument other than by legal process; or

(b) when he takes the instrument in payment of or as security for an antecedent claim against any other person whether or not the claim is due; or

(c) when he gives a negotiable instrument for it or makes an irrevocable commitment to a third person.

UCC Section 3-303. Value is not the same as consideration; *see* UCC Section 3-408. *See also* UCC Section 4-209.

Value-added tax: Tax on the value added to a product by a manufacturing or processing operation; tax on the difference between the price of finished goods and the cost of raw materials.

Value date: Delivery date of funds in a securities or foreign exchange transaction.

Value in use: Net present value of future cash flows (including the ultimate proceeds of disposal) expected to be derived from the use of an asset by the enterprise, using a discount rate that allows for the risk of the activities concerned. Financial Accounting Standards Board, Statement of Financial Accounting Standards No. 33, *Financial Reporting and Changing Prices,* paragraph 63 (1979).

Value of service: Method of setting transportation rates based more on the value of the service to the shipper than on the cost of providing the service. Railroad rates have traditionally been based on the value of service concept, resulting in incredibly complicated schedules of rates, with different rates for different commodities. Thus the rate for shipping a ton of washing machines is much higher than the rate for shipping a ton of lettuce or a ton of coal. Compare **cost of service.**

Variable rate CD: Certificate of deposit on which the interest rate changes to reflect the then current market on the date it is renewed, or rolled over.

Variable rate loan: Loan on which the interest rate varies from time to time to reflect market conditions. Variable rate loans may be related to the prime rate or other interest rate indicators.

VAT: Value-added tax.

Velocity: Rate at which money is spent on goods and services within a given period of time, usually measured as the ratio of gross national product to the money supply.

Vendee: Party to whom property is sold.

Vendor: Party selling property.

Verified: Declared to be true under oath. *See* Cal. Corp. Code § 193.

Vertical merger: Merger between a supplier and its customer. *See United States v. E. I. duPont de Nemours & Co.,* 353 U.S. 586 (1957); *Ford Motor Corp. v. United States,* 405 U.S. 562 (1972). *See generally* American Bar Association, Section of Antitrust Law, *Antitrust Law Developments* 76 (1975).

Vertical price fixing: Arrangement by a manufacturer or supplier and its dealers to fix resale prices. See **resale price maintenance.**

Vertical restraint: Restraint on resale imposed by a supplier on its customers, such as resale price fixing and territorial allocation. *See Continental T.V., Inc. v. GTE Sylvania Inc.,* 433 U.S. 36 (1977). *See generally* Posner, *The Next Step in the Antitrust Treatment of Restricted Distribution: Per Se Legality,* 48 U. Chi. L. Rev. 6 (1981).

Vessel: "Vessel" is defined under federal law as a "watercraft or other artificial contrivance used, or capable of being used, as a means of transportation on water." 1 U.S.C. § 3; 46 C.F.R. § 66.03-5. The distinction between a vessel and something else is important, because admiralty law principles and preferred mortgages are only applicable to vessels. The term has been broadly construed, without paying too much attention to the "means of transportation" part of the statutory definition, and has been held to include dredging barges (*City of Los Angeles v. United Dredging Co.*, 14 F. 2d 364 (9th Cir. 1926)), floating cranes (*The O'Boyle No. 1*, 64 F. Supp. 378 (S.D. N.Y. 1945)), and drilling scows (*Brown v. L.A. Wells Const. Co.*, 143 Ohio St. 580, 56 N.E. 2d 451 (1944)). Where exemption from import duties for vessels has been sought, construction has been narrow, excluding "midbodies," center sections of vessels intended to be used to lengthen an existing vessel. *Todd Shipyards Corp. v. United States*, 63 Cust. Ct. 165 (1969). Aircraft are not vessels, but in the United States, watergoing hovercraft are treated as vessels, although they are treated as aircraft in their birthplace, England. While under construction, a vessel is not a vessel (*Tucker v. Alexandroff*, 183 U.S. 424 (1902)), except for the purposes of Title XI construction financing. See 46 U.S.C. § 1271 (b) for the definition of vessels eligible for Title XI financing.

Vessel of the United States: Vessel documented under the laws of the United States. 46 U.S.C. § 221; Ship Mortgage Act, 1920, subsection B; 46 U.S.C. § 911.

Vested benefit: In connection with pension plans, "vested benefits" are benefits that are not contingent upon an employee's continuing in the service of the employer. American Institute of Certified Public Accountants, Accounting Principles Board Opinion No. 8, *Accounting for the Cost of Pension Plans*, Appendix B (1966).

VLCC: Very large crude carrier; tank vessel of 200,000 deadweight tons or more. A tank vessel of 400,000 deadweight tons or more may be called a ULCC, ultra large crude carrier. *See generally* N. Mostert, *Supership* (1974).

Voidable contract: Contract "where one or more of the parties have the power, by a manifestation of election to do so, to avoid the legal relations created by the contract, or by ratification of the contract to extinguish the power of avoidance." *Restatement, Second, Contracts* § 7 (1981). *See Matter of Rothko*, 43 N.Y. 2d 305, 372 N.E. 2d 291 (1977). Compare **unenforceable contract.**

Voting trust agreement: Agreement whereby one or more stockholders deposits stock with a trustee for a stated period, empowering the trustee to vote the stock. *See* Model Business Corporation Act § 34 (1979); N. Y. Bus. Corp. Law § 621; Del. Code Ann. Tit. 8 § 218; Cal. Corp. Code § 706(b).

Voyage charter: Contract for the services of a vessel for a given voyage. The vessel owner furnishes the crew and operates the vessel. See also **time charter; bare-boat charter.**

W

Wagner Act: National Labor Relations Act.

Waiver: Intentional relinquishment of a known right, or conduct that warrants an inference of such intent.

Waiver-of-defense clause: Clause in a contract, usually a lease or an obligation for the payment of money, that provides that if the contract is assigned, the obligor agrees to make the contractual payments to the assignee notwithstanding any defenses it may have against the other party to the contract. Any claims against that party must be raised in a separate action, without setoff against the contractual payments. A waiver-of-defense clause is an important element of a contract that is used as collateral for a loan, such as a take-or-pay contract. *See Bankers Trust Co. v. Litton Systems, Inc.,* 599 F. 2d 488 (2d Cir. 1979).

Wall Street rule: Rule that an investor should vote his stock as management recommends, or sell the stock. *See* J. Allen, *Exercise of Voting Rights by Large Institutional Investors: A Survey* (1977).

Warehouse Act: United States Warehouse Act; federal statute covering warehouse receipts for agricultural products. Pub. L. No. 190, ch. 313, 39 Stat. 446, 486 (1916); 7 U.S.C. §§ 71–87, 111, 113, 241–73, 2209; 16 U.S.C. §§ 490, 683; 31 U.S.C. §§ 617, 638e.

Warehouseman: Person engaged in the business of storing goods for hire. UCC Section 7-102(1)(h).

Warehouseman's lien: Security interest in favor of a warehouseman on the goods entrusted to him or their proceeds for charges for storage, transportation, insurance, labor, or other charges in relation to the goods. UCC Section 7-209.

Warehouse receipt: Under the Uniform Commercial Code, "a receipt issued by a person engaged in the business of storing goods for hire." UCC Section 1-201(45). See UCC Section

7-202 for the essential and optional terms of a warehouse receipt. *See generally* R. Riegert & R. Braucher, *Documents of Title* (3d ed. 1978).

Warrant: Right issued with securities entitling the holder to purchase additional securities of the same issuer, at a given price and within a given time. Warrants are separate from the securities with which they are issued, may be exercised without surrendering the original security, and may be traded separately.

Warranty: Undertaking that certain facts are true; a representation by the seller of property that such property has certain qualities, or that the seller has good title and the right to sell the property. In a transaction involving the sale of goods, Article 2–Sales of the Uniform Commercial Code provides that express warranties with respect to the goods are made by the seller in providing a description or sample of the goods, or making an affirmation or promise. The use of formal words such as "warrant" is not necessary and disclaimers may not be effective. Assertions of value and opinions do not constitute a warranty. UCC Section 2-313. See UCC Section 2-317 for the rules regarding cumulation and conflict of warranties. See also implied warranty; written warranty; full warranty; Magnuson-Moss Warranty–Federal Trade Commission Improvement Act. In the presentment for payment or acceptance of an instrument covered by Article 3 of the Uniform Commercial Code–Commercial Paper, or a check or other item covered by Article 4 of the Uniform Commercial Code–Bank Deposits and Collections, the party presenting the instrument warrants that he has good title to the instrument or item, that he has no knowledge that the signature of the maker or drawer is unauthorized, and that the instrument or item has not been materially altered. UCC Section 3-417(1). In the transfer for consideration of an instrument covered by Article 3–Commercial Paper of the Uniform Commercial Code, or a check or other item covered by Article 4–Bank Deposits and Collections of the Uniform Commercial Code, the transferor warrants that he has good title to the instrument or item, that all signatures are genuine or authorized, that the instrument or item has not been materially altered, that no defense of any party is good against the transferor, and that he has no knowledge of any insolvency proceeding with respect to the maker, acceptor, or drawer of the instrument or item. UCC Sections 3-417(2), 4-207(2). See **without recourse.** As to warranties in connection with negotiation or transfer of documents of title, see UCC Section 7-507.

Warranty of title: In a transaction involving the sale of goods, Article 2–Sales of the Uniform Commercial Code provides that the seller warrants that:

(a) the title conveyed shall be good, and its transfer rightful; and
(b) the goods shall be delivered free from any security interest or other lien or encumbrance of which the buyer at the time of contracting has no knowledge.

The warranty can be modified by specific language in the agreement or by special circumstances. UCC Section 2-312.

Warsaw Convention: International agreement relating to the liability of air carriers. Convention for the Unification of Certain Rules Relating to International Transportation by Air, with Additional Protocol, concluded at Warsaw, October 12, 1929, entered into force for the United States October 29, 1934, and subject to a reservation. 49 Stat. 3000; Treaties in Force 252 (1979).

Wash: Combination of transactions with no net economic effect.

Wash sale: Sale of securities, resulting in a loss, where the taxpayer has acquired or has obtained an option to acquire substantially identical securities in a period beginning 30 days before such sale and ending 30 days after. Losses from wash sales cannot be deducted from federal income tax. I.R.C. § 1091.

Wasting-assets corporation: Corporation engaged in the business of exploiting natural resources or liquidating specific assets, including patents. Wasting-assets corporations may declare dividends out of the depleting reserves of such resources or assets, whereas other corporations may usually only pay dividends out of earned surplus. *See* Model Business Corporation Act § 45(b) (1979); N. Y. Bus. Corp. Law § 510(b); Del. Code Ann. tit. 8 § 170(b).

Watered stock: Stock whose value has been diluted by issuance of shares for less than the issue price, or for which the proceeds have not been used to enhance the value of the corporation.

Water Power and Resources Service: Name of the Bureau of Reclamation during 1980 and part of 1981.

Webb-Pomerene association: Export association formed under the authority of the Webb-Pomerene Export Trade Act, with certain immunities from antitrust laws. Pub. L. No. 126, ch. 50, 40 Stat. 516 (1918); 15 U.S.C. §§ 61–65. *See United States v. Minnesota Mining & Mfg. Co.*, 92 F. Supp. 947, 965 (D. Mass. 1950). *See generally* I W. Fugate, *Foreign Commerce and the Antitrust Laws* (3d ed. 1982); Larson, *An Economic Analysis of the Webb-Pomerene Act,* 13 J. of Law & Econ. 461 (1970); *Staff Report to the Federal Trade Commission, Webb-Pomerene Associations: A 50-Year Review* (1967).

Wells submission: Statement submitted by a defendant or respondent in a proceeding by the Securities and Exchange Commission in reply to an SEC staff recommendation for enforcement action. The procedure was recommended by the SEC Advisory Committee on Enforcement Policies and Practices, the "Wells" committee, in 1972. *See* SEC Release No. 33-5310 (1972); *SEC v. National Student Marketing Corp.*, 538 F. 2d 404 (D.C. Cir. 1976), *cert. denied sub nom., White & Case v. SEC,* 429 U.S. 1073 (1977); Merrifield, *Investigations by the Securities and Exchange Commission,* 32 Bus. Law. 1583, 1623 (1977).

Wheat Report: *Disclosure to Investors: A Reappraisal of Federal Administrative Policies Under the '33 and '34 Acts* (1969), a report of a Securities and Exchange Commission staff study group.

Wheeler-Lea amendment: Amendment to the Federal Trade Commission Act expanding the Federal Trade Commission's authority under section 5. Pub. L. No. 447, ch. 49, 52 Stat. 111 (1938).

When issued: Trade in securities between the time the issue is announced and the securities are actually issued.

Whipsaw strike: Strike against one employer in an industry with the intention of prevailing over all employers by taking them on one at a time, putting each struck employer at a competitive disadvantage.

White knight: Friendly prospective merger partner or acquiring corporation. A corporation threatened with a tender offer or acquisition attempt by an entity that it considers unfriendly will often seek a white knight to merge with or acquire the target corporation to thwart the unfriendly acquisition attempt.

Wi: When issued. The term "wi wi" refers to a trade in Treasury bills before the auction.

Williams Act: Federal legislation adding sections 13(d) and (e), and sections 14(d), (e), and (f) to the Securities Exchange Act of 1934. Pub. L. No. 90-439, 82 Stat. 454 (1968). The Williams Act amendments require the filing of statements by beneficial owners of more than five percent of a class of equity securities registered under the '34 Act, and the filing of certain statements in connection with tender offers. 15 U.S.C. §§ 78m(d), 78m(e), 78n(d), 78n(e), and 78n(f). *See* SEC Regulations 14D and 14E, 17 C.F.R. §§ 240.14d, 240.14e; SEC Release No. 34-11616 (1975).

WIN: Work Incentive Program.

Windfall profits tax: Temporary excise tax imposed at the wellhead on the production of crude oil. I.R.C. §§ 4986–94.

WIPO: World Intellectual Property Organization, an international organization for the deposit of industrial designs.

Without prejudice: Words indicating the reservation of rights while performing under a contract that is subject to a dispute, so that such performance does not prejudice the rights reserved. *See* UCC Section 1-207.

Without recourse: In connection with the transfer of an instrument, meaning that the transferor declines any responsibility for payment by the maker of the instrument. Under Article 3–Commercial Paper of the Uniform Commercial Code, the words "without recourse" limit the usual warranty of the transferor as to the nonexistence of defenses to the instrument to a warranty that the transferor has no knowledge of such a defense. UCC Section 3-417(3).

Without reserve: An auction "without reserve" means that the auctioneer may not withdraw the goods after he calls for bids, unless no bid is made within a reasonable time. An auction is not without reserve unless it is explicitly stated. UCC Section 2-328(3). Compare with reserve.

With reserve: An auction "with reserve" means that the auctioneer may withdraw the goods at any time until he announces completion of the sale. An auction is "with reserve" unless it is explicitly stated otherwise. UCC Section 2-328(3). Compare **without reserve.**

Work Incentive Program: Federal program administered by the Department of Health and Human Services and the Department of Labor designed to help persons on welfare to become self-supporting. A tax credit is available to employers as an incentive for hiring registrants of the WIN program. I.R.C. §§ 50A, 50B.

Working capital: Excess of current assets over current liabilities.

Work product rule: Rule that materials prepared by or for counsel in anticipation of litigation or for use at trial are protected from discovery. Fed. R. Civ. Proc. 26(b)(3); *see Hickman v. Taylor,* 329 U.S. 495 (1947); *Upjohn Co. v. United States,* 449 U.S. 383 (1981); *Diversified Industries, Inc., v. Meredith,* 572 F. 2d 596 (8th Cir. 1977); *see generally* Block & Barton, *Internal Corporate Investigations: Maintaining the Confidentiality of a Corporate Client's Communications with Investigative Counsel,* 35 Bus. Law. 5 (1979).

World Bank: International Bank for Reconstruction and Development.

Worldscale: System of rates for the charter of oil tankers, established for combinations of ports throughout the world. Worldscale 100 is the cost per ton of carrying oil in a 19,500 ton tanker at a speed of fourteen knots, taking into consideration operating costs, depreciation, and a fair margin of profit. Charter rates are quoted in relation to this standard, Worldscale 50 being one-half of Worldscale 100, Worldscale 250, two and one-half times, and so on.

Wrap-around loan: Long-term loan arranged around a short-term loan, with payments of principal (and perhaps interest) on the long-term loan deferred until the short-term loan is repaid, so that the aggregate of the payments is level, or nearly so, over the life of both loans.

Wrap-around mortgage: Mortgage arranged to finance the sale of property with an existing mortgage, usually at a lower interest rate than the rate prevailing at the time of the sale, in which the lender (mortgagee) assumes the existing mortgage and gives a new, larger mortgage at the prevailing rate.

Written: Under the Uniform Commercial Code, "written" or "writing" includes "printing, typewriting or any intentional reduction to tangible form." UCC Section 1-201(46). The California Corporations Code includes facsimile and telegraphic communication. Cal. Corp. Code § 195. *See also* section 2(9) of the Securities Act of 1933; 15 U.S.C. § 77b(9).

Written warranty: Under the Magnuson-Moss Warranty–Federal Trade Commission Improvement Act:

The term "written warranty" means—

(A) any written affirmation of fact or written promise made in connection with the sale of a consumer product by a supplier to a buyer which relates to the nature of the material or workmanship and affirms or promises that such material or workmanship is defect free or will meet a specified level of performance over a specified period of time, or

(B) any undertaking in writing in connection with the sale by a supplier of a consumer product to refund, repair, replace, or take other remedial action with respect to such product in the event that such product fails to meet the specifications set forth in the undertaking,

which written affirmation, promise, or undertaking becomes the basis of the bargain between a supplier and a buyer for purposes other than resale of such product.

Section 101(6); 15 U.S.C. § 2301(6).

Y,Z

Yale Express: *In re Yale Express Sys. Inc.,* 370 F. 2d 433 (2d Cir. 1966). Case holding that a secured party may not be able to recover equipment subject to a security interest from a debtor in bankruptcy if the equipment is essential to a successful reorganization. *See also In re Yale Express Sys. Inc.,* 384 F. 2d 990 (2d Cir. 1967). See **adequate protection.**

Yankee bond: Bond sold in the United States, denominated in dollars, issued under United States laws, but by a foreign issuer.

Yankee CD: Certificate of deposit issued in the United States by a branch of a foreign bank.

Yellow-dog contract: Contract between an employee and an employer whereby the employee agrees not to join or be a member of a union during the period of employment.

Yield: Rate of return on an investment, usually determined by the internal rate of return method.

Yield curve: Plot showing the relationship of yield to maturity to the term of maturity of a given group of debt securities, in which the yield to maturity is the ordinate and the term of the maturity is the abscissa. A normal yield curve shows an increase in yield with maturity, that is, securities with a longer maturity have a higher yield. An inverted yield curve shows a decrease in yield with maturity. *See* H. Kaufman, *The Many Faces and Implications of the Yield Curve* (Salomon Brothers Inc, 1981). See also **spot rate curve.**

Yield to maturity: Rate of return on a debt security taking into account both the interest to maturity and the difference between the par value (the amount of principal paid at maturity) and the offering price; the rate at which future payments of principal and interest must be discounted to equal the current market price of a debt security. *See generally* S. Homer & M. Leibowitz, *Inside the Yield Book* (1972).

Yo-yo provision: Provision in transportation deregulation legislation permitting rates to move up or down within a given range without the need for approval of the regulatory body.

Zero-coupon bond: Bond that does not bear interest, but represents an obligation for a single, fixed payment at a future time. Zero-coupon bonds are sold at a discount so that the yield is de-rived from the movement of the value toward par at maturity. The advantage of zero-coupon bonds is that the yield on the investment is locked in because there is no need to reinvest interest payments. Bonds that have had the coupons stripped away (stripper bonds) and those coupons may be called zero-coupon bonds.